"Crawford is a born writer."
--*Alan J. Kaufman, Esq. Publishing Attorney*

WILDFLOWER

A Survival Story

E. R. CRAWFORD

Copyright © 2020 by Elise Crawford. All rights reserved.

Library of Congress Control Number: TXu 2-102-027

ISBN: 978-0-9600973-2-6

All rights reserved. No part of this book may be reproduced or transmitted in any form or by any means, electronic or mechanical, including photocopying, recording, or by any information storage and retrieval system, without permission in writing from the copyright owner.

This book was printed in the United States of America.

Unless otherwise noted, all scriptures are taken from THE HOLY BIBLE: NEW INTERNATIONAL VERSION®. NIV®.

FROM THE COPY EDITOR

Elise Crawford is a born storyteller, weaving her way into the hearts of her readers.

This is a true story and deals with, at times, a dark reality; yet, it is also a book filled with promise, and rays of sunshine, hope, faith and love. Elise, the author, simply and honestly tells her tale in a voice of innocence, trust, and courage, revealing her fears and vulnerabilities as well as her strength, courage, and determination. As I read, I found myself crying—alternating between tears of empathy and compassion and the tears that come with laughing so hard my sides hurt. Light and dark, funny and sad, *Wildflower* is a powerful, must-read book, written by an amazing woman.

Mary Anne Pester, Copy Editor, Proofreader

www.fourpennypages.com

A FEW REVIEWS FROM CRAWFORD'S FIRST BOOK, A PROMISE KEPT

"Elise is a born writer. *A Promise Kept* is excellent." – Alan J. Kaufman, Esq. Publishing Attorney

"This is Elise Crawford's first book; however, she writes with the skill of a seasoned author. Her powerful description and willingness to show her own mistakes, weaknesses and fears make this a wonderfully inspiring read. Impossible to put down or forget, I highly recommend *A Promise Kept*." – Excerpt from review by William R. Potter for Reader's Choice Reviews

"Elise Crawford's story personalizes one crime against society as well as any book or journalistic piece I have ever read. Crawford tells a tale that one could just as easily credit to an experienced writer of fiction, except the story she tells is absolutely true and, therefore, cuts to the bone so much so that at times the heartbreak makes it necessary to stop reading just to gather your emotions. In Crawford's telling of her story, she brings an honest strength into her writing that does not allow us to detach. Crawford does not lay out the facts of her story in a foreboding manner, or with any hint of self-pity, but with tenderness and brevity." – Excerpt from review by Jeffrey B. Allen / Author of *Gone Away Into the Land*

"*A Promise Kept* is a love story, true, but it is also a ray of hope for those that are traveling a similar road of recovery after a tragic loss. With just a few well-chosen words, Elise can draw out the readers' emotions, making them laugh at Mark's antics, cry with her in her pain, and suffer the hurt that comes with a test of faith. As a writer, I was amazed when I found tears running down my cheeks, wetting my shirt, and laughing so hard my sides hurt with just a few words. This is a must read for anyone!" – Donald Drake, *The Chronicles of the Kings of Randor*

"Powerful. I read it in one day, I couldn't put it down." – Betty, Seattle WA

"Truly wonderful. You deserve to be proud." – Jennifer, Seattle WA

"Amazing. I was just going to read a little and then pick it up again later, I read the whole book in one sitting, needless to say, nothing got done that day. And then when I watched the video of the photos and music to the book, I really lost it. I called my husband to see it, yep he did too. Very powerful." – Stacy, Seattle WA

"Very powerful. I think it would be worthwhile reading, not just for those in grief. I could really appreciate what you went through." – Richard McLane, Seattle WA

"Received the book today and just finished it. WOW! Courageous project." – Jack Carone, Los Angeles California

"Five stars on this one! And 2 THUMBS UP! It was a 'couldn't put it down' read. Congratulations Elise Crawford! Job well done!" – B. Gardner, Bloomington IA

DEDICATION

This story is dedicated to my beloved husband Roberto:

You've empowered me to believe in myself, in faith, and in my writing. You've been the greatest best friend anyone could ask for. God bless you for accepting what most could not. It's that you stand beside me and continue to try that makes me love you even more. Because of you, I can trust, love, and be loved again. It's unequivocal, you were heaven sent. You are my ultimate hero and my happy ever after. I love you so very much.

And to my beloved children, Dale, and Lexi:

I had no business bringing you into the world under the circumstances in which you both were born, but I did the best I could, and for that I was rewarded with the words for this book. I write for you. I love you both more than life itself.

You can let the life and the family you were born into dictate the definition of your very being, regardless of what you do or do not have, or, with grit, self-sufficiency, and self-reliance, you can rise above your circumstances, chart your own course and change your life, all the while empowering others to do the same.

— Elise Crawford

ACKNOWLEDGEMENTS

I am eternally indebted to all those who have traveled this journey with me, especially Our Heavenly Father, my children, Lexi and Dale, Maggie (pseudonym), Mommy, Roberto and Lucky and the countless other kindred spirits I have crossed paths with who have directly or indirectly walked this path with me; because of you, my burden has been lighter and the journey bearable.

Special thanks to the Alliance of Independent Authors for their guidance and to my publishing team, Jeff at Curiosity Press and Olivia and the cover art team at Miblart, for making this book a reality.

Publishing of Elise's writing is made possible in part by the support of the many customers of CEDAR-AL cedar oil products at www.cedaroil.com.

AUTHOR'S NOTE:

This is a painstakingly true story of how the author—guided by faith—comes to terms with the skeletons of her childhood to inspire hope and encouragement in the hearts of other survivors of mental illness and family dysfunction.

Some names and detailed descriptions of certain characters in this story have been withheld to protect the identity of the sources. I have tried in good faith to recreate events, locales, and conversations from my memories of them, from the stories my mother told me, extensive research, public records, and from interviews with family members.

Any resemblance to persons living or dead should be plainly apparent to them and those who know them. All events described within happened, though, on occasion, I have taken certain, very small, liberties with chronology and detail.

My tale is not unusual; in fact, it's just another story about one's internal strength, endurance, and ability to overcome adversity in the face of a string of incredibly unfortunate events.

It is my hope this story speaks to your heart. And, when facing any challenging situation, I hope my struggles are just enough for you to relate to, to seek hope from, to encourage you to continue forward, and to not give up.

Above all, if sharing my story makes a difference in one person's life, then my convoluted journey was not in vain.

May God's light always shine upon you, bring love and peace to all, and like Zig Ziglar once said, "I'll See You at The Top,"

Elise Crawford, *A Promise Kept*

Jesus calls the children dear,
"Come to me and never fear,
For I love the little children of the world;
I will take you by the hand,
Lead you to the better land,
For I love the little children of the world."
Jesus is the Shepherd true,
And He'll always stand by you,
For He loves the little children of the world;
He's a Savior great and strong,
And He'll shield you from the wrong,
For He loves the little children of the world.

PART I

PART I

ONE

*O*nce upon a time . . . No, that is how a fairy tale begins, a story meant to entertain children. This story is neither a fairy tale nor was it written for entertainment value. If that is something you were hoping for, you must put this book down immediately because there is no amusement to be had by mental illness and family dysfunction.

This unforgettable, true tale has never seen the light of day, until now. At times it is extremely unpleasant and rather dark, but one that must be told. Sadly, only an unfortunate few will identify with my story. It's for them I set my skeletons free. They are not alone. That is the message, no preaching, no antidotes, only to say that there is hope.

With that said, when you're ready, please join me for an incredulous journey, beginning with my conception in a janitor's closet of a mental hospital, as I pursue love, belonging, and family through almost insurmountable obstacles. Let's start with the scene where my father springs my mother out of the looney bin, shall we?

Rosemary removed all her clothes from the dresser and laid each item in like piles on the bed. She sighed in anxiety as she removed the last pair of socks from a drawer and placed them gently in the sock pile.

"Well, here it goes," she whispered.

She slipped on all five pairs of her cotton panties, one at a time, followed by her first bra. Like she did with the first, bringing the band of the second bra around her rib cage, she clasped together the last set of hooks underneath her breasts, and then twisted it around to the back.

Bending forward, she slipped the straps over her shoulders and scooped the cups of the first bra into that of the second. Then, grasping both bra bands from underneath her armpits, moving them back and forth, her mediocre breasts swaying like a pendulum, she worked determinedly to tuck in any, and all, loose flesh.

Standing before the polished metal, full-length mirror, she snickered at her reflection with its four boobs.

"Nope, that won't do," she said and shook her head at the sight.

Frustrated, she looked at the clock. Forty-two minutes left.

She reached a hand around her back and popped the clasp of the second bra and began again. This time she tucked the straps of the second bra into the sidebands of the first rather than pulling them over her shoulders.

Looking in the mirror again, she was somewhat satisfied that she appeared to have just one pair of boobs and pulled on her two slips without issue.

Taking a break, she sat on the edge of the bed to pull on her five pairs of cotton Bobby socks. Because her toes became numb after tugging on only the third pair, she lined her bras with the remaining two, one pair for each side.

The mirror affirmed once again that she appeared to have only one set of sisters.

Thirty-four minutes remained to deal with the pile of clothes still on the bed. She was already perspiring and only half dressed. She reached for a button-up blouse, and, rather than dealing with unbuttoning it first, pulled it over her head. With a firm grip, she grasped the bottom of the shirt and stretched it over her buxom cleavage.

"Wouldn't it be nice to really have this problem?" she thought as she gave it one final tug.

The three top buttons exploded into the air. She dove to catch them before they hit the floor. Having no needle and thread, she decided it would be best to tuck the renegade buttons in between the two bra bands for safekeeping.

Picking up another blouse, she unbuttoned it and put it on over the other, fastening this one only halfway. Next, she pulled on four baggy knit sweaters, each going over her head and down to her waist without incident; then she squeezed into two knit, mid-length skirts, having no choice but to leave the last one half-way unzipped. Thank goodness for the baggy sweaters that covered the waist gap in her outermost skirt top.

The clock alarm went off right on time. Twenty minutes left.

She returned a neatly folded nightgown and two remaining blouses to the dresser. Loosening the laces of a pair of saddle shoes, she wedged her feet into them.

Taking her purse to the bathroom, she stuffed it full of all her toiletries, removed her coke bottle butterfly framed glasses and washed them again for the umpteenth time. She brushed her thick auburn hair back into a ponytail and looked one more time into the full-length mirror for good measure. It looked as though she were going to football practice rather than on a date.

Returning to the bedroom, she put on her calf length, Crimplene coat with the faux fur trim, buttoned it from top to bottom, and tied a matching scarf over her head. Another quick look at the clock, four minutes to spare.

PART I

She sat on the bed and waited anxiously for the nurse's knock announcing her husband's arrival, most certain she'd die from heat exhaustion if he didn't show up soon.

An elaborate system of predetermined freedoms dictated how many nurses accompanied each patient and whether a patient could leave the grounds at all.

Freedoms started with none whatsoever and you were restricted to the ward. Next, were two nurses to one patient, then one nurse to two patients, and if you were well-behaved, you got destination privileges. That's where you called the nurse when you got where you were going and again when you were coming back.

There were also mutual escorts, two patients with no nurse, and the top rung was to wander throughout the hospital alone; each level earned by good behavior and shared trust between the nurses and patients.

Being on the not so crazy list allowed Rosemary more freedoms and privacy, in and outside the state's largest mental hospital. Preparing for a Valentine's Day outing with her husband raised no suspicions and permitted her time to get ready.

Time. The clock warned that a nurse could show up at any moment now.

❦

Clean shaven with a fresh crewcut, donned in his Sunday best, Jakob pulled up to the curb of the hospital in his cherry red, 52 Victoria Hardtop. The menacing size of the brick and sentinel marble pillars stood intimidatingly on either side of the entryway. He couldn't wait to see Rosemary again and shifted into park.

He swallowed past the lump in his throat and skipped up the steps to the admit desk, announcing his arrival to the clerk.

"Can I see your ID, please sir?"

Jakob reached into his suit and handed over his driver's license.

As if he had just asked for a hamburger, the man gave it a quick glance and gave it back to him along with a clipboard.

"Fill out the information on the first line, please sir."

Jakob signed his name on the day roster; the date and time, their destination into town, the time they would return and gave it back to the man. He spun around gallantly, skipped down the steps, and waited for her in his car.

Per protocol, the nurse escorted Rosemary off the ward to the admit desk and watched as she climbed into her husband's car. She smiled to herself when she saw Rosemary's husband lean over to kiss her hello. Satisfied, she returned to her station.

WILDFLOWER

The entry gate guard's booth seemed a million miles away. Jakob pulled a crisp, white starched hanky from his breast pocket and wiped at his brow; yet, remained as cool as a cucumber as they approached the booth.

It was a miracle they waved them past. Jakob tipped his black felt fedora hat in their direction and smiled a wide Cheshire grin.

However, they didn't stop in town; they pressed onward into the proverbial sunset instead. It was all Jakob could do not to press the pedal to the metal.

The edge of town seemed a lot further than its mere ten miles. They didn't breathe a whisper until they cleared the *visit again soon* sign.

The silence between them stretched out as far and wide as the road that separated them from the hospital. Jakob shattered the deafening quiet with a boisterous, "Woohoo!" and hurled his hat into the backseat, slapped his knee, and laughed like a crazy man.

Rosemary smiled, turned around, and looked back at the looming hospital. It shrouded the little town below it with its mysterious creepiness.

She watched until it disappeared, just, as she hoped had her past. In case they'd gained a tail, Jakob drove clear into the night until he reached a Greyhound station in the Tri-Cities.

Because they only had enough money for one ticket, they decided Rosemary would take the bus to Fargo, arrive one day later than Jakob, and meet him there.

"What's in Fargo, Jakob?" Rosemary asked.

"We will be," he replied, handing her a small carry-on bag for her clothes.

Fate was on their side when they pulled into the bus station and saw the coach to Fargo, but it was about to leave and the ticket line was a mile long. Jakob hopped out and asked the driver if he'd wait a few more minutes so they could purchase their fare.

Confident Rosemary would make the bus, and wanting to get a good head start, Jakob jumped into his car and sped away.

PART I

TWO

*I*t wasn't the first time that Jakob had come to Rosemary's rescue. They met in the community rec room of Western State Hospital late in the summer of '64. Looking beyond her plain Jane appearance and coke bottle, butterfly glasses, he saw a tall and slender dark-haired beauty and her mysteriousness fascinated him. There was something about her doe-like demeanor, her shiny blue eyes, and her haunting sadness that attracted him like a moth to a flame.

She was just as captivated by his handsome James Dean dreamy good looks. He stood about six feet tall and often wore tight-fitting Levi's and form-fitting T-shirts; the left sleeve cuffed to hold his smokes. He had a husky Finnish accent, big ocean-blue eyes, and a thick swatch of combed-back strawberry blonde hair; mutually, you could say, it was lust at first sight.

For the first couple of months, they continued to meet in the rec room where they'd talk most of the day away. Soon they were sharing their meals together and taking long walks through the hospital's beautifully manicured grounds. Powerless to the burning tension between them, it wasn't long before they stole away for brief clandestine visits in the janitor's closet every chance they could.

Everything would have been perfect had it not been for a certain male attendant who found it entertaining to harass and pick on defenseless patients. One day as Jakob entered the rec room he witnessed the man antagonizing Rosemary. The intimidating, tyrannical orderly stood well over six feet tall and weighed a minimum of two hundred pounds.

Jakob wasn't threatened by the size of the man in the least. Just a mere one hundred fifty pounds soaking wet, willing to sacrifice his freedom just to be with Rosemary, Jakob drew back his fist and threw a punch at the man's jaw.

He hit him hard enough to knock his teeth loose, an act of aggression guaranteed to lengthen his admission at the funhouse. But rather than report it, Moby Dick left them alone from then on, and Jakob became Rosemary's hero.

◈

Rosemary chewed her cuticles as she waited in the ticket line. From the corner of her eye, she noticed a security guard standing nearby. Knowing crazy and suspicious would be noticeable here, she kept her focus straight ahead, stuffed her clenched fists into her coat pockets, remembering to breathe now and again, and didn't relax until she was in the safe confines of the bus.

She was glad for the few passengers on the bus, settled in a solitary seat in the back, discreetly removed her extra layers of clothes, and tucked them into the bag Jakob gave her.

She lit a cigarette, leaned back in the soft plush seat, and tried to relax.

༄

The last day she'd seen her boys remained forever etched in her brain. It began like any other day; except the day was Christmas, and her boys were coming for a visit.

"You've got visitors," the nurse called into her room.

The hospital was cold and impersonal like any other hospital right down to its army green colored walls and its oversized vinyl chairs. Except this hospital had enforced chicken wire over the windows and an occasional patient loitering the halls in various stages of zombie-like stupor, giving an unfair misconception of all the patients admitted there.

Rosemary was excited to see her boys and couldn't get to the visiting room fast enough. She saw them waiting at a table in the far corner of the room. The baby was in his stroller, and her two other sons waited in adjoining chairs.

Even as a kindergartner, her eldest looked grown up the way he looked after his brothers, but her heart ached for her middle son, he looked sad and confused.

And the baby, so sweet and precious, she walked to him. He reached his little arms out to her, and just when she was about to lift him, her husband stepped in between them.

"I came to say goodbye, Rosemary. This is the last time you will ever see the boys and me again," he whispered rather in a cold and matter-of-fact tone and then stepped aside to let her lift the baby.

She nuzzled into the creamy softness at the nape of his neck and breathed in the essence of his being. She caressed her cheek over the silkiness of his downy hair, wrapped her arms around him and pressed his body close to hers in a loving embrace.

Her two other sons joined in for a group hug. Rosemary pulled them as close as possible and hugged them tight. She didn't want to scare them with her tears, but when they started, she couldn't hold them back.

Perturbed, her husband snatched the baby from her arms and bundled him in his stroller. He told her the judge had granted him an uncontested divorce, adding how it would be a cold day in hell before she'd ever leave the hospital. Without another word, he ushered her older sons from the room following close behind with the stroller. Her eldest glanced back at her as they disappeared around the corner.

PART I

Rosemary collapsed to the floor on her knees. She cried harder than she'd ever had before. Her heart ached, and her mind raced with the threat of her husband's menacing words.

Cut off from her family; cut off from her boys as if she'd never had them; stuck away in this hospital, so nobody had to deal with her; she wanted to die.

"My babies, my babies," she moaned as she rocked herself back and forth.

On the rare occasions that Rosemary's husband brought her boys to visit, Jakob hung back and didn't interfere. In those two brief visits, he saw enough to make his blood boil. The last visit was the worse. He'd witnessed the entire disgusting scene, and it was the last straw.

Her cutting anguish tore his heart apart. He didn't know the man, but he hated him, right down to his inner core. It was all he could do not to jump the skinny little guy and beat him senseless, but that's what got him in here in the first place.

Besides, with his sentence almost served, that piece of shit wasn't worth spending one more second than required in this cuckoo's nest.

Jakob knelt next to Rosemary and put his arm around her shoulders.

Brushing her hair back, and wiping her tears away, he whispered in her ear, "We could leave."

He leaned back on his haunches, rested his chin on his knee, and waited for her reply.

"What?" she looked up at him with swollen eyes and a tear-stained face, spellbound by his knee-knocking Robert Redford good looks and foreign accent.

"You and me; we could leave this place and start a new life. I can get you out of here," he said.

She shook her head in defeat. "No, Jakob, they'll come after me. My husband said I'll be here the rest of my life."

"I can get you out of here," he said.

Fresh tears streamed down her cheeks, "No Jakob; they'll lock you up and throw away the key too."

"Don't you want to go?"

"Where would we go?"

"Don't you worry about a thing; I'll figure it all out."

Rosemary awoke sometime later to the driver's announcement for the first stop. Spokane, they hadn't even made it out of Washington yet; it would be a long trip. She went inside the gas station and bought a soda and a Harlequin.

As the bus continued, she pressed her forehead against the cold glass window and took in the panoramic perfectness of the surrounding neighborhood; the painted clapboard houses and the just-mowed lawns, like the one she'd shared with her husband; funny how hers also had a white picket fence.

That was the way Rosemary would always remember it; the day she decided that she couldn't take it anymore.

She had been pregnant for most of their five-year marriage. Knocked-up and just out of high school, her family thought it best if they marry right away.

He was older and had a perfect job; he gave her everything and yet nothing at the same time. Try as she might, she couldn't adapt to her husband's definitions of what a wife was, creating a seething and hostile animosity a mile wide between them.

It was a warm and sunny day even for being past four o'clock. Her two eldest boys played in the sandbox, and the baby napped in a playpen close-by when her husband arrived home in a customary foul mood.

He was in a tizzy because he'd just learned that his boss and a few guys from work were coming over to their place for dinner. Infuriating him even further was the realization that his wife couldn't be depended upon to save the day.

Just as he expected, the house was a wreck and reeked of shitty diapers, dirty dishes, and stale cigarettes. He kicked a toy telephone into the wall. Rosemary watched as it smashed into little pieces, a small spring from the bell rolled across the floor and rested at her feet.

Larry screamed in Rosemary's face. "Goddammit Rosemary, you weren't listening again! I've got people from work and their wives coming any minute, and you look a mess! You've been here all day, why is this house so upside down?"

Rosemary replied, "You didn't tell me anyone was coming over. You didn't say to prepare food."

"Well isn't it obvious when I tell you to have the house spotless? Besides, you couldn't make food for a monkey."

He searched the house frantically for his sons.

"Where are the boys Rosemary" he sneered. "I'm surprised if you even remembered to change the baby's diapers today!"

"They're outside playing," Rosemary said, chewing her nails, waiting for the next wave.

PART I

He looked out the back window to affirm they were.

"Get this house together! We've only got an hour!" He poured himself a drink from the bar and flopped down in his lazy boy chair.

"Never mind about dinner, I'll order take out."

Exhausted and overwhelmed, surveying the mess around her, Rosemary couldn't decide where to begin. It looked like she hadn't done squat in the entire day.

Larry made her jump as he sprung up from the chair, "Don't just stand there dammit! Get moving!"

Rosemary cried in frustration.

Larry mocked her, "Oh now we're the victim, and I'm the big bad husband."

He drew back his hand, and it landed with a sharp sting across her left cheek.

"Now you have something to cry about. Go clean yourself up for Pete's sake before they arrive. You disgust me."

Larry walked over to the telephone and ordered a delivery of appetizers and dinner. He poured himself another drink from the bar, lit a smoke, and returned to his lazy boy.

Tears rolled down her cheeks. As hard as she tried to be like the wives she'd seen on TV, nothing was ever good enough.

Every morning before he left for work, he'd give her a list of the things he wanted to be done by the time he returned home. But it didn't matter if she'd finished them above and beyond his expectations, he still found fault in even the most minute detail.

In fact, he was always telling her what to do and how to do it, right down to the little bittyist thing, as if she didn't have a brain in her head. It was always the same scene; it was just too much.

Rather than pick up a dust rag though, she marched up to their room, pulled a suitcase down from the closet, and unloaded her dresser drawers into it instead.

She grabbed a few toiletries from the bathroom, stuffed them in with everything else, and headed downstairs for the door. As she stepped outside, she heard him hurl one last threat her way.

"If you leave, Rosemary, I'll never welcome you back, ever!"

Rosemary didn't know where to go and kept walking towards the main road where she knew the bus route was. Arriving at the bus stop, she searched her purse for change but found none. She had no money and no checkbook.

Undefeated, she walked two more blocks to the corner store and called her eldest sister collect.

It was near dark when she arrived. Rosemary climbed into the front seat and spewed all the hatred she had for her husband right into her lap, regardless if she wanted to hear it or not.

Her sister listened with tried patience, paused, and then tried to talk sense into her. She said she had spoken with Larry moments ago and he said she could come back home. Rosemary couldn't believe her ears. It was as if she hadn't heard a word she'd said.

Would she want to go back to a husband like that? I think not.

Her sister made a U-turn and headed back towards Rosemary's house.

"Don't you dare take me back there! Stop the car!"

Rosemary pulled on the door handle.

"Where do you think you're going in the middle of the night Rosemary?" her usually quiet and collected sister screamed, waking her four-year-old daughter who was sleeping in the back seat.

"Anywhere but here," Rosemary shouted back. "Now stop the damn car, or I will jump out!"

Her sister swerved to the curb just in time for Rosemary to stumble out with her suitcase, her frantic cries followed as she disappeared into the night.

The police found her some hours later wandering the solitary streets of West Seattle, picked her up, and, per her husband's request, admitted her into the state's largest mental hospital. Rosemary didn't speak to her sister again for another eight years.

～

Rosemary slept through Idaho and Montana. She awoke to the announcement for Fargo, North Dakota, gathered her things, and stepped off the bus. As promised, Jakob was right there waiting for her, leaning up against his car, looking like an outlaw with a smug smile on his face.

She ran to him.

He scooped her up and, like Rhett Butler, kissed her passionately.

"Where will we stay?" she laughed as he set her back on the ground.

"I got us a room at a motel close to here. It has a restaurant attached to it. I thought you could get a job there and I'd find work in town."

Fearful, Rosemary looked down at the ground; her face flushed. She didn't want to ruin his plans, but she'd never had a job before. He hugged her assuredly, as if he had read her mind, explaining that it would be just as easy as taking care of babies and a husband.

PART I

THREE

*J*akob was born to second-generation Finns; his father's family distilled wine on a vineyard in northern Finland, and his mother's family worked a dairy farm on the outskirts of the Laplands, on Sweden's border.

With festering and ongoing problems with the USSR and Sweden, many Finnish families, including Jakob's, moved to the United States.

The journey from Finland to England where they'd meet a ship bound for America was difficult and the damp, dark days were miserable and cold. As a result, Jakob's grandmother fell ill by the time they had reached their destination. Being poor immigrants with third-class tickets, they denied her passage until she was well enough to travel.

Not all was lost though, fate was on their side that day. Halfway through their scheduled voyage, April 14, 1912, their ship struck an iceberg and sank, resulting in the deaths of over a thousand people, most in the cheapest and least comfortable accommodations, third-class.

Jakob's grandparents never forgot that trip or the many friends they lost that day. Jakob's mother, Elsia, would always remember the horrifying story of their passage to America in vivid detail as if it were yesterday. Just fourteen, she never forgot how scared she felt during the entire trip or the stoic vigil she kept over the water for any malevolent icebergs.

Etched most in her memory, as they crossed over where the previous ship had sunk, were the mournful cries from the frightening apparitions she'd seen floating in the mist.

Jakob loved to retell that story every chance he got.

After processing successfully through Ellis Island, Elsia's family settled in South Range, Michigan where her father secured a job as a copper miner, and her mother managed a boarding house for the local miners.

Jakob's father's family settled in Negaunee Michigan, but Jakob's father wouldn't share any more about his family, except that he had a falling out with them in his early twenties and then refused to speak any further on the subject.

Although Jakob's parents grew up within a few miles of one another, they didn't meet until many years later, not until each had married, had children, and each had lost their spouses. In fact, they were pen pals an entire year through the small towns newspaper's single section before they even laid eyes on each other.

Jakob's mother told him it wasn't love at first sight, nor perhaps was it at all, but because they each longed for companionship, they agreed to marry soon after their brief introduction. His mother, just past forty, and his father, around a decade older, were ecstatic they were nearing the end of raising their nine children, his five and her four, and looked forward to the tranquility and freedom of an empty nest.

However, the day his mother arrived home from visiting the doctor for what she thought were pre-menopausal symptoms and learned that she was expecting instead, was the day that changed her relationship with his father. And was likewise the day his father moved into his own bedroom on the top floor of their home, never to share a bed with his wife again.

After Jakob's birth, lacking the energy to tend to the needs of a baby, his mother allowed him to run wild and free. His siblings' thought their parents spoiled him, and he got away with much more than they ever did, which wasn't the case, he just wasn't as harshly molded and disciplined as they had been.

By the time Jakob was a teenager, he had become rebellious and unruly with no regard for law and order. At seventeen, his parents shipped him off to the army, but unbeknownst to them the minimum age to enter the military was eighteen.

Determined not to return home, he forged his birth certificate and got himself enlisted. A year later, while serving in Korea, he returned for his father's funeral, the only and last time he ever went home again.

After the old codger was six feet under, they stationed Jakob stateside for his three remaining enlisted years. To make the time go faster, he chased skirts and partied hard, sometimes he'd get a wild hair and just disappear. His sabbaticals lasted only about a month each time, and when caught, they'd toss him into the Brig for a brief spell for going AWOL; but he didn't care; he just wanted out.

Jakob belonged nowhere; he was a misfit, a rolling stone. When the last blessed day of his service arrived, never wanting to be tied down or owned by anyone again, he found his calling and true happiness living the life of a meandering hobo, drifting from one lonely town to another.

If one day the clouds were black and ominous, and the sky threatened rain, he did not worry one bit, because he knew he could depend upon local YMCA for a dry place to sleep, a hot shower, and to wash laundry. If he needed money, there was always a small cafe around the corner in need of a dishwasher in exchange for a warm meal and a couple bucks.

And every so often, for a change of scenery, with his knack for telling tall tales and starting fights, he'd find food and shelter at the local county jail for a night. This also made him eligible for a revolving passport to the madhouse where Valium was the only thing they found to cool his hothead.

PART I

FOUR

The motel was just a few blocks from the bus station. Jakob pulled into the driveway, passed under a narrow carport with a large overhead, red neon Vacancy sign, and cruised around the circular drive to the back. The twenty-six-unit, single-story, psychedelic hotel screamed hippie, yet beckoned home sweet home.

They parked in front of room 22. He gave Rosemary a big plastic key ring tag with the room's corresponding number. Rosemary's stomach growled as a whiff of fried chicken tickled her nose. She unlocked the door and stepped inside. It smelled like a dirty ashtray and Lysol.

The walls were painted baby blue with a scattering of some southwestern-themed framed pictures. The furnishings were a mismatched set, no doubt from a going-out-of-business sale from a local used store or an estate auction.

Shoved into the corner, covered by a hideous turquoise and floral patterned coverlet, was a tidy full-size bed.

Rosemary walked into the bathroom. It was typical, right down to its Pepto Bismol walls and tiny, green, Chicklet tiled floor.

She ripped the *sanitary* paper banner off the toilet seat as if it were the Good Housekeeping Seal of Approval. The white towels, though not fluffy, seemed new.

Overall, their room was homey in its own little way. She turned and flashed Jakob a consenting smile.

Exhausted, she walked back to the bed, flopped onto its lumpy softness, and fell sound asleep in seconds flat.

Jakob left her to nap and stepped outside for a smoke. He moseyed over to the restaurant next door to get them something to eat.

He returned a short time later, set the food on the dresser, and thought to wake her up, but got a devilish idea instead.

He slipped a quarter into the coin box affixed to the headboard and held his breath as it deposited with a loud clunk.

She didn't stir. There was a buzz from deep within the bed; the fine lines on the bedspread went into soft focus. He held his breath.

Rosemary awoke in a panic to what felt as if a giant were shaking the bed as hard as it could. She gripped the sides of the mattress and rose from the depths of sleepy oblivion. In her comatose stupor, squinting, she opened one eye and scanned the room.

Consciousness hit her like a southbound train, and her heart raced. For a moment, something felt frighteningly strange and familiar. *What's happening? — was there an earthquake? — how had they got here? — where was here? — why were they...?*

The myriad of unanswered questions muddled her foggy brain. A thin film of perspiration formed on her brow and upper lip. Fear was setting in, and there was nothing she could do about it, nothing reassuring came to mind, no comforting words or thoughts, nothing.

She jumped off the bed, and the world stopped shaking. She eyed Jakob from across the room. He was laughing his ass off.

Wide awake now, she asked, "What's so damn funny? Didn't you feel the earthquake too?"

Speechless, clutching his sides, all he could do was point.

Rosemary followed the course of its direction right to the coin box affixed to the headboard that read Vibrating Bed.

"Jerk," she said.

"I'm sorry sweetie, but you should have seen your face. It was priceless. Don't worry, they don't have earthquakes in North Dakota," he half-assed apologized, trying to regain composure.

They ate in silence. Rosemary was still stewing from her rude awakening.

Frazzled from the crazy day, finding consolation in each other's arms, they curled up together and fell asleep to the gentle rhythmic rocking of the Vibrating Bed.

PART I

FIVE

The next morning Jakob headed out in search of employment. What he wanted most was to drive the long-haul trucks, but because he was only twenty-two, he had to settle for odd jobs here and there.

Rosemary, in the meanwhile, inquired with the motel and restaurant owner to see if he had any work she could do. He said he needed help at his restaurant and to meet him there around two thirty.

Arriving a tad earlier, she sat in a booth and ordered a Tab, lit a smoke, and took in her surroundings.

The diner was small and low-key; it had large sliding glass windows covered by airy yellow curtains across the length of three walls, underneath each were a pair of worn, red vinyl booths with a narrow table in between.

She watched four teenage boys eating a heaping plate of French fries and gravy but looked away when one of them caught her staring.

There was a miniature Jukebox on each table, three plays for 25c, a pair of salt and pepper shakers, a sugar dispenser, a napkin holder, and a bottle of ketchup.

Across from the booths, saddled up to one continuous counter, on a row of red leather stools, sat varying ages of men dressed in Levi's, plaid flannel shirts, and cowboy boots, their hats tucked in their laps.

The nerve-jangling bang of the order bell and the obnoxious twang from one of the waitress's startled Rosemary from her daydream.

"Table five wants his burger cremated!"

Rosemary's attention turned toward the beehive-like hum from the hustle and bustle of the two waitresses. Their uniforms were cute. They wore one-piece light pink dresses with broad, white, V-neck collars and three-quarter sleeves. Dainty white buttons ran up the front with their nametags pinned to a small hanky pocket on the right side.

A separate white apron, with a scalloped hem and pockets, held their notepads and tips and tied into a magnificent bow in the back. But, that's where the likeness stopped, each had their own variation of how they wore their uniform.

Reading their nametags as they passed by, dabbing out her cigarette, Rosemary observed how Susan was more down to earth. She was short and a little on the plump side, wore her dress buttoned to her collar bone, had shoulder length brown hair, set or natural waves she couldn't tell, pinned it back at the temples, and had a friendly face absent from makeup except for a light shade of mauve lipstick.

Then there was Luanne. Her freckled tan skin looked as though she had spent too much time in the sun and her no-nonsense lined lips were never without bright-red lipstick. She slathered it on as easy as lip balm in between patrons, applying it without a mirror, in the same way her mother did.

And her uniform, well, let's just say it was more tip-worthy. She wore her dress on the edge of flirting with the imagination. The collar was unbuttoned just enough to expose her decolletage and, even though she was tall and pencil thin, the uniform was at least one size too small, emphasizing what curves she had and a bikini panty line.

She complimented the whole show with a seductive lacey red kerchief that peeked from her hanky pocket, secured in place with her name tag. Should you miss it, there was a large, hot pink cursive letter L embroidered on her lapel to help you remember.

If that wasn't memorable enough, it was when she opened her mouth, she became stuck forever in your brain. She had a loud, sarcastic, chalkboard-grating, southern drawl, and chewed and snapped on her bubble gum like some anxious cow when she talked.

You had to pay close attention to understand what she was saying and not get caught up by the mesmerizing bright pink ball drop earrings that swayed in tempo with her jaw while she spoke.

Besides her quirkiness, she was all waitress. Luanne could carry six Blue Plate specials lined up on her arm like a charm bracelet, pour syrup like tropical rain, and keep the short-order carousel spinning like a roulette wheel. And never, not once, did she ever let a customer's coffee get cold.

"Clang, clang, clang" the banging of the order bell startled Rosemary to the present again.

"Luanne!" the cook, a husky brusque man, wearing a sweat- and grease-laden T-shirt and a rolled up white knitted cap from which thick silver sideburns peeked out, bellowed through the kitchen window.

Luanne rushed to the counter, "Oh my God! What, Floyd?" "Where's the damn fire? Give me a heart attack why don't you!"

"I see your favorite irregular is here!" He snickered waving at the owner who walked towards Rosemary's booth.

"Oh, kiss my grits." She turned and sashayed over to our table.

He sat across from Rosemary.

PART I

Poised with her pen and pad, Luanne twanged and smacked, "What can I get you, Hun?"

He asked for a slice of apple pie and a cup of coffee and then apologized to Rosemary for being late, stating how hectic it was managing a motel and a restaurant at the same time.

Rosemary smiled and told him it was ok; she had enjoyed watching all the comings and goings around there.

He got right to the point and stated that he was in dire straits for a hostess and the job was hers if she wanted it.

Rosemary blushed, "I've never had a job before."

The owner replied, "Don't you worry your pretty little head, it's a simple job, cleaning tables, filling salt and sugar jars and such."

He chuckled and dug into the steamy, fragrant pie Luanne set before him.

In between bites, he asked, "Do you think the job will suit you?"

Without hesitation, Rosemary replied it would.

Just as emphatic, he smiled and shook her hand, "Great, you can start tomorrow morning at nine a.m., just after the breakfast rush. Susan will get you a uniform and show you around for the first few days, oh and please call me Tony."

He got up to leave and added how some of her earnings would pay for her room and board, and she'd receive the rest biweekly in cash, to avoid the hassle of new employee paperwork and taxes.

Jakob couldn't believe their luck how their food was part of the deal; they had the best steaks he'd ever had.

At the end of a long day, they'd unwind with cheap cigarettes and Thunderbird wine. Jakob soon found steady work with a painting contractor and things fell into place. Everything that is, except for Rosemary, whose seams were unraveling.

Jakob didn't understand Rosemary's problems; sometimes he took his frustration and impatience out on her and the hotel room.

Often, from the safety within the confines of a locked bathroom, Rosemary began having animated conversations with herself.

"She knew when to quit, but no, not Jakob, getting all riled up about nothing at all, cursing in Finn and breaking things. Had she known this side of him, she never would have left the hospital,"

"Are you talking to the wallpaper again Rosemary?"

"Go away, Jakob. Leave me alone."

"What the hell is the matter with you? I should have left you at the hospital!" he yelled and hit the door with his fist.

"I wish you had," she muttered loud enough for him to hear, lit a cigarette, put the toilet seat down, brought her feet up off the floor to sit Indian style, and continued to process her thoughts aloud.

༄

After three months, the hotel owner had about enough of them and gave them the boot. Thankfully, Jakob had started an extra side job working nights as a janitor at the local Elks Lodge and could afford something else. They found a single bedroom, eight hundred square foot, tin can, in a run-down trailer park he'd found on the outskirts of town.

He returned home early from work one day and surprised Rosemary with a homecoming gift, a black shorthaired kitten with blue eyes about as big as its little head. Because he was an active creature with an understanding mind, Rosemary named him Geronimo.

In return, Rosemary also had a gift for Jakob. She hesitated at first, unsure of how he'd react.

"Well, Rosemary, what is it?"

"Honey, I'm pregnant."

PART I

SIX

Rosemary's parents were among the founding families of West Seattle. In fact, her grandfather was their first Fire Chief. Rosemary's mom, Jane, grew up in the University district in an impressive old house just one block from Greek Row. Jane was a late *caboose* surprise baby. Her brother Pete and sister Kate were much older, by twelve or thirteen years.

Uncle Pete was weird; Rosemary remembers fearing him when she was young. He was a loner, never married, and didn't have kids. He lived in Oregon and came up every few years to visit his sisters and their families. Her Aunt Kate married and had a daughter named Mary Jo. She was Rosemary's only cousin.

Jane was a captivating beauty, cultured, and smart in every way. Her parents raised her to be a *lady of the house* and to focus her studies on piano and dance and other similar things. When she attended college, besides majoring in French and being active in local theater, she was the president of her sorority and the drama club. Her dream was to go to Hollywood with her best friend Francis Farmer and become a movie star, but then she met Rosemary's dad, Harvey.

Harvey, president of his fraternity at the same University as Jane's, was your typical tall, dark, and handsome Romeo, a real lady's man, a skirt chaser if you will. Theirs was a true boy meets girl fairy tale, but one without a happy ending. He swept Jane off her feet and lavished her with everything she wanted, a fine big house, maids, fancy cars, and jewelry just to name a few comforts.

They made themselves at home in Harvey's family's neck of the woods in West Seattle, and he began a successful career as a car salesman not long after. As perfect as they were, Jane and Harvey's firstborn, a girl, like her parents, was flawless in every way, a shiny penny that would remain a favorite among the family. Then, there was their second child, Rosemary.

The words in Rosemary's baby book are scarce; what's not recorded speaks volumes. Born with a colloid goiter just under her chin resembling the gross swollen size of a bullfrog's neck, she spent her first month of life in the hospital inside an oxygen tent.

Lacking the strength to nurse or bottle feed, they gave her nutrition through a tube down her throat. To correct her crossed eyes, she wore thick, coke-bottle sized glasses strapped around her head and didn't learn to walk alone or speak more than single-syllable words until she was well over two years old.

Her family often left Rosemary to her own company, tied to the laundry post in the backyard by her mother *so she could keep an eye on her*. Passersby thought it entertaining in the way she tried to walk; it looked more like dancing the way she bobbed up and down.

Rosemary's mother describes her first birthday, "as rather small with a few neighbors peeking in the windows." It's also noted that she had few visitors, not even during holidays. She's described by her mother as being *ungraceful* and when Rosemary was two years old she commented, "We think she's awfully cute, but she whines a lot."

Sweet and delicate like the butterflies she loved so much, Rosemary viewed the world and everyone in it through innocent eyes. She saw only the good in others, trusted with all her heart, and never had an unkind word to say about anyone.

Rosemary was passive and not at all argumentative. She took everything personally and strived to better herself to whoever's standard she wasn't meeting.

In her late teens, the onset of schizophrenia didn't stand out because she had always behaved and spoken differently from others.

As plain as the remaining blank pages in her baby book, it was obvious she was the black sheep in her family.

Jane blamed herself for her daughter's disabilities. It wasn't long after Rosemary's birth Harvey began to chase skirts, right underneath her nose. She couldn't rely on his mother for a sympathetic ear. The woman never approved of her, and it would please her to no end to hear of Jane's unhappiness, there was no way in hell she'd give her that satisfaction.

With rumors of her husband's fooling around, Jane spiraled into a deep depression. Not even the gift of another perfect daughter, the same as her first, could bring her back from the brink of sadness and disappointment.

Not unlike a script from a Hollywood drama, Jane turned to the bottle and pills to ease her unhappiness, reflecting her misery onto her family. She thought if they didn't stay in one place for too long it would spare her of Harvey's reputation.

So, she had him move them around town, house to house, sometimes yearly to preserve what dignity she still had, but it made no difference, no matter where they went, Jane became the laughingstock of the neighborhood.

The final straw was the day Harvey kidnapped Rosemary and her youngest sister. He locked them up in a room at his mother's house for several weeks and left Jane with a pile of unpaid bills, no phone, electricity, or car and no idea where her children were.

PART I

That's when Jane got the nerve to divorce the *Pig,* as Rosemary recalls how her mother referred to him. Then everything else came undone.

Rosemary's eldest sister, only sixteen, ran off and eloped with a neighbor boy who had just joined the military and then moved with him to an overseas base.

It was incredible her parents didn't bat an eye. But boy, was there hell to pay when Rosemary found herself in a similar predicament two years later. And then when Rosemary's husband committed her to the state mental hospital a few years after that, a *you made your bed you sleep in it* sort of deal, it was just the excuse the family needed to write her off, and they left her there to rot.

SEVEN

Jacob ran his fingers through his hair several times before asking her to repeat what she'd just said. He turned and punched the wall.

Rosemary didn't understand his reaction. Jakob decided the best thing for them to do was go home to his sister Ruth's in Detroit, but they'd have to put together money first.

Jakob took on twice as many odd jobs, working here and there, around town, from sunup to sundown, and soon had a good-sized nest egg set aside for the coming baby. But, even with the best of intentions, after a series of financial pitfalls, their savings eventually disappeared, and then they got behind on the rent.

Rosemary was about six months along the day she noticed two suits with wide-brimmed hats sitting in the same corner booth for the second day in a row. They talked in quiet whispers and glanced her way occasionally. She was a nervous wreck by the time they left.

She told Jakob about them when he picked her up after her shift that night. Her suspicions peaked further when they arrived home, and their key no longer fit in the lock.

Adding insult to injury, when they went around the house to check the back door, they found all their belongings piled up on the lawn.

"Do you think they found us?" Rosemary asked.

"No, I don't think so, but we'd better get to my sister's just in case," Jakob said.

Rosemary trusted Jakob and agreed. They drove into town and rented a U-Haul with a car trailer and got a hotel for the night.

The next morning found Jakob in a foul mood. He had to load their belongings from the yard into the truck before for work, and somehow figure out their next escape.

Good thing they paid him daily, and Rosemary's payday was today too. After finishing his midafternoon deliveries, he collected his wages, stopped in the diner for a bite to eat, gathered Rosemary's check, cashed them at the grocery next door, and got busy with his plan.

By the time he picked her up, he had the U-Haul and Ford packed, gassed, and ready to go. She climbed in the passenger side, slid in close to him, and noticed a clinging Geronimo in his lap. Her face lit up as she scooped him into

PART I

her arms, it was all she could do not to cry, so relieved that he got to come along.

Then, like last time, without so much as a farewell or thank you to anyone, they disappeared into the night.

∽

Rosemary hated the way Jakob drove; he was all about getting there with no stops in the fastest time possible. She didn't see the urgency of showing up unannounced at his sister's house. They drove until just before dawn and didn't stop until they reached the suburbs of Detroit Michigan.

They found a cheap hotel where Rosemary stretched out on the queen size bed for an overdue rest. She ached all over from the jarring of the unpaved backroads and the constant kicking from the baby.

They arrived at Ruth's the next day, she took pity on Rosemary; if it weren't for her condition, she wouldn't have opened her home to them and their cat. After two months and with the baby due soon, Jakob decided they should get a home of their own. Without too much effort, he found a quaint 3-bedroom, 2-story, mother-in-law rental just behind a landlord's house.

In the brief time they lived at Ruth's, Jakob learned just enough about the tool and dye trade from her husband to secure steady work. To keep up with expenses, he also took an offer of a second job at a local Ford production plant.

He liked cars, especially Fords, he had always had one and enjoyed what some called tedious work. With an apron full of screws and an air screwdriver, he could stand for hours on end, happy as a clam, securing the chrome trim to the edges of Lincoln Mercurys' bucket seats.

Rosemary, wanting to help, found a part-time job as a hostess at a small diner within walking distance from their house. Just like she had in Fargo, she cleaned tables, filled empty salt and pepper shakers, and poured coffee, working well into the last month of her pregnancy.

∽

November arrived with its magical transformation of season and spirit. The vibrant colors of crimsons, oranges, and golds exploded everywhere in their annual blaze of color. As nature heralded the change of seasons, Rosemary and Jakob celebrated a little miracle of their own.

Retracing the worn-out path of the carpet in the fathers' waiting area, Jakob thought he'd lose his mind with worry by the time they appeared with his little bundle of joy. His heart melted the moment they handed him his baby girl.

Peering into the tiny, tear-filled, blue eyes that mirrored his own, he recalled just how he'd always wished for a baby sister and never got one. It was love at first sight.

He brought her closer to his chest and gave her a gentle hug, hoping she felt all the love he had for her.

And then she cried and cried some more; it was the one thing that Jakob couldn't stand, and he cried right along with her.

He named her after his mother and his sister, Elsia Ruth, Lissie for short. It wasn't until after the birth certificate arrived that he noticed he had misspelled his mother's name, he'd reversed the "i" and the "s". Another error, one that Jakob didn't notice, was the fictitious last name Rosemary listed for herself.

"No matter," he thought, justifying the misspelling, she still had her grandmother's name.

He loved being a father, until he had to take care of her and when she cried. He hated the annoying caterwaul of a baby's cries, his or anyone else's.

It wasn't long before Jakob became bored of the whole playing house thing, he felt tied down and trapped. He missed his carefree, party-all-night lifestyle.

Geronimo sensed his restless agitation and kept vigil over the new baby. He synced his nap schedule with that of the little human, snuggled up close to warm her body, and lulled her to sleep with his purring.

If she cried in the middle of the night and no one tended to her within a reasonable amount of time, he'd go to the parents' bed and box them in the face until they woke up.

Four months after the birth of their baby girl, Rosemary learned that she was pregnant again. Jakob's reaction hurt her feelings. The look he gave her was hateful as if she had gotten that way by herself.

Defeated, but wanting to do the right thing, since the odd jobs in Detroit were not reliable enough to support another child, and had heard of steady work in nearby Toledo, he told Rosemary they were moving again.

The day they were ready to haul out of town, Geronimo was nonexistent. While Jakob crammed the last of their belongings in the car, Rosemary searched around the yard for him.

"Geronimo . . . here kitty kitty kitty . . . where are you Geronimo . . .?" she called and called, peering into the tall grass, searching under the steps of the front porch and in all his usual hiding places.

"Come on Rosemary, time to go," Jakob called after her.

Rosemary's heart sank.

He saw the disappointment in her face when he handed her the baby.

"Don't worry, the landlady will take him in when he comes home. We have to go now before traffic gets bad and darkness sets in."

Rosemary's heart ached as they drove away. She grieved for the precious kitty that loved her baby so much but felt her place and her home was with Jakob, and she'd follow him to the ends of the earth.

EIGHT

Once in Toledo, after setting up Rosemary and the baby in a hotel, Jakob went to the DMV to transfer his Michigan driver's license to Ohio. He took a numbered ticket, sat in a chair, and was about to get comfortable when a familiar voice called his name. He looked around, it was his best friend from the army, Hank.

With a firm pat on the back and a hearty handshake, they were both surprised at their chance run in. It had been two years since their discharge, and the last time they'd spoken. Each was ecstatic to learn that the other also had a second baby on the way.

After finishing their business, Hank introduced Jakob to his wife, who had been waiting in their car with their napping daughter. When they heard Jakob and his family had only just arrived in town, Hank and his wife insisted that they stay with them until they got a place of their own. Much obliged, Jakob said they'd come by in the morning as Rosemary and their baby were at the hotel resting.

While making themselves at home in their basement, Rosemary did her best to warm up to Hanks wife, Ellen, who didn't seem as enthused about them staying there as Jakob had let on. He, by the way, and Hank were having a grand ol' time catching up and reminiscing about life in the army.

With Hank's help, Jakob got a job in town with a moving company. It was surprising how Rosemary and Jakob didn't argue the entire time they stayed with them, probably because Ellen didn't allow alcohol in her house or around her children.

With little effort, Jakob found a nice rambler for rent in the middle of a small farm vacated by ranch hands for the season. He, Rosemary, and the baby settled in for what looked like would be a long winter.

Soon after, Jakob was at work driving delivery trucks with Hank, followed by Rosemary who found part-time work at a local café, and Ellen, who surprised everyone, volunteered to stay home with all the kids.

The night Rosemary left for the hospital to have the second baby, Jakob oversaw the care of their firstborn until her return four days later.

His first night on duty, Jakob paced the floor like a wildcat, wondering what the hell he had got himself into, dreading the day Rosemary would bring another one home.

PART I

The nonstop caterwauling by his daughter interrupted his thoughts. He fed, diapered her, and did everything he'd seen Rosemary do, but nothing pacified her.

He tried ignoring her and popped open a beer, flopped on the sofa, and tried to relax. But her cries got louder and louder, echoing off of the walls, and vibrating in every corner of his brain.

Unable to reach Jakob, Rosemary and the new baby took a cab home. When they arrived, she stood dumbfounded in the doorway, and couldn't believe her eyes.

The house was a wreck, and Jakob and Lissie were asleep like drunken sailors on the couch. Strained peas decorated the kitchen wall next to a busted high chair.

Rosemary laid a sleeping Maggie in her sister's crib and then took the eldest from Jakob's arms. She slipped the wet pajamas over her head and changed her soaked diaper. Dry and comfy once again, along with a warm bottle of milk, she nestled her close to her new baby sister.

With the girls sound asleep and Jakob still passed out, Rosemary poured herself a long overdue glass of Thunderbird, sat on the steps of the front porch, and lit a cigarette. Her frantic nerves uncoiled with every deep drag of the sacred smoke as she contemplated their future.

∽

It didn't take long for Rosemary and Jakob to get into the swing of things, balancing parenting and working; Rosemary worked the dinner shift as a hostess and Jakob drove a delivery truck during the day.

As Lissie became older and able to do more for herself, she and Jakob came to a truce. Whenever she drove him nuts, all he had to do was elevate his tone a little, give her the evil eye, and she'd knock off whatever she was doing. Thank god, the second baby was quiet and didn't give him as much hell.

Hank's daughter didn't give him as much trouble as Jakob's oldest gave him. He thought their test of wills was hilarious.

"Seems you've met your match, son," he'd tease.

Jakob presumed the first one was retribution for all the wrong he'd ever done. The humdinger of all was the day he thought he lost her.

Just two years old, Jacob didn't dare take his eyes off her; she was always into everything. One afternoon he arrived home early to an unusually quiet house.

Rosemary was sound asleep on the couch. He tiptoed down the hall to the girls' room and found Maggie sleeping. Assured all was well, he turned towards the kitchen, but panic stopped him in his tracks.

Fear gripped his heart, and he went back to the crib; Lissie wasn't next to her sister. He dashed around the house in search of her, but with no luck; frustrated and tired, he shook Rosemary awake.

"Do you know where your daughter is?"

Rosemary replied half asleep, "Both of the girls are asleep in the crib."

"No, they are not," he sneered, "Lissie is gone!"

Rosemary bolted off the couch. It wasn't the first time the child had disappeared. They called her name as they searched in all the places they'd found her before, in the kitchen and bathroom cupboards, the space under the stairs, behind furniture, and under the bed.

Empty handed, they ran outside. Going in opposite directions, circling the house, they searched and searched and called for her. The putrid taste of terror gurgled from Jakob's stomach, finding its way to his mouth.

Skipping two steps at a time, he bolted off the front porch and to the neighbor's house. They watched them as they looked for her and met Jakob at the door to tell him they hadn't seen her.

He smoothed his hair back with both hands as he tried to think of where she could have wandered off to. He scanned the yard and spotted something familiar in the middle of the street.

His heart raced as he ran to see what it was. It was Lissie's t-shirt.

Rosemary stayed behind with Maggie as Jakob continued the search. He followed a trail of Lissie's clothes, a pair of socks, her pants, a wet diaper, which continued for an entire block and a half, right down to the shore of Lake Erie.

Just beyond the water was little Miss Free Spirit, playing in the water, naked as a jay bird, without a care in the world.

Her face lit up when she saw him, "Hi Daddy!"

Jakob was furious; how could she act like nothing was wrong. He grabbed her by the wrist and yanked her out of the water like a ragdoll.

Still dangling by one arm, he shook her violently and yelled, "Who do you think you are dammit! You can't just go wandering off to the damn beach whenever you damn well please!"

Lissie gave out a blood-curdling scream as he landed a severe swat on her bare wet bottom.

Rosemary ran to them as soon as they came into view. Jakob shoved Lissie at her.

"Goddamn kid!"

PART I

Despite everything though, Rosemary was optimistic about how it all was coming about. She wanted to get it right this time, even experimenting with a few recipes from a Betty Crocker Cookbook. Jakob didn't seem to mind whenever her attempts went wrong, it was food and that was all that mattered to him, the more mistakes the better he'd say.

She also tried to keep their house clean and to care for the girls herself, keeping them out of Jakob's hair mostly. Rosemary was certain she was living her happily ever after at last.

Regardless of her best efforts though, over the course of the following year, their fighting increased. The more they fought, the more Jakob drank, and the more he drank, the worse his temper got. The worse his temper got, the more she sought solace within the depths of a bottle of Thunderbird.

Not unlike the continuous unfurling of their generic cigarettes, time marched on, each day blending into another like that of the one before. Except for the afternoon three-year-old Lissie asked her mother this one little question, "Mommy, why is Daddy sleeping in the neighbor lady's bed?"

Rosemary sat on her ego and called her father; he convinced her to return home to Seattle.

NINE

Rosemary held Maggie on her right hip while she and Lissie descended the plane. The girls' platinum blonde hair shined like glory. Their chubby cheeks and pale skin made them seem ethereal; they were so tiny, so precious.

His heart swelled.

In the furthest corner of his mind, like a needle scraping across a record, the loving thoughts of his granddaughters came to a screeching halt and with the heart of a coward, he focused his steady gaze upon his daughter instead.

Rosemary saw her father waiting by his tan 66 Chevy Caprice station wagon. Even from a distance, she could see his disapproving scowl. As she approached him, two black Lincoln town cars pulled up alongside him.

She searched her father's eyes for an explanation, but he did not acknowledge her; he didn't say a word; he just nodded for the two orderlies to escort Rosemary to their waiting sedan.

They stood on either side of her and waited for the two DSHS workers who emerged from the other car to take the children.

Rosemary didn't understand the change in her father; why did he hate her so much? What had she done to deserve his betrayal? What would become of Maggie and Lissie?

Tears welled in her eyes as they took the baby from her arms, and the orderlies coaxed her to their waiting sedan.

She looked back and pleaded to her father, "No, Daddy, please?"

Then, one by one, they all disappeared through the looking glass.

༄

After six months at the same state psychiatric hospital she had escaped from, they released her to Seattle's only all-female half-way house for the mentally ill.

Nestled in the heart of one of the oldest communities, it was a safe and quiet place where she could learn the parenting and life skills required to reunite with her children.

It was a charming two-story home built in the early 1920s with four bedrooms, two baths, a dining room, living room, laundry, kitchen, and an office used for counseling sessions.

PART I

It had comfortable furnishings, near the city bus line, and within walking distance of several parks and shopping.

The home had many multi-colored leaded glass windows that shined a kaleidoscope of natural light throughout every room. The floors were hardwood with an occasional area rug here and there, under furniture, and under the dining table.

Just off the dining room, there was a brick patio and arbor with a small fenced back and side yard with hedges and trees. In the center of the yard was a raised garden bed for residents that wanted to learn about gardening, the bounty shared among the cohabitants.

Each resident had their share of the household chores and meal preparation. Rosemary blended well with the staff and other women and became close friends with her roommate.

They spent many sleepless nights sharing similar stories of how difficult it was to live with hallucinations, financial uncertainty, and loss of connection with their families, worst of all being away from their children.

Rosemary often drifted off to sleep with tears in her eyes. Her heart ached for her children. She knew she'd never see her boys again but held fast to the hope of being reunited with her girls.

Residents earned day passes to visit with friends and family or to spend the day in the community. On Rosemary's first outing, while walking around the neighborhood, she observed two pleasant women out for a stroll. She observed how they walked arm in arm and spoke to each other in quiet voices. They seemed so at peace with themselves and the world around them.

Rosemary wanted to feel that way too, so she followed them for a while to see where they had come from. They entered a quaint dwelling close to the halfway house. Without a second thought, Rosemary walked up to the door and knocked.

A friendly, handsome, long-haired, long-bearded, blonde man donned in leather sandals and a white robe opened the door. The depth of his hypnotic piercing blue eyes transfixed her.

He introduced himself as Father Divine and invited Rosemary in to have lunch with them. The smell of incense and weed wafted out from behind him. She declined to enter stating how she wasn't allowed to be around such smells.

Unoffended, he excused himself for a moment and returned with a blanket and a picnic basket. Surprised and delighted by this kind gesture, she helped the Father spread the blanket on the front lawn and lay out the picnic he had provided; and then he prayed over their meal.

As they ate, they spoke at great length about life and Rosemary's plans for her future. When Rosemary inquired about the two women she'd seen, he said they were members of his family called the Divine Family.

He explained how his family differed from the traditional kind, in the way they offered unconditional love and acceptance, freedom from one's past and from judgments of their pasts, and how members could become renewed and redefine themselves, with new names among many other benefits.

He added, by taking a different name represented a change in belief systems and a second start in life. As it was a symbolic way of reflecting unity, all members had the same first name of Divine, their second name would reveal itself in his dreams over time.

They spoke at length about her children, about children, and how one should respect and nurture them as free spirits right from birth.

He believed it constricted a child's spiritual growth if raised by one parent, and they'd become better adults if they were free and independent, loved by an entire group of parents, not just a set of two, like in his family.

They chatted well into dusk, ending their visit with discussions of his great plans for his family. He told her how he had secured two entire blocks of duplexes off the main road of a housing complex, creating his own community within a community, where they all could be together and how Rosemary was welcome to visit them any time she wanted.

"Thanks for the picnic, Father Divine."

He smiled and said, "Walk with love, Sister Rosemary."

PART I

TEN

*I*n the meantime, Rosemary's girls became wards of the state and where my story begins.

We were sent to live with the Klinger family. It is where I have my first memorable recollections. Like the smell of baking vanilla sugar cookies wafting through their house, the Little Bo Peep plaque that hung above my crib, the white gloves, navy blue dress, and matching bonnet I wore for Easter, and the Romper Room TV show I watched every morning in the sunroom.

I'll never forget one warm summer day when the sting around my thighs from the bands on my urine-soaked plastic pants made me cry. Or how I stood, trembling, and was lifted into a cast iron sink inside of a dark and dank garage by a lady with a soothing voice and gentle hands.

The warm water was calm and the bumpy metal beneath my feet felt cool. The Jergens bar soap smelled sweet as she caressed my skin, intertwining with the musky smell of the garage, and the serious looking black dog overseeing it all from the doorway spoke without moving his mouth.

"Don't be scared Lissie, Mrs. Klinger is an angel, she won't hurt you," he said.

My most cherished memory of all was the many hours I spent on a little wooden potty chair in the faithful company of the talking dog.

When I recall my childhood, I remember it in snippets, as if it were a movie, a chronological biography of significant events. Although most of it is summarized, there are moments I remember in minute detail.

One year after Rosemary arrived back in Seattle, she'd successfully jumped through the hoops to regain custody of her girls and moved into a West Seattle project community for single mothers.

Named for its proximity to the highest point in the heart of West Seattle, the High Point housing community had spectacular views of Elliott Bay, the downtown Seattle skyline, and the Cascade and Rainier Mountains.

Separated from surrounding neighborhoods on purpose, it was walking distance to the bus stop, grocery store, and local welfare office. With only one way in and one way out, the identical, single-story duplexes, with quaint, well-lit, tree-lined walkways, was a cozy and safe place to call home.

With her rehabilitation counselor's help, Rosemary secured one side of a duplex within the heart of the projects. She and her girls had a new chance at life, and a humble new beginning.

With her life on the right track at long last, she enrolled her girls in the community preschool, and volunteered twice a week for the main office.

༄

Our new house had shiny, black and white checkered tile floors throughout. It was empty except for the one bed Mommy had in her room, and the one bed sister and I would share in ours.

The first night when Mommy tucked us into bed, she gave us each a brand-new dolly. Their bodies were soft polka dotted beanbags, and they talked when we pulled their strings, "I love you, peek-a-boo, baby sleepy, go bye-bye, play patty cake, night-night." Mine was pink, and Maggie's was blue.

Our house was part of a group of duplexes set in a half moon. There was only one two-story blue house in the center. Kids of all ages poured from the crevices of each house; my sister and I were the youngest.

We hadn't lived there long when one a girl from a neighboring building ripped my new dolly from my arms. I screamed bloody murder. Mommy sprang from the house to see what the matter was.

She got my dolly back but not before they'd tortured it. The little tuft of blonde bangs was missing, and ink blackened its once pretty blue eyes.

In the process of hunting for my doll, Mommy made two new friends, a lady from across the street who also introduced her to the lady in the big blue house.

It wasn't long before the women became inseparable, their older kids looked after all the younger ones, so they could visit without interruption.

I didn't like either of the ladies, they were loud, said bad words, and smoked like chimneys. All they ever talked about was how their children were *good for nuthins,* and about the different ways they beat them to get them to behave, joking how not even broom handles or belts ever worked.

The fat lady from the blue house was the meanest, ready to swat any kid within reach with her house slipper without provocation, I wouldn't want to be her kid. And her house was the grossest of all too.

In the summer, she'd leave her front door wide open for all to see the dirty clothes and garbage strewn all over the place.

And her kids, like the old lady who lived in a shoe, ran rickshaw, in and out, and over the mess as if they'd never seen it.

PART I

I didn't like how Mommy copied the way they dressed; the nicer lady with the low, gravelly voice, and auburn hair like Mommy's, gave her some of her clothes that no longer fit.

A carbon copy of her new friends, Mommy wore coordinating polyester pantsuits, too much Avon makeup, cheap jewelry, and dime store perfume; her favorite was Jontue. Most of all, I hated how Mommy swore at us like the fat mean lady did with her kids.

Rotating between houses, the friends took turns having beauty days, experimenting with the latest and greatest Avon beauty cream, neither lady had natural pretty skin like Mommy's, or to help each other roll the other's hair in curlers.

All the fuss and primping during the day was so the women could take Mommy *out* for the night, they appointed the older kids over us younger ones, whether they or we liked it. Some nights Mommy didn't come home; other nights I awoke to the sound of her throwing up in the bathroom.

If the women didn't go out, they'd play dice or card games, or had Tupperware and Avon parties; I liked those the best.

Although banished outside, regardless of the weather, even forbidden to go in the house of the one who wasn't having the party to use the bathroom, and aware there'd be hell to pay if caught, I'd always find a way inside to sample the buffet or to scrape the candy from a coffee spoon with my teeth.

It wasn't so bad being exiled outside when it was hot. The older kids blared 70's music on their BoomBox, turned on a water hose for us younger ones to play with, and passed out lots of popsicles. My favorite was when they filled a metal garbage can with cold water and dish soap and took turns ducking us in it like we were cookies and coffee.

∽

When Mommy wasn't hanging out with her new friends, rain or shine, early or late at night, she'd take my sister and me along to visit many interesting people. She never said why we had to go or where we were going, and sometimes she took only me.

Sometimes, we visited her mother, Gram. She lived in a small apartment in the furthest corner of a cold and dark basement. The bedroom and living room were in one big room and next to it was a tiny bathroom and a little kitchen. It was as smoky as a restaurant.

No matter when we visited, Gram was in her nightgown, sitting in bed, and smoking one continuous cigarette, smoldering between her long, gnarled, and arthritic, yellow fingers.

She spoke slow and rattily and always greeted us with a hug, a smile, and a new Golden Book. Those and new coloring books and crayons kept us entertained while Mommy attended to Gram's needs, visiting with each other in quiet whispers.

The best part about going to see her was playing with the Little Kiddle dolls and the new McCall paper dolls she saved for us.

∽

Of all the places Mommy took us, two remain etched in my memory. Riding the bus into town one morning, we stopped at a dark and dingy apartment building. Walking across the lobby, we stopped at an elevator. Mommy pulled its creaky old black gates open, and we stepped inside. She pulled it closed again, shut a pair of double doors, and then pushed the number five.

When we reached our floor and opening the gate once more, we walked down a dimly lit hallway a short distance to a certain apartment. Mommy twisted a knob on the door that made a funny telephone noise.

An old man answered. He had dark skin and sparse, wiry, salt and pepper, curly hair on his head and chin. He stood as tall and as wide as the doorway and wore a faded blue shirt, baggy brown trousers, mended several times with string and held up with suspenders, and brown, tattered, house slippers.

Noticing my gawking, he replied, "You'll have to excuse me, lil miss, I never pay much mind to the way I looks nowadays cuz' I'm getting so's I can hardly see anymore, and I don't get many visitors to pay it much mind."

He smiled a warm, almost toothless grin and invited us in. He must have been as old as the building because they smelled the same. We sat at a small round table by a window that overlooked the nearby piers and viaduct.

While he and Mommy visited, I watched the seagulls dance and hummed along to the raspy voice singing low on a nearby radio. The man's hollow laughter interrupted my thoughts.

"You like that man's singing do you, little girl?"

I stared at him. His eyes were not like any I had ever seen before. Where there should have been color, were white clouds instead. I nodded my head yes in response to his question.

"Why that's Louis Armstrong singing! Such good taste for a little girl." And he bellowed another deep laugh.

While he and Mommy continued with their visit, I resumed humming to myself, keeping time with the music, swinging my legs to the song *What a Wonderful World*. That would always be one of my favorites, the words made me think of happy things. I loved most kinds of music and found it easy to get lost in it.

PART I

Another unforgettable adventure began on a dark and rainy night. Mommy shuffled Maggie and me onto a bus and towards a bench seat in the back. A roly-poly grandma, wearing a long brown coat with a funny matching knit hat, sat across from us.

Her wrinkled hands rested on the top of a shiny matching purse while she napped. She sure must have liked brown because even her shoes were the same color. She wore knee-highs like Mommy's, but hers didn't fit so well, and they had tears in them.

It seemed we had been on the bus for a long time. I wondered where we were going. I strained to see the pretty neon lights on the buildings as they passed by, but the water on the windows made it hard to see. Just after the last of the lights, Mommy rang the bell.

Mommy lit a cigarette at the bus stop. It was pitch dark and quiet; there were no cars or other people around. She pulled us along across the street, and up a steep stairway to a looming two-story house perched along a hillside. She didn't knock; we went right in like we lived there.

Once inside, we lost track of her; she just vanished. Candles flickered eerie shadows all around us. I took Maggie's hand and followed the sound of voices in search of her.

The hallways stretched on and on and around in a continuous loop with the murmurs of its inhabitants always out of reach. We stumbled across a small, carpeted stairway; I made Maggie wait while I climbed to the top to see what was there.

Using an iron handrail as my guide, I felt my way to the top step. I saw a pair of angry red eyes staring at me from across the room. I blinked and rubbed my eyes and looked again.

This time two perfect made beds came into focus, but underneath one, the pair of burning red orbs remained fixed on me, none like I'd ever see again, nor would I ever forget.

I turned and made my way down to the bottom of the stairs as quick as I could. I took hold of Maggie's hand again with even more determination to find Mommy.

But, despite our best efforts, we didn't find her, only the doorway from which we came. We sat with our backs to the door, snuggled close, and fell asleep, while waiting for Mommy's eventual return.

ELEVEN

Once Rosemary believed she was off CPS's radar, with the help from the friends she'd made on Capitol Hill, she applied to another housing project across town, the one where Father Divine promised her a place with their family.

The renovated low-income housing community sat on a hundred acres overlooking the Duwamish River Valley. The clusters of duplexes were like that of other modernized government housing throughout the Seattle area.

To avoid having alleyways, it had only two preexisting thoroughfares. The city's metro ran east and west on its north side, allowing easy access to the local small town, grocery and drug store, a variety of restaurants and entertainment, including a good handful of taverns, with connections to more buses to other nearby communities and downtown Seattle.

The road on the south side connected to surrounding neighborhoods and the heart of the little city. A heavy blanket of woods, on the furthest east and west sides, enveloped and separated the tiny oasis from the rest of the city's population.

The homes, either tan, white, or brown, faced the street and stood in identical, even rows. Most units were only 576 square feet. Individual lawn areas, mature cottonwood, and evergreen trees contributed to the visual character of the community, defining open spaces, providing canopies and shade.

The duplexes main entries were on opposite ends of each other, sheltered by a flat, black tar roof, wooden steps, balustrade, and wooden or fiberglass slats ran along the sides to provide a sense of privacy. Between each unit, was a two-car driveway and a small, cement, L-shaped containment for trashcans.

A large window, made of twelve single glass panes, complete with a window seat on the interior, enhanced the front of each house, and a gas furnace in the living room provided heat.

Each unit had a kitchen with a small eating area, a utility/pantry room, a refrigerator, a sink with cabinets, and a small counter space.

On the other side of the kitchen wall was a single bathroom with a bathtub and shower, a sink with storage underneath, and a toilet. Next to the bathroom, were one to three bedrooms, depending on family size, each with their own closet.

PART I

In the center of the housing project, there was a bustling community center which was the focus of social activities for residents, mostly comprised of single mothers, teenagers, and children.

It had a large gymnasium/auditorium, a community kitchen, a child care center and meeting space for clubs, classes, and other activities, including dances, lectures, and social and religious services.

It also had an administrative office where residents went to pay bills and to take care of other matters, a playground, and an outdoor play field. Across the street and on the corner, was a little mom and pop grocery store with an adjacent laundromat. To the north of the community center was a small elementary school.

It was like its own little city within a city.

Only the fortunate gained acceptance into this secure, Shangri-la utopia and Rosemary was among the few. She thought she'd won the lottery; it was nothing like the projects in West Seattle.

Although a unit closer to the Family wasn't available, as members had filled every inch of available space secured by Father Divine, there was a vacant single, free-standing unit next to the community center.

It was the summer of '69 and Rosemary was excited to move in with her children. Their small unit sat across the street on the south of the community center and kitty-corner from the mom and pop grocery and laundromat, a prime location for sure.

Because most of his Family of followers were misfits and society's outcasts, Father Divine created his own set of rules to keep peace among his flock. He required new members to shed their previous lives, sacrificing birth names, family ties, and all personal possessions, offering unconditional love and a sense of belonging and family unity in return.

His dominion over them was never second-guessed or questioned, some even referred to him as Jesus Christ or God.

Under his direction, to support his growing family, he required those members on welfare to turn over their state checks and food stamps each month. He asked those able to work to put their earnings into the Family pot as everything belonged to the Family; food, clothing, and, each other's children.

Also, per Father Divine, a house would not belong to an occupant, regardless if their name was on the lease or not. Members were free to move from house to house if they so choose and live in whichever one they liked.

Of all the units, only one was for storing food. Members added to the Family pot with food gleaned from the food bank every week and whatever food stamps had brought in.

Twice a week, appointed leaders delegated staples from the food house to family members. Sometimes there were vegetables, big bricks of cheese and butter, bread, powdered milk, eggs, fish, fruit, rice, and canned meat.

If you were not home when they passed out the food, you didn't eat. When there wasn't food or much of it, it was called fasting; something Father Divine expected all members to do.

Father Divine remained in his home in Seattle near the halfway house, enlisting a few appointed members as shepherds in his absence.

He returned every Sunday for devotion, family celebration, and breaking of bread. Unbeknownst to him, his appointed shepherds didn't always adhere to his faiths and practices, using psychedelic drugs, alcohol, and sex instead to control his group of followers.

∽

Soon after we'd settled into our new home was a day I'll never forget. Up early, Maggie and I ventured outside and sat on the curb of the driveway to take in our new surroundings.

There was a slight breeze and the morning sun was hot. It was quiet except for the conversations between neighbors and the maintenance workers' lawn mowers.

After we watched the owner of the small store and the Laundromat unlock them for business, we ran to the backyard to play.

The grass was brown and sharp on my bare feet. There was a clothesline with two steel metal poles close to the house, and I climbed to the top of one and sat victoriously in the center of the "T".

Assuring a good grip, I looked up at the house to see if Mommy was watching, but she wasn't. Straddling the pole, holding on with one hand, I waved towards the living room window where I saw her talking on the phone, but she didn't see me.

I wanted her to see what I could do, and I called for her two or three times more, but she still didn't hear me.

I told Maggie to toss me her plastic duck and then I threw it as hard as I could at the window hoping to get her attention, and boy did it.

"Crash!"

Of the twelve windowpane squares, one shattered upon impact from the duck. I had her attention all right, but not the way I wanted.

Before I knew it, Mommy's hands were around the scruff of my neck, yanking me off the pole. I landed with a thud to the ground; she grabbed a handful of my hair and dragged me towards the house.

PART I

"I'm sorry Mommy!" I cried in terror; I'd never seen her so mad before.

Her eyes about bulged out of their sockets as she shook me and screamed into my face.

"Why do you hate me so much?"

Once inside the kitchen, switching the firm grip of my hair to that of my neck again, she grabbed a nearby broom close at hand, and reined its blue wooden handle down upon my head.

"Crack!"

The pain of her fingernails gouging deep into my neck met with the thudding ache of the broom as it collided with my skull.

Over and over again, she pummeled my head until I fell asleep. I awoke on the couch sometime later.

"Goddammit Lissie, see what you made me do," she whispered while she wiped the blood from my aching forehead. "Mommy's sorry baby, I won't do it again."

And she never did, I made sure of that, and remained out of her arm's reach, just in case. I have a one-inch crevice in my skull from the part in my hairline to just above my right eye.

Then, not long after, I awoke one night to the smell of smoke; it wasn't the usual smell of Mommy's cigarettes but a putrid, choking, smoky smell.

I climbed out of bed and walked to Mommy's room, but she wasn't there. A green ashtray sat in the middle of her bed, and a lit cigarette lay next to it. I watched in horror as the covers burst into flames.

I ran to my bedroom, shook my sister awake, and yelled for her to go outside. Maggie grabbed her dolly and toddled half-awake towards the front door.

The smoke was getting thicker, and I couldn't see anything around me. I heard Mommy throwing up in the bathroom and followed the sounds. I burst open the door and shouted for her to get up.

"Mommy there's a fire!"

Mommy waved me away and continued heaving over the toilet.

"Throw up outside Mommy we have to go!" I persisted.

Tugging and pulling on her arm I urged her to stand. Irritated, she stood and stumbled for the door.

"I gotta get my purse and glasses," she mumbled as she walked back into her bedroom, now about engulfed in flames.

"No, Mommy!" I screamed and lunged for her legs, "We got to go outside!"

"Goddammit, Lissie! Let go!" she protested, shaking me off, and disappearing into the smoky room.

"Mommy!" I hollered in counter protest and went in after her, but I lost her again.

"Mommy, where are you?" I yelled as I felt around the room.

I tripped over her lifeless body; she'd fallen asleep on the floor. I tugged her arms with all my four-year-old might.

Once in the hallway, she woke up again, got to her hands and knees and crawled towards the front door.

But she wasn't going fast enough, so I pushed her from behind, she cursed at me all the way. Once we'd made it to the front door, we found Maggie waiting for us on the porch.

Mommy stood, gasped a breath of fresh air, and proceeded towards the curb at the end of the driveway. I helped Maggie down the stairs.

By the time the firemen arrived, there was nothing left, the house and everything in it, all gone. One fireman dropped a single charred and smoky chair abruptly on the lawn in front of Mommy.

She pulled me and Maggie into her arms and cried, squeezing me tighter and shaking, she slurred into my ear, "What are we gonna do now, Lissie?"

PART I

TWELVE

By some miracle, a vacated unit within the nucleus of the Family became available, and they welcomed us with open arms. Even though we had lost all our belongings, another member reassured Rosemary, "Not to worry sister, we take care of our own."

The new house might as well not have had a front door as it stayed open most of the time. Sometimes people even came in through the always propped-open living room window. It was the central hangout place for the Family; people coming and going at all hours of the day and night.

The Family dressed funny. Everyone had long hair, men and women alike, and the men had long beards. Some members didn't wear shoes, and others wore sandals and psychedelic clothing.

The women were always busy. They worked without stopping all day long; cooking, cleaning, and sewing. If they weren't doing those things, they made candles, necklaces with pretty beads, and colorful pillows and blankets to sell at the next festival.

They were so occupied in fact, they paid little mind to the children running amok around them, so long as they weren't underfoot. Inquiring why they were always busy one day, they said, "idle hands are a devil's handiwork."

It wasn't long before Maggie and I were running alongside the other Family children, shoeless and donned in only our underwear or summer dresses, regardless of the time of the year.

Thankfully, Maggie had tennis shoes on the day she stepped into a small hole that had broken glass in it and slashed her foot wide open.

Only one house kept food for the Family, and it wasn't ours. Once a week, alternating between houses, selected members took turns fixing a big cooked meal to share with everyone and to sing songs, hoping to get closer to god.

Women got up earlier than usual, sewed, cooked, and cleaned to prepare for the big day. I liked Mommy's goulash the best. Incense and weed intermingled with the stomach growling aromas wafting from the kitchen.

Everyone helped themselves to the food. In the winter, they'd pull the curtains shut, light lots of candles, and sit on cushions on the floor to eat, even though there was furniture to sit on.

In the summers, everyone took their plates outside and sat on the lawn. After the meal, after everybody had quieted down, guitars and tambourines kept tune with the songs a member wrote for us to sing.

At the end of the night, someone would read from the Bible and talk a lot about a man named Jesus and how we were his sheep, and then Father Divine would bless each of us, and we'd depart for our houses.

Mommy said all these people were our family, the adult women were also our mothers and the adult men our fathers, and we were to do as they told us.

Mommy had changed, we saw our other mothers more than we did her. Some of our new parents were nice, and some were mean. Some used switches, belts, wooden spoons, or their hands for spankings. I learned to stay out of their way and out of arm's reach too.

But no matter, I always seemed to be the one getting the most spankings. I didn't like Mommy's new friends and I wasn't afraid to say so; I guess that's why I always found myself over someone's knee.

"Why do you let them spank me, Mommy?" I asked her one day.

"Because you know when I start, I can't stop, and I don't want to hurt you again, so, they'll be giving you spankings from now on," she replied.

Well, that was all the elders needed to hear. I was on their radar to teach some important lessons to according to them. Often, the expressions on my face got me in trouble most of the time.

They considered grimacing, rolling, or crossing eyes, and sticking out the tongue disrespectful and no sooner had I made one of them I'd find myself hauled over a man's shoulder.

Kicking and screaming and pummeling their back with my tiny fists got me nowhere. They taught the lesson with anything close at hand, a belt, a spatula, a switch or just their hand.   And depending on what the offense was, determined how long the lesson lasted. Sometimes I couldn't sit for a while, my butt and legs stung like little bee bites. Regardless of how hard I tried, I couldn't keep the promise to behave.

They were on my radar too. I knew what was coming by a certain change in the tone of a voice, or a sudden movement, or by an odd glance or strange pause, and I'd take off faster than a second thought before they'd catch me.

One winter morning whatever I had done was so bad it had prompted Mommy to bolt from her bed, with her hair in a messy heap of curlers, dressed in a sheer nightgown with her slippers on the wrong feet, and she tore after me like a wild woman. I'd never seen her so mad or move so fast.

Quicker than a ricochet rabbit, I was out the door before she could grab ahold of my hair and ran across the front lawn and up the icy street. No one in the Family offered to help. They watched in amusement as Mommy tried in vain to keep up with me.

PART I

"Lissie, Goddammit, come back here!" Mommy slurred between her toothless gums.

Then it happened. Mommy slipped. Her nighty went over her head, and down the hill she rolled, her bare butt exposed for all to see.

She came to rest in a crumpled heap at the bottom of the small incline, the searing pain from the huge gash in her thigh made her forget how mad and embarrassed she was.

I ran to her as did some of the Family, but before I could reach her, someone snatched me in midair and flung over me over a broad pair of shoulders.

❦

Men who weren't part of the Family we were to call *Uncle*. They didn't tell us their names; they were faceless and just there, like us, like Mommy. When an *Uncle* visited, they'd send us off to do an errand.

They never paid us any mind except to give us money to buy Mommy's cigarettes at the mom and pop store two blocks away. With a note in hand, we'd run all the way to the store knowing full well there would be change for candy.

After the man at the counter gave us Mommy's Benson and Hedges Menthol Lights, he'd tell us how many pieces of candy we could take; my favorite was the banana Now and Laters.

Once back home, because an Uncle was visiting, our door was closed and locked. Until Mommy opened it again, Maggie and I'd sit on the front steps and devour our treasures.

"What did you get?" asked Maggie.

I'd open the bag just enough for her to see what was inside, and when she tried to get a piece, I'd snatch it closed again and turn away from her. Then, I'd empty the candy onto my lap and dole it out, equal and fair.

"One for you and two for me," I counted. Maggie watched with an eagle eye.

"Two for you and three for me," I continued.

Mommy opened the door in time to witness the ensuing transaction.

"What are you doing Lissie?" she yelled and snatched the remaining candy from my lap.

"I'm sharing with sister," I explained.

"She's cheating you, Maggie," she said and gave her the rest of the candy.

One *Uncle* visited in the evenings. He was older, wore fancy clothes, had big rings on his fingers, and always brought Planter's peanuts for me and Maggie. But, before he'd give them to us, we had to allow him to give us a horsey ride.

He'd cross his leg with his other and tell us to sit on the foot of the crossed leg. He'd hold our hands and bounce us up and down and sing a nursery rhyme.

"Ride a cock horse to Banbury Cross to see a fine lady upon a white horse. With rings on her fingers and bells on her toes, she shall have music wherever she goes!" and then he'd let out a hearty laugh.

I didn't see what was so funny. I just wanted it over with, so I could have the peanuts. Maggie always pushed me off for her turn. I don't think she cared about the peanuts as much as I did.

When the initiation ended, he'd hand each of us a small bag of salted peanuts and we'd disappear with our prize, hiding in separate secret places to stuff our cheeks full of the yummy treat.

The Family kept us busy and out of trouble by having us tend to the needs of the adult members and visitors, especially during parties. They'd summon us to fetch someone a beer or a lighter, to empty an ashtray, and other random errands.

We were referred to as Child since we wouldn't receive our heavenly names until we were much older when Father Divine received them from God. Although nameless, each *Child* knew whom they were being beckoned by from the direct eye contact of the adult who had directed the command.

One time, a creepy woman with glazed-over, red eyes grabbed my arm, pulled me down closer to her, and whispered in a croaky tone, "You have kind eyes Child, I can see your soul, and it is good."

Another time, while I was standing in the doorway of our house with a glass thermometer in my mouth and talking to a neighbor cat, a group of members, some sitting cross-legged on floor pillows meditating, some smoking grass, witnessed our mute conversation.

"Are you ok?" the cat asked.

I nodded that I was.

"She has E.S.P." someone commented.

"E.S.P.? What's that?" asked another.

"L.S.D." someone chimed in, and they erupted into shrieks of laughter.

Mommy crossed the room and slammed the door shut, breaking the thermometer in half.

"Knock it off Lissie!" she barked.

The thermometer fell from my mouth and shattered on the floor.

Mommy slapped me upside my head, "See what you made me do, dammit! Go to your room!"

Snickering giggles and disapproving, sneering, zombie eyes followed my every step as I walked past the group.

I hated when they smoked grass cigarettes. The smell made my stomach sick, especially when they blew it into my face. I didn't understand why they had to smoke the grass when there were plenty of cigarettes, at least with the cigarettes they didn't fall asleep like lifeless ragdolls.

One of my *mothers,* or FM, said it wasn't sleeping it was meditating and that the grass helped them in their search for the truth.

She described meditating like going on a trip, to seek enlightenment, to find oneself. And that after a trip it's very important to share your journey with others and the revelations that god gave you because the message you receive may not be for you, yours might be in what someone else received.

She said if children smelled the smoke from the grass that god would talk to them too. She said there were pills for trips too, but they were only for the adults.

Since the school was across the street from our backyard, I could see Mommy with her friends when I played at recess. One day, I saw her sitting on a blanket and smoking the grass with another Family member, smiling, and laughing, without a care in the world, floating towards the nothingness in the furthest depths of her brain. I think the teacher saw too.

THIRTEEN

The only thing I liked about the Family was my freedom. They allowed us to play anywhere in the neighborhood. Because Mommy didn't seem to care about me or Maggie anymore, nor did I care to be around her either, and, most of all, not around her new friends, I'd disappear for most of the day.

Come rain or shine, I'd wander around the projects until almost dark in search of something to do. After arriving home from school, I'd take off. On the weekends, I'd leave the house before she woke up. But in the evenings, after she'd been partying all night, I was a sitting duck.

She'd wake me from a sound sleep to say she wanted me to sleep with her. And then, while struggling to remain awake, pausing only long enough to take large drags from her cigarette, mesmerizing me with how tall she could make the ash of her cigarette before she had to flick it, she'd slur all her woes my way.

Although bored to death, the sandman threatening to take me away, I didn't dare fall asleep until I couldn't see any red on her cigarette.

Somehow, I had a way of making her feel better. I didn't have to do anything special, she just found solace in my presence, as if I understood everything she said, or could fix whatever had upset her.

As I ventured out further and further on my excursions, I came to know the north end of the projects so well I could have walked it backwards, not so bad for being a first grader.

I knew who lived in what house, if they had pets, a cat or dog, the kinds of toys they played with, when their dinner time was and what they ate, who had a car if they had one, if they had a mom *and* a dad, and if they fought.

I noticed these things by playing around each house, climbing on their garbage enclosures, and pretending I was invisible just to watch the family that lived inside. Sometimes I invited myself in for a snack and Hanna Barbera cartoons.

Every family was different, but none was like mine.

Sometimes after school, I'd stop at the rec center to play on the monkey bars and to fish out an empty bottle from the garbage to use when I caught pollywogs in the pond across from the school. If I couldn't find a bottle, I'd just chase the pollywogs and skeeter bugs until I got bored.

PART I

On rainy days, I'd hop around on the washing machines in the Laundromat until a coin popped out and then I'd take it next door to the candy store.

On nice days, when I had nothing else to do, I'd sneak around to the back side of the little store, slip under its fence, and climb onto the roof of the Laundromat, the roof edge was close to the ground, so it was easy to get on. I liked being there, I could see what everyone was doing and could have stayed there all day.

Another favorite thing I liked to do was to play around the construction site of empty houses. I'd watch the workers gather their things to go home, and then run as quick as a bunny and disappear in between the stacked wood pallets.

Once I'd found an open clearing in the center, I'd sit on the cool, cushy grass, and pretend I was anywhere but where I was.

I loved the smell of the fresh cut wood and imagined my Daddy had just cut it because he was building a new home for sister, Mommy, and me.

Sometimes I'd lay back, clasp my hands behind my head, wriggle into the cool blades of the grass, and daydream into the clouds, making up stories with every image I saw.

I liked to climb on top of the wood pallets too. Making sure the coast was clear, I'd stand in one place for a while and enjoy the silky softness of the pretty, yellow-colored wood beneath my feet. When I laid on my tummy, I'd press my nose to the wood and breath in its sweetness.

When it rained, I'd drag large pieces of plastic over the wood to make a tent, saving some to use as a coat, and then climb underneath it.

I loved the rain. I loved the smell of it and the harmony it made when the drops hit the plastic. Snuggled within my cocoon, I'd sit for hours listening to the musical patter of the pretty rain, lost in my world of make-believe.

When the men made windows, I'd shimmy up the scaffolding and pull a large piece of putty off to make a snake family. Sometimes, if no one was looking, I'd play pirate and walk the planks between the framework a few times before disappearing into my secret hiding place to play with my coveted putty.

Of all the things I found to do, my most favorite was to pop tar bubbles on warm summer days. The biggest and gooiest were the ones closest to the curbside. While trekking through the neighborhood, I'd search high and low for an elusive monster tar bubble.

Once I found one, I'd cuddle up nice and close to the curb so a car wouldn't hit me, and work at it until it popped a black sticky ooze, it was almost as gratifying as picking off a stubborn scab; I knew a thing or two about scabs, I had lots of them, or getting a big booger unstuck from my nose, I had some of those too if I didn't have the other things to pop or pick at.

After a long day of meandering, I knew it was time to make my way home when the streetlights came on. If Mommy wasn't home yet, I'd play with her small turntable and pile of 45's while I waited for her.

Even at six years old, I could sing right along with Patsy Cline, not missing a word or a note, even the high ones. I loved all the old country and folk music, like Johnny Horton's song about powdering a gators' behind and Neil Diamond's Shilo. Besides being in my alone places, getting lost in music was my second most favorite thing to do.

If Mommy still wasn't home after I tired of the records, I'd lay in my bed and listen for her, in case she fell, or threw up, or if a walker happened by. I only allowed myself to fall asleep once I was sure she was in bed.

If she stumbled in alone, I'd wait a little longer, then sneak into her room and put out her cigarette, because once she was out, not even a train through her bedroom could wake her.

One time, Mommy caught me with her records, but rather than getting mad and yelling at me, she went straight for the player's arm and scratched a deep gouge in the record.

As she raked across it, she whispered, "Shhhhh Lissie, can't you hear the birdies singing?"

I nodded that I could.

"That's not normal Lissie; birdies don't sing their morning song at night."

Then she headed for bed, leaving me to wonder about the puzzling thing she had just said.

PART I

FOURTEEN

Some Family members took turns walking the streets of the other members' houses to keep them safe, some volunteered as watch guards. Those on watch stayed up all night playing music and smoking weed.

On occasion, the walkers woke up members to assure they were OK. If children were inside a home without an adult, a walker might go in the house to check on them.

A common belief was that having sex with a member, child or adult, was not rape, but an expression of freedom; it was healthy, good, and fun.

One walker told me that the greatest love was giving your life and love to another. Because strife was not welcome in the family, he'd threaten me with his beer laden breath how violators would suffer severe punishment if they told, and how what he did was *God's word.*

At times the walker brought visitors with him. I thought if I laid still as a rock and keep my eyes closed, it wouldn't hurt, and they'd go away.

I imagined myself leaving my body, going through the wall, and falling into the soft darkness where I'd find a complete absence of pain. I knew how to do this anytime I wanted. Sometimes, I imagined going to the safety of my wooden fort.

One time, from somewhere within the darkest corner of my sanctuary, a bright light appeared, and a woman called for me ever so sweetly.

"Come here Lissie, come to the light, it's safe over here."

I wanted to stay in the painless darkness, but I went to the woman anyway.

She wrapped her arms around me. She had pale purple blossoms in her hair, the nicest flowers I'd ever smelled, and she had a matching dress that was the softest I'd ever felt. I wanted to stay there forever.

We floated to the ceiling to look down at the monsters hurting my body. They were pale without noses and had big, black eyes with wide mouths and jagged teeth.

Their arms were long with two claw-like pinchers for fingers and big ugly feet. They growled and grunted as they shoved mine and Maggie's beds around the room. I looked away.

The woman hugged me closer and said, "They can't hurt your soul Lissie."

After a time, we drifted like feathers to the corner of the room and, with our backs to the monsters, we colored pictures of my favorite animals.

While we played, the woman told me, "When they do that, we do this."

She stayed for a while longer until the monsters disappeared, and I'd fallen asleep. She came back every time the monsters returned. When I was with her, I was not afraid and felt no pain.

◊

Mommy was different. I don't remember her being with us for the rest of my childhood, even though she was around us, I don't remember seeing her. Perhaps it was because she spent most of the time with Family members at a local tavern, or because I tried to make myself invisible.

It was the trips into town where Mommy attracted and brought home strays. The worst of them was a fellow biker friend of some of the Family members.

He was long-legged, solid, and all-American, in a 'dirt, sweat, and beer' sort of way. He had iron-willed features and a sinewy 6'4" physique. As if chiseled from a slab of testosterone, he knew he was eye candy for most girls and had no trouble getting the homely little mouse to notice him.

Perhaps it was when he overheard her bragging about her beautiful daughters that he moseyed over to introduce himself. Maybe she was so taken by his undivided attention, she felt encouraged to share even more with him.

And perhaps the more he bought her to drink, the more she revealed. And the tipsier she got, the less harm she saw in allowing him to give her a ride home or to invite him in, where, after she'd passed out fast asleep, he found her sleeping angels.

One can only assume he believed he had a well thought out plan and was rather proud of the stage he'd set and couldn't wait to come back and *visit*.

That visit was the very next day. He rode in on a chopper along with a group of Family members who welcomed him into the fold with a cold beer and a hearty slap on the back. He nodded his head in appreciation, accepted the joint they passed to him, took a deep drag, and passed it on to the next person. As he exhaled the choking smoke, he scanned the yard of wild children for her.

◊

A tall, dark-haired man I hadn't seen before caught my attention with a steely blue gaze. Not wanting to get in trouble, I ran to his side to see what he wanted.

"I'm gonna go get some ice cream, do you want to go with me?" he asked.

PART I

I nodded that I did. He took my hand, and we walked away unnoticed. The furthest edge of the road felt warm on my feet as we moved along in silence until I noticed that we were going the wrong way.

"The store is that way," I said and pointed in the opposite direction.

"We are going to a bigger store; they have more kinds of ice cream." He snapped and yanked my arm to continue the way we were going.

"Can I have any kind I want?" I asked.

"Sure, kid," he said.

We walked a little further. I could see the big slide at the park.

"Can we go to the park too?" I asked.

"No. Let's take a shortcut here," he said, shoving me into the woods.

The sticks and sharp rocks dug into the bottoms of my feet. I stepped across them as we walked further and further into the woods. I made it to a tree stump and sat down.

"There's no more shortcut," I said.

He sat on a big tree branch across from me and said nothing. He pulled a big knife from a leather pouch on his belt loop and cleaned his nails with it.

I turned away from him and played with my raggedy naked Barbie doll.

"Come here." he said.

My heart pounded in my ears; I wanted to run, but I knew he'd catch me. I walked towards him, keeping my focus down at the ground and my eyes fixed on his black square-toed motorcycle boots.

"Come her," he demanded even meaner than before.

I inched closer to him and heard him unzip his pants.

"Kiss it," he commanded.

Tears streamed down my cheeks, and my body shook.

"I said kiss it!" he said louder, and brought the knife under my chin. Its pointy sharpness glistened in the sun.

Snot bubbled from my nose as I choked back tears. I closed my eyes and leaned down.

"Open your mouth, girl," he ordered.

FIFTEEN

"If you want to see your Mommy again, open your F#%$ing mouth!" I opened my mouth.

"Wider, Goddammit!" he yelled, and boxed my right ear.

My jaw felt as if it would break.

"If you bite me, so help me God, I'll chop your tongue off and cut the rest of you in little pieces," he threatened.

He peed in my mouth. I pulled away, spit it on the ground, and bawled, until he flashed his knife again.

I wiped the snot from my face with the back of my hand and sobbed to myself. Just when I thought it was over and we could leave to get the ice cream, he gave me another demand.

"Lay down."

Confused, I did as he said. He removed my panties. I closed my eyes and wished the lady would visit.

"Look at this," he said, holding up a massive, opened diaper pin. "I'm closing this pin and put it 'down there.' If you tell your mom or anyone about our secret, it will open, and you will bleed to death." With that, he shoved it in a place I didn't know existed.

I stifled a painful cry.

"Get up and get dressed; it's time to go to the store."

I didn't want ice cream anymore, but I didn't tell him. He tried to take my hand, but I pulled away. He was a nasty, beer-smelling monster, and I hated him.

After that day, I remained ever vigilant for the sound of his approaching motorcycle and was sure to hide whenever I heard it.

※

With all my wandering, I never got lost, except once. It was the time we went with Mommy and her friend to visit at her house in Ballard. This lady was meaner than the slipper lady. She was as round as she was tall with short red hair and meaty freckled fists.

She had no tolerance for back talk. No sooner had the filth rolled off your tongue, like a rubber band reflex, one of her meaty fists would come flying out

PART I

of nowhere and POW she'd haul off and smack you right in the kisser before you even knew what had hit you.

She was another person I learned to stay out of reach from. It was inevitable though she'd catch me and my smart mouth. Not paying attention one day as I made faces behind Mommy's back, I accidentally happened across her path.

Faster than a frog's tongue, out came one of her meaty claws to snatch me by the roots of my hair, and she smacked the nasty look right off my face with her other meaty fist.

And boy you'd better not cry, or she'd sure give you something to cry about. Yeah, I kept my radar on when she was around.

Most of all, I didn't like how she always gave Mommy advice about how to control her *heathens*. Unsure of what one was, but coming from her, I knew it couldn't be good. I sure hoped Mommy wasn't listening because I didn't want her to be as mean as she was.

Her boys were no angels either. One time they talked my sister and me into going to the beach with them while our mothers visited. Maggie and I walked alongside them as they rode their bikes.

They peddled in time with our steps until we got to the crosswalk of a busy street. As soon as the light changed, they took off as fast as their bikes could take them, leaving me and Maggie alone, stunned, and afraid.

The hot sun beat down on our heads. There was no shade. A warm wind blew over us as cars zoomed past in front of us. Maggie cried. I took her hand, and we walked back towards the way we came. The streets and houses all looked the same.

I looked Maggie in the eyes, "If we're ever gonna get home sister, we need to find someone to help us. I'll walk on this side of the street and you walk on that side, and we'll knock on every door until someone answers. Tell them we're lost, and our mother is at the house of the fat lady with red hair and two mean boys."

Maggie nodded and proceeded across the quiet little street to the first house. It seemed as if no one was home that day. Tears welled in my eyes as I approached the last house. Thankfully, a nice old lady answered, invited me in, and called the police. When they arrived, I sat in the back of their car as they searched for my sister.

But Maggie had found a ride with a mailman who knew of the lady she'd described. The policemen put two and two together and brought me to the right house. I need not describe the punishment that ensued after they left, just to say my legs and butt stung for a long time afterward. As far as I know, the boys never got punished.

Things worsened after Mommy married a member. He did not allow books in the house and I found that out the hard way. I had just entered the second grade and was excited to show Mommy the Dick and Jane book my teacher gave me to practice reading.

Her husband snatched it from my hands, tore it in two, and threw it across the room.

"Not allowed! Got it?"

After they married, we weren't left alone at night anymore, they'd drop us off at some stranger's house instead, sometimes for just a little while, sometimes for days. Some people were nice, and others thought we were a nuisance.

A teenage boy at one house liked to pay special attention to me. One night after everyone was asleep, he turned on the television and curled up behind me on the couch. He pet me like a cat and in some places where I don't think you pet a cat. I didn't like it, but I was too afraid to move. I was so glad we never went there again.

When they finally remembered us, it would be in the middle of the night, and I'd wake up while being carried back home.

Of all those who babysat us, I'll never forget the tall, thin girl with long, dark, stringy hair, with a scary look in her eyes, and scabs all over her face. She was just plain hateful and had her own ideas about how to treat us when no one else was around.

She wasn't just strict, she was downright cruel, and spanked us with whatever was within her reach, a spatula, a wooden spoon, or a belt, landing the blows wherever she wanted and not just on our bottoms.

On hot days, she'd take us on long walks to a park where she'd meet with her friends to smoke cigarettes, all the while barking cuss words at us if we slowed down or cried.

And if you mouthed her at all, you got a tongue full of pepper or tabasco sauce upon the return home, but the hours of torment with her was a fair trade for the park she'd take us to.

It had a space-age playground complete with a 33-foot-high tower rocket spiral slide and got crowded in the summer. At the top, you could see the ground disappear from beneath you the further up you climbed.

When it was your turn to jump into its unforeseen abyss, you didn't dare chicken out because there would always be a bigger kid waiting at the entry point in charge of pushing crybabies down the shoot.

PART I

I only went down it twice. I hated being pushed, and the trip down was too fast and scary. If you had shorts on, you'd go so fast you'd end up with a burn on one side of your legs when you shot out of its other end.

If the metal wasn't too hot, I'd play on the two different spaceship merry-go-rounds and monkey bars instead. Otherwise, I'd sit in the cool grass under a tree to watch the other kids play until she hollered for us to start on the long, hot walk home.

❦

On summer nights, we'd go on car rides with Mommy's friends. Although they were long trips and included many stops, we knew we'd wind up at Alki beach for a bonfire at the end. When beckoned for a trip to the beach, I couldn't get in the back of the car fast enough.

I'd flip the front seat forward, hop onto the long seat, and, if it were just my sister and me, stretch out on the cold leather to watch the passing streetlights twinkle above like stars.

I loved getting lost in the music on the radio, the songs City of New Orleans and The Night Chicago Died I liked the best and could have ridden around all night listening to it.

It was a whole other ball game when other kids came along. I hated how it became too crowded to lie down or hear the music.

If it was hot, we wore nothing more than shorts or panties, so everyone in the crowded back seat got hot and sticky, a sure-fire mix for a few heated arguments of "Stop touching me!"

When we became too unruly, the adults in front would flip their beer bottle tops with pictures on them into the back seat, inviting a ritualistic banging of heads as we all dived at once to be the first to grab them.

And just when one of us cried and a smackdown was about to ensue, another bottle cap would come flying from out of nowhere; sometimes we'd fake fighting just to get more caps.

The picture puzzles on the bottle caps kept our young illiterate minds entertained while the adults up front made their stops, laughing, drinking, and smoking the entire time.

At the beach, the adults would make a huge bonfire to sit around, drink beer, sing, and laugh. A portable radio blared folk music, and someone strummed along on a guitar.

They roasted hot dogs and marshmallows, and us kids would run amuck unsupervised until they corraled us into the back seat of the car once again.

Stuffed and exhausted, we'd sleep the entire way home, only to awaken in the morning with most of the menu still on our faces.

If we weren't going to the beach after a long car ride, we'd go to the drive-in. Once we arrived and were let loose, we'd descend upon the playground like a plague.

I didn't like the drive-in movies; they were always scary. I'll never forget the one with a giant spider and how some people got lost in it, and another movie had monsters.

Ignoring them, I'd always find a friend to play on the teeter-totter with, and who'd share their hot dog or popcorn and whose mom would give us chips and Kool-Aid.

Like the beach, the grownups ignored us until it was time to corral us into the backseat of the car. Although we were with adults, it always seemed as if we were alone.

PART I

SIXTEEN

One-night Mommy didn't come home, nor did anyone come to take us to a babysitter.

"I'm hungry Lissie" five-year-old Maggie whimpered. "Me too," I said, just fourteen months older than she.

I couldn't remember when Mommy left or when she was coming back and went to the pantry to find something for breakfast. There was a little bit of Puffs of Rice, so I looked in the refrigerator for milk, but there wasn't any.

I poured the cereal into two bowls and stood on a kitchen chair to get water from the faucet when I saw something move. I blocked my sister's view and picked out as many of the squirmy things as I could, focusing on the moving ones.

Darkness filled the house as evening set in; still no Mommy. The lights didn't work, so Maggie and I hid in the bathroom just in case one of Mommy's friends made a *visit*.

Crouched with our backs against the cold porcelain bathtub, we held each other tight and watched the darkness become blacker.

Too afraid to move in case a walker happened by, a stream of warm liquid seeped from beneath each of us, merging as one to form a large puddle in the middle of the floor.

Morning found us in pain, still hunkered against the tub. The ringing of the school bell startled us awake.

Not knowing if it was the for breakfast or for class—no longer afraid of a *visitor*—I found clothes for us, brushed both of our hair, grabbed Maggie's hand, and ran out the door.

I was glad the school was almost in our backyard because we made it in the nick of time for the free hot breakfast. Maggie cried when they set a bowl before her.

༄

I can't say for certain what transpired next as there are many accounts of what happened that day; I only remember the details of what became of me and Maggie. This is one version of how they busted Father Divine and the Family.

༄

Responding to allegations of child abuse, illegal drug distribution, and other related issues, dressed in military fatigues and armed to the teeth, ten SWAT officers spread out within a two-block radius and surrounded the suspected commune homes where they knew a notorious cult lived.

Going by a hunch that the leader would be present that day, a team of FBI and DEA agents, along with Child Protective Services, quiet as mice, surrounded the perimeter and two entrances of the low-income housing project.

Every window in a member's house had their blinds drawn, making them easy to spot. With their guns drawn, the officers stealthily mounted the stairs and broke down the doors of each duplex; rushing inside, they rounded up anyone within, men, women, and children.

Working catlike from the outermost buildings inwards to the central home of the cult leader, they drove every single member out into the street.

They restrained those not strung out with zip-tie handcuffs and made them sit and wait until the other buildings were empty and loaded anyone in an apparent drug stupor into an awaiting ambulance to take them to Harborview.

When they reached the cult leader's dwelling, they saw it barred, and had to use a battering ram to get inside. They found the thin, long-bearded man sitting Indian style on a floor pillow and reading a Bible as if it were any other day.

As the officers restrained him and read him his rights, he cried out onto deaf ears, "We are not hurting anyone; we are a self-sufficient community, living by God's principles!"

Shoved out into the street along with his followers, Father Divine assured his Family, "Be calm and have faith my brothers and sisters, God will see us through this trial."

Police brought the restrained members to their feet and corralled them onto a waiting charter bus. Some of the women collapsed in protest in the stairway in a fit of tears and anguish as they witnessed their children being taken away.

EMTs from four ambulances, the local police and fire department and neighboring looky-loos filled the streets of the once-sleepy community.

Just as quickly as they'd arrived, a convoy of loaded ambulances sped away with their lights flashing and sirens wailing.

Teachers at the nearby elementary school kept the members' school-age children distracted until the entire circus had cleared. Once everything had quieted down and back-to-normal, several CPS workers took up posts alongside a known path to the nearby school and waited for the unsuspecting children's arrival home.

PART I

The last bell rang announcing the end of the school day, Maggie and I crossed the street and climbed the small grassy hill behind our house.

Two strangers met us before we got to the door, a man and a lady. They stood alongside a large white sedan parked in the driveway, beckoning for us in a phony cat-call sort of way.

She's done it, just like she said she would so many times before, we had finally gotten on her last nerve; Mommy had given us away.

The condition of the two little girls approaching them surprised both officers. They were so tiny, malnourished for sure, their faded, stained, and filthy shift dresses were at least one size too small, and their hair looked ragged and dirty.

The skin on their arms and legs looked tan at first, but as they got closer, they saw it was only caked-on dirt that gave them their Sunkist look. The scabs from unhealed wounds on their legs was more than they could take, and they made their move.

Fearing their intentions, I grabbed Maggie's hand, bolted for the house, and cried out for Mommy, but she didn't answer. The strangers followed us inside, cornering me and my sister.

They lunged for us with barbaric swiftness, capturing us like wild animals, and carried us kicking and screaming to their car, releasing us only when we were inside the security cage of the backseat.

Maggie and I held onto each other for dear life as the strangers got into the front seat. We drove for a long time and didn't stop until we reached a great big brick building. The lady opened the back door, said our mom was inside, and to come with them.

They took us to a row of chairs and told us to sit and wait.

The frightening chaos surrounding us kept us distracted and entertained.

A bed with wheels, pushed by two policemen, a nurse, and a doctor, barreled through some swinging metal doors. Each one yelling instructions over the other about the man's condition; he had a knife wound.

"BP's 140 over 90, tachy at 160; minimal blood loss considering the chest laceration; gave him 300cc's of saline," shouted the nurse to the doctor.

"God, it hurts!" yelled the man in the bed.

"Give him 60 of Toradol, don't want to mix morphine with beer." said the doctor.

As they rushed past us, a scruffy old man weaved his way up to a busy desk of ringing telephones and more people giving orders.

"My chest..." the man whispered.

A nurse yelled for someone to get a gurney and then rushed him away.

From somewhere down another hall the fearful, vulgar screams of a hysterical woman interrupted my thoughts of where they may have taken the man.

Recognizing the cry, the hairs on the back of my neck stood up.

Suddenly, the scary woman was before me, escorted on either side by two policemen.

Our eyes locked. "Lissie!" Mommy shrieked. "Help me!"

Her desperate pleas ricocheted off the walls. She kicked and screamed in a relentless, violent struggle for them to let her go.

With outstretched arms and tears streaming down her cheeks, her face contorted in agony, she cried out for me, "Lissie!" "Lissie!"

The policemen held her firmly even when she hung limply by her elbows on purpose, fighting harder still to pry herself from the policemen's hold.

I ran screaming and flailing toward the policemen, "MOMMY!" but a hospital staff intercepted me mid-flight.

As much as I twisted like a snake, kicked, howled, and screeched an earsplitting "Let me go! Let me go!" I couldn't break free from my captors.

Blinded by hot tears, I stretched my arms out to her as far as they would go for her to save me.

"MOMMY!" I screamed "MOMMY!" as the mean old policemen dragged Mommy away through a pair of metal swinging doors, just like the kind at the grocery store; the echoes of her cries etched forever in my memory.

SEVENTEEN

A Guardian ad Litem introduced us to Mama Betsy, handed her a hospital bag full of medicine, and briefed her about her new charges in quick succession, promising to follow up with her in the next two weeks, and left us with this lady.

Mama Betsy aka MB had shoulder length salt and pepper hair and wore butterfly glasses like Mommy's, but hers dangled from a chain around her neck like a teacher's. She was thinner than Mommy and wore the same clothes as she did, but with a sweater. She was poker-faced; I couldn't tell if she seemed happy to see us or not.

In all her years as a foster mother, no two had ever come to her in a worse condition; we were dirtier than two little wild animals. She armed herself with yellow rubber gloves that extended all the way to her elbows, removed the de-lousing arsenal from the bag the pharmacist sent and guided us through her gravel carport around the back of the house to the garage.

We took turns kneeling on a chair, bending over a big metal sink. MB's long fingers worked, patient and gentle, as she washed the bugs from our hair. Once certain she'd killed them all, she ushered us into her house, past the kitchen, and into the bathroom.

She turned the knobs of the bathtub and filled it with water. We watched in horror as she sprinkled laundry soap under the running faucet. When the great big foamy bubbles had almost reached the top, she turned off the water, pulled our filthy dresses over our heads, helped us out of our dirty panties, and, rather than putting the clothes into the water, she coaxed us into its warm frothiness and stuffed our clothes in a trash bag instead!

Maggie and I looked at one another and giggled as we eased into the warm silkiness of the bubbles. Kneeling next to the tub, MB dipped her hands in the water, rubbed the soap in a washcloth, and washed Maggie first. Starting with her willowy arms, she squeezed the warm soapy cloth over her skin and then repeated washing the same way with the next washcloth.

We sobbed.

"It's okay," MB cooed, "I'm just going to wash you."

Maggie stopped quivering and relaxed. She looked at me and giggled again. MB took a soft brush from a shelf and worked away at Maggie's fingers and toes, wondering just how many baths it would take to get rid of the ground-in dirt.

By the time it was my turn, the water was cold and looked like mud. MB drained and filled it again with clean water and more laundry soap and repeated the entire process all over again; she had never seen two children so filthy in her life. *How in the world did the oldest one get tar underneath her fingernails?*

It was all she could do to keep her tears back as her hands caressed over the boney protrusions from beneath our skin. And the scars, the healed-over and the scabbed ones, angered her, how could anyone ever be so cruel to a child? The water was near black by the end of the cleaning ritual. For good measure, as the muddy water drained away, she turned on the tap, poured clean, warm water over our glistening pink bodies, and then wrapped us in soft fluffy towels.

She said it would take a couple more baths *before she got all the dirt out of our crevices, but we were clean enough to her liking,* and we'd have one every other night.

Dried off, we followed MB into a bedroom where pretty cotton nightgowns and white underpants awaited us. She dressed us in matching sunshine yellow robes, as soft as kitten fur, with a satin sash to tie it closed and slippers.

I dreaded the next part, combing out our hair. MB did her best, yet even with a detangling spray, she could not undo the knots from our hair. She had no choice but to cut them out, and we followed her to the kitchen for haircuts.

We took turns sitting on a chair in the center of the room. MB draped a towel around our chest, pinned it in the back of our neck, and chopped our hair in nothing flat. When she'd finished with Maggie, she looked like a boy, clean up to her ears. The look on my face made Maggie cry. MB told her not to worry; it would grow back long and pretty in no time.

I was next. She only cut mine to my shoulders. For a final touch, she combed my hair over my eyes and cut it straight across the front, just above my eyes. She said they were bangs and looked cute.

Exhausted from the grooming ceremony, we were ready for sleep, but MB had one more surprise for us. We followed her to the kitchen and sat at the table. She served the most delicious dessert ever. She said she had made it just for us, Strawberry Rhubarb Crisp.

The dessert tasted warm and syrupy, crunchy, and fruity all at the same time; but that wasn't it, she topped it off with vanilla ice cream! It was all we could do to hold back our tears.

After licking the spoon and bowl clean, we followed MB into the bathroom again for one last hygienic procedure, one, she said, we would do twice a day from then on.

PART I

MB reached into a drawer and pulled out a handful of toothbrushes and asked us each to pick one. I liked the purple one best. MB put the others back in the drawer and pulled out a tube of toothpaste. She explained that it was soap for our teeth and even though it might taste good we were not to swallow it. She put the soap on her brush and then on each of ours.

To my shock and disbelief, MB removed her teeth from her mouth to show us how to wash them. We followed along, spitting the left-over soap into the sink. Then she stuck out her tongue and showed us how to wash it. Maggie and I laughed.

She handed each of us a Dixie cup from the side of the sink, filled it halfway with water, and we rinsed our mouths out. She popped her teeth back in her mouth and plunked her brush inside of a glass. Following suit, we put our brushes next hers.

We shadowed MB to the bedroom. There were two beds stacked on top of each other. She had me climb a wooden ladder to the highest one. Maggie crawled into the lower one. I buried my face into the pillow, then into the sheets, and then the blankets. They all smelled so good just like my nightgown; I couldn't stop sniffing them.

Everything was so soft. I couldn't believe I had a sheet *and* a blanket. Winding up my teddy bear like MB showed us, I snuggled down in the warmth of the coveted cocoon and brought my knees to my chest. I hugged my teddy bear tight and hummed along to Brahms's Lullaby, neee na nee nee na nee ne na ne nee.

Almost dozing off, I bolted up wide-awake, apprehensive of the room going dark. I clutched the covers to my chin, preparing to dive under them as soon as she turned the lights out. My heart thudded in my ears; I held my breath in case the monsters might have followed us there.

But MB did not turn off the lights. Instead, she turned a nob that made them almost go out, and then clicked a button on a record player on a dresser at the end of the bed and slipped out of the room. The record did not play music like Mommy's but read a story. It seemed as if I'd stepped into the fairytale.

Remembering the possibility of the returning monsters, I took the bear with me, climbed down to Maggie's bed, curled up next to her, and put my arm around her. She was fast asleep; I stroked her hair until I too drifted off to dreamland.

EIGHTEEN

It seemed I'd just closed my eyes when MB reappeared at the foot of the bed. "Time to get up girls, get your robes and slippers on and come to the table for breakfast."

For a second, I panicked; I was not in my bed or my house. Maggie scrambled from the covers, we put on our robes and slippers, and meandered to the kitchen table.

Something smelled so good. MB told us to have a seat. Before us was a spoon on a napkin and a steaming bowl of something she called Cream of Wheat. She cut a piece of butter, put it on top of the cereal, took a big spoonful of brown sugar and put it on top of the butter, mixed them together, and then poured a little milk on top.

Giving us a nod, she said, "Be careful, girls, it's hot." Maggie and I sat mesmerized by the soupy goodness before us. I couldn't believe she called this breakfast.

MB prepared her bowl the same as ours, and we watched with curiosity as she blew on a spoonful before taking a bite. Maggie and I copied her. It was the sweetest tasting yummiest thing I had ever eaten. I smiled at MB and looked over at Maggie. Tears were rolling down her cheeks.

Maggie scooped a second bite into her mouth; a big snot bubble mingled with her tears. On cue, MB stood up, got a tissue, had Maggie blow her nose into it, and then sat down to resume with her breakfast, as if she had done the same thing a thousand times before.

We'd about finished, when MB put two pieces of bread in a toaster and smothered it with butter and strawberry jam, made from the strawberries her husband grew in their garden, she said. I didn't know which tasted better, or which I like the most, the cereal or the toast.

After breakfast, we tagged along behind her to the bathroom. Finished washing our teeth, we sat on the side of the tub and waited while she went to the bedroom and brought back two matching outfits.

Since we liked to play outside, and it was cold, MB said we could wear pants. Once dressed, she opened another drawer next to the toothbrushes, revealing a treasure trove of ball hair bands and plastic hair clips in several shapes and sizes and in every color imaginable.

PART I

She had us pick some to match our clothes. Then, with globs of some clear pink stuff called Dippity Do, she fixed our hair like princesses. Maggie snickered. This was fun for sure.

※

The next day MB took us to the doctor. We played in the waiting room while she spoke in quiet whispers with him.

"The eldest girl has vaginal scarring which is healing, but it's infected, and I want to treat her. Please give her this cream every evening before she goes to bed for a week." All I understood was I had to take medicine for a few days.

After our bath that evening, MB explained what the doctor said she had to do. So, before putting on my nightie, she had me lay on the bed and put the medicine in my pocket. I turned my head to the side and floated off to my alone place.

MB was gentle and quick. No sooner had I drifted away, it was over, and I was safely back into my panties and nightgown, all before I could shed a tear.

The days for Maggie and I started and ended the same way, and it wasn't long before we knew what to do without explanation. I looked forward to the hot breakfast, toast, and homemade jam that greeted us each morning, never cold cereal like at Mommy's.

Sometimes we had toast with raisins or toast with the jam already inside it with frosting and sprinkles on top, my favorite by far. We'd been staying the night with MB for a while now, and I wondered why Mommy hadn't come for us.

※

One day, MB announced we had to go to school. I had become used to having her near me and didn't like the thought of going somewhere without her.

For the first day of first grade, I chose a purple plaid skirt and a red turtleneck sweater. MB brushed our hair real shiny and pinned a corner of Maggie's back with one of the barrettes from the special drawer. After a big breakfast of Cream of Wheat and toast, she drove us to our new school.

Holding onto MB's hand and clutching our lunch pails, we walked through the enormous front doors of the brick building. It was so much bigger than the school at Mommy's. Everything was made of dark wood, and the floors were as shiny as the one in MB's kitchen.

Our footsteps echoed off the walls of the vast corridor as we climbed the bench length steps, crossed a great hall, and entered a busy office. We waited while MB spoke with some people.

A pretty lady took our hands and explained that she would show us around. MB said goodbye and how she'd be back in a little while to pick us up. I'd heard that before. I choked back an urge to cry.

The lady guided us down the same steps and then further down to an isolated door with a window. Next to it was a little closet to hang coats in. We went inside the room. I waited as she took my sister to meet her teacher.

Maggie walked away with her and didn't even look back. The nice lady and I returned up the stairs, past the office, and entered another classroom where she introduced me to my teacher.

The nice lady left me with her. All eyes were on me. Mrs. Flanderson showed me to my desk and gave me a coloring book and a pencil. The few hours went by fast. When the final bell rang, Mrs. Flanderson walked me to the office where I met Maggie and, just as she had promised, MB.

The next few school days, MB only walked us to the big front doors. A little while after that, parking behind the big yellow school buses, she asked if we would like to go in alone or if we would like her to walk to the door with us. Maggie didn't wait for an answer and flew off in a shot. I jumped out after her.

"Maggie, wait!" She disappeared from my sight.

"Goddam kid," I muttered to myself.

I turned around to wave at MB, but she'd left too. All alone, I walked over to the parallel bars to wait for the bell.

The only thing I liked about the school was lunch and recess. MB put the yummiest things in our lunch boxes, every mouthwatering bite was a reminder of her. A peanut butter sandwich with her homemade jam from DG's garden, a Hostess fruit pie, and a small thermos of milk.

The playground was inviting and had parallel bars like the ones I was used to. I put my sweater on the shortest horizontal bar, swung my knee over it, and pumped with my other leg to swing around and around.

Lost in the nothingness of the warm day, the taunting of some kids startled me back to the present.

"Foster kid, foster kid, foster kid!" they sang in unison.

I didn't know what a foster kid was, but they were saying it like I was one and it was a bad thing. I jumped off the bars and glared at them as mean as I could and said, "Am not."

They continued their chanting as they ran away. I crossed my arms and marched to the other side of the playground, sat on the edge of a log, and dug my heels into the wood chips.

A friendly girl from my class sat next to me.

PART I

"What's a foster kid?" I asked.

"It's a kind of kid whose mom and dad don't want them anymore. They know you're one because only those kinds of kids live at Mrs. Nelson's." Annie said.

"Well I live at that house, but my mom is coming back for me, so I couldn't be a foster kid."

Annie shook her head in agreement and became my first best friend. Sometimes I went to her house after school. Her mom was like MB and nothing like Mommy. Annie lived in a whole different world from the one I knew. She thought I was making up stories when I'd tell her about mine.

NINETEEN

The desire to hide in my alone place didn't change since coming to live with MB. My inner sanctuary was the only space where I felt safe. Every chance I got, crawling into a new hiding spot, I'd close my eyes and float away into a dark, heavenly cocoon.

I didn't sleep or dream. I bobbed away in the peaceful obscurity of nothingness, free of fear, free of pain. Sometimes I imagined I was an orphan and my real mother and father, who loved me very much, would come looking for me.

But no-one ever came; not until we lived with MB. Somehow, she'd always find my secret sanctuary no matter what and pull me out, "Go play outside, be the little girl you are and go have fun."

Outside meant in her yard. I could not wander as I liked to because I didn't know where I was. I missed looking for tar bubbles and my solitude.

The only time I could be by myself was at school, underneath dark stairwells or in the janitor's closet. This wasn't acceptable either. They expected me to be in the classroom, all day.

"Elisa are you in there?" I heard a friendly lady call after me beyond the coats next to Maggie's room.

I crossed my arms and glared at her in defiance. That wasn't my name. My name was the one that Mommy called me, but I would never tell her what my special name was, never.

I peered out to see her sitting on the stairs. She smiled at me and reached her hand out.

"Come on and visit me, Elisa." She said ever so sweet it made my teeth hurt.

I fell for that cat call once before, but she looked nice enough, so I took her hand. We walked up the two flights of stairs, crossed the hall, and up another set of stairs across from Mrs. Flanderson's class.

There was only one room at the top, and it was small with a slanted ceiling. I liked it. It was a secret hideaway.

"You live here?" I asked.

"No this is my office where I work during the day, and then I go to my home after school," she said.

"Wow, this is really neat."

PART I

"Better than the janitor's closet or stairwell?"

"Way better."

"How about if I told you that you could come here instead of going to those hiding places."

"I'd like that."

"How come you want to hide?" she asked while she laid a board game on the table.

I explained how I liked being alone, about my special place, that I missed going there, and how MB didn't like it when I did.

She nodded as if she understood.

"Is there anything else bothering you?" she asked.

After some time, I volunteered, "I'm worried about my mom."

"What is it that worries you?"

My mind wandered off. The lady sat quiet and waited.

My chin quivered, speaking over the huge lump in my throat I said, "She needs me to take care of her. I haven't heard from her in a long time. She made me promise to never leave her and if I did, she'd be scared."

"What would she be scared of?"

"Alone; Mommy doesn't like to be alone, and I make her feel better."

"How do you make her feel better?"

"I sit next to her when she's sad, and she cries and tells me things she's scared of. I give her hugs and bring her tissues for her nose and eyes, and then I climb in her bed and lay next to her so she can go to sleep."

She showed me how to play the game called Chutes and Ladders. We played in silence. She won.

"Did you like the game?"

I nodded that I did. She told me she had more games just as fun and we could play them when I visited her.

"How about we make a deal?"

"Okay," I said.

"How about if I said you could come here and play games with me every single day after lunch, but only if you promise to stay in your morning class until the lunch bell rings, would you like that?"

"Yes, I would." I bobbed up and down in my chair in excitement.

"Ok then, let's play Piggly Wiggly after lunch tomorrow, sound like a plan?" she asked, shaking my hand to seal the deal.

She walked me down the stairs and led me into Mrs. Flanderson's room. I didn't notice the stares from my classmates, I sat at my desk, and smiled; I had a secret.

The nice lady kept her promise. Although I still longed to be alone, I kept my side of the bargain and visited her every day after lunch. Back at MB's house, I continued the pursuit for a refuge of my own every chance I could.

Mommy was the only one who let me go to my alone place, I missed her so much.

⁓

It wasn't long before The Guardian ad Litem returned; I was so excited when I saw her car pull into the driveway, certain she'd come to take us back to Mommy.

MB took her to the kitchen to look out at the backyard where we were playing. "It's great what good food can do," The Guardian said, adding, "I bet Elisa has gained ten pounds. Both of the girls look so healthy, and their hair is so clean and shiny, quite a change for sure."

I wandered into the room, but they continued talking as if I wasn't there, as if I didn't understand.

"I can't stay long. I just wanted to check in and see how things were going and to discuss the future of the girls with you."

"Well," MB said, "I'm doing everything I can with the eldest one, but she likes to be in her own little world. I'm always pulling her out of little hideaways, and now she's doing it at school. The school counselor called and told me she won't stay in her classroom and isn't taking part in activities with the other children. She said she's continually pulling her out of little hideaways too, more often the coat closet under the stairwell next to Maggie's room."

In my own world, if that's what it's called when I wanted to be alone. Adults seem to have a name for everything. What's wrong with wanting to be alone? So what if their *best efforts* aren't working; I didn't want to play with the other kids; I just wanted to be left alone.

The Guardian ad Litem patted MB's hand. "You're doing a great job, Betsy, just try to keep her busy, that's all you can do."

That night, while stories filled our room with magic and faraway places, I thought about the fragments of adult conversations I'd overheard that day. Like how sick Mommy was and how it would take a long time for her to get better if she was to get better. And how MB felt about us staying with her for

PART I

an undetermined amount of time. Or how MB complained about me over the telephone, "no one could love such an incorrigible child, not even me."

What did MB mean when she called me incorrigible? It sounded like *horrible,* and I knew what that word meant cuz someone called that before. I couldn't believe she thought I was horrible. I thought I had been good. How I wished Mommy would come to get us now.

Life was not as it used to be. I didn't know where Mommy was and worried all the time about her and if her friends would find us. I had so many more things to worry about now, and it scared me to death, and there was nothing I could do about any of it.

TWENTY

*M*B and Daddy Gordon, aka DG, learned early on that they couldn't have children of their own. Supporting his wife's yearning for the completeness of a family with children, they became foster parents, the most sought-after ones at that. MB poured all her heart and soul into giving every child who entered her home the chance at a normal childhood.

Although soft-spoken and patient, MB was also rather firm and had little tolerance of any nonsense from her foster children. Neither she nor her husband ever spanked us, or yelled, or said bad words. In fact, I have no recollection of how they disciplined us, only that an occasional scary look from MB, not giving merit to my innate temptations to test the depths of the water, is all it took to set me on the straight and narrow once again.

I learned that being a pest was just the same as being good, so I gave up trying, and didn't get into trouble too often. Regardless, she seemed to like Maggie best and always saw the worst in me.

MB found great comfort in reading her Bible and attending church every Sunday. We liked going with her because we got to wear pretty dresses and munch on lifesavers while the preacher talked. We had to be as quiet as mice and sit still when the adults did their exercises, prayed, and sang.

Church was the only time MB hugged me, and it was always after the first time she'd ask me to sit still. Sometimes I'd wriggle around on purpose, so she'd wrap her arm around my shoulder.

She always wore a delicate white sweater. It was so soft and smelled like Mommy, but with a different perfume smell. As I snuggled next to her warm body, I'd play with the pretty sparkly ring on her finger and suck on candy.

When I asked about it, she said it was a wedding ring from DG, his promise he'd love her forever. While MB walked to the front of the church to get a little snack from the preacher, I closed my eyes tight and asked God to send me a man like DG when I grew up who'd love me forever too.

MB looked like an angel as she bowed her head and intertwined her pretty cross and beads between her clasped fingers. She was so serious. I hope she said a prayer for Mommy. DG never went with us; MB said it was during his sleep time. My favorite part was the chocolate donuts and playtime afterward.

Once my legs were a little longer, MB invited me to exercise with her. I felt so important helping her unfold the kneeling bench, but, after a few rounds of sit down, stand up, and kneeling on the bench, I was all too happy to resume my former station.

◊

MB always had something baking or frying. Right after breakfast, she'd prepared the dessert for after dinner and food for the next meal, I liked her glazed donuts and cinnamon sugar-coated donut holes the best.

When MB wasn't cooking or cleaning, she sewed and crocheted. She sat on the couch with her piles of colorful yarn, an eternal cigarette burning in a nearby ashtray, and make stacks and stacks of matching squares, like perfect little waffles, and pile them on the coffee table.

Then, she'd knit them together for ponchos or blankets to donate to the children's hospital or give as gifts. I'll never forget the beautiful, baby pink and blue poncho with fuzzy white pom-poms she made for us to wear over our Easter dresses one year.

As if she wasn't busy enough, once Maggie and I were in bed, she'd work until late at night on her Singer sewing machine to create identical clothes for us. If the bear or the fairy tales didn't lull me to sleep, the humming of the sewing machine sure did.

Our play clothes came from Value Village, but our special clothes, for church, parties, and other occasions, she made with her magical hands. I couldn't believe how fast she made them, right down to the cute little buttons and fancy edging.

We felt as if we were hers alone. She fussed over us like little dolls the way she combed the snarls out of our hair and pinned it back on the sides with little plastic barrettes to match our outfits. She loved getting us ready, whether it was for school, church, or anywhere.

And just as she promised, it wasn't long before Maggie's hair grew back long enough to wear braids and ponytails. Dippity Do was MB's secret to making perfect tails, a single one down the back, or one on each side.

She'd secure the ends in place with different sized colored ball hair bands or thick pieces of yarn to correspond with our clothes. I loved making my braids bounce and shaking my head back and forth just to see the pretty adornments.

MB's clothes and fancy hairdos made me feel special. The poncho she made for my eighth birthday almost sealed the deal between us. Created from a mosaic of her leftover yarn, she crocheted a patchwork design of small granny squares and two medium-sized, pink pom poms dangled in the front.

It reminded me of a country song, Coat of Many Colors; like the girl in the lyrics, I was proud to wear mine too. The poncho made me miss Mommy too because it smelled like cigarettes.

∽

Evenings were the same, but never boring. After baths and dessert, we'd lie on the carpeted living room floor and color or play with dolls while MB and her husband watched TV, the Lawrence Welk show, Mutual of Omaha animal stories, Little House on the Prairie, or The Waltons.

My favorite was the animal stories, my favorite was the one about a mother hen and her baby chicks. It was like that with us and MB, wherever she went, we followed, if something scared us, we'd hide behind her, and like the mama hen, we were never out of her sight; MB never left us with babysitters.

MB and DG had two dogs, a black poodle named Annette, and a white, long-haired, chubby shih tzu named Honey. They had their own beds in the garage just off the kitchen under DG's workbench, and a special potty area lined with newspaper at the far end of the garage.

"You can pet the dogs Elisa, but be gentle because they might nip you," DG warned when he introduced me to them.

Annette snapped at my fingers a couple times if I petted her when she was on DG's lap, but Honey never did. She even let me put doll clothes on her and put her to bed in the dolly cradle in the garage. When she was *sleeping*, I'd sit in a little chair next to the cradle and pretend to read her stories from a book, until I could read for real.

Because Annette seemed jealous and wanted to hear the stories too, I had to get another chair, and, by her own will, let her jump up in the seat, where she'd stay until she heard me say, "The End."

∽

DG was a quiet, older man who spoke little and never got mad, not at MB, not at the dogs and never at us. He liked pretty music and connected speakers from the stereo console in the living room all around the house so he could hear it everywhere.

He even drilled a tiny hole in the wall behind the radio to the garage so he could listen to it while he worked at his bench or tended to his garden. Although I missed Mommy's country music on KMPS, I came to like DG's music on KIXI too, swing and jazz from the 40s.

DG loved his garden and grew the yummiest tomatoes and peas.

"I didn't know they grew on bushes, I thought they came from cans," I observed as I popped a sweeter-than-candy, cherry tomato into my mouth.

He laughed as he filled a bowl brimming to the top with the beautiful red and green jewels.

"Please take these into mother, Elisa," he said handing me the bowl.

DG didn't seem to mind my chatter and bombardment of a million questions. He'd just listen without saying a word as he tinkered at his workbench or tended to his garden while I yammered away about anything and nothing important. He never told me to be quiet or to go away.

DG had the patience of a saint; especially when teaching Maggie and me how to ride a bike. We practiced on the back-patio after school every day. Before we knew it, the training wheels were off, and we were riding around the neighborhood.

DG worked the graveyard shift. That sounded scary, but he said it wasn't, that the Airport was easier to clean without people around.

He'd just finished his dinner about the time we arrived home from school. Donned in his army green coveralls, he'd scoop up his grey lunch pail and Stanley thermos, and head to work.

He returned home at two a.m. every morning. One night I awoke just as he arrived and walked into the kitchen to say hello. He was having his customary bowl of Grape Nuts.

He didn't get mad, instead he got another bowl from the cupboard. The cereal tasted like little pieces of rocks but was better once I heaped a bunch of sugar on it and let it sit in the milk for a spell. That night marked the first of our special time together.

From then on, I listened for his truck as it crunched over the gravel and into the carport. I met him at the kitchen table where a place setting for two awaited us, including a sugar bowl with the same funny seashell spoon MB changed her coffee spoon for. I don't remember what we talked about, but we did talk a lot, or I did anyway, and then he'd usher me back to bed.

∽

Never a dull moment, when we weren't in school or attending church on Sundays, MB would help us into the back of her two-tone yellow and brown Dodge Swinger, pop in an 8 track Disney story, and we'd disappear for the entire day.

Of the many places we went, we always went used store hopping for play clothes, to the fabric store to pick clothing patterns for special occasions, to the library, to the store for groceries, or to swimming or ice-skating lessons. The outings concluded with lunch at Arby's or McDonald's for strawberry milkshakes and Happy Meals.

Summers were the best of all. It was nonstop action. During the week, we'd wear ourselves ragged at the YMCA day camp. On Saturdays, MB and DG would take us out in their little Datsun camper for a picnic and to play somewhere. And Sundays, we'd go to church with MB and visit her friends afterward. Sometimes her friends had dinner parties. This is where we learned about Manners, Some Does Not Mean a Handful, and A Couple Means Take Two.

DG's camper was like a doll house. It had a little door in the back with two small carpeted benches on either side and speakers nestled in the corners.

With the adults in the front cab, Maggie, me, and the dogs would pile in the back and listen to stories or DG's pretty music while we headed out for the day. Often, we'd end up at the Woodland Park Zoo.

Besides his own, DG loved the zoo's garden. After he took lots of pictures and we'd tuckered ourselves out from running amok, we'd feed the bears marshmallows, watch the funny penguins do tricks, and then settle on a blanket for a Kentucky Fried Chicken picnic and a nap.

Sometimes we'd spend a day at Saltwater Park see-sawing and frolicking in the creek or doggy paddling in the Puget Sound. Sometimes, DG brought a small pop-up camper, and we'd stay overnight.

I'll never forget my first night in the wilderness, it wasn't pleasant. The loud humming sound from the kerosene lantern and the surrounding shadows terrified me. I buried into the safe cocoon of my sleeping bag and squeezed my eyes shut 'til I fell asleep, only to awaken in sheer panic a short time later.

I kicked, clawed, and screamed, but couldn't get out of the bag when all of a sudden, the world turned upside down as MB and DG worked to shake me out. Maggie was in stitches. I didn't like camping.

We took trips: on a 747 airplane to visit her parents in Boise Idaho, where the water tasted nasty, and we got awful sunburns; to Expo '74 in Spokane, Disneyland and Knott's Berry Farm in California to name a few excursions. Faraway trips included little mementos to remember it by. My favorites were the personal license plates from Disneyland for our bikes and the invisible dog on a leash from the Expo.

DG took pictures of everything and everybody on our trips. When we got home, he couldn't wait to see them. He'd set up a stand for a pull-down screen and show us a slide show of our latest adventures or holiday, including a picture or two of his prized vegetables and roses from his garden.

⁌∽⁍

MB was the best babysitter I'd ever had; our clothes, food, and seasons were the only things that changed. Each day marched along, blending one into the next, the mornings an exciting introduction of what the day would bring.

Anticipation of the bedtime ritual, dessert, and bubble baths replaced my fear of the darkness in the evenings.

PART I

    Sleep no longer brought nightmares, or concerns about Mommy, or why we were still there when my head hit the pillow at night, just contented dreams of our daily adventures mixed with the fairytales from the record player at the end of my bed. I never wanted to leave.

    After the third Christmas, I gave up the vigil of waiting for Mommy's return and convinced myself she'd died, and we'd live with MB forever.

    That is until the day that her ghost appeared.

TWENTY-ONE

One day after school, I stormed through the front door and made a beeline for the kitchen to tell MB how some girls from school invited me to join Girl Scouts, and I would be a Brownie. Halfway there, Mommy stepped out from the shadows with her arms open wide. I screamed, and then everything went black.

I awoke with a cold cloth on my forehead. Mommy was still there; her smile a mile wide. She was glad to see me and said while she was away, she'd learned how to be a good mom like MB, and how we would all be back together soon, just us, the Three Musketeers and we both cried.

"Really, Mommy?" I asked. "You promise?"

"Yes, Lissie, I promise, just you, me and Maggie; the Three Musketeers. Things will be different, you'll see."

The day she came to take us home was a sad but exciting day. My happy-ever-after was about to end, but I wasn't afraid to go home with Mommy as I was bigger and stronger now, confident no one would hurt us again.

Maggie and I were allowed to take only one toy each, leaving the others behind for the new children that would be coming to stay with MB and DG. I looked over my prized accumulation of playthings, lingered over the Barbie dolls and their accessories, but decided upon a life-size Curious George doll with baby clothes and a bottle I'd once found at the Value Village.

My third-grade teacher gave me one of the class guinea pigs to take home, the one with red fur I'd had many deep conversations with, complete with a cage and everything; I named him Redfur.

Maggie and I climbed into the back of our Grandpa's big station wagon. MB placed his cage next to me. It was hot, and the air was thick and muggy. The yellow flowered vinyl cushion stuck to our sweaty legs. Despite the discomfort, I was excited to see our new house. Mommy said it was in the same neighborhood where we last lived but on a different street.

After a short drive, Grandpa pulled into the driveway of our new home. Redfur squealed as if excited too. There was a large tree in the front yard. The branches were up high and looked difficult to climb. Maggie and I couldn't wait to get out of the hot car and see the inside.

Almost out of the car, I saw someone emerge from the house, and step onto the small front porch to greet us. It was a tall man in a cowboy hat. Mommy looked back at me with a big smile on her face. Confused and scared, I asked Mommy who the man was.

"Why that's Tim, Lissie. Wait till you meet him, you will like him a lot," she said.

I swiped at the hot angry tears streaming down my cheeks with the back of my hand and gave Mommy the most hateful glare.

"You lied, Mommy! You lied to everybody! You said it was just going to be the three of us this time, The Three Musketeers!"

I got out of the car, jerked Redfur's cage out and, with all my strength, slammed the door shut as hard as I could. With purposeful rudeness, I shoved past the man and entered the house, letting him know full well he was not welcome.

I went straight to what I assumed was my new room, put the cage on the dresser, flopped down on one of the small beds. And buried my face into a stinky pillow and cried and screamed. I wanted to go back to MB's.

Mommy entered the room and sat next to me.

"I'm sorry Lissie. We are the Three Musketeers, and we will always be, you, me, and sister, just like I promised. Tim will not live with us."

∽

Mommy changed yet was still the same. There was food in the pantry, baths, pj's, and brushing teeth before bed, with bubbles and strawberry shampoo like MB's. And Mommy fretted over keeping the house clean, always after us to pick our stuff up. But that was it. We were on our own to dress ourselves and fix our hair. Everything in the magical drawer stayed behind so we used Mommy's bobby pins and rubber bands instead.

She served dinner each night at the kitchen table just like at MB's. Mommy took her newfound culinary skills rather seriously. She'd prepare dinner, with a cigarette dangling out the side of her mouth, by studying a box of Hamburger Helper and then set about to make it. My favorite was beef stroganoff with sour cream on top.

Canned peas, corn, cream corn or green beans accompanied each meal, nothing like the kind from DG's garden. Sometimes we had fruit cocktail for dessert, Maggie and I counted the few maraschino cherries inside to assure we got the same.

One night, as Mommy stirred the ingredients together from a Jiffy cake mix, I told her about the yummy desserts' MB made and how she never got them from a box. Tears rolled down her face while she finished making the cake. Confused, I gave her a kiss on the cheek to make her feel better like I used to.

After that, Mommy only made Jiffy cakes for our birthdays and bought Libbyland TV dinners with desserts in them, like the kind MB made, instead. We could have eaten one of them every night. They came with magic powder for our milk and had puzzles on the boxes.

Like before, we were on our own for breakfast and lunch. But this time, breakfast was better than ever. When Mommy took us grocery shopping with her, she allowed us to pick any three kinds of cereal we wanted. Our favorites were Cap'n Crunch, Cocoa Puffs, Alpha Bits, Sugar Smacks, and Cheerios. MB had none of those!

After several initial inspections, never once finding a living thing inside the bowl, I allowed Maggie to pour her own. The cereal tasted way better now because we had milk in the refrigerator to put on top, brought by a milkman every other week.

We watched J.P. Patches while we ate breakfast, keeping the volume low so as not to wake Mommy. Then on Saturday's we'd stay in our pj's, load up on cereal, and watch cartoons the entire morning.

We ate lunch from the school cafeteria on school days, and on weekends and in summers we ate a bagged lunch: a small carton of milk, a piece of fruit, and a piece of bologna between two slices of bread, from the Neighborhood House at the community center.

On the days Mommy took us grocery shopping, we'd go to lunch before, somewhere sister and I could have Shirley Temples, and she could have an adult drink. Ours came with cherries. Mommy's didn't. We would only get one drink, Mommy got several.

Even though we were back in our home turf, we'd been away so long, we'd become the new kids at school again. Our school had moved to the small piece of land where our first house which burned down used to be. It was bigger with more of the same square buildings and a gym.

A larger school meant more classmates from surrounding neighborhoods. It was the kids from the outside who gave us project kids the most grief.

༄

I panicked when the teacher handed out *assignments* rather than a workbook with pictures. The piece of paper she gave me only had numbers, plus and minus symbols with equal signs.

"Ok class, we will have a test to see where each of you are with basic math. I will set a timer, and you are to complete as many as you can before the bell rings. Now go."

Everyone had their noses to their desks, some with their tongues gripping the edge of their lip and writing as fast as they could. I looked at the paper.

PART I

For the life of me, I couldn't picture how many things were for each number. With my hand in my lap, I counted the numbers on my fingers and wrote the answers as fast as I could.

At recess, a group of the neighbor kids approached me.

"Won't ya just take a look at the weirdy," the tallest girl with blonde hair said.

A sixth grader, what was she doing hanging around with the little kids? She was the one who was a weirdy.

Twice my size, she got in my face. "My mom says your mom is a retard, so that means you're retarded too, right?"

I recognized the girl. She lived two streets behind us. I was sure Mommy didn't know her mom, and who was she to say Mommy was a retard. I mean Mommy acted strange and talked funny, but I'm sure she wasn't retarded, and I turned to walk away.

"My mom says your mom's Looney Tunes, so that means your Looney too," she taunted.

"Looney, looney, looney," The others chimed in with her.

Every recess was the same. The older girl and her gang of ruffians. They pointed, snickered, and teased about how I smelled and dressed funny. They liked to joke about Mommy most of all and tease me for not having a real dad, saying how that made me a bastard.

The rest of the kids just whispered behind my back, and, after a while, left me alone for good. Funny, it's what I wanted all along.

As predicted, the man in the cowboy hat, MITCH for short, moved in; Mommy lied; it would never be just the three of us.

TWENTY-TWO

MITCH was a real dork, had goofy glasses like Mommy's, was super tall, had dark combed back hair, and always wore plaid matching polyester suits, a cowboy hat, and boots. He looked like a carbon copy of the man on Mommy's favorite show The Rockford Files, but not as cute.

"He has a good job and can help us." Mommy justified.

The day he moved in, was the day I declared war upon my mother. I cast a full-fledged Campaign of Hate upon him and anyone else who dared to take her away from us and on her for breaking our sacred circle.

I couldn't understand why she had to *have* a boyfriend and why my sister and I were never enough for her.

Sleep eluded me the first little while he lived with us, remaining ever vigilant for even the slightest movement outside our bedroom door. I prayed someone would learn that Mommy had lied and would save us before it was too late, again. When I wasn't praying, I was contemplating the details of the Campaign's itinerary for the next day.

I awoke Mommy early in the morning with a complaint of not feeling well. Then, I sneezed and held out my hands for her to see.

"Oh, Mommy, look," I said innocently, the plastic glob of Snot spread menacingly across my fingers.

She threw up all over herself and the bed. I was out the door before she could catch me.

Mommy had become talented while she was away, and MITCH encouraged her every new accomplishment. Above all, she was excited about how many kinds of casseroles she could create with a can of cream of anything soup, trying them out on Maggie, MITCH, and me.

Arriving home from school one day, I caught her in the throes of making cookies and pulled up a chair to the counter to watch.

She studied the red and white plaid cookbook with all sincerity, adding ingredients to a large green bowl as she read along, flicking her cigarette ashes in the sink in between.

She scooped out the flour with a large glass cup, splashed vanilla in the bowl, cracked two eggs on top of that, and emptied a bag of chocolate chips over it all.

PART I

I snatched a piece of chocolate and asked, "Why do you use only one bowl? MB used three."

Mommy looked up from the book, glared, and slammed it shut.

She dumped the contents of the bowl into the trash, grabbed her glass of wine and smokes, and stormed off to her room, yelling in her wake, "Make your own damn cookies!"

It was another year before she made another attempt. That time I stayed out of the kitchen. She may not have made them the same way as MB did, but boy we couldn't get enough of them.

Her prized creation was an occasional yellow Jiffy cake with chocolate frosting she always baked in the same rusty old cake pan. She was so proud of her cakes she even brought one to the Cake Walk Festival at the school.

Yep, with her goofy butterfly glasses, cigarette hanging from her lips, black curlers piled high on her head, held in place with pink curler pins and an emerald green scarf, wearing a lime green polyester pantsuit and tattered house slippers, she was proud to enter her creation into a contest, and flung it on an awaiting table. If she was trying to embarrass me that day, she made no mistake in her attempt.

Mommy may have learned a thing or two about Home Ec, but what she wasn't prepared for was how to deal with the wrath of a scorned child.

Per the rules of engagement, it was my primary goal to ruin every dinner. One night a plate of Cheeseburger Macaroni and spinach confronted me. The spinach was watery, and brown liquid seeped into the macaroni.

"The spinach is slimy and gross. I don't want it." I declared and pushed my plate away.

It didn't take long before MITCH felt comfortable enough to boss us around.

Just because he had kids of his own made him an expert with us, or so he thought.

"Eat it, Lissie, it's good for you," MITCH said.

I made a face at it, folded my arms, and refused to eat.

When dinner was over, I got up to leave the table, but MITCH told me to sit back down.

"You aren't leaving the table until it's gone," he said.

It was cold and slimier now; I would not eat it, now or ever.

Hours later, MITCH returned to the kitchen to find me still at the table.

Removing the plate, he said, "Fine, if you don't eat it now, you'll eat it in the morning for breakfast."

"Fine," I said, stormed off to my room and slammed the door behind me.

I didn't eat it in the morning either or when he sat it in front of me again at dinner. Mommy never said a word. He glared at me while he ate, and I gave him my best smirkish grin.

Back and forth the war of our wills went on until the third day when he threw it out. I pummeled at his nerves with everything I had, ignoring his demands, like putting stuff away or helping with something around the house, until the veins bulged from his temples, and he yelled and threatened to get his belt out.

I welcomed him home the same way each day after school, I'd toss my things on the couch, plop down in front of the TV, and turn on cartoons. He'd stroll into the room.

"Go put your things away Lissie," he'd say.

I'd ignore him, but he persisted.

"Go put your things away now dammit!" he'd yell, followed by the whir of his belt as it slithered through the belt loops of his polyester plaid pants.

That always got my attention. I'd stand up, grab my things, and stomp all the way to my room, hurling in my wake, "You're not the boss of me!" and slam my bedroom door shut for good measure.

I tried to be as horrible as I could whenever he was around, arguing with everyone, picking fights with Maggie, sassing Mommy, interrupting, and talk over him whenever he talked to Mommy, never saying please or thank you, and not talking to him unless I had to.

There was one bad habit that drove him hair-pulling nuts, and I only did it when I knew he was watching. I'd pick my nose with gold-digging gusto and then wipe it on the couch.

"Get a napkin for that Lissie!" he'd snap.

I'd wait until he yelled and threatened me with his belt, before jumping off the couch, stomping every step to my room, and slamming the door.

I chewed with my mouth open, burped and farted with wild abandon, and for the encore, in the whiniest annoying tone possible, I'd complain about everything.

His favorite of all was when I'd disappear until dark. Back and forth and on and on we'd go, an exciting duel to witness for sure.

I'd gotten under his skin, and that was good, and continued to challenge him every chance I got, but he still wouldn't leave.

PART I

MITCH was sick and always passing out, making the Campaign problematic sometimes. Just before his lights went out, he'd call for my mother. One time, Mommy wasn't home when it happened.

"Rosemary!" he yelled.

I looked up from my coloring book and saw his eyes rolling to the back of his head.

I ran to him. "What do I do?"

He couldn't answer as he was about to topple over any minute. I turned my back to him and pressed his body against the wall with all my might. Half his size, I somehow guided his six-foot frame to the floor just as he slipped into unconsciousness.

He lay motionless. *I hope he's dead.*

Tears welled in my eyes. "I'm sorry Tim, I'm sorry." I wept over him, wishing to take the thought back.

He awoke with a start, "Lissie?"

I stood up and ran outside.

MITCH seemed to get sick more and more, and Mommy blamed me.

"Can't you be nice to him Lissie? The more stressed out he becomes, the sicker he gets."

"Good. When's he leaving?"

TWENTY-THREE

*I*t didn't matter; with as much determination as I put into bothering him, he did his best to get on my good side as if that would change things. He took me along whenever he did errands; because he was sick, we had to ride the bus everywhere, but I didn't mind, I grew up on the bus. Of the places we went, I liked the trips to Vashon Island. The first time we went, we spent an entire day under the hot sun picking strawberries for a farmer and the second time, we rode bicycles all over the island.

His favorite place to go was downtown; he liked walking around Pike Place Market and the piers on the waterfront. We spent a lot of time poking around different stores to marvel at all kinds of weird and old things. Then, once a week we'd stop at Sears, the same store MB had taken us once for Winnie the Pooh clothes, to buy the best smelling coffee ever.

If we weren't out and about, he and Mommy hung out at a cocktail diner in town. Mommy still had some of her records, so on the nights they were out late, I'd listen to them and sing along like I used to. When bored with those, I'd listen to the radio. Whenever the song Coat of Many Colors played, it made me miss MB and think about the precious poncho she made for me. I wished with all my heart we could go back to her home.

One Christmas MITCH took us on a long Greyhound bus ride to Oregon to spend the holiday with his mom and his two kids. Sad to say, Redfur couldn't go. Mommy assured me one of the fat lady's girls, from the blue house where we once lived, would take care of him.

Upon our return, I found Redfur lifeless in his cage. The babysitter forgot to leave the heat on for him. MITCH just wrapped him in newspaper and put him in the garbage as if it were no big loss.

There were lots of kids on our street. Two sisters our age lived on the other side of the wall from us and another pair, two houses away. It seemed all they wanted to do was to play with dolls, hopscotch, drawn on the tar road with cement rocks, jump rope games, or play with our lemon skippers. I'd bring along my Curious George doll and play along, but soon tired of the monotonous boredom.

The boys further down the street were more fun; they played with marbles and cars. During recess, I watched a few games of marbles and studied the players' strategies. The object was to knock the most marbles out of the ring, a circle drawn in the dirt with a stick or a shoelace. Each player brought some of their own marbles, and their best shooter marble, and placed them in the circle, position didn't matter so long as they were inside.

The Nose Drop game determined who'd go first. Someone drew a straight line on the ground, each player took turns standing on the line, and then placed their shooter marble to their nose and let it drop to the ground. The player whose shooter marble came closest to the line went first; second closest to the line goes second, and so on.

To play, each player stood outside the circle and tried to knock marbles out by either dropping their shooter marble straight down, their toes at the line of the ring, taking aim by holding their shooter marble at about the level of their shoulder, and then dropping it into the ring, or by holding their shooter marble with their second finger of their dominant hand and sending the marble like a bullet straight into the intended target.

At the end of their turn, the player collected the marbles he knocked out of the circle along with their shooter marble. However, if they had knocked no marbles from out of the circle and if their shooter bounced outside, they had to pay one marble of their own into the circle and then could collect their shooter.

If their shooter did not bounce outside the circle, the player would lose it, allowing others a chance to win it, and then their turn was over. The game ended when there were no more marbles in the circle; the player who collected the most marbles won.

After watching and practicing a time or two, I felt confident enough to invite myself into a game. Before long, I had a big collection of marbles from my winning a lot of games in the playground, so much, in fact, some wouldn't play with me.

I had lots of matchbox cars too. I'd won them in bets to see who could jump off the highest point of the roof of empty houses or the laundromat.

Of all my friends in the projects, my favorite was the boy three doors down. His dad let us play with knives.

TWENTY-FOUR

Three doors down lived a boy from school with his older brother and father; I remembered them from our last house before we went to live with MB. His dad was short and too skinny. He always wore black clothes and motorcycle boots, had shoulder length stringy, greasy, black combed-back hair, and always had a cigarette in his mouth and a beer in his hands. If you didn't know him, you wouldn't cross him.

Everything about him and their house was dirty like the house we lived in with the Family. I couldn't stand to be inside, it stunk like cigarettes, pot, and parties. He was nice, but not to his kids, his boys were quiet, and I understood why.

When we'd play, his dad would watch us with his beer and smokes. He liked to tell us about knives, always stressing how they weren't a toy and to pay close attention when handling them and he'd teach us how to play certain knife games if we promised to only play with them when he was around.

He was a great thrower, like the kind you see at the circus, and made it look easy. He could throw it almost fifty feet in the air, and it would land, sticking straight up in the ground eight times out of ten.

There was a proper way to stand when throwing the knife, he said, "Put your right foot in back, toes at the distance mark, and put your left foot in front. Bend both of your knee, especially the front one. Let your weight rest on the ball of your back foot, and behind your toes."

Stretching his arms straight out in front of him he continued with his teaching of how to throw the knife, "Both arms are straight and point to the target. Hold the knife in a pinch grip like this. Do not stop the swing of the knife throw, go on with the movement. The right arm now makes a round and smooth swing to the back, the knife is even behind the head. Then it swings forward towards the target like you wanted it to. While swinging forward, shift your weight to rest on the front foot, with your chest following this movement. Do not move your right shoulder; it remains in a tilted line with the left. For the throw, shift your weight to the left foot while bringing the right arm with the knife to the front."

We had him show us several times. We liked watching him. He looked like a dancer in slow motion. Once we mastered how to stand and throw, he showed us some games we could play.

The first one we learned he called Split the Kipper. He had his son and I stand facing each other at about six feet apart with our legs together, and chose him to be the leading player, gave him the knife, and told him to aim and throw the knife so it would land outside my feet, either to the right of my right foot or left of my left foot.

He said the knife had to stick in the ground blade first and must be within 12 inches of said foot. If it was further away or if it didn't stick in the ground at all then it was a 'no-throw' and didn't count.

If it was within a foot and stuck in the ground, I was to move the nearest foot to where the knife landed, pull it out of the ground, and take my turn to throw back in the same way.

He explained how the game continued with each of us taking turns to throw, whilst all the time trying to remain standing as our legs got further and further apart, and the first one to fall over or gave up, lost.

He said too if one of us felt we couldn't stretch our legs any further, then that person could decide to 'Split the Kipper.' The other player would aim the knife between the other's feet, and if it stuck into the ground, that person could close their legs to the starting position.

He explained we should decide the number of times we called 'Split the Kipper' before starting, or the game could last a long time.

His pet black raven supervised our playing and cackled an annoying laugh whenever the knife didn't stick in the ground.

Once we mastered one game, his dad would show us another. We didn't share our excitement as we perfected our new-found skill with Mommy, she'd probably tell MITCH, and then we wouldn't get to play anymore.

TWENTY-FIVE

*M*ITCH moved with us out of the projects to a house on the opposite side of town. It was the biggest house we'd ever lived in. It had two bedrooms just off the living room connected by a solitary bathroom. Mommy and MITCH claimed the first bedroom that overlooked the front porch. I took the joining one further back, and Maggie claimed the smallest room just off the kitchen.

It had a basement as big as the upstairs. It was cold and smelled old and musty down there. I avoided going alone unless it was rainy or cold outside, and then only if Maggie could go with me. It was a great place to hula hoop, skip with our lemon twist toys, or ride bikes.

One morning after moving in, finding the biggest bowls we could, we filled them to the top with Honeycombs and settled in the living room for a lengthy marathon of Saturday cartoons. Just as we'd slurped the last of the milk from our bowls, someone knocked on the door.

It was a girl and boy around my age and another boy closer to Maggie's age.

"Hi. We came over to see who moved in," said the blonde-haired girl who introduced herself as Karen. She lived across the street with her mom, dad, and older sisters; her eldest sister lived with her husband and her two kids across the street from her house.

The boys were brothers, Peter the eldest and Paul the youngest, and lived with their parent's kitty-corner from us in a dark blue house.

"Wanna see my dog Hercules?" asked Paul.

"We gotta get dressed first," I said.

They showed Maggie and me the ins and outs of the neighborhood, the shortcuts to school and the nearby seven-eleven to get candy and slurpies. In the winter, they showed us how to slide down the little hill next to our house on the metal lids of garbage cans. We played all kinds of games. My favorite was *who could throw up the grossest after dinner.*

We went to separate schools but spent every moment together afterward in the street between our houses. Karen became my best friend and happy to join me as my partner in crime in the Campaign.

I kept everyone up to date about my latest antics; in fact, everyone loved pitching in their ideas for my next attack. Once, they all came over to watch TV. Armed with a couple packs of Bubble Yum, we stuffed two huge pieces of

PART I

gum in our mouths and chomped and snapped in a crescendo of cow-chewing total annoyance. Pop rocks were by far the favorite all-time nerve jangler.

Sometimes while Maggie and the brothers hung out, Karen and I would sneak around outside her house to spy on her sisters with their boyfriends or peek from my bedroom window with the lights out at the cute guys who had moved in next door.

One time, we had our first cigarette, stolen from Mommy's purse, in the backyard of a neighbor kid we were babysitting.

The most annoying thing Maggie and I dreamed up was when we invented a new language, Humshkaneese, like pig Latin. It's a "code" language created by rearranging sounds in a word moving the first sound to the end and "ay", except we added the word "inaga" and every now and then, we added the word "Alf," the furry alien from the TV show, after every consonant.

Maggie and I practiced day and night to perfect it. As convoluted as it sounded, we somehow understood each other, no matter how we mixed it up.

And boy was it was a hit. Mommy and MITCH hated it. In fact, we rarely spoke English anymore. We loved to talk about how much we hated MITCH right in front of him, and he knew it too. The more he glared, the more we'd laugh at him.

When I wasn't scheming, I'd go wandering. The perimeter of my mindless meanderings expanded beyond our immediate living space. Getting to know a new area was exciting. I couldn't believe how the blocks of houses went on and on forever no matter which way I walked.

The following summer we took a familiar Greyhound bus to visit his relatives in his hometown of La Grande again. Although we always had fun, I didn't let on like I did, after all, he was the enemy.

On the second morning of our arrival, his family packed everything except the kitchen sink, to spend the summer in their other house, in the middle of nowhere.

Sequestered to the big white house and as bored as we were, we bonded with his daughters. We spent long, sticky, mosquito-slapping days on the porch swing crooning to fifties music and guzzling Kool-Aid.

Sometimes, the family convoyed to a local river for a picnic and swimming. It was stifling hot, the sweat pouring off my body did nothing to cool me off, so I was more than eager to jump in the murky inconspicuous water with the others.

One day, resurfacing from my first cannonball, I came face to face with the cutest boy I'd ever seen. His name was Bobby. His family was friends with

MITCH's. Bobby and his brother chased my sister and me in and out of the water for the rest of the day.

Back at the summer house, just before dinner, in the middle of singing Chapel of Love, the echoing of a woman's blood-curdling screams consumed the desert air.

I grabbed Maggie's arm. The hair on the back of my neck bristled, and my goosebumps got goosebumps. We looked at each other in bug-eyed fright. MITCH's girls laughed at us city kids; they said it was just the sound of the rabbits their granny was fixing for supper.

Tears welled in my eyes as I stared at the bunny dressed in breadcrumbs on my plate, *poor Thumper*. From the corner of my eye, I saw Maggie and the rest of the kids chowing down on it as if it were Sunday chicken. I half smiled, picked up a leg, imagined it was from the Colonel and took a little bite. I couldn't believe it, it tasted like KFC, and I had seconds.

The remaining days and nights melded together, despite the splotches of Calamine lotion for the sunburns and mosquito bites, I never wanted to return home. I could live this way the rest of my life; especially, after Bobby gave me a ring and pledged to love me forever.

With our looming departure just around the corner, Bobby and I spent the rest of the time almost attached at the hip. He promised to write often and vowed he'd marry me one day.

True to his word, he wrote, sometimes twice a week, always proclaiming his undying love for me, and sometimes tucked a gumball trinket between the pages. I was proud to be the only one in fifth grade with a boyfriend.

Every day after school I waited on the front steps for the mailman. Without reason, the letters stopped coming. The mailman avoided my eyes when he deposited our letters in the mailbox, and then went on his merry way as though it were any other day.

MITCH called his mom, no one had heard from Bobby's family and didn't know how to reach them. To say I was shattered is putting it mildly, my first true love had dumped me like a hot potato.

༄

Before getting too depressed over the loss of my unrequited love, an all-encompassing, razor hot, sore throat took its place.

"Just as I suspected," the Dr. said to Mommy.

"It's her tonsils and adenoids, they are swollen, and have got to come out pronto," he added.

PART I

Mommy sat on the edge of a brick planter box outside the doctor's office and had a smoke while we waited for a cab to take us to the hospital five miles away.

Burning with fever and unable to stay awake, the nice driver carried me into the hospital. I awoke in a daze sometime later and threw up some icky brown stuff. It kept spewing out of my mouth, covering me and my bed, until I fell asleep again.

I awoke again some time later with even a worse searing pain in my throat. It scared me how I couldn't swallow or cry, and for the first time in my life, couldn't talk. Tears burned in little rivers down my face.

"Have a Popsicle," the nice nurse said.

I nodded and took the red Popsicle. I hadn't had one since MB's. The cherry flavor tasted better than whatever coated my mouth and the cold liquid quelled the burning flame. Days later Mommy took me home.

Too miserable to resume with the Campaign, MITCH took full advantage of my unguarded defenses. He showered me with everything possible to make me feel better. All I could manage was a simmering sullen look, but the ice cream, Jell-O, lozenges, and throat spray kept coming. Even after all the torture I'd given him, he still came through for me.

One night I woke up wracked by dry heaves. I staggered to the kitchen for some 7-Up but only made it to a chair. A wave of nausea hit me. I grabbed the garbage pail just in time and held onto the handle of the oven as waves of the icky brown stuff spewed like knives over my sore throat and into the can.

Tears welled in my eyes as I braced for another round; I felt a comforting hand on my back. It was MITCH. He wiped my face with a cool washrag and stayed with me until it was over, then gave me some throat spray and tucked me into bed.

After rescuing me from that horrible, nightmarish ordeal, I couldn't despise him anymore. I had failed my Campaign and hated myself for giving in. It wasn't fair. It only happened because I was sick.

Arriving home from the first day back at school, the house seemed emptier; MITCH's things had disappeared. He never said goodbye.

TWENTY-SIX

*A*fter MITCH left, Maggie woke up one morning a whole other person. A brat had replaced my sweet, compliant little sister. She challenged me on everything from the moment she threw off the bedcovers, and her feet hit the floor until she went to bed for the night.

Everything she said was sassy and snotty. We fought all the time now; they only got out of control twice. They were knee-jerk reactions; the kind you wish you could take back.

One Saturday I heard Maggie and Paul laughing and carrying on just outside the kitchen. I took the pot of boiling water from the stove, set it in the freezer, went to the window, pushed it halfway up, and hollered to Maggie, "You better stop bouncing on that tree branch, or you'll break it!"

I sat at the kitchen table to wait for some of the freezer ice to thaw. And then I heard it. A large *Crack* echoed throughout the kitchen. I leaped for the window in time to see Paul hightailing it back home and a large branch of the apple tree hanging limp to the ground.

"Maggie!" I yelled.

She sashayed into the house as if nothing had happened.

"You know Mommy's gonna be po'd when she sees the tree like it is," I said.

Maggie shrugged, "I'm gonna tell her you did it," she said and stuck her tongue out at me.

"You better not!"

"Whatcha gonna do about it? She'll believe me when I tell her you did it," she challenged.

At that moment, a most reprehensible thought crossed my mind.

I opened the freezer and removed the pot.

"Come here Maggie and taste the ice in the freezer. It tastes fantastic when it's melting."

Being summer and the day already warming up, Maggie was glad to drag a kitchen chair to the freezer to taste the cool ice. She stuck out her tongue and took a great big lick.

"Lithie," she mumbled, "Helthp me, I'm thtuck."

PART I

I laughed an evil laugh, "Good, that'll teach you," I said and walked across the street to tell Karen the cool thing I did.

Mommy returned sometime later not only to find the apple tree branch dangling to the ground, but her youngest daughter adhered to the bottom of the freezer.

It took several cups of warm water to free her, almost peeling off the top layer of her tongue.

I caught hell regardless; blamed for the condition of the tree, my sister's plight, and for not having the freezer cleaned and sent to my room until further notice.

After the freezer incident, our fighting escalated. The second bad fight we had was the day I was cooking bacon for BLT's when Maggie came flying out of her room like a bat out of hell.

"Where do you think you're going?" I asked.

"None ya," she answered in a mind your own business tone and continued towards the door.

"You're not leaving until you eat. I'm making BLT's."

"I'm not hungry," she replied.

"Well, you're not leaving until you eat."

"You're not the boss of me," she said and put her hand out for the door handle.

Without a second thought, I hurled the fork I had in my hand towards her leg, just as I had learned in knife throwing. The tip of the four prongs stuck in the back of her right calf.

She screamed; blood streamed down her leg. She reached around, pulled it out, and then came after me with it.

I bolted for the bathroom door and locked myself inside and didn't come out until I heard her leave and the smell of the bacon burning. I caught hell that time too.

༄

It wasn't long before Mommy brought home another stray, like that would help her deal with us, me most of all.

This one was short and skinny with a ginormous nose and always wore a brown leather bolo tie secured with a white acrylic slide with a real a scorpion inside, aka Scorpion Man. He had small squinty eyes shielded by black bushy eyebrows and a temper to match.

He thought he was the man for the job, but he didn't know the half of what he was in for or my capabilities. I was always up for a new challenge,

"Come on batter, batter, batter, batter, swing now!"

⁓

I can count on one hand how many times I've run away. I hadn't expected my first run. It happened the day I'd tested the boundaries of Mommy's new boyfriend beyond the point of no return.

Scorpion Man, driving, merged onto the second level of the double-deck Alaskan Way Viaduct, pulled a cigarette out from his shirt pocket, and lit it.

"Bang!" the cigarette exploded.

A shower of paper and tobacco confetti littered his lap.

Startled and confused the butt fell from his lips and onto his lap as he fought to keep the car on the road. Shook to the core and angry as hell he called Rosemary as soon as he got to work.

"That's it, Rosemary. She's gone too far this time!" I heard him threaten over the phone.

When I saw his car pull up later, I buried the remaining cigarette poppers in the trash and dived for the safety under my bed.

As soon as he entered the house, he made an angry beeline for my room. My feet were sticking out from underneath the bed, and he lunged for them.

"Come out of there Lissie! Come out right now, dammit!" he yelled.

He got a firm grip on my pant leg and pulled. I screamed and shook him off, knowing full well the belt waited for me.

"You can't do nothing right!" "You're just like your mother!"

My heart was in my throat as I dialed the phone from underneath the bed. He yanked the cord from the wall.

"Oh no you don't, you are not getting away with this that easily." He yelled and lunged for my legs again.

I kicked and squirmed, eluding his capture one more time, rolled out from the opposite side of the bed, took off out of the house as fast as I could, and ran like the devil himself was after me. I didn't think about where I was going but kept running until my lungs burned.

Certain I was far enough, I stopped and put my hands on my knees to catch my breath. I gulped in as much of the cold night air as I could unaware of the yellow Mustang that pulled up to the curb next to me.

"You okay, sweetie," Asked a friendly lady with long strawberry hair from the passenger window.

I shook my head and sobbed, "no."

The lady got out of the car along with another woman that had shorter blonde hair, and they knelt next to me.

"What's the matter honey?" the blonde-haired woman asked in a southern drawl and put her arm around me.

"My stepdad's gonna kill me if he catches me," I sobbed.

"Come, come, sweetie what makes you say that?" asked the lady with strawberry hair in a similar drawl.

In a single breath, I told them all about Mommy's broken promise, MITCH, the campaign, and how I got rid of him; the Scorpion Man and the exploding cigarette and how I couldn't take it anymore.

"Would you like to stay with us for a couple days?" The blonde-haired lady asked.

"I can ask my mom what to do; she has an answer for everything," she added.

I nodded my head "yes" and climbed into the backseat of their Mustang.

"My name is Dusty," said the strawberry-haired lady, "and this is my sister Kelly."

"I'm Lissie," I said.

Dusty turned on the radio and rolled down her window. The fresh breeze cooled my face and dried my tears. The radio played my favorite music on KJR. I laid back on the coldness of the leather seat and watched the streetlights flicker above.

We merged southbound onto the freeway and drove for a long while. Then, we exited just after Fort Lewis and continued driving down a dark gravel dirt road until we reached a small cabin deep in the woods.

I followed the ladies into their house, sat on a chair in the living room, and watched with curiosity as they hurried about lighting candles and incense and preparing a bed on the sofa for me.

The candles gave the home a cozy feeling. A crocheted blanket adorned the back of the couch, the kind like MB made. A hodgepodge of tiny knickknacks lined the shelves almost like Value Village.

Kelly brought snacks from the kitchen and sat on a cushion on the living room floor. Dusty joined her and patted a cushion next to her for me to join them. We visited and ate until I could no longer keep my eyes open.

The next morning the ladies took me to their mom's house. She stood the same height as me and was about as round as she was tall and as friendly as her girls.

"Please tell me your name and birthday, sweetie. I have to inform the police you're safe in case they are looking for you." She said with a twang just as southern as her daughters.

"Please don't send me back there." I implored.

I followed the ladies to the backyard where some friends of theirs were preparing a barbecue. The mom soon joined us. We had the best BBQ chicken I had ever tasted along with potato salad, black beans, and green Jell-O salad. We visited until late and returned to the ladies' house for the night.

The next morning Kelly made pancakes. Their mom arrived just in time to join us for breakfast.

"I spoke with your mom," she said between bites.

The pancakes suddenly tasted like cardboard. I took a drink of orange juice to swallow past the bite I had in my mouth as she told me how upset and worried Mommy was.

"Your mom said her boyfriend moved out the very next day you went missing." She continued.

"And she said to tell you she loves you very much and wishes you would come home and she's not mad, and you are not in trouble."

Tears rolled down my cheeks, and I cried. Kelly knelt next to my chair, put her arms around me, and pulled me close to her. "It's okay baby. He's gone now. He can't hurt you anymore."

"Ok then, I'll go back." I sniffed.

They all clapped and cheered "Yeah!" in unison.

"That's great sweetie. I'm so proud of you." Dusty said and kissed my cheek.

"Would you like to stay one more night and have some more of my mom's famous BBQ before you go?" Dusty asked.

I nodded that I did.

"Wonderful!" exclaimed the mom. "I'll make us a berry pie too, but first I'll call your mom to tell her you'll be home tomorrow."

Karen, Peter, Paul, and Maggie listened in wide-eyed disbelief as I told them about my great adventure of *running away*. The cigarette exploders were by far the best tactic yet.

TWENTY-SEVEN

Well, I got what I wanted; Scorpion man had enough, and it was just the three of us again, sorta. Now Mommy spent most of her time at the club or sleeping instead of being with us. We had no rules or restrictions and came and went as we pleased, set our own bedtimes, and if we were late for school, wrote our own excuse letters.

The boundaries of where she left off, and I began, blurred as I grew; sometimes it seemed as if we were the same person, as if she looked for the same love and approval from me that I sought from her.

It didn't matter what we did when we were together or if we didn't spend much time together at all; the point was, it was just us with no outsiders. Everything was just as it should have been, and Maggie and I couldn't have been happier.

For a brief while, on the first of every month after the mailman brought Mommy's check, we'd join her for an afternoon of fun while she tended to her errands, shopping was my favorite part as we got to ride home in a cab.

Once the bus dropped us off in town, after going to the bank, stopping by at her favorite place for Shirley Temples and cocktails, sometimes stopping for cheeseburgers at a local corner café called The Jungle Hut, we'd go shopping at Safeway.

Maggie and I hung onto Mommy's cart like orangutans while she searched methodically up and down every aisle for the things on her list, even if the thing she was looking for wasn't on that certain aisle.

Like before, when we got to the cereal row, she'd allow us to pick our favorite, within reason. Then, in the frozen section, we got to pick out our favorite Libby's T.V. dinners. While she shopped for other things in between, she kept us busy with tearing the food money from their coupon books. We had to be careful not to tear the money itself, or we'd risk losing one of our cereals or dinners.

As unpredictable as the weather, Mommy soon had her pole out again to reel in another victim. The elusive big one wasn't biting though; only bottom fish came and went like the perpetual seasons.

I never grew attached to any of them and made their lives as miserable as they made mine, so they'd leave, and after a while they did; but it was all for naught, no sooner had I run off one, another soon followed behind them. She just didn't get it. None of it mattered anymore and I didn't care.

Why did she have to *have* one; was it for us? We didn't want or need any of them. For the life of me, I didn't understand why my sister and I were never enough for her. I hated Mommy and life, and I vowed to never be like her, ever, ever!

My efforts to cause havoc made Mommy miserable too. And the worst she felt, the more she drank and the more she drank, the less I slept.

I knew when she broke up with one because on those nights, I didn't sleep at all. It was the same old scene. Mommy would shut herself in her room with her cheap bottle of red wine, get crazy drunk, cry, and curse at her invisible friend throughout the night.

And sometimes she'd make phone calls and rant and rave and carry on about the breakup to the poor victim on the other end.

On other occasions, I was the lucky recipient. She wanted my attention at the worse times. I seemed to be the life preserver she depended upon. Regardless of the hour, she'd drag me out of my bed to hers and fill my ears about things I didn't understand or care about.

The repetitive montage about how she lost her boys followed by a deluge of inconsolable tears was always the same. I learned to listen with half an ear. I wished she loved us as much.

If I didn't make myself available to her, before friends and above all else, day or night, she'd pout like a child and ignore me. She'd exhale the silent anger with every exaggerated drag of her cigarette, filling the space between us, so full of hate, blame, and guilt, until I felt so bad I'd give in to her to make it stop.

I hated when she acted that way. Like a double-edged sword, I wanted to comfort her, but then part of me resented that she wanted me to. Mommy had a way of making me feel as if I did something wrong even though I hadn't.

I tried to guess what she wanted and that just frustrated her. She'd say I wasn't listening or paying attention, even though I was. If I argued or talked back, she'd cry and say I didn't love her. It was a waste of time sticking up for myself, so, to keep the peace, I didn't say a word.

"I'm sorry Lissie." She'd sob in between puffs of her cigarette, rambling on and on some more.

"It's the last one Lissie, I swear." Wailing with exaggerated drama, taking slobbery, deep, exaggerated drags from her cigarette, the cherry threatening to fall to the side.

On and on and around and around she'd babble. I didn't understand what she was talking about, but I'd nod my head in response to her every question as if we were coming to some kind of an agreement about something.

She'd finish the evening off with one final promise, "I'll never bring another one home, never! Cross my heart and swear to die, it's just you, me and sister this time, always and forever."

The following morning, she'd go about her day as if nothing happened, as if she didn't remember the night before. As for the promise, well, that survived for about a month, just like all the others she'd made. With all the promises she swore not to break, I thought she'd die for sure.

TWENTY-EIGHT

To keep the strays at bay was exhausting. I figured Mommy got the hint, and I could relax at last, but it wasn't long before she brought another one home.

The summer before junior high was the worst year of my life when our snow globe illusion shattered into a million pieces. I awoke one morning to the smell of bacon and stumbled into the kitchen to see what was going on. Mommy was in her robe and slippers, frying eggs and bacon as if it were just another day.

My eyes darted to the table where a barrel-chested, hawkish looking older man with hairy grey eyebrows that seemed to have a life of their own sat in a white t-shirt puffing away on a cigarette, sipping on a cup of coffee without a care in the world.

"Hi Lissie," Mommy greeted me, "This is my friend Doug from the club."

I could feel heat as hot as bacon grease creeping up from my chest to my face. Without a word to either of them, I stomped back to my room, slammed the door as hard as I could, and flopped down on my bed.

I couldn't believe it, not again. I buried my face into my pillow and cried. For the life of me, I couldn't understand why we were never enough. Everything had been so great; we were all so happy.

As if things couldn't get worse, this one asked her to marry him, and she said yes! I didn't care if he had a good job and could take of us. He was not welcome. I did my best to chase him off, using my best tactics that had worked on others in the past, but he wasn't having it. None of my efforts ruffled his few remaining grey feathers.

Dabbing his eternal dripping nose, MORON for short, he'd say, "I know a thing or two about raising spirited little girls," as if he were an expert on me, "I have four of my own." His eldest was almost Mommy's age.

Well, he had never met the likes of me; I wasn't done with him yet. Gloves were off; I'd drawn the battle lines and declared war upon his head.

I'd made Mommy so upset and worried when I ran off before that the Scorpion Man bailed, so I plotted another trip hoping to make the MORON leave too. This time I would set out to find my father if it was the last thing I ever did, and I was never coming back either.

Mommy once said Daddy lived in Toledo, Ohio, so Ohio it was. While Mommy planned her wedding, right down to buying matching baby blue, full-

PART I

length bridesmaids dresses with matching midnight-blue velvet boleros for me and Maggie, I planned my next move.

∽

The MORON not only took away any chance I'd ever have Mommy to myself again, but he moved us two blocks south to another blue house, a bigger one with a large enough backyard to store his camper and boat.

On the main level to the left of the entry door was small a den and a flight of stairs which lead to the next level with two bedrooms on either side at the top, Maggie already claimed the one to the right, connected by a freakish crawl space, accessible by a little door in each room.

Down the stairs and to the left was the living room; nestled under the stairs was a bathroom and Mommy's bedroom. Off the living room was a large kitchen and connected to that was an enclosed back porch. Then, beyond all creepiness, a cellar door lay carved into the floor of the sunroom which led to a sinister, cold, and musty smelling basement. There was one small, empty bedroom and a large family room where the MORON set up a ping-pong table as if he thought we'd be spending time down there. A door led to the backyard and to a flight of stairs back to the sunroom.

It was the largest place we'd ever lived in, our meager belongings didn't quite fill up the colossal tomb, but I still wasn't impressed. No longer across the street from Karen, we saw less and less of each other. I had never felt so alone in my life.

Worse of all was the day when I headed out the door for my first day of junior high and got a glimpse of our neighbor. Our eyes locked for a moment. He sneered an evil grin. The acid in my stomach blazed a trail to my throat. It all came back. It was the man that took me for ice cream when I was little. I hoped he hadn't recognized me, looked away quick, and made a beeline for school.

I couldn't believe it. Was this some sort of sick joke or what? I didn't sleep sound from then on, ever vigilant of my surroundings, always checking the doors and windows were secure and locked. And, whenever I left the house, I checked from my bedroom window to see if his car was there and then walked cat-like through the backyard, into the alley, on to the main road and safety.

It was a prayer come true the day I saw a moving van parked outside his house. I caught up with the neighbor boy and asked him if he knew anything about it. He said he'd overheard his mom's telephone conversation about how the man's car went off the side of the mountain on Steven's Pass Highway this past weekend and he died. *Good*, I thought, I hope he rots in hell.

∽

Mommy and the MORON's gaggle of moth-eaten friends made their wedding a big to-do about nothing. They married on the anniversary of Pearl Harbor. *Like that day, this day too would go down in infamy.*

Unsure of when my next meal would be, I gorged on the party food. While they were away for the night on their honeymoon, assuring Maggie was fast asleep, I crept into the living room and gathered my coat and backpack from behind the couch.

All ready to go, I opened the front door and stepped out onto the porch. It was as dark as a wolf's mouth and raining. I hesitated but told myself it was now or never, how it would only get worse, and Mommy needed to learn a lesson.

I pulled the hood of my jacket over my head, tied it underneath my chin, and slipped my arms into my backpack. As I stepped off the last stair, I tripped over a tiny black kitten who appeared from out of nowhere. I scooped it up. It meowed at me plaintively and purred.

Great, now what do I do? I thought, and I tucked him into my coat. Then, we were off to find my dad. I walked fast the half block to the bus stop just in time to catch the last one for the night. I avoided eye contact with the driver and cruised with purpose to the back of the bus and got off at the last stop in Burien. The wind and rain bit at my cheeks as I roamed in search of a pay phone. I saw a light for a grocery store in the distance and made my way towards it. The kitten didn't stir; he seemed content within the confines of my warm and dry coat.

I dialed MB's house. Not disclosing my near whereabouts or my plans to find my dad, I asked her if I could come back to her house. She said there were other children living with them and there wasn't room for anymore.

Daunted but undefeated I headed back out to the road. I stared at my feet as they crunched over the gravel, and my heartbeat in cadence with my steps. My chin quivered, and hot tears splashed off my cheeks. I had hoped MB would have come and got me, but now I had to find my dad; there was no going back.

I crossed a large intersection with the walk signal. There were no cars; it was dead; everyone must have been in bed. I walked a little further, away from the streetlights, and turned to face the traffic. With blind faith, I stuck my thumb out every time a car passed.

After about a dozen, a man in a blue Mustang pulled over. He reached over and opened the passenger side door.

"How far you are going?" he asked.

"I'm going to find my dad in Ohio," I yelled over the din of the howling rain, "How far can you take me," I asked while climbing into the passenger seat.

PART I

He looked like one of the Bee Gee brothers with a beard and everything. He seemed nice enough, so I stayed.

"It's getting late, and the weather's bad; how about we get a fresh start in the morning; I just got off work and am bushed. I've got an extra bedroom at my place if you'd like to stay."

"Okay," I agreed.

I told him that my mom had died, and I was staying in a foster home and how my dad said he was coming to get me, but hadn't yet, and how they said they haven't been able to reach him, and how I was tired of waiting, and going to find him myself.

At that moment, the kitten popped his little head out from my buttoned-up jacket.

"Whoa, whatcha got there?" He laughed.

"He was a gift from the foster mom." I said.

"What's his name?"

"Midnight," I said off the bat.

"Well, I have a cat too; so, Midnight can have a snack along with us."

We drove on the freeway for a short while then exited and continued down a long dirt road. It reminded me of the road to Dusty and Kelly's house. We pulled up to a big yellow house that sat sideways to the road. There were no other houses nearby and a dimly lit, solitary streetlight flickered over it.

Something didn't feel right as I followed him into the house. He took Midnight to his cat's litter box and food dish in a room with a laundry machine and fixed us a plate of cheese and crackers with a glass of milk. When we finished, he showed Midnight and me to the guest room.

I turned off the light, tucked Midnight into my jacket, and sat on the edge of the bed. I watched the clock on the night table until an hour had passed and the house was silent; then, I tiptoed to the window and looked out.

The room was over the garage, and its roof was even with the road, just like one at the laundromat. I slid the window open as quietly as I could, put my backpack out first, and then made my escape, the second in just one night.

TWENTY-NINE

Thank god the rain stopped. I neared the freeway again when a car approached; I about dived for the bushes until I saw the car was much smaller than the man's.

I stuck my thumb out. The car stopped a few feet ahead of me. A nice lady rolled down her passenger side window and asked what I was doing out so late. I told her the same story as I did the man, about the ride with him and how I didn't feel comfortable, and that I had just escaped from the window of his guest room.

"Well then come on sweetie, get in, it's just not safe for you out here."

I climbed in. We drove to a Greyhound bus station where she bought me a ticket to Toledo and gave me money for food.

"God bless you, child," she said with tears in her eyes as she hugged me tight and saw me onto the bus.

I climbed over the runway lights surrounding the last of the large steps; the bus was almost empty, so I took the bench seat in the way back. My hands caressed over the tops of the softness of the plush seats as I made my way through the low-lit narrow aisle to the end.

I slid into the seat, scooted towards the window, and waved goodbye to the lady as the bus pulled away. I stepped inside the adjacent little bathroom, retrieved Midnight from his abyss of happiness, placed a paper towel on the floor, and put him on it. He amazed me how he knew what to do.

I took some of the cat food from the man's house from my bag. He ate some and then wanted to climb my pant leg. I pried his little claws from my jeans and tucked him back into my coat.

Using my backpack as a pillow, I stretched out on the bench seat and watched the blinking streetlights as we zoomed past them. I imagined being in the back seat of one of Mommy's friend's cars, the cool wind caressing my face and the song City of New Orleans playing loud on the radio, and it wasn't long until we were both fast asleep.

Midnight didn't stir until the morning. We went to the bathroom and he did his little number again; we had established a routine. When we returned to our seat, the bus was empty. I let Midnight stretch out on the seat and have a little snack until the driver came back.

PART I

With the roar of the diesel engine and the lights dimmed, we were off again. The steady rhythm of the tires on the pavement lulled us back to sleep in no time, just like two babies with clean diapers.

⁓

The second morning, I awoke to find a lady sitting next to me. I looked around the bus and saw that there were a lot of other seats empty and didn't understand why she had to sit in the back with me.

"I'm Colista." She said and reached out to shake my hand.

"Hi," I said, ignoring her gesture.

"Where are you going?"

"To my dad's in Toledo, Ohio."

"Cool, I live in Toledo too."

We talked for the rest of the trip. Sooner or later, I spilled the beans and told her how I wasn't going to my dad's but to find him there. She said I could stay with her until I found him if I wanted.

When we arrived in Toledo, she took me to McDonald's and then we walked a few blocks to her place.

Her house looked like the old ones back home, right down to the white chipped clapboard siding and enclosed porch. I followed her inside; it was like a time warp back to the house we lived in with the Family. The sweetish, sickening, familiar stench, was stale and putrid as if a million parties had happened there.

Colista called from another room she was showering and to make myself at home. I looked around the sparse living room. Shreds of loose threads, like the garland Mommy threw on the Christmas tree every year, adorned a rust-colored couch, yellow stuffing bulged out in several torn spots, and its two cushions sagged like soggy bread.

A voice in my head screamed, "Leave!"

The hair at the nape of my neck prickled and my heart pulsed in my ears.

I listened for the sound of the shower. Assured she was in it, I picked up my backpack, stepped out the door, and hurried back the way I remembered we'd come. Finding the bus stop and the nearest phone booth, I dialed 0.

I told the operator my dad hadn't met me at the bus station to pick me up like he said he would and how I wanted to know how to get to the police station. She told me to stay inside the depot and that a policeman would be there in a minute to meet me.

I went back inside and took Midnight to the ladies' lounge for a potty break. Funny kitten, when I scooped him up to tuck him back into my jacket, he dived into its confines, gave a couple quick somersaults, and then passed out cold.

Finding a row of seats against a far wall, keeping an eye out for Colista and for the policeman, Midnight's warmth and continual purring almost lulled me to sleep when a man's deep voice jolted me back to reality.

"Are you the girl who called the police?"

I nodded I was. He asked me to follow him to his patrol car, and we drove a short way to the police station. They asked me a ton of questions like where my dad lived, and what his phone number was. I told them I didn't know those things as it would be the first time that I'd be meeting him. They said it would take a little time to track him down and how I could stay at a house nearby to eat and sleep while I waited.

I followed the same policeman back to his car, and we drove a short distance to a nice neighborhood where trees lined either side of the street and kids played. We stopped in front of a blue house, just like the one where Peter and Paul lived.

A friendly older woman greeted us at the door. The policeman waited as she escorted me inside to a bedroom where she said I could rest and instructed me to come to the kitchen when I was ready to eat.

While the woman talked to the policeman, I extracted the stowaway from my jacket, placed him on the bed, and gave him a handful of kibbles. Since food sounded better than a nap, I stepped into the hallway in search of the kitchen and about to close the door when I heard the woman and policeman's conversation.

"It might be a few days before we contact either of her parents. I think she's a runaway." The policeman said.

"That's ok officer; she can stay here for as long as you need."

I lost my appetite. My mind and heart raced as fast as Midnight's as I returned to the room, sat on the side of the bed, and wondered what to do next. I was not going back to Mommy that's for sure, and if they couldn't find my dad, well, I'd figure something else out, but there wasn't time to worry about that now.

I searched my backpack for the money the lady gave me, and only found twenty-five dollars. Back to the doorway, I looked down the hall. I heard kids laughing in another room. Pressed against the wall, I crept to the end of the hallway where I found the woman's bedroom door ajar.

I saw her purse sitting on a dresser and made my way to it. I twisted the clasp open on the top and looked inside. There was only twenty dollars.

PART I

Better than nothing, great, now I'm a thief, I thought to myself, as I stuffed it into the pocket of my jeans and made my way back to my room. I scooped Midnight up, tucked him into the warm confines of my jacket, opened the second story window as quiet as possible, and shimmied down to freedom.

By chance, the window faced an alley. When the coast was clear, I speed walked to the nearest street. Unsure of which way to go next, I came across an older man walking his little dog and asked him how to get to the nearest store.

As luck would have it, it wasn't far. I bought a little box of Friskies, an apple fruit pie like the kind MB once packed in my lunch and asked the store clerk how to get to the bus station.

I followed his instructions and caught the city bus on the main road outside the store. Once inside the safe confines of the crowded bus station again, I joined the long ticket line and analyzed the departure board for the next scheduled trip while I waited.

When it was my turn, the man at the window peered over the counter down at me, how embarrassing.

"Where to miss?"

"One-way to Chicago please," I said.

"That'll be twenty dollars please."

I groaned to myself as I fished the woman's twenty from my pocket, *great, I was back to twenty-five dollars now.*

Ticket in hand, deciding the safest place to wait was in the ladies' lounge, I sat on the windowsill while Midnight did his business. The minutes seemed like hours. The boarding announcement couldn't come soon enough.

I knew the bus as if it were my own. The backseat was always empty and inviting. It appeared no one ever wanted to sit there, regardless of how full the bus was. That was fine by me; I wouldn't want to sit anywhere else, especially with my stowaway.

As soon as the bus entered the freeway, unwanted tears swelled and burned my eyes, a sob escaped from my throat, and then the next thing I knew I was crying like a baby.

I curled up on the seat and buried my face into my backpack. Midnight poked his furry head out from my jacket to see what all the commotion was. I managed a little laugh and nuzzled him with my chin. I was hungry and scared, and the more I thought about it, the more I cried.

A gentle hand touched my shoulder, "There, there, what's wrong child?" a sweet lady beckoned.

I swiped at my tears and managed a brave, "Nuthin."

She wasn't convinced and sat next to me. "Well it must be something, or you wouldn't be crying so hard."

In between stinging tears, snot bubbles, and half-suppressed sobs, I told her about my failed quest to find my dad, why I didn't want to go back home, and how I didn't know what to do now as I had bought the first ticket out of the city without knowing where I was going.

She listened and never interrupted, as most adults do. She said she had a sister in California who helps kids in trouble like me and would call her when we got to Chicago if it was ok with me. I said it was, and we shared the rest of the trip together.

Arriving in Chicago, I followed the lady to a phone booth and waited in a chair nearby while she called her sister. The sister said I could stay with her and for as long as I wanted.

I offered the lady the last of my money, but she wouldn't take it. She said I would need it for food for the trip.

We ate tuna sandwiches while we waited in the ladies' lounge for the boarding announcement. She laughed when Midnight popped his furry head out from my jacket; I scooped him out and handed him to her for a cuddle.

I boarded the bus for the third time, walked toward the back to claim my customary seat, scooted close to the window, and waved goodbye to Lois as the bus pulled away.

Fetching a bag of peanuts from my pack, just like Mommy's friend gave us for horsey rides, Midnight and I settled in for a long, three-day ride. If her sister was as nice as Lois, this was gonna be great.

PART I

THIRTY

Two days passed in about the same way. The driver brought me a sandwich and a soda a couple of times. I think he knew about Midnight, but he didn't let on like he did. When I arrived in Bakersfield, California, Lois's sister wasn't hard to find, and she recognized me too. I was the only lost and forlorn kid who looked as though she hadn't had a bath in a week.

"I'm Maureen." She extended her hand in a friendly gesture.

"I'm Lissie." I said and shook her hand, "And this," I pulled Midnight out from hiding, "This is Midnight."

She laughed in delight the same way as her sister had and brought him in for an Eskimo kiss. I followed her back to her car, and we drove a short distance to her house. She lived alone, no pets, no husband, and no kids. Her home was spacious, except for the many boxes piled everywhere, on the dining table, chairs, and stairway made it seemed smaller.

She showed me to my room. I put my pack on the bed and followed her into the kitchen. She must have known about Midnight because she had a litter box and food all prepared for him, and how I liked tuna sandwiches because a stack, along with a glass of iced tea, waited on the kitchen table. We talked until I couldn't keep my eyes open.

The next day and the following days thereafter were all the same. I tagged along with her to church several times a week, and to many makeup parties she gave at friends' houses, that's what was in all those boxes.

She was always busy, and we were always on the go. Midnight didn't mind being left behind; he seemed to like having the big house all to his self.

It wasn't long before I missed Karen and my friends back home. If Maureen was trying to bore me into reconsidering my plight, she was sure doing a good job. One day, I told her I was ready to go back home. Like Dusty's mom, she was glad to hear it and happy I'd had a change of heart.

Maureen said I'd find a train more comfortable than a bus, but because Midnight no longer fit in my jacket, she'd make me a deal. In exchange for him, she'd buy my ticket home.

I tossed and turned in a fit of restless sleep that night. We had been through a lot together, me and Midnight; I loved him so much and would be awful lonely without him, but not as much as Maureen if we both left. Then there was the MORON to deal with, if he was still there, and whether he and Mommy would let me keep him if he was.

We agreed I'd go home the following Saturday. She confessed how she'd kept in touch with Mommy the whole time I was there, but not to worry though, my mom was excited to have me back home.

When Saturday arrived, I gave Midnight an extra love and kiss and laughed as he scampered off across the lawn to pounce on a moving something, taking a piece of my heart with him.

⁓

As the train pulled into Seattle, I saw Mommy and the MORON waiting, apathetic and annoyed. Besides a brief welcome home hug from Mommy, nothing had changed.

Life went on as if I'd never left. Mommy and the MORON played table games with three other archaic couples on the weekends. Shit on your Neighbor, with cards, and Zilch, with dice, were their games of choice. The more they drank, the louder they became, and the more they hurled spittled swear words at each other, sure to make your ears burn off if you'd never heard them before. A memorable, frenzied party guaranteed to last well into the night.

Occasionally, because we knew there would be an out-of-this-world home-cooked buffet, Maggie and I'd tag along, suffering through the never-ending hours of the zoo and the inevitable stuff-yourself-till-you're-sick stomachache.

The fried chicken, mashed potatoes and gravy were nothing like we'd ever tasted before, even Swanson couldn't compare. It wasn't long before their friends became extended family, aunties, and uncles. They made life with the MORON tolerable and more memorable.

When school let out for the summers, the retired old farts, with the men donned in their homemade crocheted Rainier Beer hats, shorts, black crew socks and tennys and the women in their polyester matching short sets with all kinds of, eww I don't even want to see that, flesh hanging out of their tank tops, knee highs and sandals, packed up everything but the kitchen sink and headed for the mountains. No fancy travel get-ups here folks, just a group of bona fide Beverly Hillbillies and convoy of old Chevy trucks with turtle back campers.

The hot summer days of Woodstock II began late in the day with fried eggs and potatoes over a campfire and Bloody Marys for the adults to chase it down with, beer substituted the usual mixer, the hard stuff was for later; the mad hatter drinking, and gaming ensued until dinner time.

Some days, while the women did whatever they were doing, the men took the kids, who were always glad to tag along, hunting or fishing with them.

PART I

Driving with a devil-may-care attitude over the bumpy unpaved roads, KMPS blaring loud on the radio, and suds sloshing between their boney thighs, the T-shirt-wearing, chimney-smoking, beer-pull-top-flinging, balding old men could not have been any happier, oblivious to the party the kids were having of their own just behind them in the bed of the truck.

They were so snockered by the time they got to their gaming site it's a wonder they caught anything at all, and nobody died. But we survived every time, bringing enough fish, duck, and/or venison back to divvy up between everyone.

And like home, we were just as ignored and free to do whatever we wanted the entire trip, like gain a taste for Boone's Farm Strawberry wine and Mommy's Menthol Benson and Hedges. They took camping to a whole other level.

Sometimes, god forbid, the men went on hunting trips alone without the women and kids. I decided early on that gutting, filleting, pulling, and singeing feathers was not for me, yuck.

Following our first taste of the Annual Summer Bash came another year of Junior High, and boys.

THIRTY-ONE

*J*unior high opened the door for new friends and a new take on life. Like elementary school, it was quite a trek to get there, but not as woodsy, isolated, or scary, a straight shot both ways. Afterwards, I almost never went straight home. Instead, I'd stop at a friend's house for a snack and to observe their experiments with pot, hash, or speed and lengthy make-out sessions with their boyfriends.

I tried each of the drugs but didn't like how stupefied and scared they all made me feel. They thought it was fun. I didn't get it. Other times I hung out at the small mall across from the school.

Since MB's, I learned how to be the friend other people wanted me to be, to fit in and gain acceptance. With a new prospect, catching on to their personalities, I'd mimic them and talk about things they liked. Then, I'd create a likable persona and history for each of my new friends, always assuring that the new personality never ran into another friend or their friends that knew me different.

This worked on guys too. It was great fun to toy with them. I tried once to have three boyfriends at the same time but found it too much work, so I stuck to two, in most cases. If I broke up with one, no biggie, I'd string along another, letting each think I was their girl. I could be the goody two shoes or the Joan Jett girlfriend, all at the same time.

I liked the innocent wallflower boys best, the ones that sat in the back of the class with straight A's, they were the easiest to attract and never doubted my loyalty and showered me with the sweetest attention. Mind you, I wasn't a girl with a reputation; I just enjoyed toying with their hearts. Myself, I wasn't a prime choice for the all prim and proper, stick-up-the-butt, popular boys, and that was fine by me, they seemed too stuck on themselves anyway.

I can count on one hand the closest friends I've ever had. Each one has played a part in a milestone of my life, yet not one has played a role in all. My best memories are of my best friend in middle school. It was a new school year in junior high. The bell rang for 7th-grade math, and I made it to my desk seconds before it stopped. I shared a double desk with another girl. Mr. Nelson announced the impending test we were about to have that morning.

"Hi," the girl said, "I'm Kathy."

"High is not what my test score will be," I said.

PART I

She laughed, and we began the test. Breezing right through it without a sweat, her pencil was the first to click on the desk, signaling she'd finished. I fidgeted and groaned and was only three quarters done when Mr. Nelson said to pass our papers to the left.

I hated this practice, it was so embarrassing, and I hated math even more. Our classmates graded our papers as Mr. Nelson worked out the answers on the board. We received them back at the end of class. Kathy got an A. Someone wrote a big D in red on mine.

Kathy was tall and quiet as a mouse, 360-opposite of me, but we hit it off right from the get-go. She invited me to sit at the table with her and a few friends for lunch. We didn't have much in common except we all were loners and didn't fit in anywhere. I didn't share much about myself with the group as I knew they wouldn't understand.

Since Kathy wasn't allowed to ride the city bus, we could only hang out at her house, and so, I rode the school bus home with her twice a week. I couldn't believe where she lived. I'd only seen homes like hers on the TV. It was brick, bigger than a doctor's building, and overlooked the Puget Sound. Although I wasn't like them, her family made me feel just as welcome as if I were. For a brief while, I'd forget about what waited for me at home; I resented my life and wanted her reality instead.

Kathy had her own room with a TV, a telephone, from which we would talk for hours when we weren't together, and all the latest fashions in her walk-in closet. I was never jealous of the things she had. I admit I longed for some of them, but I kept it to myself.

Even with all she had, she didn't have the freedoms I had, and that's one thing I liked most about my life, to come and go anytime I pleased without restrictions.

Kathy and I were inseparable; she made everything fun. Just as she shared her world with me, I gave her a peek into mine. Not unlike the movie Grease we liked so much, I introduced her to makeup, rock and roll, and what I knew about guys. Towards the end of the year, I encouraged her to take notice of a neighbor boy two years older than her with whom she had a secret crush on.

Like Sandy, she said, "I've never felt this way about anyone before."

"Does he make your heart pound?" I asked.

"Yeah," she laughed.

"And you feel a little faint when you see him?" I probed.

"Like I'll fall over!" she said.

"And your palms get all sweaty?"

"Absolutely drenched!"

We clenched hands and laughed in hysterics.

～

Over the summer, she got to know the boy better, and they became an item.

"So, have you kissed him," I asked.

She wouldn't tell.

"C'mon, first base or second," I pressed on.

She didn't say a word.

That was one thing she kept to herself and it drove me nuts. So, I told her how far I had been. She was mortified. Talk about a real-life Sandy! I figured what was between her and that guy must have been something special, so I didn't bug her anymore about it. Unlike the movie though, I was sure I'd never talk her into being a Pink Lady if I were one.

We spent one more summer together, just before the ninth grade, just before I became a troubled teenager and lost track of her.

～

Her parents took us on a day trip to Ocean Shores. Once they let us loose, we went on our own for a hike. We followed a dirt trail until it stopped at a river. We searched forever to find a way across or around it. After searching for a solution and finding none, we discovered a narrow closing with a log stretched between each side. We climbed on top of it and inched our way toward the safety of the other side.

Slippery moss covered the log, and the thundering river rushed beneath us. When I lifted my right foot to take another step, my left foot slipped, and down into the cold water I went, jeans and all.

I gulped some air before my head went under the water. I doggie paddled as hard and as fast as I could to keep my face above the surface and to find the log, but the push of the river was too strong.

My feet swept out from underneath me. I grabbed hold of a branch sticking out from the bank. The river came alive and threatened to devour me. Beyond scared, I didn't know how to swim, and I was getting tired.

I felt Kathy's hand on mine. A strong current yanked me away from her grip and thrust me into some thorny shrubbery. Kathy ran to the bushes and jumped in behind me, kept the merciless beast from sucking me under, and helped me onto the bank. The countless hours spent in swimming lessons paid off, she'd saved my life.

PART I

Breathless and shaking, we hugged one another and laughed; then we cried like babies. No longer interested in what was on the other side, we made our way back to the car and changed our clothes. You'd think my near-death experience would have made us lifelong buddies, but my tremulous teenage years made that impossible.

∽

As I drifted away from her, I gravitated towards the school stoners with whom I could act tough, be loud and boisterous, smoke cigarettes, and swear. Like the other girls, I wore the signature San Francisco jeans with the bottom cuffs rolled up a little, the same winged blonde hair as Farrah Fawcett, and a waist-length black leather coat. I liked this persona best, just like a Pink Lady. I followed them around everywhere, behind the school portables and at nighttime parties.

For the life of me though, I couldn't decide which group I was most devoted to. I liked everything about the stoners, their attitudes and how they dressed most of all. But, because of my fear of psychedelics and how the smell of beer repulsed me, I knew I'd never be like them.

And when I was with the loners, even though it was easy to dress and act like them, it wasn't as fun as being with the other group; I was never good at being the quiet and innocent type anyway. The thing I hated most about being around the loners is how I had to check myself every time before I said something. With the stoners, nobody cared if I said something stupid.

It was all too much. Back to the tried and true, just me, myself, and I. It was less stressful being with myself. With me, I could think or say any oddball thing that came to mind without analyzing it first or worrying about any resulting repercussions. Alone has never steered me wrong before.

And then along came Tommy.

THIRTY-TWO

I first laid eyes on him in an eighth-grade history class. He was angry at the teacher for holding him back and making him retake the class with a *bunch of babies*. He had soft, golden strawberry blond hair and big blue eyes just like mine. Tommy was the hottest guy I'd ever laid eyes on.

He was from the stoner group, a loner and a rebel trying to find his place in the world like me, and just a year older and raised about the same as Kathy, you couldn't tell in the way he dressed or acted though, and had the likeness of Billy Idol, an all American bad boy, and I was in love.

But he didn't notice me because I was plain, just another ugly duckling hoping to become a swan one day. With the help of one of the stoner girls I'd become friends with, Becky, I learned a more dramatic way of applying mascara and eyeliner to make my baby blues *pop* and how to use a curling iron.

Becky and I were mirror images of one another and could be sisters. Our yin and yang personalities complemented one another. When looking to the group of stoners for inclusion, we found a mutual bond and kindred spirit in each other instead. We were like crazy glue. Funny, we also found our first, one true love within the same crowd of misfits.

After a few pokes in the eye and one or two burnt fingers, I'd accomplished a demure and subtle style all my own. Tommy noticed. He even moved to a chair closer to mine and talked away as if we were long lost friends.

One time after class and the teacher had left the room, Tommy pulled the retractable world map up to expose the blackboard underneath, drew a symbol, and then pulled it down again. He thought it was hilarious.

I learned later that the symbol was offensive to our Jewish teacher. The offender wasn't ever brought to light; I would walk over the fires of hell before ratting him out. Tommy was like that, if he knew something offended you, he'd keep on doing whatever it was just to annoy the hell out of you.

༺༻

I wanted to be Tommy's, his alone. But to my disappointment, the feelings weren't mutual. He only shined his light on me after school and regarded me as only a sister. It didn't matter though; I was glad to hang out with him, and that was better than nothing at all.

PART I

I envied Becky and her boyfriend; theirs was love at first sight. The adoration they showed one another was like the kind you read about. For me and Tommy, it was one-sided, my side.

Tommy turned the tables on me, and I got a taste of my own medicine. He toyed with my heart like it was catnip, never intending to give me his. There were other girls, straights and stoners, at his beck and call and he had no plan of falling for just one.

He grew up in a single-story house two block from me. A crazy coincidence, it was just down the street and across a four-lane highway from the project house which they took Maggie and me away from years before.

With school out for the summer and Mommy and the MORON gone camping, Tommy and I spent almost every weekend at his friend's place where he'd practice drums with his band, just like the rock star I always thought he was. He played both the left and right side of the drums like he was mad at the world.

He totally got into it, baring his teeth with ferocious determination, sweating like a pig, and thrashing his hair around like a wild man. It was loud and obnoxious. The smothering smoke-filled rooms, the drunken parties, and the bone-jarring Heavy Metal music was insane, but nothing, nothing could keep me away from him.

Since Becky's boyfriend wasn't a member of Tommy's band, the two of them ended up going their own way while I continued tagging along beside Tommy like a love-sick groupie.

When I wasn't following him around, I was working at a summer job with Becky. Since we weren't old enough to work in a restaurant, Becky's mom got us a job with her, temporary and under the table. I was clueless about what I was getting into. The job was in a dusty, hot, and suffocating potato bag factory.

Her mom, along with a row of other women, worked in silence pumping the foot pedals of an old treadle sewing machine. In cadence, they threaded twine through the needles, guided one burlap sandwich through at a time, stitched a single side and one end of the bag closed, and left an inch of string before starting on another.

The song of the machines, with an occasional back pedal and slap on the hand wheel as they turned their work, dominated all other sounds as they labored in unison.

Becky and I, a group of girls, and one woman stood on the opposite side of their machines at the ready with finger scythes on our dominant pointer finger ready to cut the long thread at the end of each bag and pile it on a flat. When it was full, we'd roll it to another room to resume cutting before the bags piled up.

It was backbreaking, sweat-pouring, callus-producing, asthma-wheezing hell, all for less than three dollars an hour.

Burlap dust matted in our hair and plastered to our skin. Beyond exhausted to care by the end of our shift, even too tired to eat most days, I was clueless how her mom did that work day in and day out.

⁓

Unlike Kathy's family, Tommy's mother didn't want him to have anything to do with me; she thought *I* was a bad example. Regardless of how much time passed, she never relaxed, I wasn't the type of girl she had in mind for him.

She fought his teenage rebellion with all she had, waiting for the day when he'd snap out of it. Little did she know, I was on to her, and working just as hard to undermine her efforts.

Because my house was always nutso, we hung out at a large park in between our houses. One day, as we scouted the adjacent woods, we found a spot in an open clearing next to a water tower and deemed it our secret place. It became our home away from home. Tommy scrounged things from his house whenever his mom wasn't around. He referred to as camping supplies and rations.

We spread a blanket on the ground and ate the yummy dinner he brought for us. Then, as we lay in each other's arms, he lit a smoke for each of us we'd stolen from our parents. I liked his better, Mommy's were menthol and tasted gross. We'd laugh and talk until dark, divulging our deepest secrets.

Both of us felt lost and misunderstood in the world and had trust issues. I held onto our relationship like a vice. Even if he didn't know it, we were soul mates. He was my first true love. There would never be another for me.

No one knew me or understood me like he did. I didn't care about anything else when we were together. It didn't matter if he never said he loved me; I knew he did and that is all that was important. I'd sacrifice everything just to be with him.

A year later while lying on the blanket and staring at the stars, I told him.

"I hate the MORON. I can't take his crap anymore."

"Then leave," Tommy said.

"Where do I go? Here?"

"I don't know. I'll go with you, somewhere far away. We'll leave after school on Friday."

PART I

THIRTY-THREE

Tommy went to high school now and got out earlier than I did. He waited for me at our secret place. Then, we thumbed our way down Ambaum and got as far as Auburn when we stopped for a snack. We sat on a curb at the side of the road as Tommy brought out our rations from his backpack, tuna fish and homemade canned peaches. He opened the fish and popped the lid off the peaches with a small army can opener, and we ate in silence as we contemplated our future.

As we continued West of Ambaum up a steep dirt hill, we rested at a trailer park. An old man approached us and invited us in for a drink. He gave us each a shot of brandy. It burned my throat when I swallowed it, but I was rewarded afterwards with a sweet taste of peaches.

He said something to Tommy to make him change his mind about running away, and we made it back home before dark. He went on to his house, and I moseyed to mine, back to the MORON, back to hell.

༄

It was great when Tommy learned to drive, but it allowed him more freedom to spend time with other friends, *girlfriends*. He loved to show off in his mom's gold Buick Electra, but soon tired of it and got his own '64 Scooby-Doo hippie van to cart his drums around to gigs on the weekends.

He painted the exterior tan and decked out the inside with curtains, carpeting, and a piece of wood that stretched across the tire wells, doubling as a bed with a place for the drums underneath, or to hide me whenever we stopped at his house to pick up stuff.

Like before, I tagged along to all his concerts, learning how to break down his drums after a show and how to set them up again before each gig, bona fide groupie stuff. I was his biggest fan and so in love.

One time he suggested we tattoo our names on one another. I couldn't believe it. It was almost a marriage proposal. A friend of his had a tattoo set, so, one weekend we visited him to do the deed.

Tommy asked where I wanted mine. I pushed up the sleeve of my blouse and pointed to my left collarbone. He tested my sensitivity with a primer poke. I jumped. I couldn't believe how much a little poke hurt and told him I only wanted his initials. He laughed.

I held my breath, gripped the chair legs, and looked away while he autographed my body in permanent green ink. I checked his finished work in the mirror. It was his signature Ozzy gothic style, making it even more personal.

His was more elaborate. He drew a palm size heart on his left forearm with a ribbon across it; then he wrote my name in pretty script in the center. There are no words to describe how that made me feel. It was if we got married.

That was all the commitment I ever got from him. His bad boy looks and ability to drive attracted other girls like a moth to a flame, and he flaunted it. No matter what I did, he still wanted his freedom.

I'll never forget the name of the one girl that hung on to his arm on purpose whenever I was around. Or the night he drove slowly past my house with her almost sitting on his lap after he'd told me he couldn't go out. I wanted to die.

Tommy's mom had his life planned out for him, and I wasn't part of the equation. It was obvious the day of his graduation party at his parents' house, and I wasn't invited.

I walked by while the festivities were underway and saw Tommy, dressed like a yuppy, wearing grey slacks, a white dress shirt under a maroon sweater, his hair combed into place, but most horrifying, was a matching girl hung onto his arm.

I watched while he laughed and joked with guests as they patted him on the back and shook his hand. That was the last I'd heard from him after that.

༄

Angry, hurt, feeling ugly and stupid, I spent the weekends skating with my sister and her friends. A cute older guy took notice of me. He was an excellent skater and took part in all the games and races. One weekend he asked me to couple skate with him. I about died. I have two left feet and am lucky just to stand in the skates. He didn't seem to notice.

The following weekend he sought me out again and asked me to skate couples with him and everyone thereafter. His strong arms and cologne were intoxicating. I lost my balance on purpose just to be close to him.

Only a couple years older than Tommy, he seemed so much more mature. Where Tommy's temperament was hair-pin explosive, this guy was always calm, cool, and collected, and he enjoyed making me laugh.

He had sandy blonde hair, a mustache to match, and an irresistible smooth southern style about him. Where Tommy was bare-chested, this dude had a thick mat of silky golden hair that peeked out from his half-unbuttoned shirt. I was hooked.

As we hung out in the parking lot after skating one night, he asked me if I'd like a ride home. Maggie said she had a ride already and to go on ahead.

PART I

He had a fantastic nice car, a red Chevelle SS with black leather seats with an awesome loud engine.

I tried not to act childish around him, lighting his cigarette piggyback from mine and singing along to the Bob Seger eight-track he liked so much. I even let him kiss me.

Before long, we saw each other outside skating. Mommy thought he was adorable. He even picked me up from school. Ninth grade was nowhere as interesting as spending time alone with him and experiencing grown-up love for the first time.

One night on the way home from skating, he dropped a bombshell. He said he'd accepted a job at a gas station in a little town near Steven's Pass, seventy miles away, and was moving there the following weekend. I panicked. Noticing my reaction and aware of my situation at home, he offered to take me with him, and I accepted without hesitation.

THIRTY-FOUR

I didn't tell a soul, not Maggie, nobody. Before school on the day we agreed upon, I packed a few of my things in a duffle bag and hid it in the closet. When the lunch bell rang, I strolled towards the main doors and met him outside. We drove to my house for my stuff and then headed East on Highway 2.

I was excited and nervous all at the same time. It was a long ride and pitch dark by the time we pulled off the highway. We passed the gas station where he'd work on our way into town, crossed over a little suspension bridge and some train tracks, and stopped in front of a small, single-story apartment building.

It was cozy. For only just renting it, it looked as if someone had lived in it for a while. The first morning I got up with him and made him a simple breakfast of eggs and toast before he left for work. Then, I tided up the place, got dressed, and ventured outside.

Although an almost-abandoned railroad town, the kind you could throw a rock clean across, the rustic old place was beautiful. I could see the whole town just from the porch. There was a post office across from the gas station, just beyond that was a white, paint chipped, three-story haunted looking hotel with a café, and next to that was a mom-and-pop grocery with a western style storefront. Behind our apartment stood a large metal garage with an oversized fire station emblem on the front.

The clouds hung low over the surrounding lush green trees. Beneath the picturesque steel framed bridge were large grey rocks that littered the shore of the river and knee-deep brush blanketed the banks. It was so quiet. The only sounds came from a symphony of insects and rushing water in the background.

Back at the apartment, I fixed him some lunch and walked the mere couple of blocks to the gas station to give it to him. The next day and from then on, he came home for lunch, and we ate together. Sometimes, we ate at the café.

Every new day was just like the one before, and I was bored out of my thick skull. There was nowhere to go and nothing to do. I read all the magazine I brought and looked at the same river so many times I could tell you how many rocks there were on the bank.

I made the mistake of telling him how I felt, a lot, and then rather than coming home after work, he stayed out late, saying, "out having beers with friends, don't wait up."

PART I

Out of my mind with cabin fever, I applied for a job at the hotel. They didn't ask my age, and I didn't volunteer. He wasn't happy about that either. His attitude changed. He became impatient, not at all like the guy I'd met at the skating rink.

One weekend he brought a dirt bike home and asked if I'd like to go for a ride. I climbed on the back and wrapped my arms around him. With my face in his back and eyes shut tight he took off like a rocket through the town and down the highway.

My heart about exploded. I'd never been so scared. Faster and faster like a bat out of hell we streaked down the highway; I wished it would be over soon and did not enjoy myself at all.

I took in a deep breath, the first since we left, as he turned off the highway. In the middle of turning around, he spun out in the middle of the U-turn, and we flew off the bike.

My right knee bit the gravel just before I tumbled over the little cross bridge just short of the creek. It happened so fast fear didn't hit me until I stood up.

A chill came over me, and every muscle in my body shook. Even my eyelashes shook. I gulped the muggy air but couldn't catch my breath. I looked at my palms. They were raw hamburger. I followed the source of the searing pain in my knee. There was a gaping hole in my jeans and saturated with blood. I didn't want to look. Tears rolled down my cheeks as I tried to contemplate what had just happened.

He called from the top of the bridge.

"You good?" he asked. "Come on let's go."

I was not getting back on that thing; not on that one or any other one, ever.

"Well, if you're going to be a baby about it, then you can just walk back, see you tomorrow." With a cloud of dust, he disappeared.

I couldn't believe it. He left me bruised and bloody in the middle of nowhere. And what did he mean, *see you tomorrow*? Was I that far from the town? Angry tears burned my cheeks as I hobbled towards the road to make my way back.

I stopped every now and again to rest and work past the pain. Infuriated, I thought of some choice words for him when I got back, that's for damn sure. There wasn't a soul around for miles. This was all so mind-boggling.

Tommy wouldn't have left me no matter what, I could bet my life on that. I was going home, and that was that. Wrapped up with myself, I didn't notice the truck that passed by me, stopped a short distance away, and backed up.

"You ok miss?"

I told him about the bike accident. He said he was one of the town's volunteer fireman and he'd take me back to the station to look at my injuries if I wanted.

Back at the station, I limped behind him to the infirmary. We winced in unison when I pulled up my pant leg to expose my knee. I held onto the sides of the chair with a death grip while he took gentle care to pluck the gravel out.

"I got most of it, miss, but some of it was so far in there that it might be with you for the rest of your life." Great, no more shorts.

He cleaned up my hands and knees with Bactine spray, glopped on some Neosporin, and plastered a humongous and ugly bandage over the whole mess. While he worked, he asked about my boyfriend. I told him we were staying at the little quad-plex across the way, and he worked at the gas station.

He recognized my boyfriend's name in an instant and said how nice of a guy he was to leave his friends and family in Seattle to move here and help with his infant son.

My ears burned fire red, and more tears made a muddy trail down my cheeks. The man offered me some Tylenol for the pain.

THIRTY-FIVE

I asked him if a bus to Seattle ever came through town. He said there was, and it stopped every day at 11am at the gift store across the highway. I thanked him for his help and rolled down my pant leg with the promise to return in the morning to change the bandage.

Making my way across the bridge I went to the hotel. I told the owner I was going to Seattle the following day; he thanked me for my help and gave me the earnings I had due.

I hobbled back to the apartment to pack my stuff. He wasn't there and didn't come home the rest of the night. I tucked the money from the hotel into a pocket of a folded pair of jeans and hid the bag in the closet.

After a sleepless night from hell, I got ready and left about ten. I stopped at the fire station for a bandage change and then gimped my way clean across town to the bus stop. When I approached the gas station, swallowing past the pain and my pride, I stood tall and sauntered, pretty as you please, past the gas station, making sure he saw me and my bag, not giving him an ounce of satisfaction that I was in pain.

I paused at the side of the desolate highway and looked both ways for traffic before crossing. He ignored me. Or perhaps he was staring in disbelief. I'll never know because I didn't look back to see. I never spoke to him again.

The bus was the same as the last time I rode on it. I took my customary seat in the back and settled in for a longer ride than the one which brought me here. Once in Seattle, I caught a city bus just outside the depot for home.

No matter how I looked at it, I couldn't come up with a good reason for my disappearing act. It didn't matter. Mommy showed no real interest in my stories anyway. I got off the bus at my street and took a shortcut through the alley to the house. I almost passed it. The MORON's camper wasn't there, and it wasn't summer.

I crossed the lawn to my bedroom window and tapped on it for Maggie to open it. She didn't respond. I tapped again; still nothing. I peered inside. It was empty. I walked around the sides of the squat yellow rambler and looked in all the windows. Vacant. Not a chair, not a puff of cigarette smoke.

I went to the neighbors. A lady in a zip up duster, matching slippers, and curlers answered the door. I asked if she knew where my mom was.

"They moved down the road not too long ago," she said, flicking her cigarette ash off the side of the porch.

Moved again? The MORON had already moved us twice before. I wonder what happened this time.

"They said you'd be along soon enough," and she handed me a piece of paper with a phone number on it written in Mommy's handwriting.

I called. Mommy answered.

"Mommy?"

"Lissie!" she half slurred, and half sobbed into the receiver. But before she could tell me how to get to the house, the MORON grabbed the phone from her.

He told me off up one side and down the other, yelling what an ungrateful and irresponsible, selfish little brat I was, and I should be ashamed of myself for making Mommy worry so. Like that was the case, one can assume he was the only one freaking out.

I held the phone away from my ear till he finished hurling insults, letting my mind wander here and there, waiting for him to take a breath. When the opportunity presented itself, to piss him off more, I asked if he'd finished because I'd only called to talk to Mommy. I just wanted to go home. I was tired and hungry.

"You stay right where you are Missy; the police are on their way," he barreled. "You wanted out so damn bad, you can just stay out," and he slammed the phone down.

Police? I had broken no laws. Jail? I called Tommy. He wasn't home. The neighbor lady put her arm around my shoulders, "Maybe it's for the best sweetie."

When the police arrived, with the lady holding my hand, I blurted out my sorry life, the men, the MORON, and how I wanted to go home but couldn't. The policemen listened, took notes, and made a couple of phone calls. They said I could stay at a receiving home until they'd figured things out.

∽

The policeman took me for a brief ride to a house on the edge of town. A nice middle-aged lady greeted me at the door and took me to a room in her basement where I'd be staying. A solitary light bulb dangled from the ceiling, providing enough light to see where you were going and that was it. There were two sets of bunk beds with an orange throw rug between them.

The lady said there were two other girls staying there, but they had left for the store and would be back later. I followed her to the kitchen where she fixed me a bite to eat. Letting me take it back to the basement, I made myself at home on one of the unoccupied lower bunks, scarfed down the sandwich, and fell into a much-needed coma.

The chattering of the other girls woke me some time later. All close in age with similar troubles, we became close friends in an instant. The home had rules, and the housemother was rather adamant about them. Some made sense, others were just plain intrusive. Of all things, smoking wasn't allowed in or around the house, and she set a curfew time in stone.

We walked to the neighboring drug store as often as we could for smoke breaks. Sometimes, one girl would leave with her boyfriend for the day. She wasn't supposed to see him and trusted us to keep it from the housemother.

For added measure, her boyfriend invited us into his van for a couple hits of grass and kept us stocked with a constant supply of smokes. I didn't partake with the weed because the smell reminded me of the Family, it intensified the things I worried about, and it made me tired.

Somehow the housemother found out about our little escapades, and she shipped us off to other receiving homes, mine was way out in Federal Way.

Although only two-stories tall, the inside of the house was larger, brighter, and looked like a hotel. The housemother sequestered kids of all ages into different areas of her spacious home.

The teens, thank god, got the basement, close to the laundry, a walk-in freezer, and pantry. Like the little woman who lived in a shoe, I lost count of how many kids lived there as they came and went at all hours and late at night.

The housemom was an older lady, as plump as she was tall. Ever present, she had the same no-nonsense, stern expression as MITCH's mom. Military organized, she took her job very seriously, much like the Brady's Alice, and managed everything without effort.

From processing the new kids, delousing them when needed, and fixing the meals, she had it all under control. She expected the troops who were old enough to help, to be her second in command, the gears beneath her mother machine.

Her husband played no part in her obsessive mission to save as many orphaned and homeless children as she could, he just existed somewhere in the cacophonous background.

I enjoyed helping her with the smaller kids, making the house meals, and cleaning. My favorite evening activity was the peanut butter and jelly toasted sandwiches she let us stuff ourselves with just before bed.

In assembly-line fashion, one of us kept the toaster loaded, two scooped the peanut butter and jelly from industrial-sized containers, one spread the precious commodities on toasted bread, and the last one dealt out the gooey masterpiece among the masses. There was no counting; she let us eat until we were full.

When it was quiet, and she didn't need much help, we'd either walk with the other teen girls to the nearby junior high for a needed smoke break or find something to do in our rooms.

One time a new girl showed us how to play what she called, The Pass-Out Game.

THIRTY-SIX

The four of us sat in a circle, the pregnant girl just observed, and the new girl stood behind the one who was up first. That person took about five deep breaths until they were lightheaded, then with one last deep breath, they held it in as the new girl tilted their head back and pressed the veins on the side of their neck until they passed out.

Once each of us had a turn and got to experience the brief floaty euphoria, she showed us how to do it to ourselves.

Shrieks of laughter vibrated up the stairs to the housemother's ear every time one of us regained consciousness. When we projected happy sounds, she had no concerns. I pretended to pass out. I couldn't get the technique just right to make it fun. It was the same with everything.

They were nice, but I missed the friends I'd made at the other place. We all had different stories, yet in a way, they were the same. One girl was in love with her dad and seven months pregnant with her brother, another girl was just as troubled as I was, and another was perfect and out of place.

Ever absent from the duties of her fellow company, the model teen had the ultimate dream boyfriend and was always with him. When he took her out, fresh, pretty flowers greeted her on the passenger seat as he opened the car door for her. She never accompanied the rest of us for the smoke break walks and, as far as I could tell, never had eaten a sweet, mouth-memory, pj sandwich either.

Sinless, she kept her bodily functions private, if she had any at all, didn't use profanity, didn't smoke, or chew gum like a cow. She never wore jeans, t-shirts, or tennys; rather, she dressed like a grown-up, ornamented in classy slacks, matching pumps, frilly blouses, and dainty jewelry. When she put makeup on, she didn't look like she was wearing any and the delicate perfume she wore was just as nauseating.

Overall, she was a goody-two-shoes, the only one of us that had their life figured out. We all envied her, and I think she knew it. It was beyond me why she was there, maybe she was a decoy; she never volunteered.

The house across the street had just as many kids, but all of them related. The eldest was a drop dead, blue-eyed California surfer wannabe, lean machine. Wow! I mean he was hang-on-your-wall cute. I tried to lock eyes with him several times, but he withstood all my attempts. He avoided the girls from the home like a plague. As if we were murderers or something.

PART I

Enrolled in the ninth grade, I tried to blend in, but somehow everyone knew I was "one of *them*," the math was beyond the realm of understanding, and the homework all but sabotaged logic. I hated school, different building, different kids, but they were all the same.

At last, there was a private stoners club where I could have a calming cigarette and be myself between classes. Sometimes I'd have my smoke as I'd walked aimlessly along the sports field or read in the bleachers.

I stowed my cigs in a salvaged empty cigarette wrapper from the trash and kept a steady supply by bumming one off everyone I saw with a smoke in their mouth. If I ran low, I'd always find a good supply of smoked stubs in the ashtray outside the teacher's lounge.

~

One day while walking the field, I saw a guy with a pet duck on the other side of the track. I walked in their direction to check it out. He introduced himself and his feathered friend. He said he lived next to the field, and pointed toward his house, and walked his duck there every day after school.

I assumed he went to the high school because junior high was still in session. He was tall, rail thin, had a Barry Manilow nose, short brown hair, wore high waters and Converse tennis shoes. Everything about him screamed Wallflower.

I saw him whenever I walked the field. Our exchanges were brief until I learned he had a car. It wasn't anything fancy, just an old, boring, faded blue station wagon; it complemented his whole look. But it was a set of wheels, so I laid on the charm just to get rides and go places.

My, so-called, flagrant truancy got me a one-way ticket to a group home in Tacoma. Geez. Give me a break. Like I was hurting anyone.

The group home might as well have been juvie. I didn't blink without permission. My wandering days were over. They'd armed the doors and windows of the small rambler home with alarms and always locked it, they assigned chores, and we had to earn privileges, like smoke breaks. We were just as supervised at school, as if we were criminals, well, I wasn't at least.

Locked inside like an unneutered caged animal, I had to be even more creative in the effort to collect stogies, wagering deals with chores or swapping privileges with housemates. I was in hell. I spent afternoons and weekends lying on my bed, staring at the ceiling, and contemplating my future. The more I thought about it, the sadder it made me, and the sadder I became, the more I stressed I was becoming like my mother.

They required counseling too, even if you thought you didn't.

"Why are you so angry?"

I looked her straight in the eye, "I hate my mother."

"Why"

"She lied. She broke her promise; she said it would be just the three of us, how it would be different this time, that's what she told everyone and us. But no, she keeps bringing guys home. When she breaks up with one, and I think I got her to myself at long last, she brings home another one. She always puts us last. She lied, and I will never forgive her."

The stupid lady replied, "She's an adult you know. It's not wrong for her to want companionship."

I wiped away at the hot tears streaming down my face with the back of my hand, stood and walked out, what did she know. Mommy lost her right to have relationships after what happened to us.

I didn't want to be at this jail, with kids I had nothing in common with. I was being punished just because I wanted Mommy all to myself. She promised. I didn't want her to share her love. For once, I wanted it all for me and Maggie. Why couldn't someone explain why we weren't enough and quit defending her?

Sometimes I dreamt about the years just before MB's. I saw the ghostly faces of the walkers and heard Mommy's promises of happiness and fun, "Just us this time, just the Three Musketeers," taunting, luring me closer and closer to self-destruction.

I'd wake up every time thrashing like a wild animal in my covers, overcome by a fiery anger and glad to be out the nightmare.

The other girls at the home made me look like a nun. Their stories were unfathomable, even for me, and nerves-in-a-blender strange. I didn't sleep sound in that place, not even once, ever vigilant of my bedroom door.

After about a month of torture, I begged the social worker to move me somewhere else, promising to be on my best behavior if she did, crossing my heart as added assurance. She arranged my transfer to a foster home, in the same neighborhood as MB's.

It was perfect: even the model teen would have approved. The foster parents were friendly retired folks; they had raised their own kids who had children of their own. They had a cozy home that overlooked the Puget Sound with a big boat parked in the front. There was a piano with sheet music that played when you pumped the foot pedal.

I had my own room with a full-size bed. A vintage mirror display tray to highlight my collection of mini perfume bottles on a matching dresser. We spent quiet evenings in the living room with a good book or homework. They included me in everything; we even made meals together.

PART I

A school bus stopped a block away and took me to the neighboring school to finish the eighth grade; it was anyone's guess if I'd ever finish the ninth. I didn't make the mistake of searching for the stoners though. This time I assumed the persona of a loner for my new role and kicked the smoking habit for good measure. Which was ok, being around nonsmokers made me forget about them.

My foster parents did their best to care for me, but it wasn't long before hair-pulling boredom set my feet itching to get away. I called Mommy during lunch one day and sobbed and begged to come home. She said I could if I got a job.

I called the guy with the duck; he said he didn't mind picking me up the next day at my lunchtime and would take me home.

As was my usual exit routine, I didn't say good-bye. I simply packed my few things in a backpack and left for school, never to see them again, kicking myself often for making them worry and for not trying harder to make it work.

THIRTY-SEVEN

With the façade of trying harder to do the right thing, as if this all was my fault, I arrived home at long last, but not to welcome arms. The MORON was not happy to see me when he arrived home from work.

"If you want to stay here, you'll get a job. That's all there is to it," he said.

If I want to stay there, hah! It was my house long before it was his. I learned a few new colorful words while at the group home and tried a few on him.

"F#@k you; you have no right to tell me what to do." I spat back.

"I'm married to your mother, and you'll do as I say, missy!"

"Asshole," I shouted and stomped out of the house.

I had no purpose or thought of where I was going, I just walked and argued with myself along the way. I was glad to work, so sick of school and the drama at home, any excuse to be away from that house was fine by me.

All the years of worrying, of not being heard, of being invisible, all the efforts to do nice things for her, to take care of her, to make her happy, they were all for naught. I lived my whole life at odds with her, fearing her erratic reactions, of upsetting her, of trying to earn her love and approval.

It was taking longer and more of an effort to get rid of that asshole. Two years of torturing him and making his life a living hell, he had the nerve to place me in a group home. Well, I wasn't finished with him yet.

With the slight blip in my life, Becky and I picked up where we left off after I returned home. When I told her about the MORON's ultimatum, she spoke with her boss at Dairy Queen and got me a job. Like before, we worked side by side like Laverne and Shirley.

Because the MORON moved us clear the hell out of town, five miles north of the blue house, I either had to thumb a ride to work, or if I could talk the MORON into a lift, he would drop me off.

I never let a perfect opportunity go to waste. I'd pummel at his nerves with everything I had about how I felt with his moving us so far from town and about how I felt with his putting me in the group home.

One time he hauled off and smacked my smart mouth; I sat closer to the door on the next trip, well out of arms reach anyway, to continue my tirade.

Although I made every trip unpleasant, slamming the door with emphasis upon each departure, he continued giving me rides.

Becky was a tireless workhorse like her mother. As with everything else, this job had its challenges too. The total bar of the archaic cash register bruised the sides of my palms, to memorize the prices on the menu and calculate individual orders twisted my brain, picky, impatient customers got on my last nerves, and the damn conveyer belt spit out buns and hamburger patties faster than I could keep up with them, not to mention remembering what went on what kind of sandwich.

And if that wasn't bad enough, there was the ice cream side of everything and the different dessert creations, their toppings, and prices to memorize. Also, the ice cream bag had to be changed out continually, the toppings and condiments refilled, and the machinery cleaned between orders. I felt more like Lucy than Laverne. All for less than four dollars an hour.

The job wasn't for me. As soon as I got home, I'd hit the sack and cry myself to sleep. Mommy liked it though, my paychecks above all and her perpetual freezer full of Dilly Bars, but six months was all I could stand.

It wasn't long before I got a job at KFC in Georgetown with a girl I knew from the Jr High stoners group days. It was easier than the DQ because we prepared most of the food ahead of time and the cash register was electric with the menu prices figured in. The hardest part was figuring out the body parts that went with each meal and cleaning at the end of the night.

I had to scrub every speck of food from trays, pots, and pans, and then load them into an industrial sized dishwasher. Then, at closing, I had to vacuum and mop the floors and sanitize all the counters, tables, and bathrooms. That was also the time I got my first glimpse of a men's urinal; gross doesn't even begin to describe it.

While opening my check on my first payday, I grumbled to my friend about how I had to sign my checks over to my mom. She told me the boss would pay me in cash if I asked. From then on, after pocketing some for myself, I paid Mommy in paper currency, and she was none the wiser.

Frustrated with restaurant jobs, vowing never to work in another one or in a factory, I tried my hand as a hotel launder and then as a maid, but I didn't like those jobs either.

One day Mommy went to the Unemployment office with me to see what else was available. *I was not going back to the group home, that's for damn sure.*

While filling out forms, I noticed a dark-haired, Elvis replica sitting across the room with a cast up to his knee on his right leg; he caught me staring, smiled, and hobbled over and sat next to me.

The Elvis replica said he was from California and had come up to Washington for work, until being hurt on the job, so, he was applying for unemployment until he was well enough to go back home. He was twenty-one.

We all stood outside for a smoke. By the end of the day, I'd enlisted in Employment Camp to learn the clerical trade, and he had his unemployment. As if he were an abandoned kitten, Mommy invited him to ride the bus back with us to our place to live until he was well enough to return to California.

She had a way with strays.

PART I

THIRTY-EIGHT

The MORON liked having him around because he helped as much as he could. Elvis stayed with us beyond the time the doctor removed his cast and even went camping with us along with Maggie's boyfriend one summer. Not long after, Elvis moved from our living room couch to my bed. The MORON was all but oblivious about our blatant love fest.

I'd forgotten about my scheduled departure for Employment Camp just after my seventeenth birthday until a letter arrived in the mail reminding me. There was no way out of it; my application may as well have been signed in blood. I once thought Astoria Oregon would be a great place to escape to and a place where I could learn office job skills at the same time, but things were different now.

From out of the blue, Tommy called. My heart melted at the sound of his voice. He said he'd joined the Army and was leaving for boot camp the next day, and then stationed in Virginia for the next four years, and if I'd like to get together before he left. He didn't have to ask twice.

I didn't tell him our current address to avoid a run-in with our boarding guest, so I met him at the grocery store down the street. Always powerless to his seduction, one thing led to another, and we ended up intertwined in the back seat of his mom's car. A few hours later, he returned me to the grocery with the promise he'd write.

The day I boarded the refurbished bus for the school my heart was heavy, and tears rained down my reddened cheeks. I hugged the bear Elvis gave me tight against my chest and fell asleep.

I awoke sometime later passing through the gates of boot camp. Well, that's what it used to be for a long time ago. A guide showed us to our assigned dorm rooms, guys in one building, gals in another, and said we had a half hour to unpack as someone was returning to escort us to the mess hall for dinner. But only one time. They expected us to remember where it was and be on time for meals. If we wanted respect as adults, then we had to act like one.

There were four girls in my room. The cathedral ceilings and checkered tile floors of the former barracks made it seem big and cold. We each had a metal single bed with a small wooden side dresser and a matching free-standing closet to hang our clothes.

After dinner, we attended an orientation to learn about the school's mission, how it was a place for adults, and what they did not allow. My ears perked up when I heard a list of violations read that would get you a one-way ticket home.

I couldn't believe when they said we'd earn a basic living allowance, paid every 2 weeks, and would increase with our training. Upon graduating, eight months to two years, depending on your program and how long it took for you to finish it, they'd help you with a transitioning allowance based on your achievements, whatever it took to prepare you for the *real* world.

The following morning after breakfast we had another orientation pertaining to the job we'd signed up for. They stressed how we had to dress according to our trade and be prompt for class each day, as it was on the job training, like in real life, and gave us vouchers to a clothes closet on base.

After dinner, we'd earned some alone time and then were called to assemble in the hall just outside our rooms. A dorm leader listed another set of rules and expectations for those living in our hall along with a chore list for each week. She was a bit too perky, one of those goody-two-shoe cheerleader type that grated my nerves, like the girl at the foster home. Thank god I only had to hear her once a week.

Overall, there were too many rules to remember. If they expected us to act like adults, then why did they treat us like kids with so many rules and earned privileges? If I heard one more thing about the real world, I would pull my hair out.

The first morning I prepared for duty, I gave myself a once-over in the mirror. OMG! I looked like an old maid! Oh, how I wanted to jump back into my jeans and Nikes. I hated pumps; they were like walking on stilts, and the pantyhose, who were they kidding? I looked more like a kid playing dress up.

My first two weeks went by in a flash; I didn't have time to be bored or miss Elvis, except on the weekends. I cashed my meager allowance in the student store and bought more smokes, stationery, and stamps.

∽

Time passed, days turned into months, and I was missing Elvis more each day. The model student, hall leader graduated, and her family came to celebrate. My graduation wouldn't be for another year. I couldn't wait that long.

In a recent letter from Elvis, he said his mom was driving up soon from California to take him home, my heart sank. And I panicked.

I reviewed the school's policy handbook and read how they considered pregnancy a medical reason for discharge. A new persona for me, I had them all convinced, even Elvis. It wasn't long before I had a one-way bus ticket back home.

PART I

I had disappointed no one; I mean since when had I finished anything? Elvis was excited to see me and about the coming baby. He had a temporary job now at a bingo parlor near Pike Place Market. His mom had arrived and was staying with friends until he was ready to go.

Tommy was home on leave, heard I was home, and how I was pregnant with Elvis baby. He called and asked to see me. Not wanting him to dupe me again, I invited him to the house. Elvis didn't know he was coming over and wasn't prepared when Tommy showed up at the front door in his Army uniform.

They argued over who might be the father of the baby. It floored Elvis to learn I'd snuck off with Tommy at about the time I would have become pregnant.

Tommy left in a huff. Elvis didn't have two words to say the rest of the night. The next day, we met up with his mom to play bingo at a little hole in the wall in town. As he opened the door for me and we started down two flights of cement stairs, his hand on the small of my back, I swear I felt a slight push, and my feet slipped from under me.

It couldn't have turned out better if I'd planned it myself. Like a real-life soap opera, I said I'd miscarried in the fall. Whew. I didn't know how much further I could make my stomach bulge out.

After recuperating for two days, I gave Mommy a big love, we packed and loaded our things in the trunk of his mom's car and headed to California.

Without a plan or money, we drifted from one of his friends' house to another. Although we started early every morning on a quest to find work, his leg wasn't a hundred percent yet and made it a challenge to find work he could do.

We counted ourselves lucky to get in one meal a day. As for smokes, we took butts from public ashtrays, or if we were really lucky, we'd find half smoked ones on the ground.

After about a month of this, he became temperamental, and impatient with me. Then, one day, while arguing in a bedroom of his cousins, he raised a hand at me.

"Wham!" across the jaw. That was it; I was going home.

When he left the room, I gathered my stuff, snuck out the ground-floor window, and walked around aimlessly until dusk. More than ever before, I wanted to go home but had no way to get there. I sat on a curb, put my head in my hands, and cried, *oh what a mess* I thought.

I'd call Mommy, but the MORON would answer, he'd think my current situation was funnier than hell. Consumed in my self-imposed misery, I didn't notice the olive-green car that pulled up next to me.

"What's the matter miss?" an old man asked.

I told him how I'd come from Washington with my boyfriend, how he couldn't find a job, how we didn't have a place to stay or money to feed ourselves, how he'd just hit me, and how I wanted to go home, but couldn't afford that either.

"Come along miss, I can't do much, but I can get you home."

He took me to the bus stop, bought me a hamburger and a one-way ticket back to Seattle.

PART I

THIRTY-NINE

Returning from work one day, the MORON found me home once again. Our wills clashed, mine, his and Mommy's, but my persistence prevailed. Defeated and disgusted, he left at long last. The week after, Mommy was more dramatic over his leaving than all the breakups before. Sure, I had her all to myself now, but it was too much, I was no longer devoted to this train wreck.

Worn-out from fighting, mumbling how *I was out of there for good this time, and going to focus on my own dreams*— when Mommy walked into the room as I was packing. Once again, she conned me into not going, pleading how she wouldn't have a reason to live without me.

Whatever, fine; and I stayed. It didn't seem as if my knight in shining armor would ever show up anyway.

She wasn't the only one with a will to die. For as long as I can remember I'd always wished for death, no more nightmares, or people to deal with, or inner turmoil.

I could have done myself in but was too chicken to, afraid of the pain and what waited for me on the other side, and how there'd be no way back.

For a while, I awoke every morning disappointed because I hadn't died in my sleep. Knowing my luck, I wouldn't die a natural death; it would be a long, drawn-out, and horrible thing, I was sure of it.

༄

It was said Tommy married the girl I'd seen at his graduation party, and they lived in a fancy apartment near the base in North Carolina. My heart deflated.

I knew he didn't love that girl the same way he did me; they didn't have a history as we had, and it was my name tattooed on his forearm.

So, I devised a plan to find them and thwart their marital bliss, besides, it wasn't too late for an annulment.

With the phone number for the base, I called and said I was his sister to get the mailing address. I poured my soul into a letter, professing my never ceasing love for him, and paid extra postage for it to reach him right away.

Then, I waited for the mailman, the same way Mommy did on payday, but his response never came. Certain I'd lost my one and only forever, Tommy called.

He said he missed me so much and didn't realize how much until I wasn't in his life anymore and asked me to join him there. Score.

About the girl, he said they weren't getting along, no surprise there, and because Army life wasn't for her, they were getting an annulment. I smiled to myself like an impish cat.

Because her parents had been paying for the apartment, he said he'd lose it after two more months, and we'd have to find our own place.

That was fine by me, I didn't want to stay anywhere she'd been anyhow. As I had enough money for a one-way ticket to Newport News, North Carolina, I couldn't pack fast enough, stuffing essentials into a duffle bag and food, lunch meat, cheese, and crackers into a small cooler to eat along the way.

No one knew about the impending trip, except for Becky. I hid the bag in my closet behind a stack of shoes. The day I left, after everyone was asleep, I snuck out my bedroom window like a thief in the night.

When the greyhound neared my destination, I changed into a white zip-up jumpsuit with light turquoise pinstripes, cute triangular turquoise earrings, a matching sweater, and white pumps, half yuppy, half gypsy, just the way he liked.

I saw him waiting at the entrance door to the bus. He looked breathtaking in his Army camouflage clothes. He smiled a mile wide when he saw me and wrapped me up in his strong arms.

My God, I couldn't have loved him any more than I did and hugged him tight in return. My ankles wobbled in the heels as we walked to his pickup truck, a '64 Chevy, white with a light blue stripe on the side.

"What's with the getup? You don't look like you."

Thank God. This tennis shoe loving tomboy was more than happy to put the heels away. I wore them one other time on a double date with an Army friend of Tommy's and his wife.

I loved the magical, colonial feel of Newport News. We wandered around several of the settler towns on the weekends. I couldn't get enough.

Fourth of July was great. Tommy brought his portable Hibachi and roasted chicken legs on the tailgate. While we waited for the fireworks, we flew a cheap kite we'd bought at the grocery, and then watched the show on the beach.

But, as with every fairy tale, when the apartment lease ended, ours came to a screeching halt. Tommy hadn't found another place for us to live; instead, he bought a canopy for the truck and said it would be home until he did. What he meant was, I'd have to live in it while he slept in the barracks and worked during the day.

PART I

He made it as cozy as possible, padding the truck bed with lots of blankets, but it was stuffy and cramped with our things. He parked it on base, with me hiding in the back.

I liked the cool evenings, but the days were hell, even if I kept the little window slits open, it still was as hot as an oven, and parking in the shade made no difference.

I didn't dare move around or make any noise for fear of being caught. Tommy stopped by the truck before work and drove to the gas station, so I could use the bathroom and stretch my legs. Then, we'd return to the base and share a stowaway breakfast from the canteen.

He'd reappear again at lunchtime for another bathroom run, and we'd eat whatever was the special of the day from the food truck.

The stretch between his breaks was near unbearable. Scared of being shot or jailed if I ventured out to find a bathroom, I took little sips of the water he left behind.

After two weeks, I'd had enough, and told him to find us another place to live, pronto, or I'd go home. After that, we spent the evenings driving around in search of another apartment.

Several days passed, but we still couldn't find an affordable place to live. Ready to call it quits for the night, as we turned around in a mobile home park, we stopped to see if they had any vacancies for rent.

They had one small trailer available, but to afford it and the bills, I'd have to get a job. With only a few places within walking distance, the base, a grocery store, a bar, and a pizza restaurant, my chances were slim.

The mobile home was a faded red, tin can with two doors, one at the front, with small, worn out wooden steps leading up to it, and one towards the rear, off the bedroom. Inside, it resembled a camper with a similar kitchen, dining table, and single bed in the back.

After we moved in, I ventured out to the bar and pizza place to fill out an application. The bar called right away; they needed a waitress. Although I was a few months shy of the legal age, I wasn't asked for proof, and I didn't volunteer.

The job was challenging from the beginning. Not only did I have to memorize a list of drink variations, figure out how to give change from the top of my head, boggling my synapses for sure, but they expected me to get dolled up and show a little skin too.

The attention from the Army guys was harmless fun. They never touched me. I only had to laugh at their jokes, and the tips poured in.

Baffled by extra money I brought home every night, Tommy stopped in at lunch one afternoon to see why.

FORTY

As you can imagine, the job didn't last much longer. Within a week, I was waitressing at the restaurant. A zombie could take orders for pizza, and the tips went hand in hand. Tommy's pride had cost us the extra money I used to rake in.

We were treading water. He wasn't happy and became short-tempered over any little thing; he chased beer and criticized anything I said or did. To be nastier, he said I fit right in where we lived, trailer trash, and I was no better or smarter than my mom.

His spoiled upbringing and bad-boy attitude exposed his true colors when he drank. He'd yell and punch walls if I argued.

He used the bar job as fodder for his outbursts, calling me a slut among other offensive things. No matter what I did, the way I cooked, the clothes I wore, or how cheerful I tried to be, nothing was good enough. I didn't even enjoy the so-called celebration of my nineteenth birthday.

As plain as the nose on my face, I realized I'd surpassed him in maturity, and had enough of his BS. I hated him; he'd pissed all over our happy ever after and I wanted to go home.

One morning, just before he left for work, I brought up the subject; if he needed another excuse for drinking, I'd just given him one.

He fussed and fumed like a pent-up bull, but I ignored him, and let his insults roll off my back. When the dust settled, he agreed to put in for a few vacation days, and drive me to Mommy's and then fly back to the base.

Far from a glorified vacation, it's a wonder how we made it to Washington alive. Tommy partied the entire trip, drinking and smoking weed with hitchhikers all along the way. I half expected the Corsican brothers to come crawling in from the back.

If I bitched, it made matters worse, so I kept my mouth shut and crossed my fingers we'd make it home in one piece.

When we happened to be the only ones in the cab, I'd sit the furthest away from him. I couldn't wait until we got home and didn't care if I never saw him again. If that was his intention, he sure was doing a hell of a job.

Somewhere along the way we'd acquired a raccoon, I can't recall how it became a stowaway or what became of it, but Tommy named it Rocky.

PART I

When we reached Tacoma, I called Mommy from a gas station to tell her I was on my way home. She cried. She said she'd divorced the MORON, about time, and now lived in an apartment north of Seattle.

Tommy dropped me off there without a single word. Fine by me. I watched his taillights until they disappeared in the distance; he could wreck his life if he wanted, but he wasn't dragging me down with him.

Mommy's apartment had three bedrooms, one for each of us. Maggie set up my room just the way it had been in our last house. She worked at a pizza parlor a block away and got me a job with her.

I enrolled in a nearby community college, finished my high school diploma, and earned a secretarial certificate. Time flew by; I didn't have time to think of much else.

One weekend I followed Maggie to her boyfriend's house to watch his band practice and to have a BBQ, and that's when I met Freddy.

FORTY-ONE

He was nine years my senior and appeared to have his ducks in a row with a good job and everything. We hit it off from the beginning. He was a shy wallflower, not cool, and kind of dumb but sort of smart, same as me. He took me out most weekends. We'd talk for hours at a local coffee shop.

Other times, because Maggie's boyfriend was his best bud, we'd hang out at his house. Before long, his, all-too-familiar, extracurricular habits got on my nerves, and I broke up with him.

When my twenty-first birthday rolled around, I celebrated it with Mommy at her favorite watering hole; becoming legal wasn't such a big deal as I'd popped that cherry in North Carolina.

A few days shy of Thanksgiving, Tommy arrived home from the Army and whined how life hadn't the same without me. It had been two years since he dumped me at my mother's.

As if before a parole board, he admitted he'd been a jerk and wanted a second chance, gazing into my eyes with his dreamy baby blues, he professed his undying love for me, apologized for the way he left things, groveled, and begged for me to come back to him. I was a goner and fell for all the BS, hook, line, and sinker.

After he had his holiday dinner with his folks, he took me to a small hotel by the airport. We were having a romantic night until he brought out the beer, then the gloves were off, his true colors reflected off him like the Fourth of July.

I'd let him use me, dammit, he was the same spoiled asshole, and I'd given in to the brat. He didn't love me. He knew how to work ol' reliable. Well, never, *ever*, again, I refused to be his plaything and told him so when he dropped me off at Mommy's.

Two weeks later, Freddy called and asked if I wanted to go out for a coffee, spinning a similar spiel as Tommy, and I fell for it, again. OMG, I'm so dumb, hello McFly, knock, knock, geez. It wasn't long before we were getting on each other's nerves and broke up a second and final time.

I was finished with the likes of either of them and didn't care if I ever dated again. With my education, I'd find a good job. In fact, I'd sign up with the Navy and see the world; I was so done wasting my life on partying and loser boyfriends.

PART I

I met with a recruiter and jumped through the hoops of enlisting. In the meanwhile, a temp agency kept me busy with a variety of office jobs. I enjoyed dressing up and being independent.

The morning of my swearing in and shipping off, I woke up with a roaring case of stomach flu.

FORTY-TWO

I bowed out of the appointment and canceled the day with the temp agency too, so glad to have the weekend to recuperate. I called Becky and told her how nausea and dizziness had kept me home for the day.

She asked if my boobs hurt too; I said they did whenever I wore my bra, and she recommended I get checked at the free clinic, just in case. I laughed at her suggestion but scheduled an appointment just the same.

Because I wasn't consistent with remembering to take the pills at the same time every day, thinking doubling up the next day was enough, but to cross it off the list of reasons, I scheduled an appointment.

"Eliza Winamucka" the nurse called.

Geeze. Were people illiterate or what. There was no *z* in my first name, nor was there a *u* or a *c* in my last, and it definitely didn't end in an *a*. Good thing I was the only one in the waiting room.

I peed in a cup, handed it to the lady, and settled in a comfy chair of a sterile waiting room to wait for the verdict. A large overhead clock taunted me with each tic as it echoed off the pristine yellow walls. My crossed legs bounced as *what if* thoughts swirled around my brain.

Just when I thought I'd lose my mind, the nurse called me in again.

"Eliza Winamucka," the same nurse called again.

Now I knew she was dumb because I told her the correct pronunciation of my name just a second ago.

As if predicting the weather, she blurted, "You're pregnant."

I stared at her like a deer caught in the headlights.

"It's okay honey. We are here to help you every step of the way."

She asked if the father and I were together. Tears burned and welled in my eyes. I told her there was no one in my life but me. She told me not to worry that there would be plenty of people to help. I stared at her in disbelief. *Easy for you to say, lady.*

I couldn't believe this was happening or had happened and gulped the air for oxygen. I wanted to cry. Not again. I had a second chance, and now I blew it.

On point, she pulled a cardboard dial from her desk, whirled the dates around, calculating my approximate last menstrual cycle and the coordinating due date. She predicted I'd conceived near Christmas and to expect my baby in late September or early October.

I was still reeling from the news as the nurse continued with her business, gathering pamphlets about the atrocities of abortion should I contemplate that option.

She showed me some pictures of what the baby looked like and then gave me a pamphlet to follow its development each month.

As a consolation prize, she gave me a large bottle of prenatal vitamins and suggested I see a doctor right away, stressing the importance of medical care for a healthy baby. I left the clinic in a daze.

Becky would be excited. But she did not know about the pot of stew I'd gotten myself in. She was with her daughter's father, and they loved each other very much. With my baby being due in September that meant the jerk I'd recently broke up was the father, and I didn't love him at all.

Becky also had her family's support. For me there was Mommy; enough said. On the way home, in the sanctuary of the back of the bus, I broke down. I was leaving for the Navy the following week, to be a nurse, to do something great with my life and see the world. But that dream went up in smoke. They wouldn't take me now.

I swore I'd never go on welfare, but now what was I going to do? So much for finishing my high school diploma and getting a clerical certificate. I was no better than Mommy and admonished myself for not taking that damn pill like I should have.

I returned Becky's call as promised. She had her hands full with a sick toddler but listened as I carried on about the unfairness of life and about what to do next.

She was thrilled, but I told her it wasn't anything to be excited about because the guy with the Corvette was the father.

Oblivious to my anguish, she yammered on as if I'd won the lotto, excited to share her maternity clothes and baby stuff her three-year-old daughter had outgrown.

I curled up on my bed and cried until my stomach hurt. Through blurry eyes, I leafed through the literature from the clinic and paused on the picture of what the baby looked like.

I patted my perfect flat tummy and said, "It'll be ok baby, we'll get through this," and then walked to the living room to tell Mommy.

She cried happy tears, astounded at becoming a grandma and not yet fifty, but overjoyed all the same to be the first among her friends.

The news spread like wildfire. The overwhelming positive consensus amazed me. This was not the way I'd planned my future. I didn't want to repeat Mommy's life, on welfare and alone.

If I conceived the baby in December, that meant Freddy was the father. Great. I wanted no further involvement with him. The last time I saw him he had been a major jerk, but he did have a good job.

The only other option I had, other than going on the dole, was to tell the Corvette guy, so, I invited him over. We sat in the parking lot, smoked two or three cigarettes, and listened to a Talking Heads CD before I got the nerve.

Dammit, like everyone else, his face lit up too. After a lengthy discussion, we decided it would be best if we married right away as his job had good medical benefits.

The following week, with Maggie and his best friend as witnesses, we found a justice of the peace and sealed the deal. I can't remember the exact date other than in January some time. The stoic occasion lacked a fancy dress, a ring, and a happy celebration afterwards; shotgun weddings never do I suppose. It was a simple, loveless arrangement with an easier to pronounce last name.

I'd grown out of the inherent desire for the Three Musketeers, but the need for it remained. All I ever wanted was to have her for myself, but it seemed that it was something she was incapable of giving me. So, I concluded, a baby was the perfect solution. Except, I'd soon learn, I couldn't have that all to myself either.

PART I

FORTY-THREE

I moved into his grandma's house where he'd been living, just a few blocks from Mommy's. Our circumstances irked her old-fashioned ways to no end, always pointing out how nothing good ever came from such sin.

I spent most days at Mommy's while Freddy worked. That is until he took his rights as a husband to a T, expecting me as his wife to learn from and emulate his mother, sister, and grandma.

So, no more hanging out with Mommy, or doing whatever I wanted during the day. Instead, he said, I had to earn my keep, making sure he always had clean laundry, preparing a lunch box for him each morning, having dinner ready when he got home, looking after his grandma, and helping her keep it clean.

The more I whined and protested, the more impatient and mean he became. I must have really thrown him over the edge because one day after work he said we were moving to an apartment of our own, twenty-five miles south to Tukwila.

My first apartment. I was so excited. It sat nestled within a hillside overlooking a slough; it had two bedrooms, one for us and one for the baby, and a swimming pool in the back.

I made it as cozy as I knew how and had fun preparing the nursery. Freddy's mother visited at least twice a month, her tone and facial expressions said she didn't approve of me or the way I kept house; what mother-in-law does?

Mommy visited, once. Around lunchtime, we walked to the bottom of the hill to a little hole in the wall to play darts and for her to have a drink.

Our little escapade didn't go over well with Freddy. He had an outright hissy fit and said no wife of his, expecting or not, would ever be caught in a bar, and forbade me to return there ever again.

Thus began our frequent arguments, or yelling matches. He wanted control over my entire life, but I wasn't giving him the reins now or ever.

The day when the doctor didn't agree with the measurements of my swollen belly, is the straw that broke the camel's back. He called the nurse to roll in an ultrasound machine to have a closer look.

Through the fuzzy image on the screen, he pointed out the pulsing black spot in the center as the baby's heartbeat. To see proof of an actual living being in my tummy seemed exciting and creepy at the same time.

The doctor said everything looked fine, but the test showed my pregnancy further along than expected. He speculated I'd conceived in November, not December, and changed the baby's due date to late August.

It didn't take a rocket scientist to do the math; Freddy shot me the most hateful look, and we rode home in silence. As soon as the apartment door closed, he changed into Dr. Jekyll, or mister pister, MP for short.

He cracked open a beer, and then another, smoked a doobie, and then let me have it. He grabbed me by the front of my blouse. I tried to run, but he had a hold of my top and yanked me back to face him. As the buttons flew off, he clenched my jaw in a vice grip, and spit the most hateful things in my face, calling me a whore and accusing me of duping him the whole time.

There wasn't a day after that he didn't push and shove me around.

Details of the remaining year under his torrential abuse is a blur; repressed and locked in the furthest crevices of my mind. What I suffered at the hands of The Family paled in comparison.

Every day his authoritarian behavior worsened. He glared at my growing belly and punched it whenever he had a clear shot.

He criticized everything I did, nothing was ever clean enough, only his way was the right way, the food I prepared wasn't fit for a dog, and saying so in front of his friends. According to him, I wasn't any better than the dirt under his shoe.

There wasn't anyone I could reach out to for help because he chaperoned me everywhere. He wouldn't even let me be alone with the doctor.

One day, we visited his mom. She took me to lunch and baby shopping. When I shared what had been going on, she explained how normal it was to overreact while pregnant, how I should think of ways to make him happy, and then he'd stop.

I couldn't believe it; make him happy? HA! I'd rather burn in hell. As you can imagine MP learned of my little disclosure, and I paid for it as soon as we got home. The neighbors below us pounded on their ceiling whenever he got too carried away and called the cops and paramedics twice.

Each time they'd ask if I wanted to press charges, but I knew there'd be hell to pay once they left, so I didn't say a word.

Because we didn't have a bed frame and the mattress sat on the floor, it was easier to sleep on the foldout couch in the living room in my final month of pregnancy.

One morning I got up to go to the bathroom but didn't make it. The water didn't smell like urine and kept gushing out as I made my way to the toilet.

Something was wrong; I didn't have a telephone to call for help as MP had yanked the cord from the wall months ago.

As if he'd read my mind, or had a hidden camera, I heard him arrive for lunch; he'd been spending it at home as of late.

At first, he bitched about the mess I'd made on the floor, then realized the urgency of the moment, gathered my overnight bag, and helped me to the car.

There was a long waiting line in the maternity ward; I swear every pregnant woman in Seattle was having their baby that day.

We hung out in a smoke-filled waiting room with a bunch of anxious expectant fathers. A few hours later when the pains began, they called me in. It's a wonder why we had to wait so long; there were only three labor rooms.

They fastened a tight seatbelt-looking thing around my protruding stomach. It had a hard hockey puck device that dug into my skin. When I complained about the pain, the nurse pointed across the room at a seismograph looking machine and said it was to monitor the baby's heartbeat.

And that was it, no more nurses, no doctors, no medical staff of any kind until several hours later when a group of hospital staff, dressed in blue PJs, booties, and shower caps, arrived with another bed to take me to surgery.

Surgery? They said I was to have a C-Section. How unfair was that? They hadn't given me a chance to birth the baby myself.

MP dressed in the same getup; then, they rolled me through a hall and into a freezing, ascetic-looking surgical room.

Everyone talked above and around me as if I wasn't there. They placed a blue cloth barrier under my chin; I couldn't see my belly. Every nerve in my body shook; the more frightened I became, the worse it got.

A doctor I didn't recognize barked from beyond the blue veil, "Can you feel this?"

Terror paralyzed the words in my throat; they were doing the surgery while I was still awake; tears seared the corners of my eyes.

My arms laid frozen to my sides; I couldn't sense a thing; the pressure and tugging were indescribable, and then I heard a baby cry.

The doctor said to MP, "There you are dad, a healthy baby boy."

I was sure my heart would stop when the doctor handed my son to that monster, the thought of him smashing him on the floor or against the wall flashed through my mind.

FORTY-FOUR

MP brought the baby where I could see him. Our eyes locked; I'll never forget the way he looked at me for as long as I live; it was love at first sight.

The nightmare of the surgery faded into a distant memory as overwhelming emotions washed over me; I knew I'd walk a thousand miles across burning sand for him.

I named him Dale, after my mother and her father. MP insisted he have his stepfather's middle name, which was ok with me because my married name was his too, not MP's.

They took him from MP to do whatever it is they do to newborns and wheeled me into a recovery room to worry about when I'd regain use of my arms and legs again.

I was almost asleep when, to my horror, the nurse nestled my son in the crook of my left arm. I told her I hadn't regained sensation in my arms and didn't want to hold him until I did. She assured me I'd be ok and left us alone.

I cried to myself as I watched him sleep, so afraid to doze off in case he slid through the bars of the bed, crashed to the floor, and died before I'd held him.

The nurse reappeared sometime later and asked why I hadn't been nuzzling with my baby, stressing the importance soon after birth. I told her how my arms still felt frozen, but my words drifted off into space, and she swept my son away.

A while later, I awoke in another room to voices in the hall.

"We're concerned because she hasn't bonded with her baby yet," said the nurse.

"It might just be postpartum depression, it's very common," said the doctor.

MP said, "Not to worry, I'll keep an eye on her and help with the connection."

Moments later, MP came blazing across the room, "What the hell is the matter with you? Why didn't you want to hold our son?"

I glared at him and spat, "He's my son, not yours."

MP grinned a satisfied evil smile, "Oh yeah?" he taunted, "He's just as much mine as yours. I already signed my name to his birth certificate."

If there was a stronger word for *hate,* that's exactly how I felt. A nurse came in, injected Morphine into my I.V., and turned to leave, but MP was hot on her heels.

"We've chosen to bottle feed. When you bring the baby in next time will you bring some formula too?"

She replied, "Your wife pumped milk for him before we gave her the first dose of pain medicine, there's no harm to the baby."

MP replied, "We'd rather give him formula, thanks."

I turned towards the window and wept myself back to sleep, a consoling place where nightmares and pain didn't exist.

When I awoke sometime later, I saw MP feeding Dale a bottle of milk, a can of Similac sat next to him on a nightstand.

I glared at him, "I want to nurse him, not bottle feed."

MP said, "Your milk is crap, at least this way he'll get nourishment. Don't think of whining to the nurses because we'll be home alone soon enough." and he smiled a wicked smile.

I couldn't move without feeling knives slitting my stomach reopen. The pain burned, it was worse than anything I'd ever experienced, worse than my tonsillectomy.

A few days later, the nurse helped me pack for my return to hell. She showed me how to change a pamper and how to care for his circumcision and umbilical bandages.

I couldn't believe she'd let me leave with him. I had no prior experience and no references. A nurse's aide brought in a wheelchair and placed Dale in my arms.

I looked into the deep blue eyes that mirrored my own and smiled, "Well, it's just you and me against the world kiddo, I hope you're ready."

They wheeled us to the front of the hospital where MP waited with a bunch of flowers and a white limo. Who was he trying to impress? I mean, what was wrong with wanting to go home? I hadn't showered in days, smelled of breast milk and sweat, and my incision hurt.

He strapped Dale into a car seat and left me to stumble into the cumbersome sedan. The driver took us to visit several of MP's friends to show off *his* son. I didn't get out or talk to anyone; I was uncomfortable and wanted to rest.

Once at home and behind the privacy of our apartment doors, MP lit into me, saying how I'd been an ungrateful bitch, and what a pouty spoiled child I'd been when he was just trying to do something nice for me.

He cracked open a beer as he continued with his pent-up rampage, lamenting how women had been having babies every day throughout history, and I was no exception.

He demanded I stop carrying on about my aches and pains and get busy fixing his dinner. The hospital stay was the only recuperation I got, it hurt too much to fight back, so I didn't.

Dale woke up and cried. I removed him from the car seat and headed towards the nursery to change him. There was a stack of crisp white cloth diapers and baby pins stuck in soap next to the changing table.

I asked MP if he knew where the Pampers were. Wrong question. He startled me with his angry response, giving me an unsolicited 101 for being ungrateful for the nice, brand-new diapers and pins his mom had set up for me.

Dale's little chin quivered with each pitiful cry, and his face began turning blue, from being wet or MP's yelling, or both.

He shoved past me, "Here I'll do it," and he yanked the baby from my arms, "Jesus, you're just as retarded as your mother," and slammed the nursery door shut in my face.

I walked to the kitchen to find a decade old Dr. Spock book his mother left on the counter. I flipped through the pages and noticed a dog-eared section of how to put on cloth diapers.

It instructed to put the diaper pins in a bar of soap, to make them slide right through the cloth, along with drawings how to fold the diaper and put the pins in without poking the baby.

The next time Dale cried, I checked to see if he was wet. As he was, I changed him per the instructions in the book. He was more than wet, and it leaked out every crevice of the diaper, covering the crib sheets, mattress, and him.

I didn't know where to begin; the baby's cries escalated.

MP yelled from the living room, "Don't make me come in there."

My chin quivered along with Dale's; tears streamed down my cheeks, and I choked back silent sobs, afraid I'd hurt him, I held my breath as I turned him on his side, and brought his arms out of the t-shirt, ever so gentle and slow, relieved they hadn't broken off.

After stripping off his clothing, I carried him to the bathroom and rinsed him off in the sink. His inconsolable cries were nerve-wracking; I cooed to him as I worked.

Although I was being as careful as I could, he screamed even louder than before; MP's taunting from the other room didn't help matters either.

After an eternity, my body drenched in a sweaty mess, I had Dale clean once more, his bandages redressed, and his bed put back together.

I cradled him in my arms, sang "Twinkle, Twinkle Little Star," and nursed him back to sleep. While we snuggled, I rehearsed the entire ordeal in my mind, so I'd go faster the next time.

Within two long weeks, we had a routine down. I knew I had improved because he cried less and even smiled at me occasionally; his approval meant more than a million gold stars on a school paper.

It took the birth of my son and awareness of my own inadequacies as a mother to overlook Mommy's flaws and love and accept her for who she was. How could I go on punishing her for something she didn't understand?

I rationalized she'd done the best for us in the only way she knew how. My son would be her second chance. Through him, our bond would be mended. As his mother, I would learn to be the mother she never had, and the one I'd so desperately sought.

One morning, while MP was at work, I heard a gentle knock at the front door. MP warned he had people watching the apartment and there'd be hell to pay if I ever opened it.

Like a frightened rabbit, I listened for their retreating footsteps, but the person stayed at the other side of the door. A woman's voice called out for me to answer.

I shouted why I couldn't; she assured me there was no one watching. I peeked outside, pulled her in, and locked it behind her.

FORTY-FIVE

*I*t was the neighbor underneath us; my face flushed. She said she knew what was happening and asked if I'd let her help. Then I lost it. She took me in her arms, and I cried my heart out.

I rambled on how he'd taken the phone and forbidden me to speak to anyone outside his presence, how I'd never cared for an infant before and only had a book to teach me how to care for my new baby, how he chided me for every little mistake I made, always calling me a whack job like my mother, and on and on.

I didn't have to tell her much more; she'd heard the details from her apartment below. With my emotions spent, wiping the tears from my face, she said she knew of shelters where the baby and I could stay.

I explained how he'd kill me before letting me go. She told me not to worry; she'd help me escape while he was at work and would orchestrate the details.

Every morning thereafter she stopped by to report how *the plan* was going. One day, she said she'd found a battered women's shelter near the University of Washington. They were sending someone to fetch me and my son the following day at 11 a.m., and they'd meet me outside the restaurant near our apartment.

She instructed I pack a small bag of necessities and hide it in my closet. The day of the escape, around 10:15 a.m., she pounded on her ceiling three times as my cue to be ready to go.

I bundled Dale up, gathered our things, locked the door to my prison cell, and flew the coop.

The driver of the van was friendly enough and secured Dale in a car seat next to me. I sobbed the entire way to our new home, scared of MP's wrath once he discovered us gone.

The driver pulled in and around the back of an older Victorian brick building. He helped me and Dale out, and a friendly lady emerged to greet us.

She showed me around and introduced me to other residents. I couldn't believe how many other women there were in the same circumstances as myself. The structure of the household reminded me of a group home with its guidelines, schedules, and rules.

After breakfast, with infants in tow and older children attending an on-site preschool daycare, we had an hour of counseling and spent the rest of the day in various classes.

I chose a parenting group to learn how to care for my baby, and classes about setting goals and becoming independent.

Man, was I so thankful they only used Pampers; I hoped to never see another cloth diaper the rest of my life.

While I recuperated, the counselor sent state officials after MP. Because I hadn't filed charges, he wasn't hauled off to jail, but they required him to complete anger management classes.

MP said I was the unstable one, always yelling and throwing things, and to blame for the neighbors repeatedly calling the cops; I guess I dislocated my own ribs and jaw too.

We could not make phone calls from the home, but there was a pay phone at the mom-and-pop deli around the corner. I seldom used it and, if I did, I never took Dale with me.

Because they discouraged us from revealing where the home was, I didn't provide specifics to anyone, just that we were somewhere in the U district and we were safe.

Two months later, MP found us and called the home. Afraid I'd hang up on him, he said all he wanted to say in one breath, how sorry he was for being such a jerk, that he wasn't mad I'd left, how he'd completed the anger management classes, that he missed me and Dale so much, and how he'd change if we'd come back home.

We spoke each night for another month before he convinced me of his sincerity. One night as the house slept, I gathered my things and baby Dale, crept out the back door, and met MP down the street.

FORTY-SIX

We didn't drive south towards Tukwila but took the exit for West Seattle instead. He said he'd found a house for us and moved our stuff there.

It was a light blue, single story rambler from the Depression era, much like the one MITCH moved us into from the projects, without the creepy basement, and on a dead-end street.

MP unpacked and put everything away as if we hadn't been gone at all. The house was near a grocery store, had a pleasant neighborhood for walking in, and was close to Becky's too.

He enrolled us in couples counseling at a non-denominational church close to the house. A few members of the congregation invited us to share potlucks every week with them.

MP's newfound patience set me on edge. His odd behavior included inviting Mommy and Maggie to share Christmas dinner with us. Despite his efforts, I kept my antennas up.

As expected, two months later, he returned home from work in a foul mood, exposing his pretentious façade. He cracked open a beer and flopped down on the couch. Twenty minutes later he opened another, guzzled it, and opened yet another.

Then he exploded. Months of pent up rage pulsed in his temples, he punched a hole in the wall above my head, looked at me like a wild man, and said, "There's nothing you can do this time, no one will believe you because I've told them all you're delusional."

"Your carefree days are over, no more unsupervised walks or telephone calls," and he yanked the cord from the wall.

Little did he know, I'd learned a thing or two while I was away and covertly devised another getaway plan. One night, while he was out with his buddies, I packed a small bag like before, nestled Dale in a front carrier, and walked to a nearby bus stop.

∽

Because the security alarm on the front door of Mommy's building connected to the police station, we stayed at her place.

I called the counselor at the shelter. She apologized for not warning me about the honeymoon phase earlier and welcomed us back to the home.

Since MP knew where it was, I couldn't risk it. She said she understood and offered to continue with our sessions by phone if I wanted.

With her guidance, I stuck a sock in my pride, got on the dole, and rented a small apartment in Ballard with Maggie. Not long after, MP found us, again.

Anxiety running the gamut, we moved to a renovated apartment in a run-down, older building near Greenlake, but this time, not a soul knew of our whereabouts.

Even though the windows had bars on them, I still couldn't sleep. The legal document to protect us wasn't any better than a piece of toilet paper.

MP sent legal papers to Mommy's address. He sought custody of Dale and was banking on my, so called, mental instability to get him.

We visited her once a week to collect my mail, changing bus stops and routes to and from home, just in case.

MP's lawyer set an appointment to have my head examined. It was their trump card, or so they thought. Convinced the doctor was on MP's side, who wasn't, when I sat across from him and shared our tale of woe, rather than interrupting and sending me on my way, he showed genuine concern for our plight.

His report was nothing MP's lawyer had painted. The doctor wrote I wasn't delusional, nor on the verge of schizophrenia, or a threat to my son. In fact, he said, I was very much mentally well with a few understandable anxiety issues stemming from spousal abuse.

It didn't matter; MP still had his circle of groupies convinced I was nuts and who took pity on him. When all was said and done, he didn't get custody, but was granted visitation instead.

Regardless of how much I protested he wasn't his son, or how he only wanted visitation to upset me, the fair warnings fell upon deaf ears. Family court said I didn't have a right to deny him his child. Unbelievable.

Amidst the anguish, I sent a heartfelt letter to Tommy's mom with a picture of Dale, a spitting image of her son. My effort was fanciful wishing though, as if they'd welcome Dale into their family with open arms.

One day on the way home from a doctor's appointment, I ran into Tommy at the bus stop. He denied knowing of Dale's existence until that moment.

I painted a picture of what we'd been through, how the courts granted MP unsupervised visitation, and how he could prevent it if he'd take a DNA test to prove his paternity.

He lit a cigarette without a response. I saw my bus just a block away. He continued to remain mute as we climbed aboard. To my back, he said he didn't want to be sued for back child support and couldn't afford the DNA test either. What a coward.

A few days later, preoccupied with everything going on, not thinking twice about leaving the front door open to let in the warm summer air, I noticed someone standing in my doorway.

I looked up to find the sexiest man I'd ever seen, tall, lean, and tan, wearing a yellow tank top, and filling my entryway with all his glory.

"I live next door with my three kids and noticed you were alone with a little boy so I'm stopping by to let you know if you ever need anything, I'm right next door."

Tongue tied, I nodded my head thanks, and he left with a knowing skip in his step. Geez, must I always be so obvious?

It was possible he knew of us the day paramedics came to rescue Dale from our foldout couch. That morning his deafening cries woke me from a sound sleep; he'd somehow wriggled to the top and became stuck in the bed frame.

Mr. Casanova, or MC for short, stopped by often to invite us along for little outings, to feed the ducks, to a park for a picnic, for ice cream cones, or to watch movies.

Only seven years older than his eldest and the same height as his youngest, we looked like his five ducklings wherever we went.

They celebrated Dale's first birthday with us, along with Mommy and Maggie. In the whirlwind six months I knew MC, after four of them I was pregnant, again.

I awoke one morning with a familiar sick feeling. But this time it was worse. The fabric of my bra made my breasts feel like they were on fire and any provocation made me puke my guts out. I bundled Dale in his stroller and with my tail between my legs I dejectedly walked into the free clinic for a pregnancy test.

I knew it before they told me. I couldn't believe it. I felt cursed. I had purposely been careful since the last time. Maybe this is what we needed in our relationship. Maybe he would quit drinking and want to be a family.

But he wasn't pleased, in fact, he was pissed. He said we already had too many mouths to feed and couldn't believe I let this happen.

We rented a house together in my old stomping grounds, near the elementary school where I attended fifth and sixth grade and attempted to blend our two families, but he wouldn't play fair.

Then, he started staying out late at night and drinking more than before. My head was so far in the clouds, a tree would have to hit me in the face before I saw the forest.

PART I

It was a miracle when I fell from the wild blue yonder, landing hard on reality and my pride. He didn't want a family; he wanted a babysitter with benefits, and to hang out with his buddies and whatever else he did when catting around. I wasn't his nanny. I told him I was moving out and if he wanted a family with me, he had to prove it.

I gave him an ultimatum, us, or his extracurricular activities, but he didn't bite. So, Dale and I moved across town to a studio apartment, next to a golf course, nestled within a steep hillside in a corner bottom unit, nice and secure, like a little hobbit hole. Mommy's current victim helped us move.

FORTY-SEVEN

We lived full circle from the blue house where we'd lived with MITCH, and down the street from Becky's place and her little family. It was roomy for being a studio. A built-in wooden partition separated three-quarters of the living room from the bedroom.

Because there wasn't room for Dale's crib, I put his mattress on the floor next to the little closet and our dressers inside. There were only two windows at the front of the apartment, across one wall of the kitchen and the living room.

With some creativity and used furniture from Mommy's friends, I made the little hole in the wall homey in no time.

The distraction of the move made me forget about my current condition until I woke one night in a full-blown Linda Blair moment. Sicker than a dog doesn't even begin to describe it, I was certain I was being punished.

It haunted my ability to sleep most nights, so, in between waves, I pondered over my predicament. *It wasn't the baby's fault it was here; it deserved a life like Kathy's, one that I couldn't provide.*

And the FOB, father of the baby, made brief appearances, pretending to care about our welfare, displaying little achievements tokens as proof he was working on his AA requirements, just to charm his way into my drawers and disappear again.

I hated myself for falling for his bullshit every time; when would I ever learn? Tired of my relentless calls looking for Casanova, his brother came clean and told me that the creep was seeing someone else, and they were getting married.

My cheeks burned as if I had been slapped. I was beyond livid. I was hit all right, with common sense.

Before long, Tommy called and asked to see Dale.

I invited him over. Right from the *Honeymoon Phase* handbook, he professed how much he missed me, how he couldn't live without us in his life, and how he'd do whatever it took to be a family.

I almost fell for it until he said he wasn't into being a father to someone else's baby and suggested I abort it. Wow.

Stunned by his horrific proposal, I explained how the new child came with the package, end of discussion.

PART I

Although he wanted to act the part, he still refused to legalize his paternity. After all he knew, I couldn't understand why he wouldn't protect his son.

With his blatant disregard of the coming baby and unwillingness to protect Dale, he repulsed me. My loyalty, my love, and my life were for my children now, so, I let him fade away, for good this time.

◇

The pregnancy didn't get any easier. Soon I was so big I had to borrow a few of Mommy's barely there Muu Muu's, in the middle of winter no less, and settle for flip-flops for shoes as I couldn't reach my feet to tie my tennis shoes; I'd run out of super glue to keep the perpetual tongue of the sole from my shoe falling off anyway.

And then I had an insatiable craving for sweet-and-sour sauce, nothing else, not the rice or anything else, just the sauce, and would turn my apartment upside down for loose change so I could get some.

Like a strung-out drug addict, although the restaurant was about five miles away and all uphill, I'd secure Dale in his stroller and make the weekly climb, until my eighth month when the awkward weight of the baby made it impossible, all for sweet-and-sour sauce.

Because I didn't drive, trips into town for doctor's appointments were humiliating. I might as well as have had a bold, purple letter A stitched to the front of my Muu Muu with a cardboard poverty sign dangling around my neck. It didn't help I didn't look a day over twelve and already had one baby. If you've ever been stared at like this, you know how I felt.

There's one such outing I'll never forget. It was right up there with one of the worst days of my life; apart from being a freezing cold, wet day, and I was ready to pop, dressed in Mommy's tent, flip flops, and a skimpy sweater, not one fellow passenger on the full bus offered their seat to me.

I was hurt and embarrassed. *Who were they to condemn me as if I wasn't already aware of my predicament? It wasn't any walk in the park believe me.*

My precious little boy had to sit on the dirty floor and hug my leg while I stood and hung onto a passenger pole all the way into town.

The baby's due date came and went, and I was getting bigger by the day. Impatient and exhausted, I picked my toddler son up and carried him around everywhere, determined not to be induced or having the baby cut out of me, seriously contemplating taking castor oil, Exlax, or anything to help get things moving.

Since the baby wasn't in a hurry, I preoccupied myself with nesting activities. I collected clothes and furniture from the pregnancy center, and had everything together, except for a girl's name.

While folding and stacking onesie t-shirts, holding the phone receiver with my cheek, and debating girl names with Maggie, a brand name of one of the t-shirts jumped out at me, Alexis.

I asked her what she thought. She loved it, but not the spelling because it appeared to read, Alex Is.

An hour later, we settled with the spelling A-l-e-x-s-i-s, Lexi for short, with her middle name to include my first and her middle.

Maggie thought her name was plenty, but as I was the mother and wanted to be part of it too, I kept both, with a hyphen in the middle, twenty-five letters total.

Mommy said the name reminded her of a not so nice lady from the show Dynasty. All the same, I cut the tag from the t-shirt and saved it anyway.

As the stork neared ever closer, nightmares of how I'd manage with two babies kept me awake. Logic said it wouldn't be fair to bring another child into poverty and to surrender it to a well deserving, childless couple who'd be able to give it a life I'd only dreamt of.

At my next counseling meeting, I told her about my decision; she was proud of my selflessness and helped me make the arrangements.

The morning of the appointment to sign the final papers, it happened.

PART I

FORTY-EIGHT

*M*oments before dawn, a few days shy from the first day of summer, I awoke from a restless night, incredibly uncomfortable and still huge as a whale, and rolled out of bed to go to the bathroom, when I felt a familiar gush of warm liquid cascade down my leg.

As luck would have it, MP arrived the very same moment to drop my son off after having him for a weekend visit. As most of the dust had settled between me and MP, and going downtown had become difficult, I allowed him to pick Dale up for visits from my place.

He offered to take me to the hospital and said he'd drop Dale at Maggie's, who'd recently married, on his way to work. I called my birthing team to meet me there.

Of all the people I didn't want to give me a ride, he was at the top of the list. But, as I didn't have a choice, I grabbed my overnight bag and an armful of towels and waddled to his car.

I did my best not to get his seat wet, but every bump, turn, and anomaly on the road caused more water to gush out. I tried to clean myself up, but it was all for naught; I gave up and swam in my own fluids all the way to the hospital.

When we finally pulled into the parking lot, I was drenched, literally dripping, and cold from being wet. MP ran in to get someone to help me inside.

I refused to sit in the wheelchair they offered simply because I was so gross and felt like they'd need to throw out the chair once I was done with it.

The birthing floor was three floors up though, of course. I was going to have a long, wet waddle ahead of me. As I began my soggy journey, leaving a dripping trail of water behind me with every step, I turned to see the corvette disappear around the corner.

The day was emotional, unexpected, and completely unforgettable. I couldn't wait for the exciting, yet frightening, moment I believed I was ready for, I mean I'd gone through it once before; it was all planned, from the type of music I wanted to the kind of birth I'd have.

This time there would be no C-section if I could help it, but with pain medicine, of course.

I made it to my room, put on a gown, and sat in a chair to wait for my cheering squad. I remembered I hadn't brushed my hair and I smelled like pee, immodest in every way, shape, and form.

The doula dimmed the lights and helped me into a hospital gown. She brought out a boom box and played classical music and some other things to help me relax.

As the birthing coach, BC, distracted me with conversation and helped me through mild contractions, the doula knitted a pair of purple booties for the baby.

After an hour, I grew restless and waddled outside for a smoke, boy you should have seen the glares, no love at all.

Back in the room, my support team took me on a hike up three flights of stairs. Oh man, did that bring on some nasty contractions, they attacked as if I'd run full speed into a wall.

Every couple of steps brought crashing waves more intense than the first. Each time my team braced into position, BC from behind with a knee for me to rest on, and the doula in front keeping my eyes in focus with hers.

"Choo, choo, choo," we chanted through each seismic wave.

The unrelenting, back-to-back pains made me a basket case. The doula walked me into the attached shower room and brought out a variety of aromatherapy bath soaps to help me relax.

As much as I appreciated her kind gestures, I couldn't enjoy them, not standing or sitting, not even on the toilet; I was too afraid the baby would fall in it.

I wanted to move away from the pain, but it followed me in relentless pursuit. The doula helped me into a new gown, and a nurse assisted me onto an exam table to see how *we were doing down there.*

The pains were going off the Richter Scale and wringing my body inside out with each contraction. I couldn't breathe through them anymore, I cried and screamed instead, regardless of any attempt to intervene.

The nurse called the I.V. team to bring an epidural. She scowled and scolded me for upsetting the other mothers whenever I cried out; I glared at her in return, doubtful she'd ever been through this.

I didn't care and thought only of my pain. I wanted to cry "Uncle," but knew that wasn't an option, and I was in this until the bloody end.

The I.V. team arrived at last. They had me lay on my side with my knees to my chest and told me to lie perfectly still. That was easy enough until another wave washed over me.

I squeezed BC's hand until her fingers turned purple. Tears poured from my eyes, certain I wouldn't live to see the baby.

The doula wiped my face with a cool cloth. Seconds after Dracula finished, the pain disappeared. I laughed when the Doula said, "Here comes a big one, are you ready?"

Another nurse came into the room with Maggie behind her. Ms. Cratchit checked me again and told Maggie she'd arrived in time for the pushing.

BC was a coach all right, she called out contractions and when to push as if we were going for the super bowl. She had my left knee and the doula my right, "Push, Push, Push," we all sang in harmony, Mozart strumming away in the background.

After a great effort, they'd lay me back to rest until the next one. BC said we needed more gravity and helped me to my feet to squat like a sumo wrestler.

After a few pushes like that, my legs turned to Jello, so they helped me back into the former position. On the next big push, the nurse lifted my gown and announced, "The baby's crowning!"

Maggie burst into tears, "It's got black hair." Then I cried; I'd almost done it.

The nurse called for the doctor, "The baby can't get past the pubic bone," she said.

The doctor entered the room and joked, "we'd better see a baby soon or we're all going to have hemorrhoids!" Everyone laughed but me.

He pulled up my gown for a look, "We'll try one last time with forceps, but if the baby doesn't budge, we'll have no other choice than to perform a C-section." He called to have the delivery room and the O.R. prepped and ready.

There was just enough space in delivery to fit my support team and the doctor. Once everyone was in position again and ready to give it one last go, MC entered the room, wearing a cap and gown.

FORTY-NINE

Maggie smiled, the audience was the least of my concerns, I just wanted this over with. Her eyes about doubled in size when she saw the two Flintstone sized, salad spoons on the table.

"You're not using those on my sister, are you?"

The doc put the archaic tongs into position, and when the birthing squad was ready, MC holding my bent right leg, Maggie the left, he shouted, "PUSH!"

Everyone took a collective deep breath; I bore down as if moving a mountain, the veins in my neck threatening to burst, and pushed as if my life depended on it.

"Whoosh!"

The doctor dropped the metal spoons in time to catch the baby.

"It's a girl!"

Everyone laughed and cheered. Yep, we'd won the game all right. I laid back on the bed in an exhausted sweaty mess. Everyone cooed over her, gave each other congratulatory pats on the back, and cried happy tears.

The nurse placed my daughter in my arms. MC leaned in for a peek and kissed us both on the forehead.

My heart overflowed, the same way it had when I'd first met her brother. I was so glad I hadn't signed the papers. I could handle one more. Although she might not have the best in life, she'd have love, lots and lots of love.

I brought her to my breast and hugged her ever so gentle as she suckled away. I didn't think it possible to love a second child as much as my first, but I did.

My lips trembled, and tears poured from my eyes as I thought about how much I loved her, "Happy Birthday sweetie, she's so pretty," I sniffled to Maggie, who was having a meltdown of her own.

When my daughter paused for a breather, Maggie reached for her, "Let me see Lexi."

Moments later, a nurse took her to the nursery, and an orderly wheeled me to recovery where a party was in full swing with all the new mothers.

I learned later Maggie had planned to call MC once the baby neared its birth. That was the second thing I'd never forgive her for.

She said every father deserved the right to be at the birth of their child. Well, not the undeserving ones, and not without the mother's consent I thought.

MC wallowed in the glory of his daughter's birth, trumpeting on and on how she was a carbon copy of himself and her siblings.

I was cheerful until the anesthesia wore off; I paid for my victory big time, every single suture, front to back, twenty-eight in, and twenty-eight out.

It felt as if a cactus was between my legs. The pain of a C-Section paled in comparison, but my doctor obliged with my wishes, even if I were a naive twenty-three-year-old.

Two days after Lexi's birth, MC took us home in his brother's, straight out of the seventies, wall to wall carpeted Chevy van, strapping her into a car seat in front, and leaving me to hang on for dear life on a bench seat in the back.

He stopped at his brothers' to show her off to her siblings, his mother, and his brother, before dropping us off at my apartment. I can count on one hand how many times he came around after that, until one day he didn't.

Maggie brought Dale home later, and then, it was just the three of us. Trying to synchronize the needs of two babies while nursing my own wounds took some imagination. I'll never understand how we survived the first three months.

With two steep flights of stairs to the laundry room, hives and asthma, to every pain pill and antibiotic the doctor gave me, two trips into town on the bus to see the pediatrician, we managed somehow. I counted every day we made it to bedtime a success.

Just when it seemed I had the swing of things; Dale's health took a turn for the worse.

FIFTY

We spent late evenings of the rest of the year at Children's Hospital in the emergency room. I loved my babies the same, cared for them the best I knew how, kept our home sanitary, the never-ending battle with the clutter had a life of its own, but it was clean, so I couldn't understand what had made him sick.

After poking him one too many times for numerous tests, they concluded he had Failure to Thrive and Asthma, and gave him several medications that made him anxious. They taught me how to give his medicine through a nebulizer and what symptoms to keep an eye out for.

The hospital sent a nutritionist to visit every Monday. Once a month, she gave me vouchers for milk and food. Following her, a social worker stopped by every other week to discuss parenting issues.

Dale loved when she visited because she brought a bucket of cars for him to venture through while we talked. After her, I was referred to a parent support person.

Diane arrived the following week, not by an umbrella, but in a shiny gold Lexus. She had an infectious smile, and the kids took to her in an instant.

She beamed like a welcome ray of sunshine, friendly, loving, and wise with the children, especially Dale, but between us though, it was strictly business.

I wasn't surprised to learn she'd broken the glass ceiling in her job as the first female senior V.P. in the way she rolled up her sleeves and got straight to work with the challenge of the three of us.

Once in a while, she visited while the kids napped so we'd get in some uninterrupted adult time. I couldn't believe she'd once been in the same circumstances as I, but with five children, and made it with the same determination as I possessed.

She said she pulled up her bootstraps and got on with getting on. This simple approach encouraged me to want more from my life, for me and my kids.

Sometimes she invited me to her office in downtown Seattle for lunch. Because we ate at the nicest places, I made sure to dress my best, fix my hair, and wear makeup.

She fascinated me in the way she carried herself, the way she dressed, the way she ate, and how she spoke with friends compared to acquaintances.

PART I

Raised in the *I Am Woman* generation, she never spoke of personal things to anyone, and never whined or complained, no matter what. I found it odd how she and Mommy were the same age.

If I sought a surrogate mother, I wouldn't find one in her. Although, I could be mistaken for her daughter as we wore the same size clothes and had similar strawberry blond hair.

In my heart, I imagined I was. The only thing missing was the warm affection she showed my children, but she was my mentor, and that's that.

Regardless, I flourished with any bit of sunlight she cast on me. As her approval meant the world to me, I always did my best to show her I wasn't a waste of time.

We had many discussions about my future, returning to school and the type of job I'd need to support the three of us. We talked about the children's futures, how not to concern them with our struggles, and how to make their lives happy with little money.

I made a list of goals and set them in stone; I wanted to break my own barriers and the statistics shrouding single mothers.

To begin on my independent journey, I met with a job counselor to chart my course, subscribed to a parenting magazine I'd seen once at the pediatrician's office, and took the kids for regular romps at the playground.

While Dale played with the other kids, and Lexi napped, I observed how other mothers interacted with their kids, how they assured their hands were clean before eating, how they wiped their runny noses with tissue, not creating a Picasso mess of their sleeves like I did, and the kinds of snacks they gave them.

One thing that came naturally was showing them unconditional love, and I did, often, always hugging and kissing them and telling them how wonderful they were, and they were.

The job counselor signed me up for a reduced housing program. Within a few months, a two-bedroom apartment north of Seattle, in Bothell, became available, and closer to Mommy, so I jumped on it.

Maggie and her husband helped me move. We had access to a grocery store, a great park with a playground, a river with ducks to feed, and the bus.

In the efforts of self-improvement, I thought a fresh new hair color, just a tad darker than my strawberry blonde, would boost my morale.

With the kids asleep at long last, I rinsed the dye in my hair and had just plopped on the couch to watch t.v. when Lexi awoke.

The change wasn't that obvious, but even in the dimness from the nightlight, she noticed. She recognized my voice but not my person and screamed when I tried to lift her.

She'd never carried on in such a way before, and it scared me. I called the nurse hotline. She suggested I put my hair up in a towel, something Lexi had seen a million times, and bring my hair out in pieces until she recognized me again.

I did as she recommended and returned to the crib. Lexi recognized me in an instant, her face lit up, and her pacifier fell from her mouth. She grinned the biggest toothless smile and held her arms out to me.

As we snuggled in a rocking chair, she reached for my hair while she nursed as usual. I let out a little strand, she twirled it in her fingers, closed her eyes, and fell back to sleep.

I never dyed my hair again.

We saw less and less of Diane because of the distance to our new place, but I think she believed she'd ignited enough of a fuse to set me on my way. Although ready to fly, I'd sure miss my alone time when she visited with the children. Because Dale and Lexi were more like twins at twenty-one months apart, keeping an eye on them was exhausting, but, I can count on one hand how many times I've screwed up, and that's not so bad, considering.

I'll never forget the day the eyes in the back of my head opened. That afternoon, I'd laid Lexi on a blanket in the living room to prepare Dale's lunch, just mere steps away, keeping her in my peripheral vision the whole time, when something distracted me for a split second.

When I looked back at the blanket, she was gone; then, I heard the most blood-curdling scream echo off the walls of our small apartment.

I secured Dale in a high chair and ricocheted around the apartment until I found her. With a tear-stained face and snot bubbles pulsing from her nose, she stood in the middle of the room with my hot curling iron stuck on top of her right forearm.

I lunged for the cord, ripped it out of the socket, and snatched the burning metal from her arm in one quick swipe.

I swung her on to my hip and ran for the phone to call the medics. She forfeited crawling for walking that day and has a three-inch scar from a second-degree burn commemorating the milestone.

༄

The following day when we set out for the doctor to have a look at it, is how we met Mark, a Seattle Metro bus driver. No matter when we set out to catch a bus thereafter, he seemed to always be our driver.

PART I

PART II

WILDFLOWER

PART II

ONE

*U*nlike other drivers who kept their foot on the brake while I struggled to board with my cumbersome load, Mark would shift the bus into "Park" and help us.

First, he'd assist Dale up the steep steps and help him into a seat; then, he'd toss Lexi into the air, tuck her into the crook of his massive arm like a sack of potatoes, fold the stroller in half, and offer me his free arm and escort me up the steps.

He continued with his route only when we were settled. He did this each time we boarded his bus; though I'm certain he helped others in the same way, I still felt special.

The rides with Mark were entertaining and uneventful. He always had candy for Dale, and some for Lex as she got older, and lots of stories for me, nothing personal just his general philosophy about the world.

He always seemed to know when I needed cheering up because on those days, he'd tell me, in full animated expression, the funniest, sidesplitting, animal stories I'd ever heard.

The more interest I took in him, the more he shared with me. His genuine friendship was infectious; the kids and I looked forward to our next trip with him.

Sometimes, if there happened to be a different driver, my quiet little boy would release his true two-year-old attributes with full vengeance.

And what a scene he'd make. It was a whole show with his lobster red, tear-soaked face, his heels dug in the ground, he flat out refused to get onto any other bus than Mark's, and that was that, end of discussion, regardless of my explanation of how it wasn't Mark's turn to drive.

One day, as we headed home on Mark's bus, he invited us to join him for lunch during his break by our place. When we arrived at the end of the line, Mark brought a camera out from his work bag.

He said he loved to take pictures and asked permission to take one of us. I didn't look my best, but he made me laugh as he clicked the button on the camera anyway.

It was a bittersweet moment caught in time, Dale, a slight, pale-haired, two-year-old little boy with large blue eyes, glaring into the lens of the camera and Lexi, a brown-eyed, chubby baby with just a tuft of brown hair on the top of her head, snuggled sound asleep inside the carrier secured to the front of me. It would be the first of many.

I'd forgotten all about that picture until I came across it ten years later. While reminiscing, for the first time I noticed a most disturbing image in the photo.

Although we were alone with Mark and parked in a secluded neighborhood, there appears to be a mysterious figure in the stairwell, just behind Lexi's head.

Sometimes we walked a half block to the Safeway grocery store to buy lunch, juice and baby food for Lex, finger foods, juice, and crackers for Dale, and deli sandwiches for us.

It was customary when we left the store, to stop at the candy machines to buy a treat for the kids and for them to ride on the coin-operated horse.

Before we ate, the birds were fed first. Mark always had birdseed in his work bag and designated places along his route where he fed them.

Like a scene from an Alfred Hitchcock movie, hundreds appeared from out of nowhere as soon as he parked the bus.

Dale watched with immense curiosity as he emptied a pound of seed the entire length of the bus onto the sidewalk. Then we'd scrambled back inside to watch them eat; his contagious baby giggles echoed off the walls.

At the end of his break, with all the seed gone and not a bird in sight, he'd sit Dale on his lap and let him *drive* us the half block to our apartment; these lunchtime visits soon became a weekly ritual.

We'd enjoyed Bothell, but it had limited bus service. Once our year lease ended, we moved a short distance south to Lake City into a larger apartment. It was within walking distance a half mile up a steep hill from Mommy's. Caught up in the routine of our lives, we lost track of our favorite bus driver.

Not long after moving to our new place, Mommy moved a couple of miles north to a government-owned apartment complex. So much for being closer.

As time drifted by, Dale grew into a handsome preschooler, and Lexi blossomed into a beautiful toddler with a head full of bouncy brown curls with the same unrelenting curiosity. Like the day she got away from me. We were on our way to the bus stop when she wriggled her hand free of mine and took off towards the busy highway.

My breath caught in my throat when I tried to yell for her to stop, but her little legs didn't hesitate, and she propelled full speed ahead towards the fast-moving cars.

I got a hold of her coat as she was about to step off the curb. The words I barked at her may have slipped my mind, but not the resounding swat I gave her on the behind.

In the same fell swoop, I gathered her into a big hug and calmed both our tears away. I'm not sure who cried harder that day, but boy she sure scared me half to death.

From then on, regardless of the stares, I tethered them in harnesses thereafter, a blue one for Dale and pink for Lexi, who had to have hers put on backwards because she always found a way out of it.

༄

Once settled in, I enrolled in a community college, a similar distance by bus as to Mommy's place, and signed Dale up for Head Start. While I studied nursing, Lexi played at the college's preschool daycare.

Each day, once Dale boarded his school bus, me and Lexi took a city bus southbound quite a distance to catch another bus back north another great distance to the school and vice versa home, rain, sleet, or snow.

By the time we returned home, it was time to make dinner and prepare for the next day, laying out clothes, packing lunches, giving baths, and reading bedtime stories; there was little time for anything else.

One day, while Lex and I transferred onto our final bus home, we happened upon Mark's bus. Lexi recognized him as soon as he opened the doors.

She squealed with delight as she tripped up the giant stairs and fell into his lap, wrapping her little arms around his stomach as far as they would reach, hugging him as tight as she could.

His face lit up, and he cuddled her in return. He was just as excited to see us again too.

I claimed my unofficial seat, the one across from his, where we could see each other best and talk in private. I rattled on a mile a minute to bring him up to date with the current events in our lives before we reached our stop, pausing only for air or to move if someone needed my seat.

Much to my surprise, my schedule coincided with his route, and before long we resumed joining him during his lunch breaks.

On one of our visits, he noticed a little Barbie doll peeking out of Lexi's carry case and asked her if he could have it.

He told her it reminded him of me and promised to take excellent care of it. She surrendered it without a second thought, and that's how I became known as Dollface.

Life was going along without a hitch until I received a letter from Family Services, MC had emerged from the rock he'd been under, and wanted visitation rights.

My opinion didn't matter. His lawyer arranged everything. Because I couldn't afford legal help, I had to play along. Since Lexi didn't know MC from Adam, the courts ordered supervised visits at the same place where I once brought Dale to exchange with MP, convenient or not.

The social worker from Children's Hospital referred us to a child counselor, whose office was a short bus ride from our apartment, to explain the upcoming events to Lexi.

Much to my annoyance, she took to her father as if she'd seem him every day of her short life. A month later, the courts granted him entire unsupervised weekends, regardless of how I felt about it.

The family counselor helped Lexi and me through the transition, taking over where Diane left off with parenting issues and the like.

After several months of biweekly trips into town for the swap, I let my guard down and allowed MC to pick her up from my apartment instead; big mistake.

One weekend he arrived during Lexi's nap time, Dale was with MP, and I was alone. I invited him in to wait until she woke up.

He chased me around the couch, vowing all the while to leave his wife, promising me the moon if I'd come back to him, and how we'd be a family just the way I'd always wanted.

A year later, he was still with his wife and making the same empty promises. As much as I wanted to pay her back for stealing him from me, it was demoralizing to be his plaything, so I put my foot down.

Well, that opened another can of worms. Not long after, a familiar letter from Family Services arrived by certified mail; this time he wanted full custody.

Ha! Over my dead body, but because he had the means, he fought me tooth and nail, he and his wife presenting themselves as the better family, with their two-parent household and resources to give her a better life.

When the battle ended, and the verdict in, the courts determined once more, I was of sound mind and, although I was a single mother, I'd always met my daughter's basic needs, and money couldn't replace the love I gave both my children.

But MC didn't stop there.

Although he didn't get custody, the judge allowed him to replace my last name with his on her birth certificate. It bothered me to no end, but at least he didn't get my baby. I kept her original birth certificate anyway, twenty-eight letters total.

Not long after, the brainwashing started. One weekend she returned from visiting with her dad and called me by my name. When the counselor asked her why she'd stopped calling me mom, she said she wasn't allowed to call me her mom while at her dad's, only the other lady, and she'd forgotten to switch back.

To make matters more baffling, they rationalized how she looked more like all of them than me or Dale, and she had their last name. To confuse things further, she didn't understand why she had to live with us at all, a huge issue that took years to unravel.

TWO

*A*s young as I was, despite the overwhelming challenges and responsibilities before me, from the day of their births, I vowed I'd never give up on them or give naysayers reason to doubt my parental abilities.

Unlike Mommy's broken promise, the three of us were one above all else. I had gotten myself into this predicament, and I'd make the best of it, come hell or high water.

～

Mark would give the shirt off his back if he thought you needed it. So, you can just imagine how hard it was for him to restrain his innate instinct to help me.

Though he couldn't comprehend the delicate sense of pride I had for myself and my circumstances, he respected my boundaries just the same, convincing me his acts of kindness were innocent expressions of sharing, not helping.

Like the clothes he dropped off for Dale that his youngest son had outgrown; or, the many times he happened by when Lex and I were about to leave to give us a lift, with the lure of apple fritters and coffee along the way.

While time evolved, so did his feelings for me. Because I regarded him as a friend and nothing more, the gradual changes in his demeanor made me uncomfortable.

Not only was he eleven years my senior, a foot and three inches taller, but he also outweighed me by two hundred pounds. Adding to that, like a Chia pet, the only hairless parts of him were on the top of his head, the palms of his hands, the bottoms of his feet, and the significant ring around his stomach from the fanny pack he wore every day.

And no matter what the season, he was a walking heater. When he wasn't wearing his Metro uniform, he wore a tank top and shorts, out of which his body hair spilled like wild ivy.

Even worse, not unlike Frosty in the Bahamas during the summer, with any kind of physical exertion, he was always dripping sweat and always carried napkins to sop up with.

Hands down, he wasn't even close to my kind of boyfriend. I had worked too hard and come too far and was not the least bit interested in repeating history.

I explained my position as kind as I could, adding how I wasn't attracted to him other than just being his friend, how I didn't want to be the *other woman*, as I knew firsthand the heartbreak of being the one cheated on, nor did I want to be his mid-life crisis, and I suggested we not see each other outside of his work anymore.

As delicate as I tried to be, it was evident in his eyes that I'd stolen his happy. Breaking his heart hurt me too. He kept his distance but continued to call to check on us to see how we were doing from time to time.

THREE

Challenged with what seemed like ceaseless and insurmountable governmental conditions, the children and I were forced to move, again.

I hated uprooting them, always zigzagging our way through the county, hoping the next place we landed lasted longer than six months.

Despite the hassle though, I found an apartment in the perfect location across the street from Mommy's apartment. Best of all, it was walking distance to the grocery store, the bus stop, the YMCA daycare, and the post office.

When I told Mark about the new place, he insisted I allow him to help with the move. Because his strength would make it faster and easier, I agreed without a second thought.

On moving day, after we'd finished, while we rested with a refreshing soda, he asked if I'd ever been to Whidbey Island. Before I could answer I hadn't, he asked if I would like to join him for a day trip the following weekend.

Against my better judgment but tempted by the chance to get away for a while, I agreed to go. And I'm glad I did; I had a great time.

While we strolled along the beach, he unfurled a fascinating tale about the island's military past. As I listened, I searched for my favorite, ever elusive, multi-colored, former hermit abodes, but only found remnants of the previous inhabitants.

Without missing a beat of the story or any great effort, my most sought-after shells would appear at his feet; unaffected by the anomaly, he'd pluck up the magical treasures and drop them in my coat pocket. Incredible.

After we'd walked the length of the beach and back, with the sun descending into the horizon, and time to kill before the next ferry, we stopped at his favorite place for a bite to eat.

A large windmill next to the front door concealed the extravagance within. I felt uneasy at first because we were a little windblown and smelled like beachcombers, but, so were many other patrons, and I let myself relax, some.

They seated us next to a fireplace at an intimate table for two. For the next hour, we laughed and joked over each course they served. He cracked me up the way he exaggerated the correct use of the polyester napkin, eating utensils, and overall appropriate restaurant etiquette.

PART II

While waiting for Baked Alaska and coffee, I noticed an unusual shadow glaze over his mischievous hazel eyes, suspending our once spirited conversation within the space between us.

The crackling fire reflected from his penetrating gaze, as though my soul stood naked before him. I tried to catch my breath, but it was wedged in my throat.

He reached under the table for my hand; transfixed by his piercing stare, I surrendered it to him. Overpowered by the once cozy fireplace, my blouse clung to my skin, and I melted into the chair; it took nerves of steel not to run screaming from the bewitching scene, certain I'd die any second.

I searched his eyes for answers. Any imperfections I'd once condemned him for, no longer existed; my heart about leaped from my chest as I realized how much I loved him, how I had always loved him, this handsome gentle giant couldn't have been more perfect.

My overall concepts about men and relationships intertwined with the smoke of the fire disappeared up the chimney, and out into oblivion.

In tune with my self-revelation, he smiled an all-knowing grin and told me how he loved me more than life itself and how he couldn't live another day without me in it.

I felt the same but looked away to break the enchantment.

Tears welled in my eyes, and my voice quivered as I explained, once more, how I didn't want to be an affair for him or a mid-life crisis. He squeezed my hand and said I meant much more to him than that.

As we drove home, my wits about me once again, I agreed to date him, but only after he had met certain conditions. Foremost, he'd have to move from the house he shared with his wife; second, he'd have to remove his wedding ring; and last, he'd have to file for a divorce.

My ultimatums didn't discourage him, nor did they put a damper on the rest of the evening. From that day forward, we were like two kids who finally got what they've always wanted for Christmas.

∽

Lexi's fourth birthday was fast approaching. She had sprouted into a willowy preschooler with a headful of beautiful, shoulder-length, curly auburn hair and just a hint of baby chubbiness in the apples of her cheeks.

One evening, just after getting her and Dale into bed, Mark appeared at my door.

He held up a piece of paper in his left hand, with a noticeable white line where his wedding band used to be, and, with a devilish grin a mile wide, asked, "Now?"

Surprised and speechless, I opened the door and jumped into his arms.

I laughed and nodded as he picked me up and swung me around. Then I cried; I was baffled how someone could care so much about me.

With unbridled passion, he pressed his lips to my cheek and, choking back tears, said he loved me beyond words. I hugged his neck in return and whispered in his ear how my heart would always be his, forever.

And then he whirled me around and around again, lost in time and space for a moment, suspended in our own fairy tale.

PART II

FOUR

*H*ell-bent on proving he wasn't like any of the other men I'd known, Mark would move mountains to assure the children and I had what we needed.

If it was broke, he fixed it; should he foresee a problem, he helped to solve it; when we needed a ride, he was right there.

If he thought we were starving, which I'm sure was always, he'd take us out to eat, buy us groceries, or give us treats.

We continued to visit him on the bus and sometimes we rode to the end of the line and visit his home base.

The kids' favorite thing to do there, besides running helter-skelter in the hallways and around the driver's lockers, was to play in the break room with the pool table and the pinball machines.

The best time they had was during one Halloween when Mark took us to a haunted house at the southern entrance of the underground bus tunnels.

When it came time to choose his routes, he made sure one of them passed by our apartment, so he could take us for an occasional nostalgic trip for lunch, candy, and junk food at Safeway.

Sometimes, we rode into town with him for a quick stop at South base to visit some of his bus buddies or the International district for a large bag of homemade fortune cookies and a huge portion of barbecued pork.

During those trips, as if we weren't already full enough, he'd take us to dinner before bringing us home, his top two choices: The Armadillo restaurant in Woodinville or Ivar's in Fremont.

But because we liked to sit in the outside dining area at Ivar's to watch the Fremont Bridge open and close and to feed our fries to the seagulls, we only ate there on pleasant days.

When he had time off, he took the children and me on mini outings to visit his favorite Seattle haunts; it was as if we were tourists in our own city.

The first place we went was to see an enormous statue of a troll underneath the Aurora Bridge. Lex sat on its lap while Dale explored around it. I thought it was rather intimidating and foreboding in a creepy sort of way, but the kids loved it.

He was a natural father to them; if you didn't know different, you would have thought he was. As I watched them laugh and play, I thought how impossible it would be to love him any more than I did, but seeing the way he interacted with my children, confirmed it tenfold.

We visited other places too, like the Pike Place Market, The Piers, The Ballard Locks, Discovery Park, and ferry rides to nowhere just to name a few.

Though these adventures might seem commonplace to any other family, for the children of a single mother who didn't drive, each new discovery was like visiting Disneyland all over again.

Of all the outings we went on, the one that made me the most nervous was the day we were introduced to his mother and the rest of his family.

PART II

FIVE

I was certain they'd disapprove of the likes of me and my kids, but they welcomed us with opened arms. His mother and I had an instant connection. She said if her son's heart was happy, hers was too.

Like two peas in a pod, referring to each other as Lucy and Ethel, we were Mark's best girls. Whenever he brought flowers for me, he'd bring her some too.

We looked forward to visiting her picturesque home, the place where Mark's family gathered for holidays, birthdays, summer games, and barbecues. Over time, we became an accepted part of it all.

∽

As our relationship unfolded, I relaxed and surrendered to all its illusions, falling with reckless abandonment, head-over-heels in love with Mark.

He was all I had ever hoped for and believed didn't exist. With him, I realized my sense of self and accomplishments. In his eyes, I saw my potential, and it made me work even harder.

The total opposite of me, he kept his heart guarded. Rather than admitting he loved me, he'd say *Remember who loves you*, and he'd cringe with any public display of affection.

When I'd tiptoe to hug him, he'd stand as tall as possible, so I couldn't clasp my fingers around his neck, forcing me to hug him around his middle, in which I could only reach part way around.

Then, rather than hug me in return, he'd dismiss my gesture with a gentle pat on my shoulder. In my world, this was a personal offense, but neither hissy fit nor standing on my head ever got me any closer to him. With all the righteousness of a saint, he'd stand by and wait for the storm to pass.

Time didn't change him either. The rule remained, no PDAs other than holding hands, ever. An unrelenting battle for sure, but I found ways around it all the same.

If his hand was all he'd give me, then hold it I would, everywhere and anywhere: while taking walks, watching TV, driving in the car, or while falling asleep.

And Lexi did too; for whichever hand was free, his pinky was reserved for her.

Although sweet nothings never made it past his lips, his kind gestures spoke louder than any uttered word. Sometimes when I arrived home from work, I'd find a box of decadent candy on the kitchen counter, or a random gift, or a fragrant bouquet in the fridge, including an occasional economy size bottle of Pamprin.

As sure as rain falls in Seattle, the surprises never stopped. And neither did the daily phone calls. Although we didn't have cell phones back then, he always called.

The first one came in the morning to wish me an awesome day. Another at lunchtime to tell me about how his day was going, to see how mine was, and that he missed me. And a final call at bedtime to wish me sweet dreams and to say, *"Remember who loves you."*

If there was an accident involving a Metro bus or driver, he'd pull over to the nearest phone booth to assure me he was all right, saying the passengers didn't seem to mind much. But I'm certain that of all of them, a few made up some of the complaints awaiting him at the bus base.

We'd formed a comfortable faith in each other, confiding our deepest thoughts, dreams, and concerns.

As we evolved, I knighted him with the endearment Hunny Bunny. He accepted it as if I'd given him a royal title or something, and never asked me to not call him it in public or in front of the children, family, or friends; so, that is all I ever called him thereafter.

If that wasn't silly enough, we had yet another set of names for one another.

Because of the special friendship Winnie the Pooh and Piglet shared, mirrored that of Mark and me, we referred to each other by these characters' names too.

He'd tell you the idea was my thing, yet he was the first to buy me Pooh and Piglet memorabilia; my favorite gift was a framed poster of Pooh and Piglet holding hands and walking into the sunset, titled, *It's So Much Friendlier with Two.*

In due process, we were introduced to his children next.

PART II

SIX

In Mark's children's eyes, I was the reason for their family's division, and nothing I said or did would ever change that.

The fact I was closer to the eldest child's age than Mark's, and that I lacked parenting maturity and experience, complicated matters too.

Holidays seemed to melt the ice a little, so we tried to make them as fun as possible.

With a celebration looming on the horizon, Mark would pump up the entire crew for the festivities with an equal exuberance, unparalleled to their own.

He was rather devout with his egg decorating ritual at Easter; he even had a special kitchen drawer reserved with an arsenal of embellishments, showing the rest of us how to make *really cool eggs*.

Even though his outshined all of theirs, they never seemed to notice; he had a way of making them feel as if their eggs were just as much of a masterpiece as his own.

Because he liked to decorate a lot of them but hated having to eat tons of hard-boiled eggs, he colored them fresh from the carton.

They never spoiled because we'd gobble them up on our next customary Sunday breakfast of green egg and ham omelets rolled in warm flour tortillas.

The icing on the cake was Christmas. My favorite photos are of the first year we decorated sugar cookies together.

I'd no sooner taken a batch out of the oven when Mark beat the kids to them and stockpiled the shapes he liked best.

The funniest picture shows a serious Dale working under Mark's apprenticeship and Lexi on his other side struggling with a bottle of sprinkles in her chubby toddler hands.

But the excitement didn't stop there. Mark also decorated the inside and outside of the house; his primary focus was on the Christmas tree, a whole other sacrament.

He wouldn't settle for an ordinary one bought from a street-side vendor like the kind my children and I knew. Rather, once bundled up like a lumberjack, his antique mitered hand saw at the ready, he'd cut down a fresh fir from a local tree farmer owned by an older man he admired.

Once tethered to the roof of his truck, he'd give the farmer and his wife a Marionberry pie, baked fresh by his favorite bakery, and render yummy treats from his pocket for their dogs.

Every year they remembered Mark's truck and greeted him with tail wagging enthusiasm as if he had only been there the day before.

Then, there were the all-out commencement of birthdays; Mark moved mountains to assure it was special for whoever it may be.

In return, I worked to make his birthdays just as memorable, like his fortieth. With his mom and his sister's help, we decorated his house with balloons and crepe paper and set out his favorite cake, angel food with strawberries and whipped cream; you'd have to be blind not to have seen it all.

He was beyond surprised when he came in the house. His beaming face in the still frames of my Kodak says it all. As anxious as if it were their own birthday, the children waited on pins and needles until he opened his gifts.

It wasn't the pewter keychain in the shape of an angel with the words Drive Safe inscribed on it that excited them, but the personal, cross-stitched heirloom they helped to create that they couldn't wait for him to see.

It took several months to put together. For the primary border, I made Celtic symbols in the colors of his heritage, Irish and Ukraine, on Aida cross-stitch cloth.

Next, inside yet another border with the same colors, I stitched objects and symbols the children drew on graphing paper that represented Mark the most.

As a final touch, I stitched a poem I composed in the center of it. Because I had to fold and hide it several times throughout its creation, it has a permanent crease down the center.

Next, I had it framed with mahogany wood and non-glare glass that made the crease almost nonexistent. It was perfect.

There wasn't a prouder bunch than when they gave it to him. It had to have been the biggest secret they'd ever kept, and for that, he loved it even more.

Before digging into his cake, he hung the masterpiece in the living room for all to see.

For Father's Day one year, each of the children cut a picture of themselves down to size and glued it onto a circle of yellow construction paper.

They opted for the caption to read: *We love you, Daddy*. I had it laminated and put into a button cover. The indescribable look on his face said it all when he opened it. He wore it that day and each Father's Day thereafter.

PART II

Mark's childish nature wasn't reserved for just the holidays. It emerged without warning or provocation like Peter Pan, infecting our brood of impish elves.

It was a waste of time telling him to act his age. Once he made me laugh, he had all the permission needed to continue with his antics, much to his captive audiences' expectation.

Sometimes it seemed as if I had five kids instead of our blended four, like the times he started the ritualistic fart on top of the boys' heads.

He'd wait until they became fixated on a video game, sneak behind them, bend, and rip a loud and gassy explosion on top of their heads. Although over and above grossed out, they'd laugh until their sides hurt.

This heartwarming display of affection would start a chain reaction of chaotic disorder, entwined with lewd and outlandish behavior. I was powerless to regain control after one of these incidents.

Then there were rituals which belonged to Mark and Lexi alone. Like the special way he picked her up. Ever since he'd held her for the first time as an infant, she had a special place in his heart.

Their greetings began with an abrupt toss into the air, a tickle grab around her ribs, and an Eskimo kiss to seal their salutation. She has a framed photo of one of those moments, just before she'd outgrown the tossing part.

Their nighttime routine was yet another habitual event. Once he tucked the blankets underneath her chin, he'd plant a gentle kiss on her little forehead and wish her sweet dreams. The boys, however; got a firm *go to sleep* before he closed their door for the night.

Then, there was the special time he set aside for the two of them, without the annoying boys or mom. No matter if they ventured off to feed the ducks or to run errands, their time alone was sacred.

Although he had three rowdy boys to roughhouse with, and even though she could be as rambunctious as all of them, and the most trying of all, she was still his precious little girl.

Immune to her incessant chatter, she could talk his ear off, repeating the most outlandish and repetitive knock-knock jokes, driving the boys beyond nail-pulling nuts, but, rather than shushing her, as he would the boys, as if he'd never heard them before, he'd give her his undivided attention, and laugh at each one she told.

The things she got away with would make your eyes roll for sure.

Our relationship continued to revolve around his bus routes. One day, the summer of 93 to be exact, while visiting him for a customary end-of-the-route lunch, he tossed something my way. I put my hands out expecting to catch a mouthwatering treat.

But I didn't catch Godiva chocolates; instead, my hands cradled a tiny, square, baby blue box with a tiny yellow ribbon on the top.

PART II

SEVEN

I looked at him for an explanation, but he continued to drive as if nothing out of the ordinary had occurred. I chose not to open the little package until we got to the end of the line, which seemed to be a million miles away.

There wasn't a nerve in my body that didn't twitch as I held onto the tiny box. Mixed emotions ran amuck in my head, anticipating what might be inside. When we arrived at long last, he parked the bus in the usual place, stood, and exaggerated a lengthy stretch.

He stopped midway when he noticed I hadn't opened the box.

"Well?" he asked, "aren't you going to open it?"

He knelt next to my seat as I untied the delicate yellow ribbon. Inside, I found yet another box; this one was black velvet; my hands shook as I pried it open.

When the light found the stone within, a kaleidoscope of colors burst throughout the bus, shimmering and dancing like hundreds of little fireflies, reflecting off my face, making the walls of the entire bus sparkle.

It was the most beautiful ring I had ever seen. He said he'd chosen the stone because it reminded him of the color of my hypnotic blue eyes, and the golden band reminded him of my strawberry blonde hair.

He removed it from the box and placed it on my left ring finger. It fit.

"Well?" he asked expecting me to answer a question he hadn't asked.

Still speechless, without concern of my mascara, tears flowed in little rivers down the apples of my cheeks, and I mumbled an indirect answer to his indirect question.

"But," I explained, "before I accept, I want to finish school, learn to drive, and to have my first permanent job."

He lifted my chin to meet his eyes. I saw my reflection in them and who he knew I was. And I saw how he was already contemplating how he'd help me accomplish my goals.

My ultimatums didn't faze him in the past nor did they now. For the moment, the best I could give him was my commitment I'd be ready, someday.

And then I cried. I cried because of how safe and loved he made me feel for the first time in my life, and because I feared how much I truly loved him.

He gathered me into his strong arms and caressed my hair, the way he always did to make me forget about whatever had upset me.

He held me even closer, whispered in my ear that he understood, and said he would wait for however long I needed, and then chased my tears away with feather-like kisses.

I nodded and hugged him in return, though my conscious-self remained unconvinced to raise the white flag quite yet.

With the blindness of a love-struck teenager, I laughed at the reality of it all, wrapped my arms around his neck, and planted a sloppy wet nose kiss on his cheek.

While we ate our lunch, we daydreamed about our future. Like the weaving of a spider's web, the more we planned, the further it stretched out before us.

He said he'd like the Armadillo restaurant to cater our wedding, imagining him and the guests in formal attire trying not to get BBQ sauce on their clothes, cracked me up, it was so like him.

You couldn't have wiped the grin from my face even if you wanted too. I wasn't just surviving anymore; life had meaning now.

PART II

EIGHT

A day didn't go by when I wasn't daydreaming into the deep blue stone. It seemed to go on forever, like my future. Not long after his proposal, we had our official engagement pictures taken.

We spent even more time together than before, including weekends.

Mark planned our brief, seventy-two-hour visits, down to the last second, making sure not to waste any of our precious time. All the same, they disappeared just as fast.

We went on outings on Saturdays and ran errands on Sundays. Because he cherished the great outdoors, the windier and colder the better, he always chose the beach first. If I thought it too cold, I'd exaggerate how much homework I had and exclude myself.

Not one to deter from his scheduled events, he'd pack up the children and disappear for almost an entire day.

Sometimes, rather than studying, I'd catch up on some crucial alone time with a hot cup of coffee and a good book, or some sleep instead.

If not at the beach, he'd scout out a new place for us to hike. He found ideas in the Sunday paper and kept the best ones in a special file; it was rare if we stole away on the same journey twice.

Just as serious as the Decorating of the Eggs ritual, the Planning of the Hike formality required as much calculation.

First, he prepared a backpack of all the things he thought we'd require, a picnic feast, a camera with extra film, a first aid kit, water, rain gear, extra hiking clothes and shoes, and birdseed of course. Bursting at the seams, he was the only one who could carry it.

The hikes in the fall were best, driving along the beautiful country roads, in awe of the tree branches that draped over their entirety with breathtaking red, gold, and orange leaves.

The hiking trails were always off the main highway at the end of rugged side roads; getting there was the children's favorite part of the drive.

Mark's stellar driving record, mingled with a cloud of dust and pebbles, scattered like confetti over the cliffs, as he made what the children called *fishtails* and *360s* until we reached the start of the path.

I swear there were times we almost went over; the more I protested, screeched, and made horrifying faces, the faster and riskier he'd drive, laughing all the while like some wild crazy man, encouraging the children to holler along with him, jangling my nerves to no end.

Somehow, we always made it to the trail. I don't know if it was his twisted way of getting the kids psyched for a hike, but it worked; they had enough adrenaline to last them the entire day.

No one ever complained about being tired or bored, not even little Lexi. In fact, I was the one pulling up the rear.

Mark made the hikes as magical as the holidays. We saw the world through his eyes and it was beautiful. He was our great teacher, a mentor, a Merlin of sorts.

As if on a field trip, he'd teach us about nature, history, and animals; about the different trees and how to tell their ages; and about plants, the kinds we could eat and touch and the ones we couldn't. It was easy to get lost in it all.

We looked forward to the yummy picnic we knew awaited us in the backpack, but the partaking of the feast did not commence until we made it to the lake or river, or the destination for that day.

After our tummies were full, Mark would break out the birdseed for his feathered friends and scatter it in the brush as we strolled back to the truck.

One hike I'll never forget, rather than tossing the birdseed into the bushes like usual, he tossed their food out on the footpath before me.

When I inched closer to get a better look at the cute little creatures, I found myself caught up in the middle of a ritualistic dance.

They swooped and flew in and out between my legs and all around me in one feathered blur, dive-bombing the ground to scoop up the offering.

We all laughed in mesmerized disbelief until our sides ached. It was an indescribable experience.

After an all-day excursion, the drive home was always a peaceful treat because the children slept the entire way back.

༄

Another place we liked to haunt was Whidbey Island. As with the hikes, there was always something new to learn. I swear we visited each fort, beach, and picnic place there. We visited so many in fact I can't distinguish one from the other in our photos.

Mark's favorite was the lighthouse at Fort Ebey; mine was the Captain's beach house at Fort Casey; and the kids, hands down, loved spending hours exploring all the island's beaches.

Because they liked to run ahead, Mark would wager a bet to keep them close to us, offering to pay five dollars to the first one to find a pure white rock, absent of any markings and larger than a quarter, but, if he found it first, the bet was off.

It worked like magic.

The best beach walks we took were at Birch Bay, just shy of the Canadian border. On our most recent trip there, Mark rented a two-bedroom condominium just off the main drag and within walking distance to the beach.

It had all the comforts of home, as was his way, nothing less than a four-star place wherever we stayed. I tried to reason with him, but it was futile, assuring we had nothing but the best made him the happiest.

The morning after we arrived, while the brood was still asleep, we took a short walk to the cafe for my morning latte.

The calm, warm air and the lazy water lapping close to the sidewalk was the perfect invitation for a story. I laughed at his recollection of childhood memories at the inlet, entwined with the area's history.

We stopped for a second to appreciate a majestic bald eagle perched above us on top of a phone pole. Mark said it had been following us since we left the condo. We stared at the massive creature a little longer and then continued with the quest for my cup of brew.

The eagle waited for us outside the coffee shop and followed us as we returned to the condo, hopping with ease from one phone pole to the next.

The bird's odd behavior invited Mark to share his theory about animal spirituality and their relationship with God, and with us.

After my coffee, we woke the children for a day at the beach. By the time we were ready to leave, sun lotion applied, shorts and tank tops on, sunglasses, beach moccasins, towels, and the camera, our regal guardian had left.

The tide was out. It was so far away we couldn't see the waves on the shore anymore. The kids took off for the shoreline.

Tiny puddles of water dotted the sand. Although I did my best to avoid them, it was useless, the squirts from the little clams under them made my legs wet no matter what I did.

Mark suggested that I remove my sandals. The water was warm, and the sand felt smooth on my virgin feet; the seaweed was slimy and tickled just like the tiny fishes that swam about my toes.

Each time a clam spurt hit me, I'd double over in a fit of laughter; it was a whole show and made Mark laugh too, setting the mood for the rest of that unforgettable weekend.

NINE

*A*s promised, Mark supported me with my independence goals. When I had night classes, he'd drive me to and from the college, care for my children, and bring me dinner, and did the same while I attended day classes when his schedule allowed.

With his support, editing and proofreading my assignments on top of everything else, I managed twenty credits each quarter, worked at the college part-time tutoring writing skills to ESL students, and maintained a 4.0 G.P.A.

But our relationship wasn't always a fairy tale. Because of the stress and fatigue from my school schedule, I conjured up several convoluted accusations and some nasty arguments too.

His calm as a cucumber attitude was frustrating. He wouldn't be goaded into fighting back, regardless of how much I pulled his tail, he refused to be disrespectful.

Issues surrounding his divorce and the blending of our two families were the greatest challenges confronting me; I was clueless about how to deal with it all; I only wanted the happy ever after.

The pressures began affecting my studies and my sleep, so, I told Mark I needed a break. Although disappointed, he granted me whatever time I needed to sort things out.

It was near impossible to avoid him during our brief separation. Although I purposely by-passed his routes, his fellow bus buddies kept me up to date how lost Mark seemed, and how his cheerful disposition was at an all-time low.

Even so, I moved on to date others, but my heart belonged to Mark, only he could fill my empty void; harnessing my inner Cimarron, I decided to give *us* another chance.

The brief pause seemed like it never happened, and Mark was soon back on the quest to help me meet my premarital requirements.

As we rang in the New Year of 1998, pledging to make it our best year yet, it began with the purchase of a new home.

It was a Hobbit-sized, single-story rambler. I wanted to be excited, but it baffled me how he thought the six of us would live in harmony under its itty-bitty roof.

Mark liked that it was close to the heart of Lynnwood and his job and met with a contractor to make the necessary size adjustments. But, no matter how

PART II

we looked at the floor plans, either up or sideways, none of them passed the zoning requirements.

I didn't understand the logistics, but with the eventual plan of adding another member or two to our family, we had no other choice but to look for a bigger house.

By mid-summer, I'd met goal number one, and graduated from college. We celebrated with both of our families, and then I set to work on goal number two, driving lessons.

I saved enough money to pay for five instruction days, including the driving test. With my limited budget, there was no room for error, and I plowed through each lesson with sheer determination.

On the day of the exam, I didn't relax until I'd neared the end of it. As I flipped the left blinker to cross oncoming traffic to return to the D.O.L, I noticed a clean slate in the examiner's binder.

An approaching shuttle bus hesitated for me to cross and I panicked. I knew to yield to advancing traffic, but the stupid van wouldn't go; it was a showdown.

Although the little impasse lasted only a couple of minutes, it seemed like an eternity. Finally, the other driver gave in and the van crept past me. As it went by, the driver put his head out the window, smiled ear-to-ear and waved a triumphant peace sign.

It was Mark; he cost me three points.

I didn't know he drove anything but a bus and was unaware he'd be around the D.O.L. He confessed later how he'd planned to drive that specific route to coordinate with my exam.

Perfect score or not, I did it; I got my license!

I celebrated my victory with my children later that evening along with my very own, one man, cheering squad.

The following weekend, putting the proverbial cherry on top, with my coveted driver's license and the rest of my savings, we headed to a car tent sale at Northgate Mall.

Because Mark knew the owners of the dealership since childhood, we didn't have the usual hassles. I fell in love with a compact, four-door, cayenne pepper red, Chevy Cavalier coupe.

All four kids begged to ride along on its maiden voyage. The thought of driving by myself and with children made me a nervous wreck.

Mark was the first one to get in; he attempted to adjust the mirrors and to assure all was in working order.

It was all I could do not to laugh as he struggled into the driver's seat, it wouldn't go back far enough, and the steering wheel was stationary.

When we were ready to leave, Mark pulled his truck in front of me, and, took off; I panicked. The once slight drizzle turned into a downpour and washed out the windshield.

I couldn't find the wiper levers; we'd forgotten to go over those minor details. Warrior drums boomed in my ears as I searched for them, all the while keeping an eye on the road and him in sight.

By the time I figured it all out, I looked like I'd just stepped out of the shower. His kids got a kick out of my driving, the way I counted at the stop signs and looked both ways, several times, before turning; yeah, real hilarious.

Dale and Lexi's infectious enthusiasm made me relax, "Hooray!! No more bussing it!" That is until Mark turned away from my apartment. He wanted to show his mom our new addition.

Once we returned to my apartment, I was high on adrenaline with my hair matted to my forehead.

Like all other new drivers before me, it soon became second nature. I'd mastered it all, except the art of parking, nor will I ever.

For the longest time, I avoided the fuel pump; it terrified me to death; I was certain the fumes would catch fire, and we'd all burn alive.

Pleased to assume gas attendant duties, going above and beyond, Mark remained ever vigilant that it was always in prime working condition, keeping the fuel topped off, checking the engine fluids, washing the windows and mirrors, and, he even changed the nail magnet tires, twice.

For added assurance, he placed a Bible, a first aid kit, a gallon of water, and a blanket in the trunk; going a step further, he hung a crystal angel from the rear-view mirror. I think he worried more about my driving than I did.

Not long after, I suggested that he buy himself a new truck. I argued how his Bronco was on its last legs, how he'd never owned a brand-new vehicle, and most important, how he deserved one.

Then one weekend, just as I was about out of my mind with worry, he pulled in the driveway with a brand-new, champagne-colored, extended cab, Chevy Truck, extra-large and powerful just like himself. I'm sure the neighbors thought we'd won the lotto.

The kids were hot on my heels as I ran outside to greet him, begging for a ride the entire way. Their irresistible excitement encouraged him to oblige. We cheered in acapella as we struggled to climb aboard.

The dashboard looked like the control panel of an airplane and the tan interior smelled like new leather. We were in awe of its enormity, oblivious to the sting under our sweaty legs whenever they stuck to the seats.

Mark flipped a switch, and a refreshing breeze cooled our clammy faces; then, he turned on the surround sound stereo; Sunday errands would never be the same again.

༄

The final goal was to land a steady job. With Mark's editing expertise, I created a resume. Since I hadn't worked before the birth of my children, it didn't look all that impressive as most of it comprised of education.

The best job I could get, not at all related to what I trained to do, was as an administrative assistant at a hospital's satellite clinic on the outskirts of downtown Seattle.

Regardless, Mark couldn't have been prouder and called me at my office twice a day to tell me so and had fresh-cut flowers delivered to my office every other week as a further reminder; I couldn't help to be proud of myself too.

Now one among the ranks of the working class, I was manning my own helm, and that's what mattered most.

I commuted to work by Metro with the rest of the sheep and left my new car at the Park and Ride, taking Mark's bus whenever our schedules coordinated.

Sometimes, he took his breaks at the Park and Ride where my car was parked to leave gifts and cards for me on the driver's seat. Although the surprises were sporadic, they always came when I needed cheering up most.

Of all the cards he left, there was one that caught me off guard. It wasn't so unusual that it had a picture of a cat on it since he and I both loved cats, but this feline wore a wedding gown.

The caption read, *No More Nights in the Alley* and it didn't take long to figure out its meaning.

When he called later that night, he confirmed my assumptions; then, asked if the following weekend would work for a moving truck to be sent to my place.

TEN

Dumfounded, speechless, excited, and nervous all at once; my mind raced around and around, was I ready? What should I say? It's what we had been working towards all along, and I had given him my word.

As promised, Mark showed up with a moving truck bright and early the following Saturday, grinning ear to ear like some love-struck fool. Because I lived in a third story walk-up, it took all six of us to move my stuff through the twists and turns of the narrow hallway from my apartment.

Since I had double the amount of household items he had, I either threw the extra stuff away, or dropped it off at the Goodwill on the way to his house; some other things I saved for a yard sale. All that remained were our personal possessions within a few boxes.

As we settled in for our first night home, I laid awake and worried how the move was the riskiest thing I had ever done since the birth of my children. I'd given up most of what I'd worked so hard for, including my independence, all for the love of one man.

To live under the same teeny tiny roof with our blended family of six was eventful, to say the least. Each of the three bedrooms had space for one bed and a dresser, no more, and it caused an instant discord among the ranks.

Mark made the final decision of who would go where, moving his eldest son to the den, Lexi into his room, and had his youngest son make room to share his room with Dale.

Despite the arrows, Mark knew how to make it fun, making sure as little time as possible was spent in the house, continuing with weekend outings and other things.

He made another major rule. One that set my inner alarms ablaze. He insisted from then on, he and the children would do most of the chores and I was to allow him to take care of me, "non-negotiable, zip, end of it."

He clarified further how I should involve myself with more enjoyable things that I loved to do, but never had time for, like reading or sewing.

His proposal was foreign to me and something I would never in a million years get used to, and I only gave in to it when he was around.

I learned so much more about Mark living with him. Not only did he feed the wild animals away from home, but he also fed any wild thing that ventured onto the back porch.

The masses that stopped by his 24-hour diner included squirrels and stellar jays, along with their friends and families; they depended upon and were expectant of their daily feedings.

The rodents with tails, as he referred to the squirrels, trusted him so much they'd take the nuts from his hand and eat them at his feet. One got so cocky one day, it invited itself into the house, cats or no cats, to get its own nuts.

We even caught one sitting inside the coffee can where Mark kept the peanuts! He put an end to that in a hurry and kept the backdoor closed from then on.

He spent as much money on animal food, wild and domestic, as he did for his family. Once a week he bought at least ten pounds of peanuts, not the cheaper ones in the bulk bin mind you, but the specialty kind in bags that cost four dollars each.

Then, a couple of times a week he'd purchase five pounds of wild birdseed and take it to work with him; and twice a month he bought fancy, dehydrated corn cob sticks and pounded them into the deck railing.

Don't let his soft side fool you though; he wasn't always Assisi with the wild animals; he detested the opossums and the raccoons. Whenever he saw one of those critters on his back porch, his personality would automatically switch from Dr. Jekyll to Mr. Hyde.

In a maniacal split-second, he'd grab an M1000 from a drawer next to the back door, light it, and throw it out after them as they hightailed it down the back cliff.

The whole backyard would illuminate and make the kids scream and laugh like crazy, especially when the aftershocks rippled through the house. I'm certain our neighbors felt them too, but for some strange reason, they never complained.

Mark preferred cats over dogs. Like our little humans, we ended up with a blended four, two he had for several years, Omar and Cinder-Mamma kitty, and two we adopted from my sister, Dinky and Amos.

With the sails for our future well underway, we enrolled Dale and Lexi into the local elementary school for the fall and set our wedding for the following spring, May 15, 1999.

The ceremony was to be held at his mother's house and the Armadillo BBQ restaurant as the caterers.

I had quite a collection going for *the day,* and his sister helped me set the stage. One thing I searched in vain to find was a Unity candle, but the perfect one refused to appear.

After an exhausting day of hunting, I stopped by a Christian store on the way home to see what they had. Tucked way back in the corner, among a display of candles, there was one that made the hairs on my neck stand up.

I stared at it in disbelief.

It wasn't the beauty of it, adorned with faux pearls and lace, that caught my eye, but the name of the manufacturer written in bold letters across the top that caused me to take a second look.

Lillian Rose. The very name we'd chosen for a baby girl should we have one someday; Lillian, after his favorite Aunt, and Rose after his mom.

Convinced it was a sign, besides a fitting scripture on the front; 1 Corinthians 13:4-8, it sold itself; I couldn't wait to show Mark.

Once settled in our new home, he pampered me more than he'd ever had before. When I got home from work, he'd have me sit in my favorite chair, prop my feet up on a footstool with a pillow, and give me something cold to drink.

Who would pass that up?

Twice a week he had a warm and scented, candlelit, bath waiting for me, and when I finished, I'd find my pajamas, still warm from the dryer, folded and waiting for me on the bed.

As if that wasn't enough, he'd lie on my side of the bed until I finished dressing, so I had a warm spot to climb into. When I told him how he made me feel like royalty, he'd laugh and say, "Yeah, a Royal HighnAss."

As much as I tried to relax and enjoy my new life, I couldn't, all of it seemed too good to be true.

With November, just after my thirty-third birthday, my new job announced a departmental layoff at the end of the year; my name was on the list, "Last one in, first one out," they said.

Ever confident, always seeing life as half full, and respecting my innate independence, Mark helped me with job-hunting as he had before.

While waiting for a bite on the line, I took a flexible weekend job as a cashier at J.C. Penny's. Since he had some paid time off to use, he planned a trip to Canada for just the two of us to visit some of his relatives and celebrate my birthday.

When the day arrived, as was his way, we rented what he referred to as a big butt car, a brand-new white Cadillac, and drove in comfort and style all the way to Vancouver.

Although his family insisted that we stay with them, Mark took me to the Weston hotel instead. I'll never forget walking through the elegant, enormous entryway, wondering what others thought as we both were in sweats and tennis shoes, carrying luggage in one hand and several plastic grocery bags with boxes of saltine crackers in the other.

We must have looked like some poor folks who'd just won a night's stay at the hotel and couldn't afford anything else to eat.

After a night on the town, we checked out the hotel's swimming pool. Feeling self-conscious in a bathing suit, I told Mark I wouldn't get in if there were a crowd of people. He assured me it wouldn't be as it was late in the evening, but that was not the case when we arrived.

Without a second thought, Mark tossed his robe onto a lounge chair, sauntered to the side of the pool as if he were about to jump in, and it vacated in less than two seconds.

I'd seen nothing like it before and about died laughing.

We jumped in the water, I wrapped my arms around his neck and planted a big ol' soggy kiss on his cheek. Like a paternal gorilla, he swung me around to his back and pulled me all around the pool.

Time seemed to stand still while we splashed and played, our worries and responsibilities miles away. We watched a movie later, or tried to, but ended up dropping off into a sound sleep instead.

Early the next morning I was awakened by the screeching of hundreds of gulls, not unlike that of an Alfred Hitchcock movie. I searched for the source of the noise and found Mark standing on the balcony flinging saltine crackers at them like a skeet shooter.

With an evil laugh, he asked if I wanted to join him. I meandered half-awake to the balcony but stopped at the threshold when I saw several of our neighbors glaring at him. I ducked back in, declining participation in the maniacal ritual.

That afternoon we joined his favorite Aunt Lil and her family for Dim Sum, walked through Stanley Park with his cousin, and then headed back home. Although brief, it was a memorable birthday for sure.

We'd only just arrived when Mark's mom called. Recent test results revealed she had only months left to live and not likely to make it for our wedding.

We went to our bedroom and closed the door. He laid down on the bed, took me in his arms, and cried.

My heart ached for him. I'd never seen him cry before, or any man shed a tear for that matter and didn't know what to do other than to hold him as close as I could.

I cried along with him and worried about the challenges that lay ahead. After a while, we shared the news with the children.

The following week was short because of the upcoming holiday. Although it wasn't time for my customary flower delivery, he made a surprise visit to my office following his appointment at the dentist, with grocery store flowers.

He couldn't stay long as he had to return to work, but Safeway flowers and a personal visit from my Hunny Bunny, no matter how short, was a fair trade for delivery flowers any day.

Thanksgiving was split amongst our families. Mark's children would visit with their mom for a while, and we'd visit mine until it was time to pick them up.

After that, we'd have the traditional turkey feast with all the fixings at his moms, and then the following day, Mark, the kids, and I would have our own dinner at home.

But this year would be different, the somber thought of how it might be the last Thanksgiving with his mom, weighed heavy on the family's hearts, making it difficult for anyone to be in the holiday spirit.

To lighten the mood on the way to her house, I asked the kids to share what each was most thankful for, but before they could respond, Mark did me one better, and bellowed, "Good gas!"

This outlandish outburst was followed by a tremendous evil laugh, echoed by screeching laughter and armpit farts from the kids.

I flatlined that one and never learned what they all were most thankful for.

More relatives visited that year than before; choosing to ignore the reality and seriousness of her fate, his mom went about dinner like she always did year after year, smiling, laughing, and joking, with not a care in the world.

The kids played with the other young relatives while the adults visited. Everything was as it always was. And what we thought would be a solemn Thanksgiving turned out to be one of the better ones.

Because Mark and I had to work a half shift the next day, with Lexi's insistence, his sister said she could stay the night until I picked her up on my way home from work the next day.

With a final round of hugs and kisses for all, Mark, the boys, and I headed back to our place. The drive was quiet. My mind was preoccupied with the thought of how devastated Mark would be without his mom, and how learning to live without her would be our greatest trial yet.

PART II

ELEVEN

*U*p early, I skated through my morning routine, excited for one last day of work before the holiday weekend. Mark's shift, a half day substitute route, started later than mine which allowed him more time for shut-eye.

I collected my purse, keys, and lunch, and stopped by our room to say goodbye. As I leaned over to kiss him on the cheek, I about jumped out of my skin when he grabbed my arms and pulled me closer; I thought he was asleep.

Ignoring his subtle intentions, we went over the plan for the children: Lexi would remain with his sister and mom until I picked her up; his oldest would be at work until late; his youngest would stay home alone, and my son Dale would go to work with him.

His assurance to call during his break wafted in the wake of my urgent departure.

As Mark and Dale were about to leave a few hours later, my sister Maggie, who lived on the opposite side of town, lurched awake from a sound sleep.

∽

Like the vicious beating of Jumanji drums, her heart pounded so intensely that it jolted her from the depth of her unconscious sleep. She sat straight up in bed, still caught up in the nightmare she couldn't shake and tried in vain to make sense of it. Shook to the core of her soul, she had only one, consistent, overwhelming thought; she had to get her nephew Dale. She fumbled in the darkness for the phone and called her sister's house.

∽

Mark heard the phone ring as he and Dale climbed into his truck. He hesitated, but decided there was enough time, and ran to answer it. It was Lis' sister; she was crying and hysterical. The most he could make of her rambling was that she wanted him to leave Dale at home and be allowed to pick him up.

Confused by her irrational behavior, but without time to argue or to call Lis at work, he agreed to leave Dale at home. Without so much as a thank you or see you later, she slammed the phone down, and, forgetting her coat, flew out the door in her pajamas.

She looked like a wild woman, with makeup from the night before now smeared down her face from the tears she'd been crying and her hair a tangled mess, as she jumped into her car.

When she reached Dale, at last, Maggie took him in her arms and hugged him with all her might, crying harder than she'd ever had before.

She realized she'd confused and frightened him and explained how she'd had a scary dream, and just wanted him to visit her for the day.

I called home a few hours later to assure Dale had gone to work with Mark and was none too pleased to learn my sister had taken him instead.

I couldn't believe it. Mark knew we never went against *the plan* without talking it over first. I couldn't wait to see what kind of reason he had for letting Dale go with her.

He called a little before 2:30 p.m. and said he had a reasonable explanation for leaving Dale behind, but because he was a little late leaving from the Aurora Village to downtown, he would have to fill me in after he got home.

Annoyed or not, for the time being, I had no other choice but to settle for his brief explanation and wish him, as I always did, "Drive safe. I love you," and let him go back to work.

I was not looking forward to the inevitable confrontation with my sister when I picked Dale up later.

On the other side of town, sitting at his kitchen table in his dreary apartment, by the dim light of a 40-watt bulb, Steven Gary Cool impatiently strummed his fingertips across the Formica for the umpteenth time. The clock on the wall said it was 2:15 p.m.

Cool, 43, raggedy, tall and lean, a steely-eyed petty thief, Peeping Tom, a onetime Boy Scout, favored sunglasses at night, collected pornography, ate dinner at street missions, and lived off free money from his parents. It was not unusual for those who rode the metro on Aurora Avenue to see this scruffy character; that's why only larger, more intimidating bus drivers drove this specific route.

Cool suffered from both severe chronic back pain and outward signs of paranoia; he so feared and disliked drivers and other bus riders that he exposed a handgun to one fellow passenger, bragging how he was *gonna get a second* so he could deal with the *mean people who ride and drive buses*.

His first attempt failed. He'd walked up to the driver, pointed a gun at his head and pulled the trigger twice, but the weapon misfired. In the panic of the moment, the driver slammed on the brakes and opened the doors by mistake, allowing him a chance to escape.

Cool continued to strum his fingers; he couldn't take much more of the silence. He stood in haste and turned towards the kitchen to pick up a piece of paper from the floor.

PART II

Underneath the stove drawer, he found a grease laden pencil and wrote himself a note for later, "Don't put plastic containers in the oven," and then tossed both onto the filthy tile, adding to the confetti of other written reminders of the simplest of tasks.

Although Cool had been renting the sparse one-bedroom apartment for the past thirteen years, his place looked as though a transient occupied it.

A refrigerator stood empty and unused in the kitchen. A huge stack of outdated Metro bus schedules cluttered an otherwise empty bookcase near the entry door. An upright inflatable bed leaned against a wall. Tin foil covered all the windows. And in the bath, an aging clutter of creams and ointments littered an unused sink.

Cool glanced at the clock again; time to go. He pulled the fleece collar of his brown bomber jacket up to cover his ears, put on his sunglasses, stuffed his hands deep into the pockets of his coat, stepped out into the crisp November air and dashed the one block to the bus stop.

⁓

Mark's seventy-two-foot passenger articulated diesel bus continued to trundle southbound on Aurora Avenue North, stopping for passengers amid the strip malls, motels, and parking lots. Several boarded with Christmas packages from shopping and others were on their way into town for more shopping.

Some boarded for a spontaneous journey just glad to be outside after a week of pouring rain. Some seemed content just to be off their feet after a long work shift, looking forward to settling in for a brief nap during the ride home, while others headed off to work.

A few passengers read while others visited with each other. It was a quiet ride even with thirty-two passengers on board.

They occupied the seats in no specific order and only one passenger, the last to board, sat up front across from the driver, the seat Dale would have occupied had he gone to work with Mark.

As the bus approached the Aurora Bridge, that same passenger stood up and approached the driver as if he wanted to ask a question.

But the man didn't say a word. He pulled out a gun, pointed it at Mark, and shot him twice in his side instead.

It happened so fast Mark didn't have time to hit the emergency alarm. The man grabbed for the steering wheel, but Mark fought him off, struggling to stay alert and in control of the bus.

Their confrontation shattered the once lulling quiet. There were more popping sounds from the firearm. A passenger in the back yelled "Gun! Gun!!" In a panic, riders fell to their knees and covered their heads.

Before losing consciousness, Mark pushed on the brakes with the last bit of energy he had, leaving a permanent scar on the pavement. Despite his best efforts, his firm grip lessened, and he slumped unconscious over the steering wheel.

The bus torpedoed onward, veering left and skidding another hundred feet before losing control. It swerved into oncoming northbound traffic, hit a van, crushing it all the way to its bumper, jumped a fifteen-inch curb, and slammed into a guardrail.

Metal grated against metal and concrete as the bus ripped through a twenty-five-foot section of the railing, barreling right into a light pole, bending it in half.

And then Bus 359 flew off the Aurora Bridge.

PART II

TWELVE

Somebody yelled, "Oh my God! We're going off..." Passengers braced themselves for the impact, certain they would die, and the airborne bus fell as if in slow motion some forty feet to the ground. The sleepy little neighborhood with Colonial style homes would never be the same after what happened next.

The front end of the bus smashed onto the entry level of a two-story apartment complex. It slid down the side of the tenement, tore through evergreen trees, and ripped off porches and stairways on its way down.

Mark, not buckled in, was ejected headfirst through the windshield and onto the roof of the building. It sounded as if the bridge itself had imploded as the 40,000-pound bus crashed hard onto the front lawn of the dwelling.

Mostly in one piece, it wrapped itself around a tree in a V shape, almost coming to rest in the lap of Mark's beloved Fremont Troll.

Giant chunks of concrete followed its descent, showering whatever was below it with a swirl of glass, metal, and blood. People were screaming, seats were breaking, and 75 gallons of diesel fuel from a ruptured fuel tank, threatened the neighborhood. The exact location was fateful. Five seconds later it would have plunged over a hundred feet into Lake Union.

A man who lived in the apartment building was sitting on his front porch when the bus passed overhead. Another was taking a shower when he felt the building move.

He grabbed onto the sides of the tub, bracing himself for what he thought was the granddaddy earthquake of them all, and rushed dripping wet from the bathroom to grab his clothes. He looked towards his main entry and saw the door was ajar.

With caution, he approached it and looked outside. His front porch was gone; he looked down and stared into the frightened faces of people trapped inside of a broken bus.

Just a few feet away, another resident witnessed the same frightening scene, made the sign of the cross, and prayed, "God help them."

∽

The city's emergency dispatch radioed West, East, South, North precincts to the scene along with all enforcement agencies to stand by for possible mutual aide. Ten off-duty firefighters, five medic units, and twenty-seven aid vehicles were already on the scene.

Emergency vehicles, everything from ladder trucks to technical rescue teams, crowded the narrow streets. The quiet little neighborhood soon became a mini war zone. Sirens filled the air; orders screamed from the rescuers echoed through the street.

News crews descended upon the scene like vultures. Reporters narrated the setting right down to the grisliest detail.

The injured were twisted and scattered about like dolls, each crying and moaning for help. The smell of diesel fuel soaked the air; firefighters feared a catastrophic explosion would happen any moment.

Onlookers became rescuers, sixty-five to be exact, and others, looters, plundering anything worth value left behind.

Heroic bystanders labored together to release the front doors of the bus, while terrified passengers within pushed in desperation to force them open.

Once they gave way, dozens of paramedics and firefighters worked in quick succession to pull bloody riders out from the interior of the shattered bus.

With the entry cleared, they inspected the tail end for more victims and found several piled up in the rear stairwell. Lying at the bottom, was a man with his head stuck in the undercarriage, and they brought in the Jaws of Life to free him.

Alongside him, lay another victim's upper torso, the rest of him dangled outside of the ripped-open bus. A passerby saw this, pulled the man all the way out, and placed him on the ground.

On the lawn of the apartment, another passenger's screams pierced the cold air as a medical team worked to put a splint on his leg bone that stuck out the side of his pants.

Those injured the most were lifted onto backboards and out the side windows while, only by miracle, others walked out on their own.

As the evacuation continued, rescuers yelled into the bus, "Where's the driver? Has anyone seen the driver?"

One of the injured whispered, "He's been shot. Somebody shot the driver several times!"

Diesel fuel saturated the interior of the bus; it flowed onto the ground and down the street, spreading fumes throughout the scene, coating anyone and anything in its path, making rescue efforts difficult and dangerous.

Outside of the bus, firefighters worked at a frantic pace to connect a generator, hoses to nearby fire hydrants, and lights.

Even more firefighters worked above the scene, at the top of the bridge, to tie off a part of the east guardrail and secure a light pole that dangled over the side.

Other rescue teams searched the apartment building for casualties, and found none, only minor injuries, ordering any remaining tenants to evacuate.

They disconnected the electricity and worked at a steadfast speed, using whatever force necessary to enter each apartment that wasn't damaged or unsafe and flip the circuit breakers off.

A dog team searched the entire scene for victims that may have wandered off and collapsed but found none.

A police officer approached a semi-hurt but conscious victim and asked if he had witnessed the shooting. He said he had and described the shooter as a white male in his 40s, about six feet two inches tall, 190-200 lbs., wearing a tan hat and coat, dark glasses, and carrying a bag of some sort.

The officer asked if he'd walk around the scene with him to locate the suspect. They searched the entire area and the crowd of onlookers, but he couldn't identify the suspect.

Although bodies were strewn all over the place, the driver was not among them. The police declared the horrific scene a homicide investigation.

They cordoned off a large area and posted a few officers to guard it, assigned others to establish crowd and traffic control so rescue vehicles could leave with the injured, and had several others search for the missing driver.

A firefighter paramedic arrived on the scene; he put on an orange colored vest with the word TRIAGE written on it in bold black letters and sorted the injured victims.

His job was both simple and agonizing. He had to decide who needed immediate help, who could wait, and who was beyond help.

A quick look or a hand on the chest measured respiratory rate, a flick of the fingers on the wrist found both pulse and blood pressure to determine if a victim was bleeding out, and some quick, simple questions gauged mental status.

Each assessment took about five seconds. If a victim failed one test, they got a red ribbon wrapped around their arm for priority treatment and taken immediately to the hospital.

The walking wounded or uninjured got green tags; serious but responsive, yellow tags. Those not breathing got one last chance, if they didn't breathe or were beyond help at the scene, black tags.

He tagged about three-fourths with red ribbons. Next, he assigned each of the injured a number. A police officer stood by the final victim the firefighter had to assess. He told the officer the man fit the suspect's description.

Covered in dirt and blood, he had a light pulse, shallow breathing, and dark circles around both of his eyes, indicative of a head injury.

Upon further inspection, he found a single gunshot wound to his head. The policeman searched his body for a weapon, but it came up clean.

Medics intubated the victim and continued to breathe for him as they strapped him to a backboard. The fireman tied a red ribbon around his arm, and one of the waiting ambulances took him to the hospital.

Rescuer worked on the bloody passengers in relay, untangling I.V. tubing, preparing O2 bottles, C-collars, tape, and ringers, making them ready as fast as they could, stopping only when a bleeding victim needed CPR, or to insert a breathing tube down their throat, or to assist another with a ventilating bag.

Like a well-oiled machine, they took and recorded vitals, summarized and bandaged injuries, and then strapped the victims onto backboards and loaded them into waiting ambulances.

Local area hospitals scrambled to empty beds as fast as they could for the influx of incoming casualties.

A command officer on the phone with a doctor from Harborview Medical Center received directions: I have two yellows and a red, "Go to Swedish;" I have three yellows, "Go to Ballard;"

Volunteers comforted the injured waiting in stunned silence for their turn to go to the hospital. Within two hours, all the victims had been taken to area hospitals.

❦

Around 3:30 p.m. a friend of mine called me at work; she seemed upset.

"What route is Mark driving today? Was he going to be traveling on Aurora?"

"Yes, he is substituting on the route 6 and will be driving on Aurora. Why?"

"There has been a terrible accident..." her voice trailed off.

I didn't hear the rest of what she had to say. My heart pounded loud in my ears and my stomach turned and twisted. I swallowed past the sickening burn of bile in my throat and started shaking as if I were freezing cold; yet, I was perspiring.

The room seemed to close in around me. I couldn't catch my breath and searched in my purse for my inhaler; I took two puffs, but I still couldn't breathe.

PART II

∽

A firefighter looked up at the roof of the apartment building and noticed a pair of legs dangling, but not moving, over the side. He called for a rescue team to grab a ladder, their equipment, and supplies. They approached the injured person and recognized the familiar uniform, they'd found the missing driver.

Mark was lying face down. They rolled him over and observed several gunshot wounds. Unable to detect a pulse, they worked on his chest with dedication.

Defeated and powerless, their lead instructed them to stop helping him; they were too late.

Mark's eyes became fixed and pale gray, and his respirations slowed. With one final breath, he whispered "Lis."

Despite their best efforts, he was pronounced dead at the scene.

∽

Numb, I stared at the phone, waiting for Mark's call to reassure me he was all right, yet somehow, I knew it would never come.

I rubbed my eyes. When I opened them again, they came to rest on a poster on a wall next to my desk; it read, "Trust in the LORD with all your heart and lean not on your own understanding." Proverbs 3:5.

A doctor from the clinic approached my desk, "Are you all right?" he asked.

His lips moved, but I couldn't understand his words, and mumbled how I wanted to go home.

In a daze, I made it to the bus stop, and sat toward the front as it traveled North on I-5. Strangers strained to see out the west side windows at the commotion happening across the water.

A battle ensued in my head. One side told me it was Mark, and the other shrieked for it to *Shut up!*

I wanted to put my hands over my ears and scream, but most of all I wanted to shout for everyone to *Sit the hell down and quit staring out the windows!*

∽

At 4:45 pm officers located an AMT Backup .380 pistol near the front door of the bus and collected more evidence at the scene. They directed detectives to each of the hospitals to interview witnesses and identify the suspect.

∽

It seemed to take forever to reach the Park and Ride. When we arrived at long last, I ran to my car and drove home on auto-pilot. When I pulled into our driveway, I jumped out of the car, burst open the front door, and turned on the TV.

The clash in my head ensued as I watched the calamity unfold. To convince the pessimist in my head, I said aloud, *See, it was the 359, not Mark's 6. He'll be calling soon to say so.*

⁓

Firefighters stood by with a hose line while other firefighters placed several large rescue-lifting bags under the bus. A large, heavy-duty, Metro tow truck backed up to the wreckage, and together they lifted it. Rescuers checked underneath for victims but found none.

⁓

The phone rang, startling me out of my self-argument, but my excitement was brief. It was only his sister, also as upset as I was.

She said she too believed it couldn't be Mark because he'd told her he would be driving the number 6 that day, not the 359 in question.

A car pulled into the driveway. I looked at the TV again. The news media showed firefighters performing CPR on the driver.

What transpired next seemed to happen in slow motion.

I looked back at the familiar white sedan parked in the driveway. My heart sank; for a moment I remembered city officials in a similar car coming for my sister and me.

It hit me like a ton of bricks when I realized why they were there. The phone slipped from my hands, and I walked towards the door.

"He's gone! He's gone! He's gone!" my mind screamed; I pressed my hands over my ears to quiet the noise.

The car doors opened, and two individuals climbed out. I yelled for them to go away.

My knees turned into jelly. Like Alice in Wonderland, I felt myself falling into some nightmarish reality. "No! No! No!" I screamed, and my body crumpled.

Strong but loving hands caught me by my elbows and stopped my fall. The two people were Mark's supervisors. They told me what I already knew.

I found myself back at the phone and cried to Mark's sister how Mark's supervisors were there and said it was his bus, and they'd come to take me to the hospital.

PART II

I babbled and cried the entire trip, and don't remember a thing I said.

∽

With the attention and efforts of four firefighters, a ladder truck carefully removed Mark's body from the apartment roof. The media recorded its slow descent, etching the scene permanently into the minds of thousands of viewers.

On a backboard, secured and far from the media, his body, covered with a yellow rescue blanket and a tarp, laid waiting under the bridge for the coroner.

∽

Like a Hollywood movie, the police surrounded the hospital. News crews and cameras were in full force. Metro officials ushered me away from them through a side door and into a private waiting area.

It was like Grand Central Station. I'd never seen so many people in one place before. King County Executives filed in and out of the waiting area offering their deepest condolences.

Their voices blended together, monotone, and garbled. A sea of arms came to hug me from all directions. I clung to each one, desperate for their energy, hoping it was enough to snap me out of my nightmarish dream fog.

But my efforts were in vain; no number of hugs or energy could bring me back to the reality I sought.

I begged the hospital staff to take me to Mark, but my requests fell on deaf ears. A hospital counselor came in. She explained it was because authorities considered his death a homicide, and they wouldn't allow me to see him just yet.I didn't care what her rationalization was. Through tears, and near hysteria, I pleaded "Please at least allow me to touch his hand, so I know it's true!"

I wanted to touch him as I remembered him, warm, not cold, not dead.

She told me she couldn't; that she wasn't allowed to. I cried harder; I couldn't understand her reasoning. Nothing made sense; all I wanted, more than anything in the world, was to be with him and see for myself.

Amidst the confusion, my best friend arrived. Like a protective mother, she shooed all of them out of the room, regardless of authority, and took me into her arms. She rocked me gently and stroked my hair, in the same way she would soothe one of her daughters.

Once I had my wits about me, she led me out of the room, down a back hallway, and to her car where her husband was waiting to take me to my house.

She offered how I could stay with them, but I declined, I just wanted to be alone.

Once at my house, she walked me in and asked again if I'd be all right. I assured her I would and hugged her goodbye.

Exhausted, I prepared for bed, skipping the Pooh and Piglet flannel pajamas Mark had given me for my birthday, choosing a t-shirt of his from the laundry instead, and changed into that.

I also found a fragrant work shirt of his from the day before, pulled it down over his pillow, and climbed into bed.

For the first time, my side of the bed was as cold as his. Shivering, I curled my body around his pillow, buried my face into the smell of his shirt, and cried.

I prayed and cried until my throat and eyes stung, *please don't let this be true, please, please Mark, come home.* And somehow, I fell into a deep sleep.

PART II

THIRTEEN

Daylight filled the room, my head pounded, and my eyes hurt when I tried to open them. I stretched across the bed to pull Mark closer, but didn't find him, and figured he was up already.

Then, I understood, and terror seized my heart like an unforgiving vice as the events of the day before spun around in my mind.

I gathered his pillow to my chest and cried myself back to sleep.

Sometime later, I awoke to the sounds of someone in the house. To this day, I couldn't tell you who it was; sweet and soothing like an angel she called for me.

I felt like I was in a dream; everything seemed to happen in slow motion. With love and patience, she guided me through the motions of preparing for the day, and then drove me to Mark's mom's where Lexi waited for me.

My appearance frightened her. She lowered her tear-filled eyes and hugged me as if I were a delicate flower. I sat at the kitchen table. His children were there. They didn't approach me.

The house buzzed with people dropping by to offer their condolences, or to leave warm food for the family.

Occasionally, I'd overhear someone say, "She's not up to visiting right now."

The television on the counter blared news reports of the incident as if on repeat. Hours later, she returned me to my house. Maggie brought Lexi and Dale home with her.

Like the movie Mark and I loved so much, the same scene played over again for several days. I didn't understand why I had to go every day, but I went. Each time I sat at the kitchen table near the window where I could see Whidbey Island in the far distance, evidence the fairy tale had once existed.

An occasional tear welled in my eyes and streamed down my face. I wanted to detach from the world that continued to move around me, so, I stared into space until she took me home again.

What I wanted was to be left alone, and to stay in bed until I withered away and died. What I wanted most of all was Mark.

I found peace within the safety of our home, but the reminders were there too. Each day I returned, I'd find several business cards wedged into the cracks of our front door from the news media who wanted an interview, but the possibility of that ever happening was inconceivable.

I'd forgotten to feed Mark's animals from the bracken, and one by one they stopped coming to the deck for food, all except for a solitary stellar jay.

Sometimes I paid him homage with a few peanuts from the offering can, and no matter if I remembered or not, he still came.

Having our number listed in the local directory kept our phone on a continual ring, flooding our answering machine with messages. Before long, I yanked both from the wall just to make it all stop, to keep the outside from coming in.

Flowers and letters continued to multiply on the porch. To read them only reminded me of what I was so determined to deny, and I tucked them all away for someday instead.

The food, flowers, and notes from strangers, so many affected, like ripples in the water, by the same senseless act on that horrible day. As much as I wanted to separate myself from it all, I felt uplifted by their thoughtfulness at the same time.

Soon the day to assemble funeral clothes for Mark settled its heavy burden on my shoulders. I felt perplexed about the task before me as I sat at the end of our bed and stared, for what seemed to be an eternity, at our closet.

He'd always dressed himself; wearing either his work uniform, sweats, or shorts with t-shirts. I'd never seen him in a suit before, or monkey suit as he would have called it. We hadn't even bought his tux for the wedding yet. Anything formal would require a custom fitting.

I said aloud, *A funeral, what would you wear to a funeral?*

Suddenly, the door on Mark's side of the closet shook and rattled. Unfazed, I slid the door open and found a dress shirt and blazer on the other side of his work clothes, the same set he wore a few years earlier for his eldest sister's funeral, but I couldn't find pants.

I called his mom and explained the dilemma.

She called back a short while later and said the funeral director told her not to worry, as he could keep Mark's lower half covered during services, omitting the need for pants.

How like him to be in his underwear for his memorial service.

◌

A man from the Big Brothers program, Jim, brought Dale to the scene of ground zero the day after it happened, as he wanted to put flowers on daddy Mark's chair.

Metro officials didn't mind postponing towing the wreckage for a few more minutes, and lifted the crime scene tape, allowing them to board the mangled bus.

They stared at the empty driver's seat in silence. Dale choked back tears as he placed his bouquet on the seat. They stepped off the bus and watched as it was towed away.

∽

Metro returned Mark's belongings to his mom. Any money he had in his possession they gave to his sons. I asked for the keychain I gave him for his birthday years before and his workbag.

The cheap little sack hadn't suffered any damage outside of the usual wear and tear. I unzipped each of its pockets and investigated their contents.

I laughed when I came across some holistic medicine he had been using. He used to tease me about my naturopathic cures, referring to them all as hocus-pocus.

After examining each little nook and cranny, I zipped all the pockets closed again, careful to leave everything just as he'd left it.

The little doll Lex gave him was missing, and it broke my heart. I wiped at the tears beginning to trickle down my cheeks, I mourned for the doll too.

Although the bag might seem trivial to others, for me it was priceless, and I would treasure it always. The insignificant thing affected his eldest sister's cat, a chubby orange- and cream-colored tabby named Marmalade, whom his mother inherited after her death.

She wouldn't let anyone near her except for Mark. Whenever he visited, she'd plop herself at his feet, and roll all over the floor until he stopped whatever he was doing to pet her.

The day his bag arrived, she somehow knew it was his. Her owl-sized eyes turned into narrow slits as she scrutinized my every move. No longer had I put the bag down, she pounced on it, purred her loudest, and rolled all over it with wild abandon.

She startled me even more by what she did next.

Without a second thought, she jumped up on my lap, did a somersault, almost falling off as she wriggled and squirmed, and settled in for a deep massage.

I kept my hands away from her until I was sure she wouldn't take one off. Starting under her chin, she continued to purr like a steam engine, pausing only to nudge my hand if I stopped scratching.

She down shifted her loud drone into a low consoling hum, and remained that way until I left, and continued with the same ritual whenever I visited thereafter. It seemed as if she was saying she missed him too.

∽

As time waits for no one, cleanup crews erased the aftermath of the scene. The whole thing seemed nonexistent if it hadn't been for the media continuing to air the details.

Someone taped a metallic teardrop under one of the troll's eyes, covering its lap in a shrine of flowers and candles. Another person cut our engagement photo from the newspaper, enlarged it, and taped it onto one of the bridge's supports where even more flowers and candles grew.

Throughout King County, government buildings flew their flags at half-staff for a few days. At all the transit bases, Metro set up a table for mourners to leave cards, donations, or to write remembrances in a journal. They even created a web page where mourners could leave their thoughts and condolences.

∽

The cacophonous atmosphere of visitors and media subsided long enough to make funeral arrangements. Mark's family organized the details and ran them by me on occasion to see what I thought, but I refused to be part of it.

I believed if I didn't go along with the idea he died, it would make it untrue.

All that crazy thinking stopped the day Barry Samet, the President from the Union who represented all the Metro employees, entered my life.

Although he was a kind and funny man, he was also firm in all he believed in, making it his sole mission to involve me in the planning of Mark's memorial service, whether I wanted to or not.

He wouldn't let me sit on the sidelines, and wither away. Unlike others who'd ask me a question, and walk away if I didn't feel like answering, he'd wait for as long as it took until I did, not allowing me to hide behind the curtain I'd put up for myself.

You can imagine how shocked I was the day he called to ask how Mark would want us to remember him. I wanted the world to swallow me up.

Remembered? If we're remembering him, that would mean he's gone somewhere.

No, we will not remember him!

A large lump formed in my throat, aching worse than the tonsillectomy I had as a kid, and I struggled to swallow past it to answer him.

PART II

Unaffected by my display of defiance, he waited for a reply. A swell of burning tears cascaded down my cheeks.

Only one word found its way to the surface, "big."

FOURTEEN

*J*ust when I thought things couldn't get worse, came the day of the viewing. All day and into the evening Mark's closest friends and family gathered at his mom's house and drove in little groups to the funeral home. They invited me to go along, but I avoided the dreaded ritual with the excuse of not being ready yet.

With the last of the visitors gone, convinced I'd succeeded and about to relax, my best friend arrived. Not willing to take no for an answer, along with loving intervention from Mark's sister, they coaxed me into going, even if it was the middle of the night.

As we entered the building, they stood on either side of me with their arms wrapped secure and supportive around my waist.

For a funeral home, it was inviting, not cold and indifferent as I had imagined it would be, but it was too quiet.

Candles burned throughout, creating a tranquil ambience that calmed my nerves some. I scanned the room in search of Mark's body and breathed a sigh relief when I didn't find him.

The girls guided me towards a pair of large white double doors; somehow, I knew Mark lay beyond them. They each opened a side panel to another room, much darker, more solemn, and foreboding than the foyer.

They guided me in, but my knees buckled, and my heart skipped a beat.

Like a fish out of water, I gulped in the stale air and struggled to catch my breath.

To save myself from any more unforeseen trauma, I dug my heels into the carpet, and cried, "No! No! No! Not yet! Not yet!"

With all the love and patience in the world, they guided me away from the room to a bench just outside the door, and we sat down together.

They wiped the tears from my face, stroked my hair, and whispered consoling words. When I was ready to try again, we stood arm in arm and walked towards the darker room once more.

But again, I only made it as far as the edge before fear, greater than my dread of spiders, shot through my body with lightning-bolt sharpness and made my legs buckle.

I couldn't make myself go in there. As tolerant as saints, the girls walked me back to the bench until I was ready to give it another go.

PART II

I don't know how many times it took to get me past the threshold. They deserve a Medal of Honor if there were one for such heroic efforts.

I sat next to Mark on a bench next to his casket; my body shook uncontrollably as if I were freezing cold. I took a deep breath and stood beside him. My knees wobbled as I reached out to touch his hand. It felt like ice.

I laid my head on his chest. It was as hard as cement. I leaned into the casket and wrapped my arms around him and cried like I've never cried before.

My tears made his face wet as I kissed his cheeks, his forehead, his nose, and his eyes. I nuzzled into the familiar nape of his neck and buried my face into his hair, seeking his warmth, his smell, expecting the stroke of his hand to assure me everything would be all right.

But nothing happened. I hugged him even tighter and cried harder, "No! No! No! Hunny Bunny, Hunny Bunny, please! Wake up! Wake up! Wake up!"

I cried and cried. The mournful song of my wounded soul echoed throughout the corridors. I wept until my throat, my jaw, my eyes, and my heart hurt.

The girls were beside me again. I reached into my coat pocket and brought out the Father's Day button the kids made for him years before, and the guardian angel key chain he always carried.

My hands shook as I secured the button onto his lapel and placed the key chain in his breast pocket. I kissed his face one more time and let the girls guide me out to the car, and back to his mom's house.

That night I fell into bed exhausted, but even as tired as I was, sleep eluded me. I had never been so sick or drained in my life. There wasn't a smidgeon of my body that didn't ache, and none as throbbing as my heart was.

I tried to etch in my mind right down to the simplest detail our nightly ritual, and spoke aloud to the darkness, *"I miss the way you warmed my side of the bed, and the sucking noises you made while you flossed and brushed your teeth as you walked around the house, securing it for the night."*

"I miss the way you cracked me up in the way you exaggerated spitting the depleted toothpaste into the sink, and the even louder spitting and gargling noises as you swished the water inside your cheeks."

"I bet you heard me laughing, and that's why you'd do a final encore of sucking your teeth on your way to bed."

I couldn't chase away the image of Mark lying in that coffin from my mind. Nothing made sense; what once was a bright and promising future had become an eternal black hole.

My heart ached when I thought of the years we'd worked so hard to bring our lives together, and I cursed myself for the precious time I'd wasted with my stubborn independence.

I mourned too for our daughter, Lillian Rose, who would never be.

I sought his pillow for comfort but discovered that his scent had worn away, and found only sorrow instead.

Unafraid of the stillness of the night or the footsteps pacing outside our bedroom, I found comfort instead and drifted off into a deep sleep.

⁓

The following days and nights blended together in a sea of tears, causing me to drift further and further away from Mark. The farther I drifted, the more afraid and insecure I became.

Soon, the night of the family's memorial service was upon me. I allowed Dale to be a part of it, but not Lexi, she was still too young to understand.

The media was already swarming when we arrived at the church. They asked how we were doing. How do you answer such a question? Mark and I were private people, unknowns until now; I felt as if I were in a glass bowl, all eyes on me, judging each reaction.

In all honesty, I didn't know how I was to react.

As much as I fought back tears for fear it was too much, it was no use. My emotions had taken over, and they came at will.

Uncertain if it was appropriate to smile at well-wishers, I received them with blank stares instead. The worst moments were the times when I *should have* been crying but didn't have a single tear left to shed. What came out instead were more like the moans of a wounded animal.

Adding insult to injury, was when I overheard someone say, "She really puts on a great show, huh?"

Several hundred mourners came to pay their respects and to offer their condolences. Because there wasn't enough room in the church, they had to televise the service in another building. Although I knew they meant well, I resented the words, "I'm sorry for your loss" and "It's better to have loved and lost, dear, than to have never loved at all."

Their words echoed in my mind like the chants from the children who taunted me in elementary school. It was all I could do not to scream and lash out at anyone who uttered them, as if all of this was their fault.

Among the mourners were dozens of Mark's Metro colleagues. Each wore black armbands and black buttons with Mark's work ID number 2106 printed in white on them. As well were many longtime passengers and some of his friends from his high school days; I'm sure he didn't know just how many lives he'd touched.

PART II

At 7 p.m., coinciding with the starting of the services, Metro's General Manager requested through each coach's PA system for all operators to stop their buses at the safest location for a brief tribute to Mark.

The memorial service was as surreal as it was overwhelming. The church was beautiful. Mark's photograph, flowers, wreaths, and personal mementos surrounded the priest podium. Among them was the heirloom I'd sewn for his fortieth birthday.

I turned over his funeral announcement and smiled. At the bottom of the page, was a cameo replica of his little lost doll, his precious Dollface.

The unceasing tide welled in my eyes, the thoughtfulness meant more to me than the person who placed it there would ever know.

His sister and I clung to each other throughout the services. I stood proud for Mark, maintaining composure throughout most of the service. The greatest test of my resolve were the times when friends of his spoke of things they'd most remember him for.

After, the priest blessed Mark and all his mourners, and led the procession out of the church. Family members placed a single rose on Mark's coffin as it passed by, filing out behind it in procession for the viewing, followed by the rest of the mourners.

Later, some gathered in the reception hall to visit, but I didn't want to be around so many people, nor did I want to be fodder for the evening news, so my best friend snuck me out the back door and into her car.

Against her better judgment, she dropped me off at my house. It seemed as if wanting to be alone wasn't an appropriate reaction either; what was wrong with being alone?

It seemed all anybody wanted to talk about was the day it happened, or to ask how I was feeling, and I didn't want to talk about either, or anything at all for that matter.

Home alone at last. I curled up with Mark's favorite pillow on the living room couch and spoke to him. *"I still laugh when I think about your daily return-from-work routine, how you'd make a beeline to our room, strip out of your uncomfortable work clothes as if you were shedding the shackles of the day, and then, once free from their confinement, how you'd dance around naked, announcing with delight to one and all you were doing the dangle."*

And then I laughed, a real, from the gut, chuckle, the first time in what seemed an eternity, and continued with my conversation,

"After your moment of insanity, you'd put on your cotton shorts and tank top and head for the kitchen in search of food. Sometimes it hurt my feelings when you didn't want what I'd fixed for me and the kids for dinner.

"You said a heavy meal late at night would upset your stomach, and you'd rather have popcorn instead. Then, with your meal of choice, a supersized glass of ice water, your favorite tattered pale green pillow, and your newspaper, you'd find a comfortable spot on the living room floor to unwind.

"Though you seldom got any time to yourself, your downtime always interrupted with the children's incessant chatter, me, or the cats laying in the middle of your paper, you never complained.

"And I remember how you loved the times I rubbed your feet while you relaxed, I'm sorry I never softened that hard patch just underneath your large toe."

I returned to the present and walked to the hall closet in search of another piece of clothing with his cologne on it.

The flannel shirt-coat he wore when he worked out in the yard, the one he wore to chop down our annual Christmas tree, was the last of his things with his scent on it; I wrapped it around his pillow, curled myself around it, and drifted in and out of sleep.

⁂

I dreamt Mark and I were visiting on a park bench, but it didn't seem like a dream; it seemed real. I saw and heard him as plain as day.

He laughed at my continual string of questions and answered each one of my concerns; I woke up before we could say goodbye.

I struggled to fall back to sleep, hoping to continue with our visit. My mind raced as I rifled through the recesses of my brain, in hopes of holding onto our conversation, but all was lost. For the life of me, I couldn't recall one word.

Not unlike our favorite movie, Ground Hog Day, every morning seemed like the last, reminding me of what I fought so hard to deny. I could think of nothing else, and soon forgot what life I had before *it* happened.

The morning brought Mark's burial. It was too much. I couldn't take anymore. No sooner had I made it to the surface, another wave would drag me under.

I wanted to stay in bed with the covers over my head. My entire body hurt; I felt like something the cat dragged in and spit out, no, worse than that, what they'd buried in their litter box.

But hiding wasn't an option. Just as I was about to fall back to sleep, my guardian angel arrived to pull me back into the world of the living.

PART II

FIFTEEN

As much as I dreaded and wanted to avoid the day, I went about the preparations in a brain fog. I didn't have a set of funeral clothes in my wardrobe either, so I settled for a black pair of slacks and a blouse.

It was a fitting day for a burial; just above freezing, calm winds, overcast, and gloomy. The family assembled at Mark's mom's house.

Mark's brothers and his sons, including Dale, would be the pallbearers. Lex stayed with my sister. Several black limousines arrived. It wasn't how I'd planned my first ride in one. The drivers escorted us to the sedans.

The inside of the fancy Lincoln distracted the children for a moment. I wanted them to sit still, to act respectful, but I reminded myself they were just children.

Multitudes of people gathered at the church, thank god the car had dark windows.

We stopped, and to my horror, Mark's sister-in-law reached inside, and motioned for me to come out. With sympathy and understanding, she coaxed me out of the car, explaining how we were to see Mark one last time, rushing me past the crowd, and into the church.

The family assembled around the casket. I stood next to his eldest brother who flew in from California. The priest said a final blessing and reached to close Mark's cocoon. I lost it; my legs buckled.

I grabbed onto the eldest brother's arm with one hand and reached for Mark with the other. He put his arms around me, and whispered lovingly like Mark, "You have to let him go now."

Like the wounded animal in my soul, an uncontrollable cry from deep within my heart exploded, "No, no, no, Hunny Bunny, noooo!"

He pulled me back to allow the priest to close the casket, and then Mark's sister-in-law assisted me back to the car.

They hadn't even had the interment yet, and I was already a mess. The children stared at me. I turned away and looked out the window. I chastised myself for the way I'd reacted, or overreacted.

My poor Dale. He had never seen me behave like this before. I tried to give myself some credit, I mean, how was I to prepare? Would I have reacted differently had I known ahead of time?

These kinds of crazy thoughts chased around in my head. I might as well have had boxing gloves to hit myself with.

To brighten my mood some, Dale pointed towards the back window and told me to look. Stretched two miles deep or better, a convoy of Metro buses and vans, official cars, and other mourners in vehicles of various shapes and sizes, lined up behind us.

On both sides and in front, several motorcycle police officers escorted the family along the entire six-mile procession to the cemetery, stopping traffic at all the intersections to allow the massive convoy to pass.

It was impressive. The heaviness in my heart lightened a little, and I smiled at Dale.

Once at the cemetery, I joined Mark's mom. We walked arm in arm in quiet reverence to our seats next to the burial site. My heart ached for her. She'd walked this same path recently, burying both a husband and a daughter, in the same place where they were about to lay her favorite son, and where she herself would soon rest alongside them.

We waited in silence as the pallbearers brought Mark's coffin to rest before us. Although the smallest, Dale walked proud and brave as he helped to carry the casket of the only father he had ever known.

I was so proud of him. I'm sure it would be the most gut-wrenching thing he'd ever have to do.

My best friend stood behind me and placed her hands on my shoulders throughout the ceremony. It was a miracle I'd kept my composure. Afterwards, family and friends gathered at his mom's, many of whom I had never met.

Even there, my home away from home, I sensed a cold indifference. It made me feel awkward and uncomfortable, so I had my best friend take me home.

I missed the kids and needing their distraction I called Maggie to bring them home, she couldn't have been happier.

Their presence seemed to give the neighbors the green light. I didn't realize how many wonderful people lived around us, but it was just what I needed.

For a while, they brought much-appreciated food and conversation. No one talked about *it*; little did anyone know, that gave me more comfort than anything else.

Sweet notes of condolences and flowers brightened our front steps, and one time the children found stuffed animals on our back porch.

Dale and Lexi gave my life purpose. When I cared for them, I thought less of how miserable I was and managed through each day.

One thing challenged my autopilot like no other, keeping the house warm.

PART II

To cut heating costs, Mark had dismantled all the wall heaters in the house when we moved in and deemed a wood burning, potbelly stove our primary source of heat.

That was fine and dandy while he managed the thing, but now with the match in my hands, I couldn't get the miserable monster to start regardless of what I did.

I stared at the menacing stacks of wood and kindling in our driveway Mark's friends continued to bring.

It didn't matter. Regardless of which method they shared for the fine art of fire making, going to great lengths along with step by step demonstrations, it still wouldn't catch a flame for me, and kicking, berating, and hitting it with an iron poker wouldn't make it work either.

When had I become so helpless?

Before I caused too much damage, a neighbor and her husband offered to drop by in the mornings to get it going; my challenge was to keep it going.

The house stayed cozy most of the day but morphed into a meat locker in the middle of the night. To keep us all warm, I brought the children into our bed for the rest of the night. They slept like newborn kittens, cuddling in a heap of arms, legs, blankets, and pillows, but not me.

I laid awake, whiling away the long, exhaustive hours, tossing and turning, dreading the dawn of a new day. The images of Mark lying motionless in that box, beneath the cold, wet ground, haunted my efforts to sleep. He did not like to be cold or dirty.

꼭

Before long, there was another memorial for Mark to face. This one was larger, planned for all Metro employees and the public to pay their respects. When the day arrived, the family gathered once more at Mark's mom's, this time I allowed Lexi to attend.

Metro officials picked us up in company vans and brought us downtown to Metro's South Base. From there they escorted us onto a waiting bus. To my great surprise, Barry and his wife joined us.

The bus was older and painted a pretty fire engine red. Its directional sign displayed Mark's badge number and had a funeral wreath attached to the front. I remembered riding on one like it with Mommy.

As the driver brought the family bus around to the street side, I saw the most beautiful decorated bus, a replica like the last one Mark drove. It had a black wreath fastened to the front between the headlights, and Mark's ID number, 2106, emblazoned on the top and sides.

On either side of the carriage, draped over the advertising space, was a cloth with Mark's photo, his memorial date, and a message thanking him for 20 years of service. On each side of the front of the bus, black flags with the number 2106 printed in white waved proudly.

His work jacket hung on the back of the driver's seat along with a black ribbon affixed to the top of it; each of the surviving passengers' seats had purple ribbons tied to the top, among them, a sole black ribbon honored the one passenger that died. There wasn't a ribbon for the shooter.

The driver's seat remained empty, pulled along instead by a tow truck, bearing another memorial wreath. With two Seattle Police Officers on motorcycles as escorts, the procession began.

Our coach was next, followed by a bus carrying Metro officials; another with Metro drivers and employees, and yet another followed carrying the same.

Memorial wreaths adorned each bus with Mark's ID number displayed on their directional signs. Some even had notes of condolences written on their bulletin boards on either side of their buses.

To my disbelief, beyond them, stretched out as far as one could see, a sea of busses joined the convoy just like the day of Mark's funeral procession. Barry said there must have been 80 or more from all around the U.S. and Canada, including area fire engines and various transit vans too.

Just as thrilled as the kids, I felt excitement bubble in my chest, but I didn't dare show it. Unsure of what my reactions should be, I sat alone in my seat in quiet, stoic reverence.

We traveled at a slow pace up 4th avenue. The following convoy merged into two columns, side-by-side, in silent solidarity. Crowds lined either side of the street. Several people carried signs thanking the drivers; some cried, and others saluted, even Seattle firefighters stood by their ladder trucks in solemn salute.

Some placed their hands over their hearts, and others waved. Lexi was beside herself with concern, she wanted a reason for all the fanfare; why was daddy Mark's picture everywhere and why hadn't he come along with us. My heart ached worse than ever as I explained the best as I knew how, in words I hoped she'd understand.

Undaunted, she squealed in delight and ran to the window to wave to those we passed, as if to thank them for their show of respect of her daddy Mark.

Her smiles and laughter were infectious and brightened the mood in the bus. Dale joined in and saluted back to all those who acknowledged the bus.

PART II

The procession ended at the Key Arena for Mark's memorial service. They wrote his name and memorial on their lighted announcement board in place of the night's upcoming game.

I hugged Barry and told him how Mark would have loved all of it. As we left the bus, he gave each of us a black memorial button with 2106 printed in white on them.

Ushers escorted the family inside towards a stage where they'd set up a tribute for Mark. My heart skipped a beat. A larger-than-life photograph of Mark and his boys stared me in the face, it didn't include me and my children.

As we approached it, a familiar sense of foreboding came over me, just like I'd experienced at his mom's house. They led us to front row seats facing the stage and some estimated 5,000 people joined us in the remaining seats behind ours, well beyond the *big* I'd expected.

Over the next two hours, Mark's fellow colleagues paid tribute to him. Emotions ran the gamut for all in attendance. Some of the speeches and the music made us laugh, and others moved us to tears.

Aware I was in full view of the media and public, I kept my emotions in check for most of the service, but when Barry offered me a memorial flag from the King County Honor Guard, followed by Taps and bagpipes, the unraveling began.

To keep the teetering tears at bay, I held my breath while Barry announced Mark as the honorary Operator of the Year; he would have been so proud.

And just when I thought I had made it scot free, came an unexpected announcement that echoed eerily throughout the massive space.

Over a loud speaker, a dispatcher called out for Mark,

"Operator 2106....... *static*...... moment of silence...... Operator 2106....... *static*...... silence. Operator 2106 is now out of service."

The finality of the abrupt disconnection was mind-numbing.

There wasn't a dry eye in the house; it was a relief not to be alone.

SIXTEEN

Relieved to be back in the safety of our home, alone and away from scrutinizing eyes, I walked straight to our room, closed the door, flopped down on the bed, buried my face into my pillow, and screamed and cried until I was hoarse.

I assured myself that this wasn't real, it wasn't happening, I'd been in a terrible car accident or something, and in a coma, having a horrible nightmare of *what if?*

I turned towards the ever-present dark shadow in the corner of the room and cried out,

"I know you were always proud of my inner strength, independence, and resilience. Those things are what you said you loved most about me. You are the only one who loved, believed in, and accepted me for who I am. I've assented the trials and tribulations of single motherhood, life on public transportation, along with the humility and sacrifices of poverty. But please forgive me, Mark, this one is too much! This one I cannot do! I can't go on! I'm so lost without you! I miss you so much it hurts!"

My head fell back onto the pillow; I buried my face into its softness and cried until the sandman found me.

༄

Sometime later, Lexi and Dale crept into the room. As quiet as church mice, they asked what was for dinner. For a second the fog lifted, but then I realized I was still in the nightmare as I looked upon their sweet faces. My heart hurt for them. They had never seen me cry before, not like this. I wish I could give them their Mommy back.

I climbed out of the bed and followed them to the kitchen. The food in the fridge from our neighbors was a blessing. I fed them and stared into space as they ate. From the corner of my eye, I saw they were waiting for me to eat too.

For their sake, I pretended to. Although I was starving, my stomach twisted in knotted somersaults, and the thought of food made it worse.

The following days melded together and time marched selfishly along. I resumed driving but having the children in the car made me more nervous than before; yet, being in the enclosed space and listening to my favorite music seemed to renew my broken soul.

Whenever a song reminded Dale and Lexi of one that Mark liked, *I wish I was in Tijuana eating barbequed iguana...*, they'd yell in unison, "Turn it up! Turn it up!"

The happiness Mark had brought them resurfaced in their excitement. Familiar tunes, singing, and acting goofy helped us forget, even for just a little while.

As much as I yearned for it, the holiday spirit avoided me. I wouldn't be making cookies, decorating, or visiting the tree farmer and his wife this year. Not even for the children's sake.

So much for New Year's resolutions, I might as well have thrown 1998's calendar into the recycle bin. But didn't; I would always treasure the weekly events Mark penciled in our last year together.

His sister brought over a tree and hung an angel ornament on it. But even that didn't do it for me. It wouldn't be Christmas without Mark.

A few days shy of Christ's birthday, me and the kids awoke in the wee hours of the morning to loud voices coming from the living room.

I wrapped myself in a robe to investigate. It wasn't Santa paying us an early visit, but Mark's brother and his sons in a hurried frenzy packing and taking what they thought they had a right to.

I stood among them, but as if I were invisible, not one acknowledged me.

A cold draft swept through the room. I looked around and noticed all the doors were wide open, letting out the precious heat, and allowing the December cold to come in.

My polite request to close the doors fell upon deaf ears. They replied they wouldn't be much longer. I returned to the bedroom, shut the door, crawled back into bed, and snuggled next to my children.

It wasn't long before the chilly air found its way under the door and the blankets, waking the kids. We huddled even closer for warmth as we waited for our uninvited visitors to leave.

Just as Lexi's little body began shivering and her teeth chattering, the disconnected heater the bed was up against, blazed on in a burning glory of instant warmth.

We jumped off the bed to move it away from the wall. And just as quick, bounded back underneath the covers. Oblivious to the miracle we'd experienced, they cuddled even deeper into the cozy folds and fell back to sleep in an instant.

I curled up next to them and thought how someone might think I'd made it up if I shared what had just happened.

Comforted by Mark's enduring love and support, I cried myself back to sleep.

When we awoke a little while later, the house was cold and almost empty. They'd left a mess in the wake of their evacuation. There was a gaping hole in the center of the wooden console where the TV and stereo used to be; they'd rearranged the furniture and taken all the boys' belongings.

I couldn't believe it. I did my best to explain what happened, but it didn't sink in, the kids just wanted to watch cartoons.

Later, Mark's sister stopped by. Her frazzled demeanor spoke volumes. In so many words, she said the children and I had to leave.

Her words floated around me. *What was she trying to say? First Mark, now this? Not only were we being rejected from the family we'd always thought we were a part of, but now they wanted to evict us from our home as well?*

She said she hadn't played a part in the decision; the family said because I was unemployed, they wouldn't be able to provide for us until I found another job, and so we had to go.

Then the hammer fell. She said her brother would be coming first thing the next morning to evict us, and he'd instructed her to help me pack, to assure we didn't take any of Mark's things.

In disbelief and in my defense, I explained what we had of our own wasn't much more than personal belongings as we had done away with a lot of our things when we moved in.

I pleaded with her not to force us to leave with nothing, not at Christmas.

With consideration of the situation we both faced, she said, although she had the family's trust, she'd allow me to take all the necessities I needed that I could fit into my car.

I wanted to hug her for her mercy but hesitated. I doubted her loyalty, or how genuine her concern for us really was, and if I would ever trust her, or anyone in Mark's family, again.

I insulated my feelings by staying focused on the urgency of all I had to do. But that only lasted for so long. Soon the numbness wore off and shock set in as I contemplated what was about to transpire.

I choked back tears as I thought how I should have been wrapping presents, not packing. *Where would we go?*

Mommy lived in subsidized housing and would risk eviction if we landed on her doorstep, and it was out of the question to ask my sister, also a struggling single mom, to take us in, besides we'd end up killing each other after only a couple of days.

As I racked my brain for solutions, a neighbor stopped by; surprised by the chaos and to see me haphazardly stuffing things into hefty bags, she asked what the urgency was.

In a zombie-like stupor, absorbed in my thoughts and the daunting task before me, I explained the situation.

Mark's sister drove to the store to see if they had one or two boxes, while I sorted through the linen closet and the kitchen cupboards. All I now owned would fit into just a few of them.

Lexi and Dale looked over the disarray. To put them at ease, I made up an adventure story as an explanation for why we were leaving, but because tears rolled down my face while I told it, they didn't buy it.

I folded down the back seat of my tiny coupe and stuffed it as full as possible, leaving just enough room for the children and me. They cried when it was time to leave Mark's sister.

The neighbor who stopped by earlier returned just as we were getting into the car. She handed me a piece of paper with an address written on it and said it was somewhere we could stay for as long as we needed.

She whispered in my ear as she hugged me farewell, "It will be okay. Be strong. Your children need you." Near tears, I nodded, hugged her in return, and thanked her.

I put on a brave face for the children's sake, but inside my bones rattled, I'd never known a greater sense of fear than I did that day.

With empty pockets and heavy hearts, in the middle of a cold December's night, like exiled refugees, we left our home, our happy-ever-after, and Omar, Cinder-Mamma Kitty, Dinky, and Amos.

Only looking forward, we drove off towards an uncertain future.

SEVENTEEN

The directions seemed to have a step missing. I pulled into a parking lot to take another look at them and rechecked the address; yup, we were at the right place.

We hadn't arrived at someone's home, but at the grandest hotel in Lynnwood, The Embassy Suites!

We stared in awe at the magnificent building; what a Christmas gift for sure. In the even grander lobby, the manager greeted me and the children with open arms.

She gave me a key to room 231 and said we could stay for as long as we needed, adding how breakfast was on the house.

When I opened the door to the room, I laughed and cried all at once, convinced Mark had played a part in it somehow: luxurious furnishings, elegant wallpaper and decorations, tranquil ambiance from the soft light of the table lamps, a private bedroom, a living room, a mini kitchen with a little refrigerator, and a spacious bathroom welcomed us.

Surreal couldn't come close to describing the extravagance. Dale made a beeline for the TV and set about preparing it for his video games. Lexi ran straight to the single bedroom and jumped up and down on top of one of the oversized, cushy, queen size beds.

We returned to the car to park it closer to make it easier to bring in some of our belongings. It was near midnight by the time we finished getting ready for sleep. Lex and I shared one bed and Dale had the other, the biggest bed he'd ever had all to himself.

After tucking them in and reading a story, I switched off the lights, and turned to walk out when I heard Lexi sniffle. I gathered her in my arms. She said she missed daddy Mark; Dale whispered he did too.

Desperate for a Band-Aid to patch their broken hearts, I told them I'd read if we spoke out loud to him, he'd hear us.

Lexi stopped sobbing, contemplated this possibility, and they let loose at the same time. Always the gentleman with his precious sister, Dale paused and let her go first.

She rattled on and on, leaving nothing out about recent events. When she stopped long enough for Dale to speak, he couldn't, the ache in his throat hurt too much.

My heart ached for them more than it did already, and even more as I realized there wasn't anything I could do about it.

After they'd each had their say, and snuggled into bed once again, Lex interrupted the silence by asking how we'd know if he was really there. Baffled, I suggested she ask him.

And so, she did.

She'd only rolled the words off her tongue when a resounding *crack* thundered from the corner of the room.

Great, now she was wide awake and as excited as if it were Christmas day.

"He's here! He's here!" she shrieked, bounding up and down on the bed, clapping her hands in amusement.

Dale joined in, "Dad is it true? Are you here?"

Another rumble responded. Lexi squealed in delight. A little spooked by the occurrences, I told them perhaps dad was saying it was time to go to sleep.

Their silliness stopped on a dime, and they scrambled underneath their covers; "Good night daddy," Lex said before she fell sound asleep, at long last.

I laid awake a while longer and then, finding comfort from the ever-present dark shadow in the corner of this strange room, turned to face the wall, and soon fell fast asleep myself.

I had the strangest dream I'd written a book. I saw it as clear as day, the beginning to the end, the book cover, the title and its placement, the format of the contents, the main text, the index, the whole thing.

It was so impressed in my mind I couldn't forget it even if I wanted to.

I awoke before the children and stumbled into the bathroom to have a peaceful shower. I looked at the reflection in the mirror and didn't recognize the person staring back at me.

"Where did she go?" No wonder the kids seemed afraid of me. I washed my face, but the haunting image remained unchanged.

The dream took the forefront as I showered. How did someone with limited education go about writing a book? Such a craft belonged in the hands of a more cultured person. I disregarded the notion as only a dream and shoved the thought to the furthest corner of my mind. Lord knows, I had enough to worry about.

I put on some makeup and reevaluated my reflection. It was still the same.

Grief aside, I called Barry. Dumbfounded by our situation, he assured me we would be all right, and he'd research our options.

A little while later he called back with bad news. The law didn't recognize Mark and me as married by common law; therefore, my children and I would not receive any of Mark's pension, his social security, or any of the funds donated by the public.

With a defeated *goodbye*, I hung up the phone, walked into the bathroom, shut the door, and sat on the edge of the bathtub.

Man, I screwed up this time. We were up a creek without a paddle, no, worse than that, our boat had run ashore on top of rocks, in the middle of nowhere, with a hole in the bottom and broken oars.

My god! Would I ever right it again?

Besot by the irony in my life, I shoved my face deep into a luxurious hotel towel and cried the makeup away.

With the kids on winter break, it was a relief not to worry about school for a while. As for food, thank God for the free breakfast.

In the mornings we stuffed ourselves to the gills, and harbored more to our room, hoping it would get us through until dinner.

I called the social service office to learn they couldn't help me. According to their charts, I'd made too much money in former months to qualify, even though I didn't have a pot to pee in presently, go figure.

Discouraged but not defeated, I found I qualified for unemployment benefits; as luck would have it, they wouldn't be available for another two weeks, and not very much; but it was better than nothing. In the meantime, I was given an appointment to see a social worker about finding a job.

When the day arrived, I hesitated as I extended out my hand to introduce myself. As an unwilling participant on this road less traveled, I decided—if I had to start my life over, then my name would change too.

I would no longer go by the childhood nickname my father gave me, Lis or Lissie, but by the name Lexi carried for her middle name, and the one her teacher addressed me by, Elise.

Within two weeks, I'd had numerous job leads, enrolled the kids for medical benefits, and learned of several area food banks and the times they operated.

The only written rule for the food bank was the hours, the assumed ones we figured out the hard way. After waiting for what seemed an eternity in the freezing cold and pouring rain, we learned to dress for inclement weather and to get in line early because dairy products went first.

With our modest rations in hand, keeping in mind the compact refrigerator at the hotel and the size of my car trunk, I picked through them and kept only what we needed, the remainder I shared with my mom and the tenants who lived in her building.

Although most of the food had ingredients I frowned upon, it kept us alive, and for that I felt grateful. In my heart, I knew it wouldn't always be this way.

The kids couldn't believe their luck, "Cookies and SpaghettiOs!"

EIGHTEEN

*W*inter break came to an end, and the children returned to school. Because we no longer lived by the school bus stop, I had to drive them back and forth each day.

While they were away, although I would rather have climbed back into bed and hid away from the world, I spent the long hours researching for solutions out of the mess I'd gotten us into.

I went to appointments, ran errands, applied for available jobs, and made time to visit Mark. My first visit was unnerving.

Although I had made a mental note of the surroundings and the landmarks of the precise place where he lay the day of the funeral, it still took forever to find him.

Freshly dug earth and a tiny burial tag were the only indicators of his resting place. I draped my coat onto the ground under which he slept, laid on my stomach, and, wanting to be as close to him as possible, pressed my cheek firm to the cold, damp earth.

I closed my eyes and stretched my arms out to embrace his grave. With each hand, I gripped the fresh seeded soil and let my fingers sink as deep as they could into the silky softness, hoping to find him, and cried.

While lying there, the sky opened, and rain poured down on me like tears from heaven. I welcomed it; the water falling from the clouds, the dark and gloominess of it all. It seemed as if Mark was crying with me.

I kept my eyes shut, ignoring the ever-increasing dampness of my clothing and hair, and whispered how much we missed him and what was happening with us.

After some time, regaining common sense and composure, I kissed his tiny, temporary marker tenderly, wiped the dirt from my hands and the tears from my face, gathered my coat, and headed back for the hotel.

I visited him each week thereafter and always left a gift, like a laminated picture of us or some flowers, but for some unknown reason upon my next return, my mere tokens of love had disappeared. Many items of remembrances and flowers remained, as did other gifts on other graves, but not ours.

The most devastating of all was the mysterious vanishing of the mini potted Christmas tree we'd decorated for him.

PART II

No matter though, in my heart I knew there was one thing they couldn't take away from us, and that was Mark's love.

I decided two could play their game and tucked secret mementos in and around his grave when I visited. They were the tiniest and most insignificant gestures of love: a button from my blouse, a ribbon from Lexi, and a wisp of some of our hair, just to name a few.

Each visit thereafter, I was content to find the obscured gifts from the time before were just as I left them.

∽

Like a ghost from the past, Lexi's biological father resurfaced. With much discussion, I decided it was best for her to stay with him and his wife until I got back on my feet; until then, she'd visit on the weekends.

They lived in Lacy, which might as well have been in New York. The day I gave her away, was yet another one of the *worst days of my life*. The aching desire for all of us to be together again, was the incentive I needed to pull up my bootstraps and rebuild our lives.

Back at the hotel, we got a surprise visit from two of my former coworkers. I was glad to see them again and receive their warm hugs. They gave me a card with many heartfelt condolences written within; a lump formed in my throat as I read them.

There was also a letter inside, it was from the hospital where I'd worked, they'd created a donation fund for me and my children.

The girls offered me another gift. Nestled within delicate white tissue paper, lay a beautiful piece of translucent, beveled crystal glass. Pressed in its center, sealed with gold color led, were petals from the last bouquet Mark gave me, the day before he died, Safeway flowers, and I cried.

It was a priceless keepsake, the most sentimental, unique gift I'd ever received, words couldn't express my gratitude.

As if that still wasn't enough, the one closer to my age surprised me further, and offered her home to us, insisting we could stay with her family for as long as we needed.

∽

Dale and I were more than obliged to accept. Although the hotel spoiled us, moving from its sanctuary was just the propulsion I needed.

With her guest room's two full size beds and bathroom, it was almost as large as our suite at the hotel. They were so gracious and shared all they had with us.

I was glad the weekends passed by fast as they brought Lexi home again. Even in this new place, the kids continued to listen for Mark's familiar noises before going to sleep, and he never failed them.

Evenings were the worst for me. The inability to run away from my worries, as I did during the day, held me captive. One sleepless night, my face buried into the pillow to stifle my frustrated cries, I felt someone sit next to me on the bed.

I reached out to assure them I was all right but didn't find anyone. I turned to see where they were but saw no one.

Yet, the warm presence remained, with a clear indention on the bed. Indifferent, I stuffed my face deeper into the pillow and cried harder than before.

The warmth moved from my side to the length of my back and across my arms, the same way Mark once held me to sleep.

It didn't matter which way I tossed or turned, rubbed at my arms, or moved my legs, the sensation endured. Somehow, I found comfort in the strange phenomenon and gave into it, surrendering to a welcomed sound slumber.

The friend we lived with worked with doctors who specialized in grief. I felt self-conscious whenever I was around her; only I understood my new sense of reality.

Although she wanted to be close, I preferred to be alone. I know she only desired to help, but I wasn't ready to listen. Bit by bit, I pushed her away, and everyone else, including my best friend and myself; I avoided them all.

I didn't want the comfort of a well-meaning hug, and I most definitely did not want to hear the dreaded words of condolence. All of that reminded me how I wasn't in a coma, and Mark wasn't coming home.

Anyone who suggested I celebrate Mark's life, rather than consume myself in the sorrow of his death, or to move on or forward, or commented how it was better to have loved than to never have loved at all, became my enemy.

I didn't expect anyone to understand my feelings, rational or otherwise, and I felt smothered by any attempt to make it better.

Mark's death left a huge crater in my heart. Somewhere along the way, I'd lost my sense of self, allowing his former existence to define my ultimate happiness.

A willing victim, I turned inward and isolated myself, detaching from the world, losing the sound of the rain falling, the wind blowing, and the birds singing.

Grief aside, with mouths to feed and wanting Lexi home above all, I applied for an office assistant job with King County.

They called me in for an interview and then another. I was excited when I got it; although it was a challenge to concentrate and process like I used to, it wasn't stressful, and the coworkers made it fun.

By March, I found an affordable, small, one-bedroom apartment next to the park and ride where I once rode the bus to work. Even though I traveled into town on a Community Transit bus rather than on a Metro, occasional compassionate stares took some getting used to. Sometimes I'd smile back to reassure them all was right in my world, even though it wasn't.

While getting back into the swing of my daily commute, I noticed how the world continued to revolve as if nothing extraordinary had happened. Everyone seemed in high spirits, with goals and a purpose.

There wasn't a day that went by without a reminder in it, a metro bus, an exact replica of the last one Mark drove, a metro driver in uniform, Mark's friends, and tons of Pooh and Piglet stuff.

All of it affected my overall mood. If I didn't have children to provide for, I would have run screaming back home and buried myself under the covers.

Since that wasn't an option, I gathered my own reminders, hoarding anything related to Mark and the day of his death, whatever provided proof of his existence; media, pictures, condolence cards, gifts, etc.

Then, without reading or opening any of it, along with my conviction *it* didn't happen, I packed the entire collection in a large Rubbermaid storage container, never letting it be far from me.

※

The apartment wasn't any bigger than the hotel, but it was a start, and with what little belongings we had, it was just right. My mom stayed with us for a few days to help where she could, and to keep the children entertained.

Even here, as I tucked them in at night, upon their beckoning, the unexplainable noises echoed throughout the room until they drifted off to dreamland.

As well, the familiar warmth lulled me to sleep, and a joyful song from a stellar jay greeted me in the mornings, somehow finding us no matter where we ended up.

With life falling in place, it was time for Lexi to come home, permanently. But her father wouldn't return her without a fight.

With the help of a pro bono attorney, I won her back, but with a price of $2,000 for child support for the few months she'd lived with him, even though he owed me much more.

To add salt to the wound, he said if I wanted her so bad, I had to drive down to get her, eighty miles south to Lacy.

NINETEEN

The thought of driving to Lacey about sent me over the edge. But the love for my baby superseded all uncertainties, giving me the needed courage to bring her home.

I began the dreaded journey from the Park and Ride after work one Friday. All was well until the dark of the evening settled in and a menacing wind along with it.

The winds howled and whipped around my little coupe and about jerked it out of the lane. I fought the steering wheel to keep it straight, but mother nature wasn't done with me. An incredible monsoon about swallowed my car.

Because the windshield was slanted, the wipers proved futile, even on the highest setting. I moved up closer to the dash, but still couldn't see a thing. It felt as if I were a toy boat washed away at sea.

As I continued the fight with the helm, my knuckles blanched white, my forearms numbed to pinpricks, and my chin quivered; I didn't know how much longer I could hold on.

I wiped at the tears with the back of my hand, and smeared a cobwebby mess across my face, making the visibility worse.

I cried out to Mark.

Moments later, the exit sign to Lacey illuminated in my headlights. Singing praises in my head, I left the highway from hell, took in a deep breath, the first since beginning the voyage, and turned into the gas station where they waited for me.

Exhausted and drenched, I cleaned the sticky mess from my face with some napkins and climbed out of the car.

Lexi ran toward me. Too drained to have words with her father, I gathered her into my arms in one victorious swoop and headed back towards the dreaded interstate.

The squall had passed, Amen. Lexi, being her mother's daughter, sensed something was wrong, turned the car radio to our favorite country station, and encouraged me to caterwaul along with her all the way back home.

All was complete with my precious baby girl home.

With the commute of my new job and the children busy with various activities, our visits to Mark's grave became fewer and shorter, and then only on special occasions.

PART II

The busier I kept myself, the easier life seemed to manage. With that in mind, I jumped on whatever opportunity there was available to keep occupied and distracted.

To be on autopilot, going through the motions of daily life, was the easiest way not to think about *it*. I'm sure some held their breath, waiting for the other shoe to drop, but it never did.

I didn't know if I'd ever meet up with my old self again, but for now, being lost within my inner turmoil made me happy, glad to be nonexistent without a sense of time.

The children continued to thrive and push on ahead even without all of me present. My one true regret though, is that I missed out on the joys of their final years of childhood.

◠

If I hadn't flown over the cuckoo's nest yet, I found controlling my immediate environment the most challenging.

I obsessed over avoiding all that reminded me of *that* day, zeroing in on all parks and towns anywhere near ground zero.

So, poof! One day they no longer existed, no more Woodland Park Zoo, Greenlake, Freemont, or any of those places, all gone.

And to make sure I didn't happen by those areas, I never rode as a passenger in another vehicle again, avoiding the chance of being taken there *for my own good*.

To add to the craziness, I became over-vigilant with my children and all those I loved, certain if I didn't protect all I held dear, I'd somehow lose it again.

I convinced myself the world was not a safe place, clouding my belief anything would ever be okay again, interacting and speaking only to Mark.

Confident I'd always managed before, and certain I still could, my stubborn pride keeping me from asking for the help we desperately needed, it somehow came anyway, and always when we needed it the most.

Stranger yet were the pennies from heaven: rebate checks from various bills overpaid from years before, which made little sense as I would never overpay anything, spontaneous, anonymous checks came in the mail, and untraceable payments made on utility bills.

Then there was the extra money that manifested in my bank account without a transaction ever being made.

Besides our divine financial security, I also had a celestial copilot. Odd as it may sound, I didn't hear voices per se, but I had inner thoughts besides my own, and they guided me through each day, from mundane decision making, to caring for the children.

I never second guessed them; I just went along. They never pointed me in the wrong direction, so I came to trust and rely on them for everything. Most important, they consoled me whenever my heart seemed the heaviest, with them I never felt alone.

After all we'd been through, and what was about to be mine and Mark's wedding day, I planned a trip to Disneyland. It was just what the doctor ordered, known for being *the happiest place on earth*.

I made the travel arrangements on a lunch break. The representative made me laugh. Not so much by what he said or the sound of his voice, but by the uncanny way he spoke.

It was verbatim, the same quotes and phrases, the way Mark would've said them. I'd almost forgotten the way he spoke until that phone call.

Afterwards as familiar tears welled in my eyes, a co-worker knelt next to my desk and put her hand on my back. I told her of my experience.

To further corroborate Mark's influence, later that day while entering data on the computer, the background on the screen changed from black to florescent green. I showed the same colleague.

Neither of us could explain it. Then just as quick, it changed back to black again. I laughed to myself while fighting back tears, green was Mark's favorite color; call it what you will, but I thought it made perfect sense.

When we left for our vacation, my newfound neurosis threatened to poison the trip: I organized the whole itinerary to the last second, squeezing the life out of the mighty dollar, and ran our retreat like a boot camp.

Despite my crazed demeanor, the kids had a great time, and relinquished months of pent-up emotion by climbing on whatever fast-moving ride they could find. They even tricked me into riding on an enclosed roller coaster, never again; enough said.

In the evenings, they unwound in the hotel pool, and when their heads hit their pillows, they fell into an exhausted sleep, forgetting just for a moment, letting go just a little while.

Watching them play, laugh, and have fun again was the purpose of the trip. I hadn't seen them smile that much since the last hike with Mark.

Upon our return, commuting home from work one day, I noticed a book the person next to me was reading, Talking to Heaven, by James Van Praagh.

She told me a little about it on the way to the Park and Ride, and then gave me a business card with the name Ralph and a phone number written on the back of it.

She said he, like the author of her book, was a local medium she'd sought guidance from for many years and felt certain he could help me too.

Out of sheer curiosity, mostly because Mark had spoken of these kinds of things, I called the number as soon as I arrived home and set a date to meet this Ralph.

TWENTY

On the day of the appointment, the directions took me to a gift shop. I looked at the paper again and compared it with the address, certain I had arrived at the right place.

A store clerk within noticed my uncertainty, and guided me towards the back of the store, up a short flight of stairs, and into a large and candlelit room.

I've transcribed the recorded session as it unfolded.

Incense permeated the area, wax dripped from the various candles around the room, and a parrot cackled somewhere in the background.

I sat across from an enormous man. More skeptical than afraid, I said little, if nothing at all, to test his authenticity.

He put a cassette into a tape recorder and, in a friendly, heavy English accent, told me things I wouldn't understand until much later, until I had all but forgotten my visit, and the predictions he made that day.

He asked about a ring, like a wedding ring, and said he could see it upside down, and how it was rotating about, and asked if I had recently become single.

Not wanting to give him any cues, I tucked my left hand with the ring on it under my leg and prepared to keep my emotions under wrap.

His ramblings and mumblings were a challenge to follow. They twisted and turned, on and on, around and around, in no sensible sequence. In this odd place, it seemed as if I was in a real-life Wonderland, and with a real-life Mad Hatter.

Ralph explained how everything around me was *really weird at the moment*. Although the ring he envisioned wasn't broken, he sensed the relationship connected to it had ended somehow, and he perceived there was something about me and this relationship that wasn't sorted out, that it was on pause, and yet there was life still in it.

Ralph stopped for a moment and shook his head. Rather perplexed, he asked if the man had left me. He continued to mutter to himself as if trying to unravel a mystery, asserting aloud that the strangest thing was that although this man was away, he sensed that he was standing right next to me.

He snapped his fingers and nodded with firm assurance and asked if the man had passed away. Then, his thoughts took a three sixty flip, and he prophesied, "When you are in bed at night, and you get the feeling he's there, he wants you to know that he really is there. Though he is not with you every second of the day, he truly misses you as much as you miss him. What we have here are two people in a terrible situation. It is going to take some time, but it is something that you will be able to work through. He still finds that he needs to be around you and that at the times when you're distracted but suddenly think of him for no reason, not to be sad because it's at those times he's checking on you."

Without missing a beat, he added, "He has been trying to show you that he is with you by tilting pictures, hiding your keys, and that sort of thing."

Off course once more, he said, "It sure was a lovely ring," drifting further, he blurted, "I'm getting the word *shithead*." I couldn't help myself, and laughed, convinced now more than ever of Mark's presence.

Ralph looked distressed, and a shadow of sadness crossed his face. He asked if he had died a sudden death, adding, "I get the feeling that although it was sudden, it seems as though it was predestined, a pre-arranged thing. As if it was his time to go, though his conscience didn't know it, but his soul did. The adjustment is going to be difficult for both of you because there is work still to do. But you will eventually heal and move forward, some days will be easier than others."

Distracted for a moment, he continued, "You will live to be quite old because you have many things still to do." He stopped mid-sentence and muttered something about my eyes. He asked if my eyes were what Mark was first attracted to.

At that moment, I remembered the first song Mark played for me, U2s *I Will Follow,* and I lost it. Great; I had done it now. I had given the guy the lead he needed to continue.

Nowadays, once the unraveling began, there was no way back, but some of his prophecies were too close to home. In my heart I wanted to believe, I mean Mark did talk a lot about my eyes after all. He loved them, and always commented on how they were hypnotic like a mermaid's siren, just like the blue stone in my engagement ring.

I sniffled as Ralph continued.

"Have you been having dreams about visiting with him? They aren't dreams. You need to keep a journal of his visits. He needs you as much as you need him."

He continued, describing mine and Mark's personalities, stating how I'd always made him laugh and made him feel good about himself.

Then he changed course and foretold of my future and about the many great things still to happen. I thought it ironic when he said I shouldn't worry about money.

He ricocheted his thoughts again and exclaimed, "He loves children, doesn't he?"

With even more surprise, he asked if I was a mother. I opened my mouth to respond, but he interrupted, nodding his head with firm conviction, and stated how I'd had two pregnancies, and then asked to see my hand.

He looked at my palm and interpreted the lines he saw there. Blunt as usual, he said he saw a broken one, and asked if I'd married before.

He returned my hand and changed the subject, "What a great mom you are! You have the mind of an adult as well as that of a child. Your children will be fine. You will always make things fun for them, they will never lack in love, and they will not end up drug addicts or have any serious problems."

His thoughts zigzagged yet again, "You will never look your age, and this will piss off a lot of women around your own age. You have an extremely full life ahead of you. And although you are a very independent lady, and could never be accused of being easy, men will continue to hit on you. And although you will never show any interest, you will definitely marry again."

He paused as if listening to something and then muttered the name, *Martin*. He asked aloud to no one who this was, and repeated the name again with more conviction, "Oh, Martin!"

Ralph shook his head as he pondered this revelation, "It's either part of his first or last name." After a moment, smiling like a Cheshire cat, he exclaimed with even more sureness, "It is most definitely a part of his last name!"

Confused, I asked whose last name he was referring to, and he answered in a matter-of-fact tone, "It is the name of the man you will marry someday, but not for a long while."

Our visit concluded with his premonition of how my present journey wouldn't be easy, but I wouldn't be walking it alone as I had a lot of protective spirits around me who would remain by my side until I didn't need them as much.

He stressed how my intuition level was high and when someone of that degree gets an emotional hurt, it's devastating, the worst, and that although some people might drift away because they don't know what to say, not to let it consume me as my guides would help me.

Ralph affirmed with utmost certainty no other catastrophes lie ahead for me. He popped the cassette out of the player and said how wonderful it was to meet me.

I hugged him in return and thanked him for his time. It wouldn't be until much later I'd learn just how accurate Ralph's predictions were.

PART II

TWENTY-ONE

I arrived home from my bizarre meeting with Ralph, wrapped the cassette in tissue paper, placed it into Mark's coveted box, regarding the experience as no more than a grain of salt, and tucked it in the further recesses of my mind.

Tired of the grey cloud hovering above me, wanting an instruction manual to manage the unfair rite of passage in my life, but I didn't know how to go about looking for one.

What was I supposed to feel; how was I supposed to act; what was normal? I wanted to give my children the answers they sought, something in stone, black and white, something that didn't require too much thinking.

There had to be a book out there. But regardless of the tons I researched, I didn't relate to any. How was I to lead my children when I didn't know the way?

In an ironic twist, the more hopeless it all seemed, the more I dreamt about *the book*. As much as I tried to ignore it, stuffing it back with *the box*, it haunted me anyway.

How in the world could I write my story if I hadn't been through the journey it foretold, one I was none too eager to begin?

The days without Mark rippled ever further from reach. My children became my only reason to get out of bed and face the world each day.

Barry and I continued to meet on occasion for lunch. I'd tell him how my life was going, and he'd tell me about the security changes happening at Metro, like how a new Transit Security Program was in place with off-duty police officers on buses, and how security cameras had been installed on all the coaches. Ironic how hindsight is twenty-twenty.

Summer snuck up on me, bringing Mark and Lexi's birthday with it. I placed a single red rose on Mark's grave, kissed his new gravestone and threw a surprise party for Lex. From an outsider's point of view, it appeared as if things were getting back to normal.

Midsummer, the kids left for a two-week YMCA camp. Moments after waving goodbye to their bus, I was beside myself. I tried to enjoy the time I had alone, but my rambling thoughts made it impossible to sit still long enough and enjoy my favorite hobbies: sewing, and reading.

I knew there was one person who could use my expendable energy, my mother. So, I spent every waking moment, cleaning, cooking, and running errands for her. She even enticed me into a few games of dice. Before I knew it, the children were coming home.

Next on my to-do list was to find a permanent place to live. I came across a cozy three-bedroom townhouse on the corner of a private cul-de-sac in Mukilteo, but I had to clear a few hurdles before getting it.

To make ends meet, I had to cut a few corners. The most heart wrenching of all was trading in the beloved little coup Mark had chosen for me, the one Lexi named Lilly, for an even smaller, used Geo Storm.

Upon satisfying a never-ending checklist, the house was ours at last. To get it ready to move into was the most time-consuming. I wasn't handy with tools, and I lacked the redecorating skills required for the expectations my imagination conjured up.

Naïve of how much effort the work called for, just wanting to get settled in and on with our lives, I forged full-tilt ahead, and spent many sleepless nights fixing it up.

In the evenings after dinner, I'd drive out to the house, and spend several hours scrubbing, wallpapering, and painting until I couldn't lift another tool. Then, I'd return to our apartment in time to catch a few hours of shut-eye before going to work the next day.

Four weeks later, frustration, impatience, and exhaustion had me in their grips. I stood in the living room, the last area to clean and paint, and gazed up in awe at the height of the cathedral ceilings and the length of the walls before me and lost it.

I collapsed to the floor in tears and pummeled at its unforgiving firmness with my fists, crying like I have never cried before.

"Why?" I screamed. "I can't do this by myself!"

My meltdown lasted until I'd excised every emotion.

Drained, relaxing into a full child's pose, I buried my nose into the dusty floor, and prayed for strength. I left the unfinished living room for the next day and drove back to the apartment. Believe it or not, I got it done by the end of the week and must admit I did an outstanding job too.

We moved in just before the start of the 1999 school year and celebrated with a housewarming party. Even with so much to rejoice in, my heart was still heavy. I felt guilty for not feeling exuberant about all the hurdles I'd cleared so far.

It was quite an adjustment settling into our new home. With what little belongings we had, the house, with its tall ceilings, and vast spaciousness, seemed cold and empty.

Because we'd always slept within a stone's throw from one another, and since Dale had the bigger bed, we camped out in his room for the first month.

Even though the children no longer sought Mark's reassuring presence before they fell asleep, a crack or two from the walls and ceilings continued to echo a soft lullaby throughout the slumbering quietness.

The enveloping warmth I'd come to rely upon to soothe me asleep had disappeared. In its place were endless nights of tossing and turning, worrying, longing for Mark, and for what once was.

Sure, we had come a long way since the hotel, but I didn't want these new things, these new changes; I just wanted to be home with Mark, in our cramped little house, among the things we'd made a life out of.

Aware of the fact there were no do-overs in life, I got busy with settling in, it was way more fun than redecorating for sure. Consumed with the task, I forgot about my recent prayer request, yet, an answer was well on its way.

TWENTY-TWO

One day Lexi ran into the house and announced how her new friend had found something exciting. She pulled me towards the main entry where Sasha stood. I laughed and followed along, expecting to see something unexciting.

Sasha approached me, cradling something as tiny as her hands. It a was black and fuzzy animal with a nub for a tail; I was certain it must be a hamster.

Sasha pleaded in desperation, "Can you save this kitty? Its mother has killed its four brothers and sisters, and I just got this one away from her as she was biting on it, she bit its tail off, see, and your daughter says you're a nurse, and I was wondering if you would save him."

My daughter was jumping up and down and begging me at this point.

I wasn't a practicing nurse, and my specialty did not involve animals, but I scooped the tiny thing into my hands anyway. As I held up the pint-sized creature and gazed into its eyes, a mysterious, enveloping warmth radiated through my hands, up my arms, over my chest, and straight into my heart.

My motherly instincts took over and I gave it a quick once-over. I determined *it* was a *he*, his eyes and ears hadn't opened yet, and he appeared to be no worse for wear other than losing a slight chunk of his tail.

He was so little and vulnerable, *caring for him wouldn't be any harder than mothering or nursing,* I justified as I hurried into the house in search of a towel to wrap him in.

I passed my daughter along the way and heard her shout, "Yeah!" behind me.

I nestled him as snug as a bug within a thick cotton bath towel, climbed into my truck, tucked him into my lap, and headed for the vet who cares for our other cats.

Once there, I learned of his fate. He weighed in at only two ounces and had a mere thirty percent chance of survival.

The vet shared her concerns about my recent loss, and how it might affect my ability to handle the additional grief if he didn't live. She recommended I find someone else to take on the responsibility.

Well, I wasn't about to abandon him; not now. And I persisted. I assured her I could handle it no matter what the outcome. Unconvinced, she pulled out her pen and wrote instructions on how to care for him all the same.

With my maternal instincts in full bore, I re-wrapped him in the towel, and headed for the pet store where I bought kitten formula, a tiny syringe, and a kitten care booklet.

Back home, I glanced through the important sections and set about tucking him in for the night. It suggested he have a quiet, warm, dark place to sleep and a windup clock close to him, so he would think he was with his mother.

I wrapped him secure within the warm folds of the towel, nestled the sleeping kitten into the corner of the couch, and set out on a scavenger hunt to find all the things he required.

In my garage, I found a small cat carrier, an old sweatshirt from my closet, a hot water bottle from the bathroom. I filled it with warm water and wrapped it in a kitchen towel and wound up an old clock from a yard sale box.

Then, I assembled a cozy nest within the portable confinement, and the fun began. I followed the instructions on the canister of kitten formula. Since I'd nursed both of my children, I found this bottle making stuff foreign overall.

I pierced a hole in the top of the nipple of the tiny bottle with a sharp sewing needle. Per the vet's instructions, I propped him up in a semi-sitting position and put the bottle in his mouth.

It was challenging as it was scary. No matter what sized hole I poked in the nipple, he still couldn't find satisfaction. After several attempts, we both gave up and settled with a needleless syringe the pharmacist once gave me instead.

At first, I worried I was pushing the plunger too fast, certain he'd drown for sure. But, not to worry, the little piglet sucked the plunger down faster than I could push it, content with how little of an effort it required of him.

The guidelines stated to feed him only a specific amount to a certain ounce in weight; but he was the exception to their rules, and guzzled super-sized amounts, every three to four hours until his belly looked like an over-filled water balloon.

Certain his cat mother would have done the same, I let him be the judge of how much he needed, continuing with the vet's instructions, and turned him on his tummy to wipe his bottom until he eliminated, this also made him burp.

I was as excited as a new mother; that was until the process became messier. Sometimes I didn't have enough tissue on hand to sop it all up, and it ended up on me, causing my hands to blister from repeated hand washings.

Once assured he had a full belly and was clean, I kissed the top of his tiny head, the start of an expected night-night ritual, and put him to bed on top of an old shirt, next to the warm, towel-wrapped water bottle, inside of the carrier.

Comforted by the warmth, he curled up next to it; the rhythmic ticking of the windup clock lulled him to sleep in no time.

Nestled within the surrogate cocoon, on the throw rug next to my bed, he slept like a baby with clean diapers, oblivious to the cruel world from which he'd been saved.

After tucking my children in for the night, I snuggled down in my bed, and prayed the little nest I'd prepared for him would suffice for the mother that wasn't there.

That first night, we both fell asleep quickly and soundly; but it was short-lived; he awoke for a feeding a prompt three hours later.

I once thought only the shrill ring from an alarm clock or a cry from my children were the only things that could wake me from a sound sleep, but his plaintive yowling was louder than he was big and surpassed them all.

Half asleep, with one eye open, vowing under my breath never to have another baby, human or animal, cradling the screaming baby kitty in my arms, I stumbled into the kitchen, and prepared the required apparatus for his midnight snack.

It didn't take long to learn to prepare, including an extra batch or two of formula, prior to bedtime.

With only the glow from the overhead stove lamp and his feeding and toileting arsenal at hand, I sat cross-legged on the rug in the middle of the kitchen floor and began what would become another evening routine for weeks to come.

It took almost an hour to prepare him for bed again, in addition to the ten minutes it took to re-warm his water bottle and change his soiled bed, but once we'd nestled in our beds for a second time, falling asleep was easy for both of us, him from a full tummy, and me from new kitty-mommy anxiety, and pure exhaustion.

The kitten posed another dilemma. I had to work the following Monday.

I called around, but there wasn't anyone who had the time to take on the responsibilities he required in an eight-hour workday, let alone for the next month or two of workdays.

As much as I didn't want to, I had to call my boss. She said my newborn could come to work with me, suggesting he sleep in the conference room while I worked.

When Monday morning rolled around, I awoke earlier than usual to get the both of us ready on time. I packed a makeshift diaper bag with his feeding and toileting apparatus, along with my lunch, wrapped him in one of my daughter's doll blankets, since it was early fall and the mornings were becoming cold, stuffed him into the cat carrier, hollered after-school instructions to my children, and walked out the door.

PART II

It was awkward carrying so much stuff the three long country blocks to the bus stop. I wished I still had a baby stroller, but that would bother the other commuters on the bus.

"*Oh well,*" I sighed aloud as I thought about doing this for the next three weeks, "*We'll live through this.*"

Once at the bus stop, I set down my cumbersome load and reached into my purse for my bus pass but found something wet instead.

The kitten milk I'd packed and fit into my purse spilled. I panicked. He couldn't go an entire day without his formula, and kitten milk wasn't available at the corner store. I had no other choice but to trudge all the way home and make more.

In a sweaty, frustrated hurry, I cleaned out my purse and put a new batch of milk in securer container. Because I had missed my scheduled bus, I had to drive to the nearest Park and Ride to catch another one. It was a miracle I made it to work on time.

The kitten was the main attraction where I worked. My coworkers celebrated with me when he first opened his eyes and ears and took his first steps.

As the days went by, he grew bigger and stronger, gaining an ounce or more each week. The vet couldn't believe how well he was doing and assured me he was well out of the woods.

He adjusted well to the daily hour and half bus ride to and from work and kept our fellow commuters amused with his growth and development milestones.

But it wasn't long before he protested his confinement in the carrier. He was loud and holding him was the only way to calm him, regardless of the bus policies.

Although I risked a long walk home, I harbored him in the folds of my jacket or put my hand in the carrier to console him. In my heart, I knew it was time to leave him at home, but, since he still seemed so young, I waited an additional week before attempting it.

When the time came, organizing his care around mine and my adolescent children's schedules, unconvinced they were ready to handle him, as the toileting task really grossed them out, they proved to be just as careful as I was, and my morning commute returned to normal.

Because he'd spent most of his early life in transit, he expected we take him along whenever the family went out. One Saturday I brought him with me to have lunch with Maggie. She doted and gushed over him, parading him around her office, showing him to all her coworkers.

She even insisted on being the one to feed and toilet him during our visit, that's just the type of Auntie she is, and then asked what his name was.

I said one hadn't caught my attention yet, it was like the conversation we had when I was eight months pregnant with my second child and hadn't decided on a girl's name if it were one.

She said ever since the kitten had come into my life, I'd been a different person, almost like my old self before Mark died.

An aching lump formed in my throat at the mere mention of his name, inviting grief to engulf me in its grips once again. I nuzzled the kitten for comfort, burying my face into his fur, fighting the urge to cry, and she continued.

Maggie said she believed Mark sent him to me. Her admission was surreal, she had always denied the possibility of such a thing. To consider him continuing to look out for me made my eyes burn and swell with tears.

She didn't stop there, and said the kitty should have an angelic, guardian sort of name, and suggested he be named Spirit.

Tears splashed down my cheeks. I cried for my angelic gift, and for my beloved. I nodded in agreement; it was a perfect name. A kitty who cheats death, and brings hope to a grieving family, must be a divine spirit.

PART II

TWENTY-THREE

It was unfathomable the first-year anniversary of Mark's death was just around the corner. Barry held a memorial at the foot of the troll. Many of his co-workers, union leaders, some family members, and Dale attended. Lex and I stayed home. It was noticeable how well I wasn't doing, and, above all, I didn't want to face the reality of the bridge.

The city dedicated a memorial plaque in Mark's memory to honor his heroism on that fateful day, and had it attached to the pillar where his bus impacted.

Metro held another ceremony at North Base; they unveiled an additional memorial plaque and placed it in the courtyard.

In the base's foyer, within a glass case, a display showcased the many achievements and awards Mark had earned over the years.

Later, I created a shadow box with an assortment of Safe Driver Award badges and pins Mark had saved. Barry placed it front and center within the display case.

Lexi had an extraordinary request from Barry; he shared the idea with Metro's operating manager, who shared the idea with the Red Cross and the Spangler Candy Company in Bryan, Ohio.

It wasn't long before Barry called to say they'd granted her wish. Spangler offered to donate 25,000 candy canes to Metro in memory of Mark, and not the customary red and white striped type, but the rare flavored kind that Mark liked to hand out to the children passengers during Christmas.

Even more incredible, the trucking company, Dawes Transport, offered to deliver all fifty-eight cases of the candy canes across the country, in blizzard-like conditions, for free!

It was amazing how it all came together. Lexi was beside herself. Just two weeks before Christmas, while the sweets made their way west, me and the kids worked with Barry on the candy cane drive, making life-size posters and flyers for each base.

A large easel propped up the announcement alongside a large barrel for the collection. During the next two weeks, candy canes of all kinds poured in.

When the day arrived at last, Barry invited the kids and me to ride on a route to help pass them out. Our excitement for the festivities masked our fear of the bus as we handed them to the kids who boarded. It was a great success, and we looked forward to doing it again the following year.

∽

Spirit grew in leaps and bounds over the next two summers, continuing to hurtle many obstacles along the way, acing all the kitty milestones without issue; amen he found the litter box a no-brainer.

He learned to walk by chasing my feet when I scooted backward, revving up to a full gallop in no time, trotting alongside me, with lazy, horse-like clippity-clop steps, echoing mine.

His body developed faster than his head did; but, not to worry though, my pin-headed kitty grew into himself in due course.

The vet predicted he'd weigh fifteen pounds by the time he finished growing, but he fooled them. At his final kitten check-up, he weighed a little over twenty pounds, making me wonder just what was in the kitten formula.

He was very serious about his self-ordained duty of watching over the family. In the evenings, as we slept, he'd rest his head on his outstretched paws, lay a bit on his side, ears at the ready like a canine cop, and doze lightly on the hard floor between our rooms, sounding the alarm by breaking down our doors with any unfamiliar noise, including falling leaves and thunderstorms.

While on duty, like an unmovable marble statue, he wouldn't budge, not even if we stumbled over him in the middle of the night to get to the bathroom.

His vigilance intensified if illness befell any of us. When my son and I had bouts of asthmatic coughing, he insisted we keep our bedroom doors open so he could check on us.

Woe was us if we forgot, he'd keep us awake all night with his worrisome yowling, and banging around until we allowed him in.

He'd carry on at meal time when he wanted a bite of what we were eating, or if we left without him, or shut him out of a room we were in, like the bathroom. But once he laid eyes on us again, all was forgiven, and he'd greet us with a hearty "Meow." I bet his picture is listed in the dictionary alongside the word *dramatic*.

His antics were just as entertaining during the day. If we didn't get up when our alarms blared, he'd bump, scratch, and rattle the doors 'til they about came off their hinges until he saw the white of our eyes emerge from our caves.

∽

With the new millennium came a tide of challenges. The first one being the high price of maintaining our new home, expensive heating bills and others I hadn't expected.

In addition to after-school care, groceries, and gas, it wasn't long before the expenses piled over my head and stretched beyond my grasp.

What I thought as a probable solution to my financial troubles, I'd signed up for a couple of credit cards, became an even bigger, scatterbrained plan of mismanagement, because I had to pay for those too.

To top it off, the used car I bought began acting up, so, I traded it in for what I believed was something better, my ignorance served me well.

The shark at the car lot talked me into an older Eddie Bauer Ford Explorer. He said it had room for the kids, all our stuff, and an adjustable front seat and steering wheel; but, they failed to mention how it would eat any remaining penny I had for gas and insurance.

Then, as the calendar passed the first anniversary of my job at the county, an all too familiar rumor of layoffs circulated in our office.

Always a step ahead, Barry offered me a position at the Union as a secretary which paid more than my county job; so, I jumped at the opportunity.

But after only a few months, once I'd adjusted to the fast-paced work environment, and the extra bus I had to take in the mornings, the Union elected new Officers; Barry wasn't one of them. Under the new regime, they phased my job out too.

Even worse, the new administration ruled there would no longer be any special recognition planned for Mark, including Candy Canes for Kids the following Christmas.

None of my explanations helped to patch Lexi's broken heart. And there it lay. Without official power, Barry could do no more, and he went on to resume his previous position as a driver.

The cherry on top was the day I received a letter from the IRS to audit my 1998 taxes.

TWENTY-FOUR

Besieged by uncontrolled asthma, burning eczema sores on both hands and fingers, throbbing bursitis in both hips, gut-eating ulcers, mind-numbing headaches, a weight gain of over forty pounds, and hair loss among others, I tucked in my tail and sought a doctor's care.

He said there was a name for what ailed me, Broken Heart Syndrome, and insisted I seek a counselor's help. But that wasn't all. He discovered something else, brought on by genetics which only surgery could correct.

He wrote a few prescriptions, assuring they were just short term. I took the pieces of paper with reluctance, knowing I had to comply for the children's sake, and then we discussed the grisly details of the impending surgery.

Amid the insurmountable bills and the uncertainty of the future of my job, I decided it best to sell our new home.

Of the friends we'd made in our cul-de-sac, a single father offered to share his place with us while I recovered from the surgery.

The children and I lugged most of what we had back into storage and moved into the kind neighbor's house. I hated myself for disappointing them, yet again.

Our new living quarters seemed shoe size, eight people in less than eight hundred square feet, three bedrooms, and one bathroom. I was thankful his children only visited on an occasional weekend.

Since my mom and sister had the same surgery without complications, I wasn't afraid of the procedure, that was until I awoke in a foggy, surreal state to learn they'd cut me from hip to hip, and given me a partial hysterectomy; they'd found cancer on my uterus and cervix.

They assured me all the diseased tissue had been removed, and I wouldn't require further treatment. While I recovered, I learned I was allergic to all pain medication.

With each new drug, I'd be consumed by severe hives and asthma. Tylenol became my only option, but it did nothing to mask the pain from the slightest movement.

The only saving grace from this horror is that it blanketed the grief in my heart. Several months passed before I could walk upright and resume my usual routine again.

Mindful of the doctor's suggestion, I sought the guidance from a counselor, although I knew I wasn't mentally ill, or suffering from some serious psychiatric break, or was I?

I tested the waters with a pastor recommended by a friend. He listened as I exorcized all my thoughts, feelings, and unusual experiences right into his lap. Spent but satisfied, I was certain he'd understand, and grant me a magical fix-all blessing.

Indifferent to my confession though, he asked point blank if I believed in God, and if so, did I blame Him for what happened.

Remembering the years of biblical lessons Mark taught me, I told him I believed, and it hadn't crossed my mind to blame Him.

He brought out a Bible and read from Exodus 22:22, Psalms 68:5, 146:9, Deuteronomy 10:18, and 1 Timothy 5:5 about how God takes care of the widows and the fatherless. It was ironic how I'd become a widow before becoming a bride.

He read from Job how God is always with us, whether we're good or bad, and several comforting passages from Psalms. Then from Mark 9:23, John 20:27, about holding onto trust and faith, and poignantly from Proverbs 3:5-6, the same passage I'd read from a poster the day *it* happened.

When he finished, I asked him why he thought God would concern himself with me when I wasn't a Christian, that I'd always considered Him an urban legend like the Easter Bunny, nor had I lived a moral life.

With reverent assurance, he explained how God loves us all, imperfections and the whole lot, how we are all His children, and He knows when we need Him the most, whether we feel like we're deserving, or not.

He said he believed we had truly witnessed God's love and grace, and perhaps through Mark's death, I was to learn about Him.

We talked in length about grief, the process, and how one moves through it. He explained the importance of prayer and of faith and said I could share all my worries and concerns with Him any time I needed. And then we prayed my first prayer together.

I followed the pastor's suggestions and talked about Mark to anyone who would listen. Most helpful were the prayers; I prayed all the time, for guidance, strength, and most of all for direction. I prayed right through the days that were the hardest to get through, and somehow felt better.

Then I sought grief counseling but found talking about it made it hurt even more. The counselor signed me up for a bereavement group, but I did not find comfort in hearing about another soul's pain. I wrote in journals, took walks, and went to a healing retreat.

My roommate went with me to visit Mark's beloved Whidbey Island. I brought a metal security box filled with a few of mine and Mark's special things: a lock of my hair, his ponytail he'd cut off once before, some mementos and pictures, and buried it underneath the Deception Pass Bridge.

I lit a green candle and sat next to the shore with reverent thoughts of saying goodbye and letting go, until the candle burned to the end of its wick.

As I was about to leave, within arm's reach, a large white seal with grey spots popped its head out of the water, held me captive with its immense black eyes and steady gaze for a moment, and then disappeared under the water again.

The experience was comforting. Remembering Mark's lessons about animal spirituality and their relationship with God and us, made the perfect ending to the ritual.

Always in tune to my emotions, Spirit seemed to sense my current disposition, and became even more vigilant than usual, not letting me out of his sight, doing all he could to distract me from the ever-present grey cloud over my head.

When he wasn't in my shadow, he'd hide in some unexpected place, and wait to ambush me the moment I walked by. Although I knew he'd fly from out of nowhere and tackle my ankles from behind, he still terrified me half-to-death when he did. I'm certain my dramatic reactions encouraged him to keep up his little game.

If he didn't scare me out of my funk, he'd go to the next level to make me laugh. Like the time I caught him stealing my cherry cough drops. He had opened and climbed into my toiletries drawer somehow and was about to fish out a lozenge when I startled him.

He popped his noggin out of the deep compartment with the bag stuck over his head; the remaining drops cascaded down his body like an upset apple cart. Mission accomplished; I never laughed as hard as I did that day.

Despite his best efforts though, and my faux optimism, nothing helped. The wound in my heart was as deep as the Grand Canyon and just as fresh as the day it tore apart. In my mind and in my heart, Mark wasn't really gone, and no one could convince me otherwise.

I didn't want to *process through grief*, ever; I just wanted him to come home. As a last resort, I tried acupuncture and several antidepressants, but they proved to be just as ineffective as the rest. At an end, and out of ideas, the doctor told me there wasn't a magic pill or remedy to mend my broken heart, it was something only time could heal.

PART II

TWENTY-FIVE

With spring, came renewed physical health, accompanied by a deeper depression that worsened with any new confronting challenge. I returned to work at the Union, but only for a brief time before being let go because of another initiative that passed, or so they said, I'm sure it had nothing to do with my current lovely outlook.

With my tail between my legs once more, I retreated to the all too familiar unemployment line, where even the staff knew me by my first name. I sent out numerous resumes and cover letters for various jobs, and reapplied with the County, which wasn't hiring; or rehiring, boy did I chastise myself for moving from that job.

Whenever I found work, it didn't last long. Keeping full-time employment seemed more and more of a challenge. I just couldn't function like I used to in a work setting, with coworkers, or in the overall real world.

It wasn't long before our tiny living quarters turned into a battleground for our two families. One day I came home to an empty house. My roommate just up and moved out. To make matters worse, the landlords were his parents.

I breathed a sigh of relief the day they agreed to let us stay. I signed a new contract for a reduced rent and an agreement to vacate the premises within four months.

To save money, I traded in the Ford Explorer for an older MPV, resumed my place at the food bank lines, and spent hours sorting through our storage unit in search of expendable things to pawn to pay the rent and other bills.

It took a lot of effort to minimize the urgency of the situation I had gotten us into, yet again, and to keep up the facade of normalcy to the outside world, including my children.

With the dawn of each new day, it was all I could do to get out of bed. Exhausted from running from something I didn't understand, I found little joy in anything anymore. There was nothing to laugh about. The world was no longer beautiful, nor was I. The weight of it all was upon my shoulders, and I was crumbling from beneath it.

My body ached, and my legs felt like lead. I had fallen into a deep dark pit with no way out, becoming more like Eeyore than Piglet nowadays.

My emotions came and went like the tide, their intensity varied hour by hour, and day to day. When the tears started, the anguish in my heart was quick to follow. Any little thing made me cry, even if someone asked how I was, or to say, "I'm sorry for your loss."

Whenever I heard those words, they'd rip the scab off my heart to reveal the overwhelming sorrow that dwelled in there, tearing away my insides, leaving but an empty shell. I allowed myself to become lost, discombobulated, and alone.

All I'd worked so hard and sacrificed for, aspired and hoped for, died with Mark. I kicked myself for my stupidity.

I lost sight of the future; a cold and black, empty void filled its space instead. I felt orphaned now more than ever, convinced no one would ever care for me in the way he did.

Spirit, true to his loyalty, dialed in to my dismal disposition. Whether lonely, or missing Mark the most, he'd stand on his hind legs, lean on me with one paw, reach out with the other, and meow, as if to say, "I'm here."

Then, when I picked him up, he'd wrap his giant gentle paws around my neck, and let me hug him as tight as I needed. If I felt the urge to cry, he'd allow me to bury my face into his soft furry neck until the storm passed.

He'd purr, loud and consoling, into my ear the whole while, unconcerned about how wet my tears made him, or how constricting my hugs were. There's not a written word to describe the love I felt for my one in a million, irreplaceable kitty.

I wallowed unashamed in my pain and misery, all I could think about was that day and nothing before. I didn't want to celebrate anything, not holidays or birthdays, or life for that matter. The more I let doom and gloom consume me, the more I beat myself up for feeling the way I did.

One day I decided I'd had enough and contrived a plan. I'd drive to the Aurora Bridge, around one in the morning when there would be little or no traffic, make myself drunker than a skunk with an entire bottle of vodka, and gun my car as hard as I could over the bridge, right into Mark's waiting arms.

The plan is all I thought about, certain it was the only way to relieve the consuming pain in my heart, and the only way I could be with Mark again.

It clouded my judgment and reasoning. I didn't even consider my precious babies, I believed they'd be better off without my ever-increasing instability. My absence would spare them from being dragged down into a bottomless abyss of sadness and despair.

The night of, as I put them to bed, I kissed and hugged them more than usual; my heart ached at the thought of how much I'd miss them.

PART II

When they were sound asleep, I went to the kitchen and pulled out the bottle of vodka I'd stashed in the back of a cupboard, put it in a paper bag, and crept out to my car.

TWENTY-SIX

While I traveled south on the interstate towards *the* bridge, thoughts that were not my own screamed for me to pull off the next exit. Bewildered but compliant, I pulled off the freeway, the exit for my mother's place.

I knew she would still be up, and sitting in her easy chair, absorbed in a Harlequin romance novel, without a care in the world.

I surprised her when I rang her apartment on the security phone. She was waiting for me when I arrived at her door, certain something was wrong.

She asked several times what the matter was, as I guided her back to her chair. Lost for words, I could only shake my head through tears.

Once seated, I knelt beside her. Her hands shook as she lit a cigarette. As if I were seven years old again, I rested my head in her lap, and cried, oblivious to the suffocating smoke swirling about my head.

To see me shed tears made her cry too. Concerned and desperate, she pried for an explanation behind my extraordinary and unexpected late-night visit and asked why her grandchildren weren't with me.

Between sobs, I explained I'd come to say good-bye.

My intentions hit her like a ton of bricks. She slid down from her chair to sit beside me and looked me square in the eyes.

Shock and fear overshadowed her ageless face, as she took mine in her hands, and pleaded for me to not even consider such a thing.

Then, she gathered me into a fierce embrace, and rocked me back and forth imploring,

"No, no, no Lissie!"

I told her the pain was too much, and I couldn't live with it anymore.

"But," she pressed, "Don't you see, I can't live without YOU! Who will take care of me? All I have is you. We all love you Lissie! Me and the children, we need you!"

With that, she wept and moaned like I'd never heard her before, the same way I'd cried for Mark the first time I saw him lying in the casket.

Her body shook, and her tears soaked my hair and face, as she kissed my cheeks.

PART II

"Mommy's here baby, you just hold onto me when you can't take it anymore. I can't fix it, but I can hold you. Please Lissie don't, please don't do this thing."

I'd frightened and hurt her, and I hated myself even more. We hugged and rocked for what seemed an eternity.

"It's okay Mommy, I won't; I'll keep trying, I promise."

I left sometime later, assuring her I'd call when I got home.

And home I went.

After calling and reassuring her I'd arrived safe and sound, I crawled into bed, and curled up with Lexi. I whispered how sorry I was for contemplating such a thing, and quietly wept myself to sleep.

The following evening, Maggie called to invite us over for movies and pizza. The movies she chose were too close for comfort, City of Angels, What Dreams May Come, and The Sixth Sense.

In an in-between-the-lines kind of way, the movie's message, What Dreams May Come, was loud and clear. If I ever wanted to be with Mark again, I could never give up, or I'd end up in some God-forsaken, horrible and lonely place, far away from him, my family, and my children. And unlike the movie, there would be no way back.

To fathom never seeing my children again, the possibility of being stuck between two worlds, and to have to suffer the pain I'd caused everyone for eternity was too much. No thanks, no matter how hopeless it all seemed, I would find a way to tough it out.

Even though I watched the last movie between my fingers, its ending was so surprising, yet so profound, I bawled my eyes out.

Maggie seemed a little miffed. I know she just wanted me to have fun for a while, but as usual, I got all shook up instead.

On the way home, I thought how reassuring it was not to be alone in my feelings or experiences. Whoever wrote the scripts for the movies, didn't just have vivid imaginations, their inspiration must have come from personal experience.

∽

I'd saved enough money for us to move, again, to a charming duplex across the speedway from where we lived, allowing the children to stay in the same school district.

It was a relief to move our stuff from storage, and to be among our personal things again. All seemed peaceful and right again in our new home.

By the second day, I'd about unpacked and put away all our things, but I couldn't find mine and Mark's engagement picture. I rifled through the last remaining boxes in the garage to no avail.

As I searched, a familiar maternal voice in my head said, "Look in *the box*."

For the first time, I ignored it. I wasn't ready to open *that* box. Frustrated and exhausted, I sat in a defeated heap and cried.

How had I accumulated so much stuff, even after all I had taken to the pawn shop?

As I contemplated where the picture might be, the thought became more consistent.

"Okay, okay," I said aloud, and approached *it*.

I almost screamed when I pried the box open. There it was, on the top, front, and center of everything, alongside his burial flag. I couldn't remember putting it there, nor would I.

Oh well, I thought, and snatched it out, quick to reseal the tomb in a mere two steps.

My soul at peace at last, I dusted it off, and placed it on the nightstand closest to my pillow.

Mark's presence seemed to linger around me more than usual; I felt guilty for not letting him rest in peace, hanging onto his memory with an iron fist.

This may have been the very reason why the unexplainable resurfaced again.

PART II

TWENTY-SEVEN

The strange occurrences didn't scare us. They made us laugh for the most part. It became commonplace for one of us to chime, "Dad's here!"

But sometimes the kids didn't think his visits were so funny, like when they wouldn't listen, and I'd become upset. Just when the veins in my forehead threatened to burst, and my asthma hindered my ability to yell, the lights in the room would turn off and on, until they hopped to whatever I'd expected of them.

Boy, you never saw two children move faster than they did when that happened. For whatever it was, it worked. And being children, you can imagine why none of their friends asked to stay the night, especially after the experience of one of Lexi's friends.

One day, as we pulled into our driveway, we saw her friend running and screaming from our house.

She said she'd invited herself in because the door wasn't locked, and, while waiting for us at the kitchen table, she'd heard a noise from the other side of the house, and, assuming it was one of our cats, went to investigate.

When she approached the hallway, she didn't find a cat, but rather a large man standing in the doorway to my bedroom, with an angry scowl on his face, and pointing toward the main door.

She described the man in precise detail; Mark fit the bill. Since she hadn't been in my room to see our photo, and there were no pictures on the walls yet, she wouldn't have known what he looked like.

As well, Lexi hadn't spoken about him to her before, so she wouldn't have known the way he pointed at her was the way he did whenever she, or the boys, had pushed him too far.

It worked every time, without a word, he'd just point. The sternness in his face and his pointing finger was all it took for them to heed to his authority.

He was telling the child she was inside without being invited, and to get out. She never visited again. Money couldn't buy a better security system.

To be certain there wasn't an electrical problem, the landlord sent an electrician to give the house a thorough once-over. As I figured, our five-year-old duplex got a clean bill of health.

Besides Mark's sporadic visits, our benevolent spirit bird, the mysterious stellar jay, continued to watch over us. Because the children noticed him, confirmed I wasn't halfway over the cuckoo nest.

One ear always at the ready for the familiar cacophonous squawking, hoping to be the first one to see him, the kids would look high and low, through all the windows in the house until they spotted him.

"There he is, mama! There he is, there's your bird!"

If all of that wasn't unfathomable enough, an occasional blanket of cold air hung around me like Saran Wrap, and I couldn't shake it off no matter what.

It fascinated the kids, that is, until the day it touched Lexi.

One morning I found her alone at the kitchen table crying. In between mournful sobs, she said she had been thinking about daddy Mark when she felt something cold on her hand, and then on her cheek.

She said she knew it was daddy and cried even harder. Before I could say anything, she burst out laughing, about as hard as she had been bawling, and could only point at me as to why.

I looked in the bathroom mirror and freaked. My long hair, Mark's favorite part of me, stood straight up like an orangutan's.

For the next half hour, we laughed as the static fluctuated in my hair, regardless of where I stood. Logic aside, it was just like Mark to make Lex laugh her unhappy tears away; and so, began the static moment's phenomenon, a gratifying, instant mood lifter, a surefire sign of Mark's presence; like the bird, the children kept a vigilant eye out for them.

Convinced of his presence, without missing a beat, they'd tell him as much as they could before my hair resettled around my shoulders.

Although these unexplainable occurrences wouldn't make sense to anyone else, and maybe there was a rational explanation behind them, they comforted us. Believing he was still around, nothing else mattered.

Spirit's third summer, Mark's birthday to be exact, began one cool evening with his daring escape out the front door.

PART II

TWENTY-EIGHT

*A*lways hoping for an out through the incoming traffic, his efforts paid off at last, and he was free from the confines of the inside. My mind numbed as I watched him disappear around the corner.

I chased after him, but, faster than any free bird had ever flown, he vanished. I called and whistled for him at hourly intervals, but he didn't return.

Sleep evaded me, ever vigilant for his meowing or scratching on the door, but none ever came. The next morning, I resumed the search, but there was still no sign of him.

As I hurried Lexi towards the door for the school bus, a stampede of footsteps on the porch startled us. It was a group of my daughter's school friends.

They were breathless and appeared as if something had frightened them. They begged me to come to the bus stop, muttering something about finding Spirit, and took off down the street.

With a sick sense of déjà vu, I ran after them. I wiggled through a group of kids to find Spirit lying motionless on the sidewalk. In my mind, I saw Mark.

Oblivious to the stares from the children and the neighbors, I screamed, and collapsed into a weeping heap at my precious guardian angel's side.

Someone offered me a blanket. Just as I had done three years before, I gathered him within its folds, and took him home.

I placed him in the back seat of my truck and went inside to tell my daughter. From the familiar look on my face, she knew something was terribly wrong.

"What?" She implored, "What's wrong Mommy?!"

With her friends looking on, I took her into my arms, and told her the heart-crushing news.

"No!" she screamed and burst into tears.

She buried her face into my chest; the pain in her soul vibrated through mine.

I held her as close as possible, until the heaving sobs left in her body.

My God, how would I ever fix this?

She insisted on carrying Spirit's body in her lap while I drove to the school.

Her friends left for class, and I excused Lexi for the day, so she could go with me to the animal hospital.

I hesitated before surrendering our precious, tear-soaked, angel.

They understood without my saying so, and told me about a man who lived in the community who cremated pets, and made special pine boxes to hold their ashes in.

It was just what we wanted.

Within a week, we had Spirit back with us in his own special box. Although his love for Lexi was unequivocal, we were each other's guardian angel. Brought together in our most desperate hours, we'd saved each other from uncertain fates. He kept me from wallowing in depression, and I gave him life-sustaining care.

A short while later, Dale got his first job as an assistant at a veterinary clinic on the other side of the Speedway. He hadn't worked there long, when he came home one day with a woeful tale about an unadoptable kitten with a chronic sinus infection.

PART II

TWENTY-NINE

*D*ale knows I am a sucker for sick animals. So, of course, it was a shoo-in after I'd seen the sorrowful kitten for myself, adding one more to our growing fur family, who became known as Sniffles.

Her coat was as black as night like Spirit's, until she passed kittenhood, then, a white layer of fur grew in near her skin, only seen if she was petted the wrong way.

Without skipping a beat, Sniffles took over where Spirit left off, but in a motherly type of way. Although she was more petite and daintier than Spirit, she was serious about her charge over me. She would even growl at the window if she didn't recognize the person approaching our house.

Because she required regular checkups, we became close friends with the doctor. Towards the end of Sniffles' first year, he invited us to see a Christmas play at the church he attended. We hadn't been to a house of worship before, but after all the unexplainable events we had experienced since Mark's death, we were eager to check it out.

The congregation welcomed us with open arms, as if we were members of their family. The kids never complained about getting up early to attend the services. In fact, they were the ones rushing me out the door to get to the church on time.

We joined many of their family functions. The kids participated in their youth group, sang at events, and took part in plays. They even became members of their Christian missionary group, traveling all the way to Mexico one time, and volunteered as counselors during the summers for the little kid's annual day camp.

After attending for about a year, the pastor asked us if we would like to become official members of the church. They didn't have to ask twice, and we spent the next several months preparing for the ceremony. If I had a list of the best days of my life, the morning they baptized us together would be one of them.

With the congregation as witnesses, we knelt before the pastor and a senior elder, the vet no less, and shared the most beautiful moment of our lives as a family. Afterwards, we stood before the gathering and took turns reading scriptures fitting for the special day.

I read 1 Timothy 5:5, Hebrews 13:20-21, and said a brief thank you to the congregation. Dale read Acts 4:32 and 1 Corinthians 13:13. And Lex read

Hebrews 11:1 and the Advent reading. We finished in unison by wishing the audience a wonderful Easter. There wasn't a dry eye in the pews.

As official members, we were encouraged to take part in different activities; the children dove right in, but I continued to prefer to be alone. Although I was excited about the new path we had chosen, it still wasn't enough to take away the painful gloominess I'd struggled with for so long, and I didn't want to burden anyone else with my issues.

To avoid bringing attention to myself, I joined a few bible studies, participated in their weekly potluck gatherings, volunteering to host one or two at my house, and that's about it. I couldn't trust the church family, or anyone, not to take it upon themselves to help through my grief.

With all my heart, I believed Mark wasn't gone, and I'd wake one day to find everything back to normal. Not wanting to hear otherwise, I drifted away from the church by taking a weekend job.

The children continued their involvement a while longer, but when Dale became wrapped up with the final requirements to graduate from high school, his band practice, and job, and Lex busy with her own activities, they too faded away from the gathering. I'm sure I was a little to blame for their eventual lack of interest.

I continued to worship on my own. My relationship with God was mine, within the secure privacy of my heart, where I kept Mark. With Him, I could grieve without opinion, expectation, or a timeline.

༄

Any extra time I had, I looked after my mother. With her, I found solace and could be myself. She never played judge or jury. She was the only person, other than Mark, and God, who understood, accepted, and loved me for who I was, no matter what; as I did her.

Sweet and delicate like the butterflies she loved so much, Mommy always viewed the world, and everyone in it, through innocent eyes, seeing only the good in others, trusting totally, and never had an unkind word to say about anyone.

Although I'd been more her mother, more than she mine, for as long as I can remember, she was still my best friend. We were two peas in a pod; we thought the same things were funny, enjoyed similar TV shows and movies, and we loved to play dice and cards, Yahtzee, Zilch, and Shit on Your Neighbor, for hours and hours, in which no one, not even Mark, would make time to do, or enjoy like she and I did.

In her early sixties, she suffered from a variety of lifelong disabilities and was in poor health. Unable to work most of her life, she survived on a meager living expense from the government.

As well, years of sitting like a stump in her ratted easy chair, smoking like a chimney, and not caring about what kinds of food she ate, had taken a toll on her body, affecting her ability to care for herself.

I quit my weekend job and didn't bat an eye the day they laid me off from my weekday job, to give her the extra help she needed.

The government paid me a trivial supplement to take her to doctor appointments, do her shopping, errands, laundry, housecleaning, and personal care, but it wasn't enough.

Between unemployment benefits and several part-time jobs, I made ends meet. I can't say how I did it, but somehow, things always worked themselves out.

By hook or by crook, I never missed the children's school bus; thankfully, it stopped between my apartment and hers. Trust me when I say, they were not inconvenienced in the least when they had to visit their Grammy, and I'm sure it had nothing to do with her pantry shelf full of junk food.

There wasn't a day I didn't work like a mad woman, practicing all I'd learned in nursing school to lessen Mommy's pain, hiding from the grief in my heart, and dodging the truth of what had become our new reality.

I changed her diet, enrolled her in a smoking cessation program, gave her daily hot baths and massages; but, regardless of my best efforts, her pain triumphed over it all.

Her doctor determined she needed two different surgeries, one for her back and the other to replace her hip. With much discussion, it was decided her back was most important.

It was all planned. The papers were signed, allowing me guardianship should anything go wrong, her suitcase packed, and her neighbor's promise to look after her kitty while she was away.

After a successful surgery and recovery, with my help and a visiting physical therapist, she'd come home to get healthy for the next surgery.

But that's not the way it unfolded at all.

THIRTY

Scared to death of the hospital and all the strangers, she held fast to my promise I had it all under control, and she was safe. Pulling the curtains closed around us in the prep area, I whispered we had one more security measure to cover.

I explained that, regardless of her religious convictions, she had to get right with Jesus before they hauled her into surgery, just for good measure. Much to my disbelief, she didn't get bent out of shape by the idea.

Not unlike that of a frightened child, she held tight to my hands, squeezed her eyes shut, and nodded every so often as I prayed over her.

With what I learned from my time with the church, I asked if she believed Jesus lived, died, and rose again so we would be forgiven for our sins.

She whispered she did, and then I prayed for His protection and healing for her surgery. All securities locked and loaded, we hugged, and I smiled as I wiped away the tears that spilled down her cheeks.

"I love you, Lissie."

"I love you too, Mommy."

When I opened the curtains, there wasn't a dry eye in the room; they'd overheard the prayer.

The surgery lasted ten hours. I thought I'd go mad waiting, so I called the pastor from our church. Then, I tried to read, but kept repeating the same sentence.

I must have downed all the hospital's coffee and worn a hole in the linoleum by the time the doctor reappeared to say the surgery had been a success.

While she rested in recovery, I curled up on one of the waiting room chairs, and fell into a sound sleep.

Little did I know, a series of unfortunate events would bring about a tragic and painful end for her, and yet another test of my resolve.

After a couple of days, as I prepared to take her home, the doctor stopped in to explain how she'd require more physical therapy before releasing her, nine days' minimum, two weeks max.

My hands were tied; another promise I had to break; *how would I tell her?*

Of course, my confession upset and alarmed her, she only trusted me to take care of her.

PART II

I did an extensive search for the best rehab facility close to us, one that would give her the same care I would. My sister and I chose one near Richmond Beach, and the hospital sent them her paperwork.

Assured of an effortless transition, Maggie rented an apartment close by, and moved in straight away to share in Mommy's care.

On the day of her hospital discharge, the nurse at the facility called to inform me there had been a mistake. They understood my mom's insurance was Medicare, not Medicaid, and said they didn't have a vacancy for my mom's type of insurance.

Unbelievable, Maggie and I were beyond furious. With just hours until her release, I found another facility closer to my house that would take her insurance, in the center of my route between work, the children's school, and home.

The whole ordeal was a nightmare. Although I conveyed my mom's delicate emotional, mental, and physical health, stressing to the director of the faculty how important it was to give her psychological medication on time, the staff still didn't treat her with much regard, which only exacerbated her anxiety.

Maggie and I decorated the corner of her room as cheerful as we could, brought her treats and homemade food, and spent as much time as possible with her, always promising how she'd be returning home soon enough.

I did my best to make her comfortable, and only left her side in the evenings, but it wasn't enough. The place and the roughness of the staff frightened her. She cried the entire time I was away, delaying her body's ability to heal.

On the morning of the third day, I returned to find her missing from her bed. In an all-out panic, I searched the bathroom, the dining area, and the TV room, but turned up empty-handed.

I inquired of her whereabouts at the nurses' station. As if giving the weather report, they said she'd been taken to the hospital.

I ran to my car and drove as fast as possible to the emergency room. All the while, a dreadful sense of déjà vu gripped its familiar, cold, and clammy fingers around my heart.

As they escorted me to her trauma room, I got a grip on my breathing and tried to calm myself, but it was all for naught.

I couldn't wrap my mind around the scene before me; the room spun when my eyes found Mommy, hooked up to every wire and tubing imaginable.

Someone sat me in a chair; a doctor approached me; her mouth moved in garbled words, taking me back to the waiting room of Harborview Hospital. My eyes stayed with Mommy. The doctor said she'd aspirated and had a severe stroke.

A bitter sense of betrayal tightened around my heart like I'd never felt before. I pulled a chair close to the side of her bed, held her hand, and rested my head on her chest, amid an array of wires and tubing.

In-between an inconsolable flood of tears, apologizing over and over for breaking my promise, regurgitating the familiar, sickening, suffocating ache all over again, in my throat, my eyes, and my heart.

And then I got mad.

I jumped out of the chair, and demanded to know how this had happened, but my barking fell on deaf ears, and only made me hoarse.

Over the next few days, her condition worsened. She couldn't talk, or stay awake, and, because she couldn't swallow without choking, she had a feeding tube inserted through her abdomen.

Even worse, because of the threat of another blood clot, they had to slice the calf of her left leg wide open and leave it that way.

One morning, I returned to find her missing, again, and panicked. They'd discharged her to a nearby nursing home. I ran across the street to the place where they had taken her. When I inquired at the nurses' station of her whereabouts, no one had heard of her, or what room she was in.

As if the star in my own horror movie, my heart pounded in my ears like a gong, and sweat dripped from every pore in my body, as I raced up and down the halls in search of her.

I found her in a room the furthest back; she was dangling haphazardly from a bed, and I rushed to her side to set her right.

Her semi-conscious body burned with fever as I cradled her in my arms and rocked her back and forth until I'd calmed down some.

And I cried for the both of us, "I'm sorry Mommy, so, so sorry."

I left her just long enough to yell for a nurse. My frantic, shrill cry echoed throughout the quiet corridor. It was like a ghost town, no patients, no staff.

When I located one, I pulled her into Mommy's room. Not well versed in the English language, she didn't understand what was wrong. I snatched the stethoscope and electric thermometer from her pocket and dialed 911.

Mommy's temp was near a hundred and three, and her blood pressure had about bottomed out. A chill ran up my spine at the thought of how I'd almost lost her. The medics brought her back to the hospital ER.

In a trauma room once again, I began shivering uncontrollably; I'd never been so irate in my life.

Maggie arrived not long after. We cried on each other's shoulders and hugged with the same desperate fierceness as we did when frightened as little girls.

Free of our pent-up emotions, wanting to calm our nerves, we did the most unordinary thing. Beyond the brink of reasoning, we searched the contents of Mommy's purse, found a pack of her nasty, dime store cigarettes, walked to the parking lot, smoked one, then another, and returned to the hospital.

We found Mommy resting peacefully and stood on either side of her; Maggie held her hand while I wiped the perspiration from her brow with a cool washcloth.

The doctor came in. He said the stroke had paralyzed her throat muscles, and she risked a ninety-nine percent chance of repeating an episode like the one she'd just had.

He asked us if we thought she'd want to live the rest of her life that way. Maggie and I looked at one another, his suggestion taking mere seconds to seep in.

Without conviction, our hearts knew what mommy would have wanted. Deprived of her Irish cream coffee and Dr. Pepper soda, Harlequin romances, the Eagles club, chocolate and treats, double cheeseburgers, cards or dice, it would not be a quality of life for her.

I promised the day of her surgery, if it ever came to this, I would not let her live her life as a vegetable. Tears welled in our eyes as we squeezed her hand.

Maggie looked away while I arranged for hospice care, had them remove her tubes, and assured she was given morphine to keep her comfortable.

Then, I signed her death warrant.

THIRTY-ONE

It was the utmost, second worse day of my life; I felt like crap because I didn't even get to say goodbye; I never should have left her alone.

The next day, they transferred Mommy to a hospice care facility, located across the street from my sister's apartment, the exact same place that turned her away a few days earlier.

Her insurance would cover hospice at this facility, but not rehab, go figure.

With Maggie living nearby, it was easier to share in the care of each other's children, and keep a constant vigil next to Mommy.

Like the other place, we decorated her little corner of the room, and fussed over her like we'd never had before.

When it was my turn to sit with her, I took my anger out on the staff by barking at the nurses if she wasn't clean and chased away the male orderlies if they even thought of stepping into her room.

I wanted to be alone with her, to tend to the open wound on her leg, and to care for her as only I knew how. I spent hours reading all the Psalms to her until my throat ached, hoping to find salvation for both of us. Despite my best efforts though, atonement never came.

One morning I awoke to a cold and stormy day. The wind was blowing something fierce by the time I left to visit Mommy. Halfway there, in the middle of a busy highway, the serpentine belt in my Ford Explorer snapped.

It was fortunate Dale was with me that day, and how it had happened in front of a mechanic's shop. We fought the elements and the stationary steering wheel and guided the truck into the garage.

Maggie picked us up. She said she thought Mommy wasn't doing so well, and that we should have the children visit her right away.

The wind had knocked out the power in the nursing home. It was dark and as quiet as a morgue, except for the steady hum of a generator.

When we entered Mommy's room, it was just like Maggie had said, something didn't seem quite right.

Within the dimness of a flashlight, Mommy's three grandchildren lavished her with teary hugs and kisses and said their final farewells; Maggie almost had to drag them away from her.

I stayed behind for what I thought was the final vigil and whispered beautiful words from my Bible to comfort both our souls, concentrating on Psalm 23.

Lost in the moment, I about leaped from my chair when Mommy sat straight up, pointed at the corner of the room, and exclaimed, "The man!"

I shined the flashlight around every corner. Although no one else was in the room, I was certain we were not alone. Seeking solace for the both of us, I gathered her in my arms, stroked her hair, and rocked her in the quiet darkness like she did for me whenever I was sick as a little girl, like she did for me a few months earlier.

I told her how it could've been a man, an angel, or Jesus coming to take her home, and not to fear whoever it was; I elaborated about the wonderful place where she was going, and how the rest of us would join her there one day.

Tears of regret, guilt, and blame dripped onto my cheeks as I assured her I'd be okay, and how she had our permission if she was ready to go.

I held her for the longest time as she labored for even the tiniest of breaths.

Near midnight, unconvinced that tonight was the night, I kissed her forehead and returned to Maggie's place. As I walked away, I was startled by the sudden return of the power, shining bright like a beacon in the night, as if illuminating some invisible path.

We stayed the night with Maggie, just in case. The death knoll came by way of a shrill ring from the telephone at three a.m. I stumbled through the unfamiliar darkness towards the sound, smacking my shin on the coffee table along the way.

It was the hospice nurse. She told me what I already knew; the angels had taken her home; Mommy was gone.

My sister and I threw on our coats and ran across the street to the facility. The atmosphere in her room reminded me of the peculiar stillness of the funeral home. But this time I wasn't afraid.

I laid down beside her, wrapped one arm around her lifeless body, buried my face into the softness of her hair. and released all the tears I had kept from her.

After expunging my soul, I wiped the tears from my face, and whispered in her ear, "Goodbye Mommy. Please forgive me. I'm so sorry."

Comfortable with our final respects, Maggie and I walked back to her apartment. Silence filled the space between us as we tried to digest what we'd experienced.

We reached for each other's hands, our grasps even more desperate than ever before because this time we knew she wouldn't be coming back.

The absurdness of the entire ordeal didn't end there. Neither Maggie or I had the money for burial expenses, and Mommy didn't have a life insurance policy, so the funeral home suggested a cremation; but, before they would do it, they required a down payment of $150 upfront, and the remaining $350 to release her ashes.

They said they would keep her in a refrigerator until we could come up with the money; unbelievable.

While Maggie made phone calls, searching far and wide for the funds, I took on the challenge of cleaning out her apartment of fifteen years.

Somehow, I had it vacated before the following month's rent was due, most in part because of the many neighbors who were glad to have the furnishings and other possessions I gave away.

It took almost two weeks to raise the cash for Mommy's release. As macabre as it may sound, we had her ashes put into two urns, one part of her for each of us.

Mommy arrived in two small aluminum containers, not unlike the cheap candy tins she bought at the drug store, but she was with us again, and that's what mattered most.

Amid all the heartache and confusion, my thirty-eighth birthday came and went. No Betty Crocker mix in a blackened cake pan with frosting and sprinkles to surprise me this year, or ever again.

Just when things seemed to settle back in place, the fifth anniversary of Mark's death reared its ugly head.

Without a word to anyone, I closed the bedroom blinds, crawled into bed, and prayed for the holidays to be over. I felt more alone than I ever had before; I'd lost my best friend, and my handsome prince had fallen from his horse.

Pushed to the limit, the familiar comfort of defeat and the reluctance to go on weakened my heart, but I knew I had to push on. I promised Mommy I would.

With the gradual strengthening of my resolve, I compelled to forge ahead, if only by faith and hope.

PART II

THIRTY-TWO

I'd smoked off and on in my teens and twenties, but I kicked the habit for Mark back in '93. I'm not sure he ever knew because I felt ashamed of it and kept it to myself.

Mommy's death shoved me off the wagon. One day, while the children were away at school, I searched the garage like a madwoman for her purse. Rummaging through its contents, I found the very thing I was after, her cigarettes.

I took them to the back porch and lit one. It was stale and nasty tasting; I'd sealed the deal with the unhealthy habit once again, hoping they'd cause me a somewhat natural death.

I only indulged in the fixation in private. As a former closet smoker, I knew how to keep it under wraps.

I stashed all the necessities required for my *I hate smoking* campaign in my car: a toothbrush and toothpaste, gum, breathe lozenges, a washrag, liquid instant soap, a bottle of water, and my inhaler, just in case.

Because I hated the nauseating stench, and even worse aftertaste, my cleaning ritual extended beyond the obsessive and ridiculous. Sometimes I rubbed the skin in and around my mouth raw just to get rid of it.

Too embarrassed to smoke in public, the more opportunities I had alone, increased the number of cigarettes I'd burn through, resulting in an insatiable craving.

If I couldn't be alone, I'd become agitated and irritable, consumed by a vicious cycle of panic attacks. I discovered private places to park and smoke: behind school buildings, in old abandoned parks, and behind grocery stores to name a few.

Somehow, they made me feel better; yet, they made me feel worse at the same time. It wasn't long before the cravings kept me awake at night, so, I took a risk, and lit up on our back porch once the kids were asleep.

They almost caught me several times, and I don't think I fooled them either, one more thing to beat myself up for.

Common sense said it was probable I'd live to be a million years old, with or without the cancer sticks, before ever seeing either Mommy or Mark again.

So, in addition to the smoking, hoping to make time go by faster, I planned to work myself to death, taking on a variety of part-time jobs, right through the weekends, busying myself with the children's activities, and cleaning the house beyond compulsiveness.

But, no matter how much I did, I couldn't make up for the money that time didn't make, and soon was way in over my head, forced to file for bankruptcy.

None of it mattered though. I didn't care about my credit, or much of anything anymore, not even the failing of my health again, absorbed with only one goal.

Along with the bankruptcy came the repossession of my car in the middle of one night. Since we lived in an area with limited bus service, and the children had extracurricular activities scattered throughout Lynnwood, we found ourselves paralyzed without a car.

The church loaned me some money, and I purchased an Uncle Buck station wagon for a thousand dollars. Our home was next on the chopping block, forcing me to find something less expensive.

It didn't surprise me when a brand new, two-story townhouse, dropped from the sky, within walking distance from where we lived. It was much larger than the duplex, had a considerable sized yard, was right on the school bus line, and the rent was two hundred dollars cheaper.

With the help of the church, we zigzagged our way, yet again, back across the Speedway.

Amidst it all, the book continued to haunt my dreams, and once we moved into the new place, it consumed my thoughts throughout the day too.

One day I gave into it. I quit looking for that elusive, full-time job, settled with an occasional temp assignment, and concentrated on my book.

I can't explain it, but, with that brave leap of faith, every little thing seemed to take care of itself, convincing those within my inner circle I'd lost my head for sure this time.

For encouragement, like a town crier, I told anyone who was interested about the book, believing the more I spoke of it, the likelier it would manifest.

Those who were interested inspired me to go for it. I always meant to start but found plenty of reasons not to each time.

The painful reality of Mark's death, and the fear associated with that realism, superseded the motivation I had started out with.

To fathom he'd never come home again was unbearable. And, because the book required a lot of soul searching, remembering, and processing, it became the most challenging thing I had to face and overcome.

I found refuge through my weekend job. When I'd applied for it, I assumed it would be easy, something to get lost in. *I mean how difficult would it be to pet dogs for four hours?*

It turned out to be much more than that and served the purpose of distraction I sought. I was in my element; it was the perfect job. I worked solo, and the animals gave me a kind of pet therapy.

The job was anxiety-producing at first, accustomed to people approaching me with a concern, not vice versa. But, within in a year, and with practice, I got my sea legs, and looked forward to the weekends, interacting with the customers, co-workers, store employees, and competitors from other pet food companies.

While working at one pet store, near where I got my driver's license, others encouraged me to notice a silvered tongued, Latin competitor.

I slowed down long enough to consider his handsome face, and my heart skipped a beat.

His mere presence confused my dormant soul. I'd concentrated for so long for a way back to Mark, and not once in my wildest dreams had I ever considered dating someone else.

That, and I'd kicked my appearance to the wayside since Mark's death.

We danced around the feelings between us for another year, before either of us had the nerve to make the next move.

One night before another weekend shift, I had a passionate, real-life dream about him, and couldn't put it out of my mind for the life of me.

When I saw him at the pet store the next day, and he stopped to say hello, my face turned as red as a lobster. With a twinkle in his eye, my obvious embarrassment made him grin a mile wide.

My breath caught in my throat. *How did he know?*

I was never as glad as I was when my shift ended that day. It was clear our friendship had turned, and it pleased the others to no end.

I was excited yet did not understand how to proceed. Part of me wanted this, but another part was beyond petrified.

One day, throwing my long-held convictions about Mark and caution to the wind, I made the first move and asked him if he had a camera.

He said he did, so I invited him to Dale's high school graduation, June 6, 2005.

PART III

WILDFLOWER

PART III

ONE

That was the beginning. Soon we were having dessert and coffee in the evenings at my place; he even brought a whole pecan pie to share on his fifty-second birthday and made flan for me on my fortieth a couple of months later.

We enjoyed each other's company, and never ran out of things to talk or laugh about. Sometimes, when we met at his place, he'd entice me to dance.

Both awkward and excited, born without rhythm and two left feet compared to his years as a professional salsa dancer, he didn't seem to mind when I'd stumble over his feet while attempting to keep up with his lead.

It was odd to be in the arms of someone other than Mark. Roberto was the extreme opposite of him. He stood only a head taller than me, and my arms reached all the way around him.

Although a year older than Mark, he seemed much younger, a spitting image of Cheech Marin, and not only had impeccable taste in food, but how he dressed as well, slacks only, he detested blue jeans.

His favorite music was opera and nothing else, mine has always been country, so comical, like a song from a seventies show.

His demeanor, his thick Spanish accent, and his respect for women was spellbinding. We had little in common, yet, we clicked like two missing puzzle pieces.

Of all the things I shared with him, I spoke little about Mark. The more I avoided that subject, the more he pursued it. He understood all too well how much I hurt, because he'd also lost his true love.

Over twenty years ago, his young wife died in a horrific car accident as she passed over a railway, right into the path of an oncoming train. Like me, he also received the devastating news while at work.

He never remarried nor had any children and came to the states alone a few years after her death. Penniless and fluent only in Spanish, he made a new life for himself in Seattle.

We shared a parallel experience so profound, only a fellow traveler on the same journey could comprehend its complexity and turning point in one's life.

He said it took several years to face his own reality, and to heal. Mindful of the consequences of denial, he made it his mission, or obsession, I begin the process I so wanted to avoid. His lure was through my book, always needling me to get going on it.

All the while, with a headstrong determination that rivaled my own, he chiseled at the fortress around my heart where I kept Mark alive, and one evening he succeeded.

We'd just finished our dessert and coffee when he brought the prohibited subject up again. Annoyed and frustrated with his constant meddling, fighting the urge to cry, I walked into his living room to hide my reaction.

But he knew; somehow, he always knew. He approached me and wrapped his arms around mine in a gentle embrace. His masculinity tugged at the chains surrounding my inner fortress, making me aware of the depth of my suffering.

He continued to hold me. My lower lip quivered. Bit by bit, the retaining wall I'd fought so hard to hold back, the buried thoughts, feelings, and sensations crumbled.

He turned me around to face him. The never-ending depths of his soft brown eyes broke my reserve. A sob forced its way to the surface, and then another, and another, and others thick and fast.

He held me even tighter. Helpless, I gave up the struggle, and cried free and open. It was all over; I was sure I had lost what I'd only just found.

But, rather than recoiling, he held me closer and whispered,

"I am on your side, Elise, I believe in you, and I will be here whenever you need me."

His unbendable perseverance astounded, yet intrigued me, I had met my match, and none of the hundreds of excuses I concocted to delay setting pen to paper dissuaded him.

Nor did my so-called fragility, or that most of the information needed to begin, was in *the box*. With or without my cooperation, he planned its resurrection.

To plan was one thing, to carry it out was another. With the upper hand, I delayed the event for as long as I could. He wasn't fooled nor put off by my purposeful procrastination.

One Saturday after work, he escorted me to my house to oversee the exhumation and transfer of *the box* to his house.

When we arrived at his place, I couldn't believe what I saw. He not only had his living room prepared in advance for the dreaded, impending event, but he also had an inviting lunch set out for us.

PART III

I stretched our meal out for as long as I could. Immune to my dawdling, as soon as he finished, he set straight to work, announcing with business-like purpose,

"Come on, let's get started."

My cheeks flushed hot, and the color drained from my face as I looked across the room at *the box*. It was like revisiting the funeral home all over again.

Dread, like wild ivy, wrapped its tentacles around my heart. My body felt like lead, I couldn't move from my chair; more than ever before, I wanted to leave.

In tune with my disposition, with the patience of a saint, he linked his arm with mine, and, in quiet reverence, guided me toward *the box*.

I followed his lead, and we worked nonstop, side by side, in silence sorting and making various piles of things: media videos, newspaper clippings, condolence cards, pictures, etc. It was amazing how much I'd gathered in seven years.

From memory, he labeled the names of each of the chapters on boxes and envelopes from each of the piles. His genuine concern touched my heart. If he was out to earn his wings, like Clarence from my favorite movie, he was on the right path.

I came across the special glass frame that held my Safeway flowers. Paying careful attention when unwrapping and re-wrapping it, it occurred to me, that while I had spent a lot of time and effort protecting and preserving some of Mark's most sentimental things, I'd ignored and abused his most precious treasure of all, me.

With that profound revelation, lost in the memories, I wept to myself. As I continued to sort through the piles, like the wrath of the sea, waves of emotion rippled and crashed down over me.

Held hostage by the shadowed obscurity of the reality of it all, crying one minute, and laughing the next, it went on like this until darkness covered the room.

But we forged on anyway, and finished by the dim light of a lamp he brought in.

Sometime later, from out of the fervent silence, his familiar, tender voice broke through my grey barrier, and announced, "We're finished. Elise, you did it!"

For a moment, I stared at him in disbelief, and then laughed.

He took me in his arms and said how proud he was of me. And then I lost it, again. Like a break in a damn, I sobbed, "He's gone."

The words seeped into my very being, swirled around in my brain, and made me cry harder. I hadn't had a meltdown like this since Mommy died.

With that thought, I cried even more. My throat ached, and my eyes hurt.

I held onto him even tighter, as my knees buckled, "He's really gone Roberto..."

PART III

TWO

I am returning to write this story after two days of procrastination, for fear of what happened while writing the unfinished sentence in the last chapter. After typing the words, "He's really gone Roberto...", my computer screen went berserk, as if hijacked.

I fought with the keyboard and tried to finish the sentence, pressing the correct letters with intent for each word, but it refused to obey.

When I pushed the apostrophe key, a quotation mark appeared. If I attempted to move some highlighted words to another place, they scrambled. Whenever I wanted to capitalize a letter, the shift key would make it lower case, with or without the caps lock on.

I tried one last time to move the cursor into the correct position, but it took off like a possessed bat out of hell. Entire paragraphs highlighted off and on, and the letters on the keyboard played like a piano

The little hairs at the nape of my neck stood up, and I broke out in goosebumps from head to toe. I picked up the phone and called Maggie. I sobbed in hysterics about what was happening.

Also spooked, she suggested I save my work if I could, turn off the computer, and to go enjoy the sunshine for the day.

After the call, as I turned to leave the room, large snapping flames shot out from the HEPA filter; I turned it off and ran out of the house.

Beyond shaken, I about left skid marks as I sped away; I didn't return until the following day. Rather than writing though, I brought the HEPA filter to the store where I'd bought it. They said something had fried the insides and it was beyond repair.

I didn't have the courage to return and continue with my story until the following day.

౭ఇ

My heart hurt as I released the wounded animal within; Roberto held me tighter as I submitted to seven years of pent up emotions. "It's okay honey. It's okay. Let it go. You have to let it go."

I clutched a handful of his shirt, holding on as though my life depended on it, and cried even louder. He stayed the course, cradled my head to his chest, and continued to whisper sweet, consoling words in my ear.

As he wiped the tears from my face, I smiled at him, and gave him a tender kiss. Captivated by the depths of his deep brown eyes, seeing a familiar friend within my reflection, I believed things would be all right again.

My soul stirred in his secure embrace; I felt safe once more; my heart recognized the transformation and wanted to stay there for eternity.

He returned my kiss, further stirring the sleeping winter in my soul, melting away feelings of fear, guilt, and despair, replacing them with life and love for a second time.

I snuggled closer to him. For the first time in a long time, hopeful was no longer a far-fetched word.

My spirit seemed lighter after we'd finished *the box*. But it was only one of the many hurdles I had yet to face before putting my fingers to the keyboard.

The following weekend curled up safe within his masculine arms, a box of tissue at hand, we watched all the videos I'd collected.

He held me even tighter if I sobbed or let out a deep sigh. With each clip, one consistent message pounded away at my heart, *it was for real, Mark wasn't coming back.*

The next task was to sort through all the typewritten articles. As I reached into a box labeled 11-27-98, and pulled out a pile of papers, an audio cassette fell out. I laughed as I recalled my strange encounter with Ralph.

Excited to share it with Roberto, he popped it into a cassette player, and we listened with intense curiosity. Our hearts about stopped with Ralph's last prophesy.

He paused as if listening to something and then muttered "Martin?" He asked aloud who this was and said the name again, "Oh Martin!"

Mumbling some more, he shook his head with utmost certainty and said, "It's either part of his first or last name."

After a moment, he exclaimed with even more conviction, "It is most definitely a part of his last name!"

Confused, I asked whose last name he was referring to. He replied matter-of-factly "It is the name of the man you will marry someday, but not for a long while."

In disbelief, we rewound the tape, and put our ears closer to the speaker to hear it again. For a brief time, in awe of what may or may not be, neither of us spoke.

PART III

My eyes met his, this most wonderful and incredible man's last name was none other than, Martinez. By pure coincidence or divine intervention, like something out of the movies, I laughed a genuine laugh for the first time in seven years, wrapped my arms around my hero, and planted an appreciative kiss on his baby smooth cheek.

He grinned and returned my kiss, "See, I told you it was meant to be."

Ralph's revelation was all we needed to break the last piece of ice between us.

Some never find true love, and a few only find it once. To receive a second chance was unheard of. For us, it was unquestionable, and we dove in headfirst, with our eyes wide-open, we vowed to love each other to the fullest from that day, October 14, 2005, and every day thereafter.

No longer a solitary traveler, I was ready to take the first steps on my journey, but there was just one thing that threatened our new-found happiness, my clandestine affair with the Marlboro man.

The day I confessed to it was devastating and embarrassing. The disappointment in Roberto's eyes made me flush with shame. Even worse, he professed an outrageous ultimatum; it was him or the cigarettes, no if, ands, or butts. He would not hang around to watch me kill myself.

Stunned by his directness, I knew what I had to do.

THREE

*I*t wasn't until I attempted to put the nasty things out of my life, that I realized how addicted I had become to them again. Armed with some holistic calming aids, lots of mints and gum, assuring I was never alone for the first two weeks, I quit cold turkey.

It was hell, but I would rather have walked over hot coals before losing Roberto.

The book kept my mind preoccupied, sorting through mounds of material, highlighting important facts, and shredding duplicate info. Like with the videos, the more I read, the greater the message drove home, and the stronger I felt.

While I organized a momentous number of notes, Roberto prepared a desk for me right next to his and furnished it with the things I'd need: pens, pencils, a dictionary, a thesaurus, and an endless supply of candles.

The most thoughtful of these were two prayer books; my favorite, a pocket book titled, How to Work with Angels, complete with prayer decrees for angelic guidance, inspiration, healing, and comfort.

Then, with an archaic computer he had stashed away, outfitted with Windows 2003, I was ready to begin; but the blank page confronted me, I didn't know where to begin.

Always with his antennas up, Roberto returned to the room to see how it was going. He dimmed the lights, placed a few burning candles around my desk, put the two prayer books in my hands, suggested I pray for guidance, and then left me on my own.

And I prayed. I pleaded for His infinite glory, along with all the angels in heaven, to give me the words; but something still wasn't right. Roberto reappeared. I explained how it was too quiet.

As if reaching in a magic hat, he found a soundtrack from an older movie, *Somewhere in Time,* that I enjoyed, and set it on repeat. It was like food for my inner writer; it inspired and encouraged me regardless of how many times it looped.

I placed my fingers into position on the keyboard, as if transcribing from a recorder, I know it sounds cliché, but the story poured out of me; it was indescribable. One by one, with each blessed word, the kryptonite links around my heart fell away, taking the heaviness in my soul along with them.

PART III

The release was unimaginable and captivating. I wanted to stay in the moment forever. As if dictating from a pre-written text, the words came whether I was ready for them or not. Like Mickey Mouse and The Magic Brooms, they were unstoppable.

Momentous and strong, the story forced itself through my fingers. Incessant, even when I wasn't at the computer, they haunted my dreams more than the book ever had until I wrote them down. I stayed the course for hours at a time, oblivious to the carpal tunnel in my wrists, and wrote the first thirteen thousand words in nine days.

Since we were long past the newness of our relationship and feeling comfortable with one another, I told Roberto about the incredulous and strange occurrences I'd experienced since Mark's death.

He corroborated the part about the spirit bird with his own eyewitness and told me of a day when he left me to work on my book, when he saw a solitary stellar jay, sitting matter-of-factly on a wire just outside the window where I was writing, not once, but each time I came to write.

My first thought was that he was being condescending to make my story seem plausible. But the next morning when I arrived to write, leaning over my desk, searching the skies for my elusive feathered guardian, Roberto more hopeful than myself, we saw it.

We didn't have to strain our necks for long; my reverent bird, sat ready for duty on a wire over the neighbor's house, with a clear view of the room I was working in.

I laughed in disbelief and tears flooded my eyes.

My writing ritual remained unchanged; for me it was sacred. So much in fact, I couldn't begin the process without the candles, the music, or the prayers and prayer books. They filled me with peace, and the quiet discipline required to listen and heal.

Sometimes the book was so overwhelming, I had to get away from it. There were days I flat out avoided my desk, before getting the nerve to face the story again, despite the nightmares that taunted me to get back to it.

Delayed by fear of the blatant reality between the pages of the second and third chapters and besieged by further nightmares of the horrifying incidents within each, it took several months to describe their actual events.

The thoughts, the process, and the pain was sometimes so unbearable, I wasn't sure if I'd ever finish the story.

Strange as it may seem, contented, blissful peace would be mine once I resumed writing.

My one-man cheering squad pushed me when I didn't want to budge and praised me onward through its progression.

One worry interfered with my productivity, though. It was a struggle to balance writing with earning a living. But, not to fret, Roberto had an answer for that too, and offered me a job. I thought he was joking. I mean, it wasn't possible to have an answer for *everything*, was it?

He told me about how he'd acquired a small business, a one-man band which had once made a name for itself, but because of his full-time job, he hadn't had time to nurture it back to life.

The position wouldn't have a salary per se or the perks of a regular job, but he'd help with my bills until I got it up and running, adding how it would be my baby if I accepted.

Wow. He didn't have to ask twice, and I jumped on the opportunity without reservation. Because it wasn't demanding, I found it to be the perfect job, and one I could manage while writing at the same time.

Yet again, Roberto and I worked side by side, and we resurrected the little business.

As with writing the book, I had no prior training, but once I took hold of the reins, it seemed to take on a life of its own.

I relied upon mentors at the local S.B.A. to steer me in the right direction with bookkeeping, advertising, and taxes among others. With their help, I created an online store too.

Sometimes the undertaking frustrated me to no end, but the website turned out rather cute, bright colors, animated bugs, and articles with more than you wanted to know about repelling insects.

Before long, the products were on the shelves of several western Washington stores, including one in Florida.

With Roberto's suggestion, I posted a picture of the former label, back when the products sold in Eddie Bauer stores in the 90's, on the website, and sales took off.

The job gave me a sense of purpose and accomplishment, more so than any other work I'd done before. Roberto was the dream boss, he believed in, and trusted me with all he had.

It also came with a mascot, Roberto's handsome and gentle, black, medium-haired with a tuxedo bib on his chest, Norwegian Forest Cat, named Lucky.

He took to me like a magnet. The feelings were mutual. Just a year old, he'd sit beside me, sometimes for hours, and wouldn't move a muscle until Roberto arrived home from work.

On a rough, emotional writing day, he'd jump into my arms, wrap his little paws around my neck, and purr until the storm passed, just like Spirit used to.

I wanted to finish the book by Roberto's birthday, eleven months later. But, 2006 disappeared in the blink of an eye, and it still wasn't finished.

One part remained, the ending.

And as you may have guessed, Roberto had an answer for that too. The following weekend, Lexi, Roberto, and I took a little field trip to *the bridge*.

I tried to talk him out of the idea, but my protests fell on deaf ears. He said he would be with me the entire time, so, there was nothing to fear. Easy for him to say.

We parked underneath the bridge, alongside the Troll. The cold wind blew sharp on our faces as Lexi led the way up the stairs to the top. She stopped when she reached the concrete pillar with Mark's memorial plaque.

I put my hand on the railing and felt the newness of the pieces that replaced the ones torn away that fateful day. My heart skipped a beat when I looked over the edge at the top of the apartment and recognized the large replaced sections of the roof, it was Mark's final resting place.

A lump swelled in my throat, and tears spilled from my eyes as I thought about how frightened he must have been. I couldn't believe the distance between the bridge and the apartment.

Lost in the thought of how horrific his last day must have unfolded, Roberto gave my arm a gentle squeeze, and I pulled him closer.

I placed my hand on the memorial plaque, closed my eyes, and whispered a silent farewell, "Goodbye Hunny Bunny, my love."

The words stung like hot daggers in my throat, worse than when I had my tonsils removed. Burning tears continued their descent down my cheeks, but I continued,

"I will never love you any less, and will continue to care for you forever, but, from this day forward, I must go it alone."

As I let my hand slip from the pillar, the heaviness in my heart and the weight on my shoulders lifted, caught up in the slight current of the wind, and floated away with my words.

Then, as if in silent reverence, bus number 358 whooshed past us, blanketing me with a warm and gentle breath. I smiled. I was free at last.

Roberto reached for my hand and wrapped it secure within the crook of his arm. Lexi led the way; with our backs to the never more dark and ominous bridge, we walked towards a new beginning.

My journey was complete, I was ready to finish the story, or so I thought.

FOUR

Roberto lived almost a mile away from me in a senior mobile home park. Although he was a few years' shy of the age requirement, a retired friend of his convinced him, stating he needed help with a promising business venture, to buy the trailer next to his, with the pretense he was buying it for his elderly mother.

For the next couple of years, Roberto did what he could to help his friend get his idea off the ground but was unsuccessful. So, besides his full-time job, he took an extra job on the weekends, and that's when he met me.

With my unpredictable schedule, and wanting to assure Lexi finished high school, I planned with her eldest brother and his wife, who lived just on the other side of town, for her to complete her final year with them.

Because I spent most of my time working and writing at Roberto's, and my weekend job at the pet store was only two blocks from his place, it made sense to move in with him.

I asked Dale if he wanted to bring in some roommates to finish out the rental contract for our condo; he jumped on the opportunity right away; Sniffles, Foxy, and I transplanted to Roberto's, moving my belongings to storage, again.

My presence in the park eluded the residents as they were used to my visiting. I think the owner knew what was going on, but he never let on like he did.

∞

The following two years were well and quiet. Dale finished the rental contract on the condo, and then joined the Navy. Roberto thought it was the next best thing to pecan pie, but I felt betrayed. My son made the decision without me, in the middle of a war no less.

My firstborn headed off to boot camp winter of 2008. The few, but brief, letters I received were better than none.

I sensed the frustration in his words as he wrote about how disappointed he was, how it wasn't like the recruiter had told him, how the conditions were miserable with subzero temperatures, how he hated the days beginning at four each morning. and the suffering he'd signed himself up for.

Worse yet, he said he was sicker than a dog with a sinus infection, pink eye, and a horrible case of athlete's foot.

And even more unbelievable, he said, just when he thought he'd missed the pain of the penicillin shot, the dentist told him all his wisdom teeth had to come out.

Worse still, he was sent back to training soon after. I guess he got the last laugh.

Roberto, Lexi, and I headed to Chicago for his graduation ceremony in March. Dale was right, it was like the North Pole.

When the snow fell, it looked like a huge pillow fight, not like the wet and hazardous kind we have in Seattle. It was a community effort to keep the roads clear. Regular trucks outfitted with plows cased the streets, spewing huge mounds of the fluffy stuff onto the sidewalks.

We got a rental car and headed for the hotel; well that was the plan anyway. The mosaic of exit and merge lanes on the freeway were not straightforward like those at home, making it impossible to get out where you wanted.

The Google maps directions I printed and brought along stated we were to take the Milwaukee exit. After about an hour of heading in the wrong direction, we pulled off on a random exit, and asked for guidance at a mom-and-pop store.

We showed them the instructions we had. They laughed and said we should look for the Wisconsin exit. We felt dumb. It didn't even occur to us Milwaukee was a city in Wisconsin, but the rental agency stressed we were to look specifically for the Wisconsin sign.

Oh well, it wasn't much longer before we found the hotel. Although cheap, decent, and sparkling clean, I still wiped it down with Lysol and sprayed the beds with our cedar oil, just in case.

There was a family diner across the highway that had great home-cooked meals. I brought along a Chicago Entertainment book I'd dogeared with a few fun activities we could do with Dale.

The graduation ceremony was boring and the stadium where it was held was meat locker cold, but the inconvenience was worth having Dale in my arms again.

As families and visitors gathered, I noticed how my son wasn't the only one sick, the entire base was a cesspool.

A blizzard rolled in during the ceremony. When we headed to the car for a fun filled afternoon, we couldn't see beyond the windshield, and never made it to Chicago, or five minutes from the base for that matter.

It was a miracle that we happened upon a little Mexican restaurant and stopped for a quick bite. With most of his free time spent in the car, we arrived back at the base within minutes of the expiration of his pass. With a quick round of hugs, he skipped off through the gates.

I didn't understand his excitement. My children had always been within arm's reach, or at least inside a mile of them, but now it was as if my apron strings had been cut at the quick.

I wouldn't see him again for four more years.

The Bootcamp Plague followed Roberto back to Seattle, somehow Lexi and I dodged the bullet. He woke up the following morning on death's bed.

He looked like Rocky at the end of a fight. His chest was so full I thought he'd drown for sure, it was all I could do to keep him from going under.

In the throes of the worst of it one night, he called out for his baby sister, a year older than me, Isabelle. She died from an unexpected brain aneurysm just before we'd met. The last time they spoke is when Roberto learned about it.

He told her he didn't think they'd ever see each other again, but asked her to promise she'd come back to see him.

I snuggled up to him and patted his back. Suddenly, the light from his cell phone lit up the room; it stayed on for an entire minute. It was one a.m., fifteen minutes later it illuminated again for another minute, and continued like this in fifteen-minute intervals until two a.m.

The strange occurrence repeated the same pattern the following night, and every night thereafter. Roberto pulled through in two weeks. Once he recovered, we took his phone in to exchange it for another.

But, even with the new phone, the same phenomenon occurred. For peace of mind, we exchanged it one more time for a different model and waited for the bewitching hour. Sure enough, it lit up like before.

There's no doubt in our minds it was Isabelle. After my experiences with Mark's spirit, who was I to say otherwise? The power of love is an amazing thing. Her visits remain steadfast to this day, regardless of Day Light Savings Time or change in time zones.

In fact, we've taken *her* to Mexico to show Roberto's family. They were so excited when they saw it with their own eyes.

Each time it lit up, through tears they'd rattle off in Spanish all the things they wanted to share with her, one night she even kept the phone lit for thirty minutes.

All the while Dale was away, Lexi graduated from high school, moved out on her own, and got a job as a teller for a local bank. We acquired a fourth cat,

PART III

a stray we named Fluke because we'd mistaken him for Lucky when he first came around, until we noticed the white toes on his back feet.

I finished writing the book, organized all of Roberto's financial affairs, and got his little sole proprietorship business up and running.

When the mobile home park owner moved away without forewarning anyone, our tranquil oasis skyrocketed from bad-to-worse in a hurry. He hired a senior husband and wife managerial team to administer in his place.

They ruled over the peaceful dominion with iron fists, raising the rent, rearranging the guidelines to suit them, and giving hell to residents whose lifestyles they didn't approve of.

It was people like Roberto's elderly friend, whom I referred to as Uncle Mike, a hoarder and chain smoker, and us, that really got their goat.

One afternoon the manager's wife saw me at the mailbox. The next morning her husband approached Roberto to inquire about our marital status. Roberto, a patient man to a point, replied we were not.

Without explanation, the manager demanded I leave the park by the subsequent weekend, or he'd face eviction.

Roberto tried to enlighten the positive influence I'd had in the small community over the past three years, and how the park had become my home.

He elaborated how I'd volunteered nursing care to those with an urgent need, fed the shut-ins when we had extras, and baked Christmas cookies for residents each year.

Above all, he asserted, there wasn't anywhere else for me to go.

Despite his best efforts though, his pleas fell on deaf ears. The manager stood firm; all inhabitants had to be 55 years or older, only spouses could be younger.

Roberto countered his conviction, and said we'd wed right away if it would suit him; but, the man stood his ground. He said it was too late; occupants were to be married prior to the new rule.

And so, our quest for another home began.

FIVE

*O*ver dinner one night, upon learning of our plight, a friend of ours whom we refer to as Grandma Faye, offered to rent her house to us.

She said her little lakeside cabin would be perfect. It was a solitary place where I could write, had a large shop to accommodate our growing business, and our kitties would just love it there.

Without missing a beat, she added how the last anyone had lived there was almost thirty years ago and might need a little work.

Roberto and I drove out to visit her lake house the following weekend. High hopes filled our hearts, and The Jefferson's theme song played in our heads.

With a final turn into a dead-end street, we grinned a mile wide while admiring the surrounding neighborhood and fine homes; we couldn't believe our luck.

But our excitement was short-lived when we pulled up next to the mailbox with the coordinating address. We checked the numbers again. There was no mistake; we were at the right location.

Because blackberry bushes stood well over eight feet tall on either side of the muddy, boggy driveway, we had to drive up an adjacent dirt road to reach her property.

To say it was a jungle would be an understatement. Mammoth sized, deep orange maple leaves blanketed the mucky ground. There were two campers to our right, one a vintage, moss-covered, replica of Donald Duck's trailer, and the other, a large seventies Dodge motorhome.

On our left, parked alongside a little barn shaped storage shed, sheltered by a small grey tarp, secured with a rusty lawn chair and some bricks, was a classic, olive colored, Dodge Swinger, like MB's, except hers was yellow.

Straight ahead was a looming, corroded brown outbuilding with two large barn doors. The Sanford and Son theme drowned out the joyful melody we'd hummed only moments before.

Since Roberto had been to the property in the past, I asked him if he remembered where the house was. He approached the barn and opened one side, it almost fell from its hinges when he did.

He canvassed the musty crypt with his flashlight until it lit upon a machete leaning on the opposite door.

PART III

He chopped a clearing adjacent to the shed to make a path to where he thought the house might be. I followed right behind him, aware of each little creepy crawly thing along the way.

Just before the porch, we got a clear view of it. A sad, Bavarian style cottage with scalloped trimming sat amid an overgrowth of vine maples, blackberry shrubs, and ivy.

Like Sleeping Beauty's Castle, a thick layer of clinging moss smothered the roof, thorny branches of a holly berry tree consumed one entire side, and ivy wrapped its never ending tentacles tightly around the structure, cracking its wooden shingles.

Several more holly bushes, blanketed with a sheer veil of spider webs, stood guard near the front porch, shielding the little abode from the world for the past thirty years; another decade more, the earth would have swallowed it whole.

We couldn't venture outside the path we'd just cut, but we could see a lake beyond a forest like clearing. Roberto snapped pictures to share with Grandma Faye, and then led the way up the porch steps.

The curtains on all the doors and windows were closed, and piles of stuff from the inside leaned against them, blocking our ability to peek in.

He put the key in the door and turned, but it wouldn't open. He positioned his shoulder against it and gave it a firm push.

Whoosh!

Like a long-sealed tomb, a cloud of dust and hot air shot out of the house. We coughed and covered our faces. It only budged an inch, just enough for Roberto to stick his head part way in to peek inside.

"What is it? What do you see?"

He made room for me to peer in. We were in awe of what we saw. It was stacked solid, clear to the ceiling, with who knows what and how deep, all the way to the door.

I couldn't escape the suffocating smell even when I breathed through my mouth, the stench was inescapable.

I turned my head and gasped for fresh air. Overwhelmed, I sat on the porch and cried. Roberto approached me from behind and squeezed my shoulders.

"Let's go," I sniffed.

"Go? Come on Elise, we can do this. It's a pretty place, quiet enough for you to write, large enough for our business, and safe enough for the cats."

I stood up.

"We can do what, Roberto? Just look around you. We're damned if we do and damned if we don't."

I stormed down the stairs, folded my arms across my chest, and faced the lake in defiance. We spent the next few minutes debating whether this venture was worth pursuing.

First, we couldn't continue harboring me in and out of his mobile home. Second, this place needed more work than we could manage. And third, it would be a long time before we could move in, and we required somewhere to live, now.

Around and around and back and forth we debated. I said we should consider looking elsewhere; he said my glass was half full.

And then he did what he always does to persuade the donkey, he wrapped his muscular arms over my shoulders and whispered in my ear.

"I'm sure with a little hard work we can figure out whatever it requires to make it livable." His notable strength and warm breath melted my resolve like butter.

"But Roberto, we're middle-aged, I just don't know..."

The sun was setting on the horizon over the lake. A group of ducks wished each other good night, and a choir of croaking frogs and singing crickets played an enchanting orchestra in the background.

I looked back at the house. I can't explain it; but it seemed to pull at my heart like a stray cat; and I caved. We would make this place our home if it was the last thing we did.

"I'm in, if you are."

PART III

SIX

We returned to the front door. Roberto pushed on it harder than he had before but couldn't get it to budge any further. He reached inside and pulled out handfuls of junk.

A shower of rat poop and dead bugs rained over the top of us as he hauled out several plastic grocery bags full of washed Styrofoam hamburger boxes, soup cans, and other cleaned trash.

Five hours later, we got the door all the way opened.

We stood dumbfounded as we took in the mountainous landfill before us and beyond as far as the eye could see.

Large dusty cobwebs, like the kind in scary movies, hung from ceilings and corners of the house. I shuddered at the thought of the species of spiders who created them.

The nauseating pea soup, colored walls made my skin crawl. A sickly black path lined the tops of them, just above the trash trail.

Rectangular insect traps and long pieces of sticky bug tape dangled from the ceilings like a frat party gone wrong. If Roberto hadn't been with me, I would have sealed the crypt, and never returned.

It was getting dark, and I'd had enough. As we were about to leave, a little plastic grocery bag, full of the same stuff we'd encountered, sailed from out of nowhere, and landed at our feet.

We looked at one another for confirmation the other had witnessed the same occurrence.

Then another bag came in from our left, the kitchen, then another from our right, the laundry room. We weren't scared; the implausible notion of what was happening only made us laugh.

It wasn't a *get out* kind of gesture, but more like a reminder there was more garbage to take. Familiar with unexplainable happenings since Mark's death, I spoke aloud to reassure whoever was there, we would return to finish purging the mess, and make it a home again.

We waited a moment. Nothing more happened.

Satisfied, we turned off the hall light, stepped out onto the porch, and closed the door. It was as dark as a wolf's mouth.

I held onto Roberto's arm. I wasn't afraid; I almost felt sad for the little house. It was as if it needed us as much as we needed it.

The following Sunday, during a dinner with Grandma Faye, we showed her the pictures we took, and described the condition of her lake house, making sure not to elaborate on the hoarding aspect of it. To say she felt devastated was an understatement.

But all was not lost. Before the night's end, we had her blessing to go forward, a project plan, and a budget to work with.

Restoration would ensue on the weekends, beginning the following Friday when Roberto finished his day job, through Sunday.

The first item on the list was to empty the entire house, all sixteen hundred feet of it, thank goodness it was a single level with only a half basement.

We stopped at Lowes for supplies, heavy duty, 3ml construction garbage bags, chemical respirators, like Darth Vader masks, mine was pink, gloves, and a gallon of Lysol cleaner among other odds and ends.

Roberto also brought along fifty empty paper case boxes with lids from his job if we happened upon anything salvageable.

Evening was just settling in when we arrived for our first day of labor. Autumn clouds hid the moon and enveloped our surroundings in a spooky darkness. I'd never encountered that kind of pitch black before, blind as a bat past six p.m., even in the best of conditions, my imagination threatened to run away with me.

We fumbled around in our supply box for the flashlight but came up empty-handed. What a great way to start, of all the things to forget.

Unconcerned, Roberto picked up the supplies and walked toward the house. I held onto his arm as we inched along the beaten path.

Halfway to the porch, the lights turned on. I wanted to run back to the car. Indifferent, he shouted a friendly, "Thank you!" He wasn't afraid of anything, if he was, he never let on about it.

We put worn-out clothes over of our good ones, donned respirators, and gloves, and then forged ahead into the great unknown.

I started by clearing a path to the kitchen; Roberto took on the laundry room.

The rats hadn't missed one square inch with their urine. They spared nothing. They found their way in drawers, shredding and pooping on anything, inside milk cartons to have their young, and on clothing, hung or not. It was too awful for words.

I was so glad the obvious stench could not permeate the mask. I can't even describe the things my gloved hands touched, or how many times I wanted to hurl.

We documented what we cleaned with photographs, filled umpteen humongous garbage bags with rat nesting and bug laden items, and packed the rest into the case boxes.

Roberto stacked the trash within the dilapidated gazebo, a stone's throw from the porch, for when we made a dump run.

We worked nonstop, except when we had to dash outside to wipe the sweat and slobber from the interior of our masks.

After a few backbreaking hours, ready for a rest and some fresh air, as we were about to step through the door, we heard, "Achoo!" from the laundry room.

Roberto moved a mound of clothes where the noise originated and revealed a large hole. We heard scampering little feet disappear into the recesses of the wall.

We had to laugh. We were kicking up so much dust even the rats needed respirators. As we turned to leave again; the entire area lit up in a flash of light.

"BOOM!"

My heart skipped a beat. Should we run?

Roberto found a flashlight, one among several we'd come across, and peered into the hole.

There were loose, almost chewed through, sparkling wires hanging by a thread, and water was leaking on them from somewhere. It was amazing the house was still standing.

After a brief rest, assured there was no longer an impending threat, neither of us having an appetite for the snacks I'd brought, we carried on.

While acting out our own version of Man of La Mancha, we worked side by side as we dug through the landslides of ick, stuffing garbage into bags, sorting through the salvageable, and packing sentimental stuff into boxes.

Once Roberto removed most of the clothing and debris from the laundry room, he discovered two large free-standing freezers, the same obnoxious color as the walls. They were still functioning and preserving the food inside.

All the contents had expiration dates from the late sixties and early eighties. Without hesitation, he bagged all of it and carried it to the gazebo before it thawed. The stench was unimaginable, and then he unplugged the units to empty them out.

As he tackled the nasty chore, I was having fun of my own in the kitchen. While I worked, I made grossed out faces under my mask and breathed through my mouth as if I could smell the stuff.

The refrigerator had to be replaced. By some miracle, the root beer colored, 1950's Westinghouse double electric stove didn't need replacing; it functioned just fine and only needed delousing and a good scrubbing.

Once I removed all the rotten and moldy food from the non-functioning fridge, I set up a small ladder, pulled a garbage can close, and tossed out the staples from the cupboards.

Little bugs, some the same kind I once picked out of Maggie's cereal, and others I'd never seen before, were everywhere. Believe it or not, a few of them were still alive! Funny how they never touched the sugar though.

It killed me to see so much food wasted, but like Roberto had found in the freezer, the expiration dates on boxes and canned goods were about the same age as I was, and not worth salvaging. Some cans had even exploded, forever stuck to the shelf in a gross molasses ooze.

Lost in my thoughts, I almost fell off the ladder when I saw a tall man walk past the bay window before me.

PART III

SEVEN

My heart beat like wild horses in my chest. I couldn't wrap my mind around what I had just seen. There was no way anyone could have walked by, tall or otherwise, there was too much growth, and they would have tripped on something as dark as it was.

I called for Roberto. He checked outside with a flashlight, but to no avail. He agreed with me it would be impossible for anybody to cross by the window and assured me of no impending danger.

We worked like robots for two more hours, only seeing him again when he stopped by to replace my full garbage bags. Unable to bend or stoop any longer, usually the first to cry Uncle, Roberto would sterilize the entire house in one visit if I let him.

We disinfected our masks and hung them on nails to dry, shook out our hair, changed clothes, and then stumbled to the car like zombies, looking forward to a nice and warm, sanitizing shower at home.

The subsequent weekends repeated themselves. It didn't matter how hard or fast we worked, it seemed as if the never-ending garbage reproduced itself.

We determined our little ghosty must be Grandma Faye's deceased husband, Jim. He greets us with the porch lights when we arrive and guides us when we need help. He seems friendly enough, and his presence has become commonplace.

∽

In the meanwhile, life at the trailer park has been no picnic. I cannot go out during the day for fear of harassment by the managers. Because their place is within sight of ours, we keep our blinds pulled, so it looks like nobody is home.

One day, without thinking, I ran the garbage disposal. In a matter of seconds, the manager's wife was banging on my front door.

"I know you're in there, Missy! You better answer this door!"

I cowered in our bedroom while she banged and yelled for who knows how long. When Roberto arrived home later, an eviction notice greeted him at the door.

One thing for sure, their continual harassment pushed us to work even harder on the lake house.

After emptying the kitchen, I continued into the adjacent dining area. Once it was almost cleared, I propped up a ladder next to a mountainous wall of junk and looked over the landfill to see it connected to the family room.

Roberto brought the ladder around to the other side, just off the foyer, and peered over the barricade of stuff.

He challenged me to a cleaning contest from opposite ends to the center; he was on.

As it's the largest part in the house, the process took weeks, but I won, and got to have my choice for dinner.

Underneath the tons of garbage, straight out of the Twilight Zone, was a fully furnished, flashback to the seventies style living area, and it appeared as if someone had been there only moments before.

A Sony T.V. was still on, it's off-the-air fuzziness glowed eerily in the dimness of the room. A pair of glasses and a bowl of decaying snacks sat on an end table alongside a black leather, blanketed in white mold, lazy boy recliner, and a pair of black leather oxfords, the inside heels worn to nubs, were tucked underneath.

Next to that, was the most exciting find, a brick fireplace with a bench seat. It was one thing Jim's chair was near it, but we couldn't understand why he also had a portable heater beside it. Or why there were heavy insulated draperies covering the six bay windows.

All around the hearth, and the entire length of the far wall, was a single piece of mahogany panel board. Between the living and dining rooms a jagged square hole had been cut into the wall. Perched precariously in the center of it was an unfinished garden window.

Overlooking the chaos, was a polished, Redwood oak, cathedral ceiling, divided into two sections by large solid beams. A ceiling fan was its only accessory.

Roberto learned later it all was a facade. The magnificent woodwork was only a thin sheet of plywood with hollowed out pieces of particle board for the rafters. The designer forgot to install a three-quarter panel to separate the living room from the attic.

Next to conquer was the hallway and bathroom. I took on the former.

Occasionally, Roberto called me to witness some exciting blast from the past he'd found. Because Grandma Faye had so many interesting things, although corroded with mold and mildew, I was always eager to see a new treasure.

I'll never forget one prank he pulled. Hanging by the tail in his gloved hand, a dehydrated rat greeted me, white with beady red eyes.

I fell for it each time.

Another month passed before we finished those areas. Ironically, once the hall was clear, we discovered a plaque of The Declaration of Independence hanging on the wall.

There seemed to be no end to the mess we'd gotten ourselves into. We'd worked almost sixteen, thirty-two-hour weeks, and hoped to finish and move in by June, six months away.

In the meanwhile, we received a second eviction notice.

∽

The bedrooms were next, I seized the smaller room, leaving Roberto with the larger mess at the end of the hall, and then we resumed the monotonous chore of sorting and packing.

One afternoon, while Roberto hauled more garbage bags to the gazebo, I took a break from my task to see how he was coming along.

He'd cleared the entry and made a path to a wall with an unfinished sliding glass door. Now I understood why the whole house was such a freezer, and why there was a blanket of white fuzzy mold over everything.

Whomever Grandma Faye hired to put in the door hadn't finished it. Like a loose tooth, the same as the garden window in the dining room, it rested in the jagged hole cut out for it. Worse yet, the supporting beam across the top didn't meet the ceiling, leaving the attic without reinforcement.

The outside elements flowed into the house through a gaping opening to the left of it, disguised by the slats of the exterior trim. A branch of ivy weaved its way around them through a gash at the bottom, allowing passage for an entire army of rats.

A couch in the middle of the room had a blanket on it, like someone had just slept there.

Although all the comforts of home beckoned the laziest of squatters, I am certain the insurmountable garbage heap was what deterred them from taking over.

Several vintage dressers lined two walls. Roberto opened some of their drawers. Rats soaked the contents with their urine, even shredding money.

A cool looking, antique brass book resting on the top of one bureau caught my eye. I tried to open it, but it wouldn't budge. I attempted to bring it to the floor for more leverage, and almost dropped it.

Roberto returned to find me all but standing on it. Rather than taking over and opening it like usual, he took it from my grip, and turned it on its side to reveal the title.

It was Jim's urn.

Mortified, I apologized aloud with wholehearted sincerity, and never touched it again, unless I absolutely had to.

I must admit—it made for great storytelling though.

Back to my assignment in the other room, under stacks of bags, boxes, and clothes, I found her bed. Like all I'd seen thus far, the sheets, blankets, and mattress were stained with rat urine.

I found an unwrapped package of cookies hidden under one pillow, and an opened, gnawed on, King James Bible under the other.

A wainscot theme dominated the room, with paisley patterned wall covering on the top, and mint green wooden panels on the bottom.

I peeled open a corner of the paper to see how hard it would be to remove it and jumped back in revulsion; there was a thriving colony of silverfish. The walls would have to be replaced. Thankfully, the ceiling was salvageable.

The bedroom window was yet another unfinished remodeling attempt, just like the ones in the dining area and the backroom sliding door.

The never-ending mess and the shoddy carpentry jobs were getting to me. It was incomprehensible how some took advantage of the elderly. *Why did a discounted project mean having to settle for incomplete, less than quality work?*

I walked outside, sat on the steps, removed my mask, and bawled my eyes out. Regardless of how many hours we put in, it's seemed like we'd never finish.

It wasn't supposed to take this long.

Always on his radar, Roberto came to see what the matter was. As I cooled my heels a while longer, he plugged in a seventies cast-off, digital radio he'd found next to where I was working and set it to the swing band station I loved.

After a good venting, I pulled up my big girl panties, donned my protective gear, and got back to work, finding solace in the uplifting music.

While sorting through the contents of a top drawer, I heard a sickening scratching sound coming from within the walls.

Focusing on the songs, humming even louder to the Andrews Sisters, it persisted, competing with my concerted efforts to ignore it.

I shook out a handful of the nesting material into the garbage, trying to understand how the rats had gotten hold of so much human hair, and about died on the spot when I grabbed for another, and realized the hair had come from the head of one of Grandma Faye's dead relatives.

Disgust curdled every cell in my body, and I dropped the whole mess in the trash.

My eyes were drawn to the corner of the room where the rat noise originated.

And then I saw it.

EIGHT

Without thinking, I lifted my mask and screamed for Roberto. He didn't answer, and I grabbed my phone to dial him. "Honey, where are you? You have to see this!"

"I see him, sweetie! I'm outside at the bottom of the stairs."

A stellar jay had made his way through a tangled net of ivy and holly berry thorns and was tapping incessantly on the window until I noticed him.

My heart lighter, I smiled to myself, and resumed with the dreaded chore at hand.

Before we left for the evening, Roberto took pictures of what we'd accomplished for the day. In one photo, we learned later the baseball-sized, shiny globe of light, right next to where I'd been working, was an orb.

The following week we returned to the smell of a wet dog, and little, soggy, doggie paw prints in the foyer. We searched around the house but couldn't find the culprit.

Without further delay, we continued with the day's task of emptying the garbage out of the gazebo. By nightfall, we'd hauled eight tons of trash to the dump, and moved over a hundred boxes to her storage room.

We were only halfway done.

Later, when we asked Grandma Faye if she ever had a dog, she said she'd had one once, but locked him in the basement by accident, and he died.

With most of the clutter gone, the rest of the cleanup went by in no time.

The attic was next, accessible only through a pull-down stepladder in the laundry room. Daunted by the possibility of finding it stuffed to the rafters with the same old crap, we were relieved to find only a small amount of junk just at the top of it.

Roberto was thankful she hadn't made it further.

I waited on solid ground as he slid odd and ends down the ladder into my waiting arms, showering me with a cloud of dust, dead spiders, and rat poop.

I heaped the stuff into a wheelbarrow, hauled it to the living room, dumped it in a pile for sorting, and returned to receive more.

While anticipating the next delivery, I glanced out the window in time to see a man approaching the porch.

I removed my mask, and opened the door to greet him, but found no one there.

I resumed my position at the ladder and played the scene over again in my mind. The more I thought about it, the less it made sense.

It wasn't possible for anyone to cross the front yard the way he had, yet I saw him do just that, and it was the same man as last time, tall with curly beach blonde hair.

I tried to shrug it off, but it still bothered me.

The best find in the entire house was in the attic, a working shop vac. Without a second thought, Roberto put it to work for poop duty.

He was crazy obsessed with the thing, zapping little brown turds with tornado-force gusto, nearly overflowing one of the industrial sized bags by the time we'd left for the night.

It was also the day we learned of another ghosty, a woman entity who didn't like loud noises, especially that of the archaic shop vac.

She began with a warning cry, "HONEY!"

And then wouldn't let up until he turned it off. Roberto checked the motor to see where the whining was coming from but couldn't find anything amiss.

So, he resumed his work with the vacuum when he heard the demanding voice again. Regardless, if it made a loud noise, she'd scream for him to turn it off.

At first, he thought I was yelling for him and came to see what I needed, but each time he'd find me with a respirator shielding my mouth, absorbed in a task, and in complete denial of calling for him.

Creeped out, yet wanting to keep the peace, he gave her a heads-up before he started from then on, but it was to no avail though, she still didn't like it.

◌‿◌

We saved the basement for last. Armed with our decontamination paraphernalia, Roberto cut a path to two small barn-like doors on the side of the house.

The first one led to a drafty crawlspace with a dirt floor. It wasn't something either of us wanted to venture into, the exterminators would have to deal with that; so, we opened the next door underneath the office.

Upon opening it, as if it were taunting us, we were greeted by the same insurmountable chaos we'd just finished cleaning.

The thought of starting all over again was like salt-on-a-wound, and more than I could bear. I wanted to cry.

How one little elderly lady had stuffed so much in such a small space, was anyone's guess. Roberto put his arm around my shoulders, gave me a brief pat, along with an awkward grin, and handed me a pair of gloves.

After a day of getting nowhere, we secured the tiny door closed once again, and made our way back to the porch to close for the night.

As we were about to climb the second set of steps, we saw someone leaning out of the doorway, as if they were looking for us.

The outline of its form was well-defined, but not its features, and it was faceless, like a white cartoon.

Before you could blink twice, it disappeared, but the image remained, seared into the depths of our minds. It happened so fast, it was incomprehensible.

Rather than dropping our supplies and running for the hills, as any sane person would have done, we laughed an anxious laugh, and agreed to let the *landlord* know whenever we planned to work outside of the house thereafter.

It was unanimous, we had over-extended ourselves, or something.

∽

Some weeks later, after clearing out the last of the stuff in the basement, we found the water heater, not replaced since 1985, and discovered a corner wall had melted away from a misplaced drainpipe.

The hole was so huge, a bay window could have fit in its place. Only a miracle had kept the room above it from sliding down into the lake.

Roberto took several photos of the damage and then, as a temporary fix, hoisted up the sagging deck with a car jack.

Incredibly, while reviewing the pictures later, the image in the photo before last, had a large mist on its left side with a figure of a man inside it. Grandpa Jim, we supposed. We'd finally captured our little ghosty on film.

The exterminator arrived not long after. When she emerged from the recesses of the crawlspace, she looked like a Sleestack, covered in spider webs and dirt.

As if she'd won the Olympics, she held up the carcasses of several dead animals in her gloved hands. I wouldn't do her job for all the money in the world.

After a thorough assessment, she recommended clearing the entire foundation of trees and brush, so treatment could begin. Adding, in all her years on the job, our house had the worst rat and bug problem she'd ever seen. How humiliating.

∽

PART III

It took Roberto most of an afternoon to hack his way around to the back of the house. He removed the growth from underneath the porch and steps and raked off two inches of moss and wet leaves from the deck, which hadn't glimpsed the light of day in years.

The roof appeared in dire straits; but because there wasn't a muscle in his body that didn't ache, he thought better of tackling it just yet, as well, cleaning it might cause it to leak.

We updated Grandma Faye during our next dinner date. It was mutual, finishing the inside of the house was more important than the outside. A specialist would have to come in to expose the foundation.

After a couple of bids, we settled for a family-owned, husband and wife tree-clearing team, and showed them around the property.

We explained what we wanted, and then let them have at it.

NINE

When we returned the following week, my heart about stopped as we approached the house. It was as flat as Kansas, all four hundred feet of it, from the mailbox to the lake, and eighty feet from one neighbor's property to the next, exposing all Grandma Faye's dirty underwear.

We asked them to thin the brush not clear it, but, like a tribe of wild goats on steroids, they'd mowed it all down.

I had a headache for three days, worrying about how to break the news to Grandma Faye. When I got the nerve, she simply said, "No sense in cryin' over spilled milk."

We tried not to show our disappointment, I mean they couldn't put it back if they wanted to, but it would take another year before enough grew in its place to camouflage some of the eyesores.

Their two sons, around my kids' ages, helped with the project. One of them ran into an enormous hornets' nest and was stung three different times. The same son fell into a well they happened upon. A well of all things! Thankfully he wasn't hurt.

Besides the gaping hole, they dug up almost a half a ton of trash beneath the ivy and brush, as if it had been someone's personal garbage dump, and pointed to the gazebo where they piled it all.

At least we were rid of the mountain of blackberry bushes in the front, and we had a driveway we could use.

The backyard clearing took my breath away. It was unbelievable. The sun twinkled enchantingly over the lake and smiled sweetly upon the house for the first time in decades.

I had to wonder how our neighbors felt, they hadn't seen anything from their north side window in over twenty years, or us.

When we closed up for the night, we saw three displaced bunnies in the driveway. They looked around perplexed, as if to say, "What the heck, what has happened to our house?"

The following day, on the heels of the tree company, the exterminators returned. They parked their loudly advertised vehicle in front of the house weekly for the next six months, to swap out traps and spray more poison.

In the meanwhile, the other half of their team *cleaned* out the attic and crawl space. Roberto had them return three different times to get the last of the rat droppings they'd missed.

When he installed a few boards in the attic, he found more they'd overlooked. Instead of wasting his breath with the company, he vacuumed and disinfected the area again himself, sterile enough to eat off the boards.

We won't even discuss the crawl space; he had to go over it a second time with the shop vac and Lysol too.

They might not have cleaned to our liking, but boy did they wipe out the bugs. To assure they remained evicted, armed with a caulking gun and Great Stuff, Roberto sealed every nook and cranny my flashlight shined through.

We worked in tandem, sealing all covert openings in and around the house. When we finished, it was as secure as Fort Knox, nothing was getting back in.

With the land cleared and infestation exterminated, it was time to assess inside damages, and plan for repairs.

TEN

*W*e found the reason for the leaking water between the wall separating the laundry and bathroom. In one of the few remodels, someone had done a half-assed job sealing off the chimney of an ancient wood cook stove.

The river trail revealed yet more damage. It had all but destroyed the makeshift bathroom counter, the ceilings, adjoining walls, and tile floors of both rooms. It even found its way under the kitchen tiles. All of them had to be ripped out and refinished.

We were relieved the smaller bedroom only required the replacement of one wall connecting to the bathroom, a lot of old fashioned elbow grease, and repainting.

The exterminator said the black tracks above the trash line was oil from the bodies of the rats, a calling card to others, and the only way to assure they didn't return was to paint over them, duly noted.

Water damage to the dining room ceiling revealed a leak in the roof; fortunately, it had spared the walls. But before raising a new one though, the entire thing needed to be washed, inspected, and patched.

The carpeting, draperies, stand up freezers, refrigerator, washer, and dryer, and all her furniture had to go, along with a few irreparable kitchen cupboards and the corroded tile counter.

A local recycling center offered to pick up the appliances for free, as is, washed or not, and that was music to our ears.

Through word of mouth, I found an affordable contractor to finish the two windows and the patio door in the back. For a little extra, I talked him into replacing the French doors in the dining room with a sliding glass door.

Besides the roof, the entire house needed rewiring, it was a tinderbox waiting to ignite, and should have been condemned; even so, we refused to give up on it just yet.

After reviewing the list and pictures, Grandma Faye gave us the green light to continue. But because of our inexperience, I recruited some extra hands to help.

First, I came across a retired electrician on a job board of a local senior center, who was also a jack of all trades, and agreed to rewire the house for next to nothing.

Then, as Dale was in the Navy, Lexi and some of her friends committed to some time when and where they could.

And last, wanting to nurture a relationship with my estranged father who was well versed in construction, I invited him to help. Honored I'd asked, he readily agreed, clueless to what he was in for. And that was it for my home improvement team.

∽

As my dad lives some 200 miles away in Portland Oregon, he had to stagger the time he stayed around the needs of his cat.

Every few days, he made the long journey to his place to empty a bag of food into a soup pot, fill another with water, and refill the litter box.

It was a relief she preferred to be outdoors. Our cats are so spoiled they wouldn't have survived past the first day.

He volunteered all he had to our cause, insisting, even though he had to sleep on a cot in our living room, that home-cooked meals, a perpetual thermos full of coffee, and gas money for his round trips home, were more than enough for compensation.

Because diabetes and years of hard labor had taken a toll on his body, limiting what he could do to help, and because he loved my cooking so much, but doesn't like it prepared in a filthy galley, he took complete charge of that section.

Once we'd ripped out all the wall-to-wall carpeting, Roberto helped my dad move all the appliances into the living room, as it was the largest space in the house it became the official command center where we tackled most projects.

My dad set out for the lake house well ahead of us each morning and worked until supper time. Regardless of when we arrived, we'd find him hard at work, in his coveralls and floppy fisherman's hat, either blasting away with a steam cleaner or sitting on a stool concentrating on some intricate thing.

He was quick, too. Within a week, he'd sanitized, caulked, sanded, and restored all the cabinets and their sliding tracks; they were impressive and appeared fresh off the assembly line.

Between the two of us, we burnt through two new, 1500-watt, portable steam cleaners. Apparently, they were not pre-tested for house restoration.

One morning we arrived to find him going to town with a plunger in the kitchen sink. He said he'd already tried Drain-O and it hadn't worked.

Roberto attempted to snake it, but it wouldn't budge. He dug open the ground on the other side of the wall to check the pipes and continued to dig until he had unearthed half of the front yard, reminiscent of the movie Caddyshack.

The last few inches revealed a shattered clay pipe and a small wooden barrel connected to the end of it. Dad explained it was a grease trap and how turn of the century kitchen sinks were plumbed to one, like ours.

It was as plain as the nose on Roberto's face, there was no other choice, the sink would have to be rerouted to the septic tank.

Thankfully, the electrician said he knew a thing or two about plumbing as well and offered to do the job once he finished the electricity. Grandma Faye would flip over this latest development.

The floor underneath it had to be cut open to make the detour. To get inside the space, the cast iron enamel basin had to come out.

With some serious elbow grease, a smattering of Spanish curse words, and an engine hoist, Roberto and dad finally got the thing out. The chance of it ever finding its way back in service was pretty-well zero to none.

While the electrician worked on the bypass, my dad surprised me by making a space for a dishwasher and a skinny pan-cupboard alongside it, I've always wanted one of those.

While he toiled away on my dream kitchenette, Roberto and I made a trip to the south side of town in search of salvaged counters for the bathroom and kitchen, and a toilet.

It took several trips before we found a counter to fit between the stove and fridge, a steal for twenty-five bucks and it only needed a touch of TLC.

Unfortunately, we couldn't find a replacement for the counter in the privy. We'd have to refurbish what we had and buy a new commode.

Because the hinges and screws for the French-style doors on the bathroom counter were antique and its replacements hard to come by, my dad sanded off the present peeling color, and I repainted them to match my other accessories.

I hung the hinges on twine over the garbage pile in the gazebo, pounded the screws in a small piece of wood, and spray painted the whole lot vintage bronze. They looked brand new; Martha would be proud.

❦

I had to laugh when Lexi first arrived. She wore a fresh off the rack, matching Carhartt outfit, a fashionista even in construction. She didn't stay tidy for long though.

While the carpet and laminate floors were being ripped out, she was right in the middle of the fray, removing the bathroom tile all by herself.

We were pleasantly surprised to discover maple hardwoods underneath the rugs. As original hardwoods are hard to find nowadays, we abandoned the idea

PART III

for new carpeting and chose to refinish the wood floors instead; the how we would figure out later.

When it was time to gut the bedroom walls and the bathroom ceiling, Lexi was at the ready with her tools. I'm sure her expressions in the photos I took meant, *enough with the camera mom.*

While vacuuming the inner framing, light shined through some holes in the black paper covering them. In fact, the only thing separating the wall from the exterior shingles was the thin sheet of paper.

Come to find out, the entire house was lined the same way, absent of an outer, three-quarter board. Therefore, insulating was out of the question.

My dad suggested to have some blown in; but, if we did, all the siding would pop off like a cork. Because there was neither the time nor the money to put in the missing panels, we settled with lining the wall shared with the bathroom with insulation, at least the bedroom would be warm.

Then, demolition Lexi filled what holes she could with Great Stuff.

It was no wonder why Jim had a heater near his chair and why they had wall to wall carpeting and heavy curtains.

Just as we were finishing, Roberto ran into the house to show us a picture he'd taken just moments before of some prehistoric looking spider.

"Look at this sucker!" And then he high tailed back to where he'd found it.

Lexi was hot on his heels. I heard her scream. It was then I knew it was nothing I wanted to see. When she returned, she was smiling like a Cheshire cat.

"I squished it mama, and it popped like a big ol' zit."

Gross.

Roberto and Brent, a friend of Lexi's, took down the hidden chimney, an all-day job. Lexi brought them supplies, running up and down the roof ladder with ease; her each descent scaring me half to death.

Roberto worked on the moss while he was up there, pushing it off to the yard below. Between watching him scurrying all over like some damn fool, and Lexi's acrobatics on the ladder, about turned my hair white.

It was irrefutable, all the roof shingles needed replacing, but it would cost more than the house was worth. Roberto dreaded the effort it would take to keep it from leaking.

Our ghosty seemed to be as excited as we were, as he'd been active during the entire restoration project. I think he must have been getting bored though, because as soon as the walls and ceilings came down, things started disappearing.

All those who've worked on the house have lost one thing or another they'd swear they had in their hands only moments before.

Like the day when Roberto walked from the bedroom, where he was writing on drywall with Lexi and Brent, to the kitchen and back again, misplacing his glasses somewhere along the way.

He found them three days later in the shop, and he hadn't been in there for almost a week.

Then my dad saw it.

PART III

ELEVEN

*H*e described it as the same white form we'd seen, something we withheld on purpose so as not to scare anyone away. He said he caught a glimpse of *the spook* from the corner of his eye as it paced several times, back and forth, past the doorway to the dining room.

Well, that was all Lexi needed to hear, and her visits became fewer and far between; she never stayed past dusk again.

It wasn't long after my dad's encounter, that he proclaimed his health was making the 400-mile roundtrips home difficult, and therefore couldn't stay any longer either.

To top it all, our electrician claimed he had a family emergency, and had to be absent for a while too. He hadn't mentioned if he had happenstances with our ethereal friend, nor did we ask. I don't know if he would have admitted it if he had.

Within two weeks, I'd lost all my help.

೧೨

Roberto and I were now at the mercy of YouTube how-to videos, and the employees of the local hardware stores to finish the house. As we ventured further into the unknown, almost insurmountable obstacles bombarded us every which way we turned, testing not only our individual resolve, but the foundation of our rock-solid relationship as well.

For example, when Roberto asked if I thought his measurements appeared correct, and I said they were *too much*, he'd interpret it as, *in excess*, and cut off a little more of the Formica, molding, four-by-four, or drywall, and we'd have to start all over again.

At the time, the comical Ricky and Lucy moments weren't so funny.

೧೨

With the water heater replaced, we looked forward to washing in hot water at last; but the house didn't let us down. When we arrived the following day, we were welcomed by a small flood in the laundry room. A stripped pipe leaked a little river down the new drywall overnight. It was a blessing in disguise nothing else was spoiled.

Roberto followed the perpetual trickle and discovered a large section underneath the existing underlayment damaged from years of leaks, the present seepage turned it into mush.

So much for a *simple repair job*.

Because the last of the remaining sinks was off limits for a while, the front yard became the official washing headquarters, a bucket to wash supplies, one to rinse, and one for personal use.

It took three weeks to finish the laundry area, but so worth the effort, it's just stunning, I can't wait for Grandma Faye to see it.

༄

The dining room ceiling was the largest and most difficult to swap out. I talked Lexi into helping with that one last thing, early in the morning mind you. Along with Lexi's boyfiend's help to balance it, Roberto got it secured into place.

One day, while digging new holes for the back-deck post and beam blocks, and pouring fresh cement around them for added measure, he dropped his bucket and doubled over in pain.

I heard him holler for me, but not in the same way he usually does. I ran to his side, helped him to the car, and headed for the hospital.

It was the last thing he'd fix for the next four weeks. All the heavy lifting had taken a toll on his body and resulted in two hernias.

The rest was on my plate, for a while.

On the first day of working solo, I walked around back to check on the curing of the beams, and noticed our names etched in the cement; it was a Hallmark moment for sure.

While Roberto convalesced at home, propelled by the urgency to finish, and be moved in by the time he was well again, I forged ahead, hell-bent on completing the tasks he'd started.

It was an arduous process, but it wasn't long before I could wield a mudding spatula, seal exposed seams, dings, and nail holes, and file mudded joints to a smooth perfection.

༄

There were days when I didn't think I could do it though. The archaic sanding machine, called a Jigger, became a two-ton brick after a while, and made my entire arm ache when I tried to lift it beyond my elbow.

Although the hand sander was lighter and easier to manage, it took forever. By the end of the day, I looked like a transplant from Area 51.

Most nights it felt as if I were a victim of a voodoo doll, stinging pinpricks ran up and down my arms and kept me awake; but, with sheer stubbornness, I *got 'er done*.

PART III

It was a relief Roberto's surgeries were spread-out, so he could help some.

Any sarcastic remark about my finishing skills hurt my feelings. Like how I tried to match the bald spots created by sanding with the original bumpy surface on the walls.

As spray textured paint was common in the olden days, finding something comparable to it was almost impossible.

The last thing on God's green earth like it was liquid sand. Since I'd mastered the mudding and sanding technique, I didn't think it would be any harder to apply texture.

The guy at the paint counter told me how easy it was to put on, but recommended I be quick with it because it dried fast.

He said it was easy; all I had to do was scoop it from the bucket with a trowel, slap it on the surface, and scrape off any excess.

Well, that turned out to be easier said than done. I started in the office, where mistakes would be less noticeable, and worked my way out to the foyer. I think I got more on me and the floor than the wall.

Regardless of how much I sanded it after it dried, I couldn't get it to match the look of the original texture. It wasn't until I reached the hallway, I'd figured out a simpler method.

I scooped a little glob of the sand with a small sponge and slopped it on the wall, gave it a flamboyant twist, and *ta-da*, the result was a pretty, Picassoesque swirl.

It looked much better than where I started in the office anyway. If no one glanced up at the ceiling or stared at the walls for any length of time, they wouldn't be the wiser.

Not until Roberto noticed my artwork and about died laughing. He said they reminded him of continents. Funny; I wasn't aiming for a global theme.

Ten months into the restoration project, the prep work was finished, and the painting could begin at last. As I opened the door to head out for Lowes, a third eviction notice fluttered to my feet.

I bought all the required supplies and several buckets of warm-colored paint, gold for most of the walls, creamy white for the ceilings, sky-blue for the bathroom, and a soft grey for the kitchen and dining rooms.

On my way to the house, psyching myself into the foreboding task awaiting me, I was ready to rumble until I opened the door, and found a bunch of dimples in my newly prepped walls.

My finishing work had caused some of the original nails to bulge out. A quick-fix trick on YouTube suggested just to smack them back into place, and then drill a drywall screw in above them.

But that was only the half of it, the new spots needed mudding and sanding too, and delayed the painting for yet another day.

While the new spots cured, I spent a few hours fighting with the painter's tape. It looked as though Harold went postal by the time I'd finished.

When I returned the following morning, I received a suffocating welcome. I sealed the house so well, it about doubled the outside hundred-degree temp. I was certain I'd die that day.

It took hot yoga to a new level, Habanero caliber even, it was if I were painting in the desert, sweat poured from places I didn't know existed.

To make things worse, the paint wouldn't co-operate; I'd met my match, it proved more stubborn than myself.

Although I bought the kind with primer, with the thought of having to apply just one coat, it refused to take to the archaic walls, and sucked it up like a dehydrated sponge.

Dejected and exhausted, I cried Uncle, and dragged my pathetic carcass to the hardware store for primer. As much as I wanted to avoid doubling the chore, it was the only way it would work.

It wasn't long before my temper surpassed that of the heat. By the time I'd made it halfway down the hall, I was in a full-blown argument with myself.

"How did I end up being the one to paint the entire house? I didn't sign up for this!"

"Oh, yes you did Missy! You wanted this little cabin on the lake just as much as Roberto, you know you did, so buck up girlfriend, pull up them bootstraps, and get back to work!"

Despite the soul-sapping task, I wouldn't have had it any other way. I'm rather particular about details and Roberto is better at fixing things, so yes, without a doubt, the painting was my job.

Once the office was completed, I brought my mom to be with Grandpa Jim, setting her candy tin of ashes by his on the window sill.

They must have had a grand ol' time, because when we arrived the next day, our nostrils were accosted by several strange smells, fried eggs and bacon wafted in from the kitchen, Mommy's musky, Jontue fragrance, fused with a hint of tobacco, hovered in the bathroom, and a man's Wild Country cologne permeated the office.

The moldings were the last to repair. I found a nice walnut color to match the originals. While Roberto sanded and prepped them for me, I applied the same paint to the trimmings.

Now I know I'm the crazy cat lady, but I thought it was hilarious when he suggested I also decorate the wood trim on the sides of the kitty door.

Going a step further, with glittery stick-on letters, I added the names of our four fur babies along the edges as well.

When we left for the night, I'd finished painting the details, all the doors, and created a column around the living room entry to match too; I slept like a hibernating bear that evening.

September snuck past us as did the first anniversary of the restoration project. The mobile park manager was breathing fire by now and stuck a fourth eviction notice on our door.

TWELVE

*A*t night, for the time being, I need to leave my van at Lexi's apartment. It's nice because we get to visit for a while until Roberto can bring me home.

Once we enter the park, I must recline my seat back, cover myself with a blanket, and, when we reach our place, sneak in the rear entrance, so far so good.

We are forced to continue with this charade until the lake house is finished. Depending on its cooperation, I can't say for certain when it will be ready as the remaining work requires a lot of effort, instalation of two sinks and a toilet, sanding 750 square feet of wood floors, cleaning the air ducts, and laying tile flooring in three rooms.

～

We set our minds to focus on the bathroom first. Prepared, yet anxious for any unsuspecting challenges, we laid the tile, applied Brewster's swan wallpaper, and put in the new commode without a hitch, knock on wood.

Of all the adjustments Grandma Faye had made, the most disappointing was the missing bathtub. She had a plumber remove it some years back. Now there was only a small, closet-sized shower. I'd mourn for my weekly candlelit, glass of wine, and Epsom salt soaks for sure.

The final work required most of Roberto's brawn and know-how. To appear helpful though, I stuck close to his heels, at the ready to lend him a foot, or a hand, and fetch him a tool at any given moment. It reminded me of assisting in the O.R., "Phillips, clamp, saw, hold this still."

The tile floors were a bear to make seamless. My hands and knees ached for days from crawling around on them to seal each little groove. But, if I had to choose, I would rather have done that, than finish the walls again, no doubt.

To wrap up a few final touches in the laundry room, I had Roberto climb up in the attic to get something, but before I could whistle Dixie, his leg came through the ceiling, dangling right over my head.

I wanted to laugh my socks off; he was fortunate to have only hurt his pride. The delay to make repairs cost us half of a day, so much for my flawless ceiling.

Last, the bathroom counter got an overhaul. With the broken tiles and the moldy three-quarter board removed, my refurbished hardware put back into place, and a coat of baby blue paint to match the walls, it looked new again. All it needed now was the original pink cast iron sink and Formica.

∽

We continued to work in quick succession; the kitchen underlayment was next. As with the shop vac, Roberto went nuts with the nail gun. He was sure the more nails he used, along with the adhesive underneath, the less noise the floor would make.

Despite his best efforts though, it continues to squeak. Mums the word, I know I'll bite my tongue off one of these days.

The Formica for the two kitchen counters was next. Because the hardware store put the fear of God in us when we told them we were installing it ourselves, we saved that task for last on purpose.

I sacrificed my tail end to secure it in place while Roberto traced the outline of the sink, it also gave me a chance to rest a second.

Hah! It wasn't that bad after all.

It cut easy enough with a box cutter and super-duper construction glue, with our abilities, there was no way we'd attempt to use contact cement, total visual there.

Afterwards, we set several cans of paint, and whatever else we could find that was heavy, on top of it while the adhesive set. And it did just that, giving us the confidence to place it on the refurbished counter and the one in the bathroom.

As Roberto prepared to tile the kitchen floor, I gladly headed to the back deck to paint ceiling moldings. While they dried, I tackled the panel wall with gel stain in Provincial tint and polished it to a new perfection.

The transformation of the house was exciting, the kitchen most of all. With the appliances returned to their places, a country-themed border applied around the top, and a cute, lace gauge, rooster valance hung over the window, it looked like those I'd seen in a home décor magazine.

Next came the sink. No matter how many MacGyver ideas Roberto conjured up, almost bringing down the cupboards at one point, we couldn't get the original cast iron sink back into place. So, we had to settle with a clearance, light-weight, stainless steel model instead.

The last task to do was the wood floors. Roberto studied Youtube videos for two days until he was ready to try it. In the meanwhile, I sat for hours picking dehydrated, timeworn grout from the cracks in the floor. I worked until the filler and dirt lines blurred into one and my spine screamed for mercy.

The sanding machine we rented was a monster. It seemed to have a life of its own, and made the lights dim as it sucked the electricity from the walls. It was so loud, Roberto couldn't have heard the ghosty if she had protested.

Impatient with its little progress, he swapped it for a scarier, roller type. I thought we wouldn't have any floor left for sure. Especially when he left it spinning in one spot, even for just a second.

After the floors were finished and the air ducts cleaned and repaired, we were able to remove our respirators for the first time in thirty-two weeks.

Those final repairs took six months to finish, but it was all done, and we were finally ready to move in.

∞

For peace of mind, with the Ghostbusters being inaccessible, following the instructions for a spiritual home cleansing, I opened all the cupboards, windows, doors, and attic access, and *banished* any lingering bad spirits with a smoking stick of sage.

For added measure, after moving in our belongings, but before staying our first night, I called a Catholic priest from down the road for a house blessing.

He sat across from us on the loveseat and listened as we enlightened him about our renovation story and the experiences we'd had with the ghostys.

Just as we were getting into the witness accounts, a loud crash, like a box of nails strewn all over the attic floor, echoed above our heads.

PART III

THIRTEEN

The priest stood, ready to tango with whatever it was, and followed Roberto to the attic access. There were no nails lying about, nor had anything fallen onto the narrow quarter board floor. We returned to the living room, and the priest prayed over us. Then, he began his blessings in the attic.

He read passages from the Bible as he made his way around the house, making signs of the cross with his crucifix and flicking about Holy water as he did.

He wrote a symbol over each doorway and window with Holy water, blessing Jim and Mommy's urns too, insisting they be removed from the house as soon as possible.

A final blessing and prayer concluded at the front door, he left a series of numbers and letters written in chalk at the top of it, 20+C+M+B+11, and there they remain.

A few days later he emailed a list of his concerns. Because he had been taunted by a spiritual presence several times during his visit, he said the house was the center of a supernatural vortex, stating how he felt it wasn't safe for us to live there.

He said his main concern was for our overall health if we chose to continue with our plans to move in, as the living and the dead shouldn't knowingly cohabitate.

Without hesitation, we moved Jim's urn to Grandma Faye's storage, and Mommy, well, since we had nowhere else to take her, we placed her behind some books.

We saw no harm in keeping *Isabelle's phone*, so, we propped it up against a mirror on our dresser, on top of a jewelry box, with a picture of Our Lady of Guadalupe laminated on it, that one of Roberto's sisters made for me.

Since there was no other option for us, we stayed.

After the blessings and shifting stuff around, we noticed an immediate difference. The atmosphere seemed lighter and more positive than before.

For added measure though, we hung crucifixes around the house, a portrait of Our Lady of Guadalupe on the wall at the entry of our bedroom and displayed several pictures of Christ on either side of our bureau.

Thankful for our tiny bed, we were able to move it and a single nightstand in the remaining space, leaving just enough room to shimmy sideways between the two.

Last, but not least, we brought all four fur babies to their new home, two male tuxedo Norwegian Forest Cats, Lucky and Fluke, a female black domestic short-hair, Sniffles, and her daughter Foxy, a calico; cozy and protected; we hoped.

⁓

The little town where we lived didn't have a historical society, so I began my investigation with the local property archives.

I learned how the house started out as a tiny hunting shack in the thirties, and in the forties, a nice couple from Germany bought and remodeled it, four times in all, turning it into the Bavarian Cottage style, family home it is today.

Combined with what Grandma Faye remembered, and the recollections of some of the neighbors, the names of the original owners were Einar and Agnus Zimmerman.

When Einar wasn't making wood furnishings for the folks around town, you could find him tinkering away on his house. Agnus worked just as hard perfecting the inside.

He and his wife coveted their beloved cottage on the lake and put their heart and soul into all its little details. Overlooked by the Stork, they fulfilled their maternal needs by supporting the local children's hospital, and Agnus taught at the town's first elementary school.

Overall, their lives were complete and uneventful. Until, just after they'd entered their seventies and were enjoying the fruits of retirement, Einar met his fate in a fatal traffic accident.

Grief-stricken, Agnus sold their beloved home to the only interested person, Grandma Faye, left most of their belongings behind, taking only necessities, and without a word, disappeared, and no one ever heard from her again.

Grandma Faye and her husband, Jim, moved the Zimmermans' possessions to the half basement to make room for their own belongings. Since he seldom frequented the shop, Einar's tools remained on his workbench just as he had left them.

Two years later, Jim died without warning from a heart attack. Fast forward to today.

Like the movie, Beetlejuice, Roberto and I believe Einar and Agnus are the spirits living with us. As they are not malevolent, none of the casting-out prayers worked to evict them. I'm sure it delighted them to not only have their precious home restored, but it had received a priest's blessing no less.

PART III

It was quiet in the beginning after we took up residence, but then the noises in the attic and the kitchen started up again. It appeared Agnus' major pet peeve was having dirty dishes left in the sink. We jumped when we first heard her clanging around, but now we laugh to ourselves and assure her the sink will be empty by morning.

Occasionally, after a good rain, a loud smack from the ceiling brings us to attention in a hot second. The first time it happened, Roberto checked the attic for the culprit and found a leak in the roof in the exact place where the noise came from.

We're convinced Einar is keeping an eye on it; Roberto depends upon his messages, discovering a new leak every time.

We've learned one other thing Agnus doesn't like, and its cats, most of all in the kitchen or bedroom. Our eldest, Lucky, hasn't taken well to being ordered about by someone he can't see and began marking her prized oven in defiance.

From what I gather, it was her first electric stove, a welcomed relief I'm sure from the wood burning kind she had before, the one we'd found leaking behind the laundry room wall.

Thankfully, their standoff didn't last long, and they reached some sort of an agreement. Nowadays, he comes and goes as he pleases, and her beloved range is left unfouled.

Although, she remains steadfast about the *no cats in the bedroom* rule; hallelujah, he's never sprayed in there.

Lucky and I have an evening ritual, and it's always been the same. Once settled, he'll snuggle next to my shoulder, stretch his paws across my chest with the greatest care, and lull me to sleep with his gentle rhythmic purring.

But, not in this house, as soon as we turn the lights off, he'll jump to his feet, hiss, and disappear, scaring me half to death each time.

In defiance, he will return a short while later and snooze at the foot of the bed, or on Roberto's side. He's relentless, determined to battle this one out with her until the bitter end. I bet she's never seen the likes of him before.

Another thing she doesn't like, and I don't know if it's a pet peeve or if she is playing an affectionate game with me or what, is how I position my antique, tin, spice containers on the shelf of her stove.

In about three weeks, each one will straighten ever so slightly, until they are horizontal with the ledge. When I put them back the diagonal way, it isn't long before they're straightened out again.

Mind you, this isn't happening with the use of the oven. We don't use it very often because it causes the electric meter to spin like a top.

Speaking of spinning, just about half of the discount we'd earned on the rent, fed the electric company, a shocking hike compared to what we'd paid at the mobile home.

The archaic heater in the basement makes the meter spin the most, so we mothballed it without a second thought. So much for having the ducts cleaned to use it.

After sealing off the floor grates, the temperature inside wavering about twenty degrees more than out, we were hard pressed for another means of warmth.

At first, we thought the fireplace would be our saving grace, but it only warms the area in front of it. So, after a few purchases and returns, we settled with some portable space heaters that didn't break the bank, or cause the meter to whir, one each for the office, the bathroom, and the living room.

The Zimmerman's presence has become commonplace and not at all foreboding. In fact, we feel like they have taken to me and Roberto, as if we are their kids. Above all, they've given us a real sense of being *home*.

Curious to know more about our invisible hosts, delving even further into the spiritual unknown, reading up on ghost hunting and how to do our own, we set about capturing them on audio.

PART III

FOURTEEN

The first night, we set the recorder in the laundry room and listened the next day with unbelievable fascination. The next night, and those thereafter, we put it in various other locations to see if there was a difference in sounds.

We scared ourselves silly, but we couldn't stop.

Their days seemed to start when ours ended, with the most movement between one and four in the morning. It was typical daytime activity overheard in any house on an average day, constant footsteps up and down the hallway, knocking on doors, the shuffling sound of objects moving, and polite conversation between two people.

Funny how we couldn't hear all the commotion without a recorder.

Their speech wasn't always discernable, yet, it was apparent one was a male and the other a female. Most of their conversations were warbled and muffled, like the way the adults talked on Charlie Brown. Sometimes, they spoke in rhythmic syllables, their words clear as a bell, like "thank you" and "you're welcome."

In the first recording, we heard cascading water in the background. We took the recorder to the store, played it for the manager, and exchanged it for another, testing it before we purchased it.

When we replayed the next night's noises, the trickling sound was still present. We thought perhaps they wanted us to turn on our little waterfall we have in the foyer, so we did.

When we listened again the following day, we heard only a slight dripping from our fountain, a bit of comprehensible conversation, and a lot of activity.

We heard someone knock twice on our bedroom door and a woman ask, "Is anyone here?" In two, thirty-minute intervals we heard a loud screeching sound, followed by an exasperated exhale, and someone moving about.

A couple of hours more into the recording, we heard a rapid knock and a door opening on a rusty hinge.

The next night, our fountain was the only thing we could discern. It seemed as if the activity was stronger with the waterfall on, but the noise from it stifled their dialogs.

The subsequent evening, they must have been having a party. Besides the same inaudible conversation, there was laughter and the popping of a cork, twice, fifteen minutes apart.

An hour later a man groaned, and a woman asked, "What?"

The rest of the time was more back and forth muffled conversations, a distinct "Thank you" and "You're welcome," a thunderous smack on something, and a bang.

We recorded only one more night of the same sounds.

Just after we'd turned on the recorder, I got a loud and clear message in my mind to cease and desist. I climbed into bed, cuddled close to Roberto, and switched off the lights.

Just then my slippers scuffled ever so slight on the wooden floor next to my side of the bed. My heart pulsed like a wild drum, and I scooted closer to Roberto.

Suddenly, as if someone had kicked them, my slippers took off across the room, and a voice screamed and vibrated off the inner walls of my skull, "KNOCK IT OFF!"

I buried my face into Roberto's back and cried out for him. Startled, he fumbled for the lamp. We were alone. We peered cautiously over my side of the bed to find my slippers positioned in perfect attention, pointing towards the headboard, unlike the usual haphazard way I kick them off.

I shared what I heard in my head with Roberto. Without another thought, he got up and stopped the recorder, decommissioning our ghost hunting adventure then and there. Regardless of any strange happenings since, we've kept our curiosity in check.

I slept with the lamp on for the next two weeks.

PART III

FIFTEEN

Overall, we are enjoying our little money pit in the woods and are having fun making it our home. We've made friends with some of our neighbors, including a squirrel companion we named Peanut. We thought it was a boy at first until we noticed she'd been nursing babies.

As the name Peanut can go both ways, we stuck with it. She's so funny. She'll disappear for most of the spring and summer, and just when we think something's happened to her, I'll hear her knocking at the window for nuts.

I'm serious; she does. She will search all the windows in the house, including the clear panel of the cat door, until she finds me, and then acts out charades until she gets my attention. In fact, she's looking at me right now.

She must've bragged to someone because there's been an influx of squirrels at the mission morning chow line, no doubt all her friends and relations, who expect their breakfast, mixed nuts, and cracked corn, served promptly.

In addition, a whirlwind of ravens and stellar jays have joined in on the cacophony. If I'm late, it's a mutiny, sure to bring a neighbor's complaint one of these days.

Roberto balked at first, complaining how we couldn't afford to feed the neighborhood, but now he beats me to the serving line each morning.

Of all of them, Peanut is the only one to take the nuts from our hands and to sit next to me while she eats; she's quite the listener too.

∽

We also share our property with the nighttime wild, namely coyotes. They come from across the main road in the early hours of the morning, under the cloak of darkness, to prey upon the domestic pets in the neighborhood.

We learned our lesson about them the hard way with the capture of our beloved Sniffles. Several months later, we lost our precious Fluke. We weren't sure if a coyote got him, or if he was taken.

We honored him with an altar inside of our unused fireplace, adding his photo and favorite white toy mouse, a lit candle, and began a dedicated prayer and meditation ritual.

Even Lucky contributed all his energy, love, and support to the effort. Sometimes during mid-prayer, he'd jump on my lap and purr throughout the remaining meditation, regardless if it was for fifteen minutes or thirty.

If Fluke was still alive, we hoped he felt our love and knew his entire family wanted him home. To find him became a family effort that even extended to my father.

He drove the long and strenuous 200-mile trek from his home to ours to keep up the prayer vigil while we were away on Christmas vacation.

We returned home just after the New Year to find Fluke's favorite chair still empty. Roberto was heartbroken; although there would always be a place in his heart for Lucky, Fluke had his heart and soul.

The overwhelming grief on his face frustrated me, but there was nothing more I could do. No number of candles, prayer, or meditation had brought Fluke back.

Undefeated, I created one hundred *Lost Cat* posters, hoping to pull at someone's heartstrings I added he had a health condition and the enticement of a $150 reward, lying down about that much at FEDEX to print and laminate them.

The following weekend we stapled them to phone poles and stop signs all over our neighborhood, in local pet shelters, community centers, convenience stores, and restaurants throughout neighboring towns.

And then we waited.

PART III

SIXTEEN

Whenever I wash the dishes, I scan over the property as far as I can, ever hopeful of seeing our precious bundle of fur lumbering up the walkway, or a car coming up the drive to bring him home.

But neither of these scenes played out. After three weeks with no response from the posters, I printed, cut out, and laminated small rectangular cards with a revised reward sum of $250.

We spent two more weekends reapplying them to the posted notices, but despite our best efforts, there was nothing.

The first anniversary of Fluke's disappearance was upon us, and we were no closer to finding him. A thick layer of soot formed on the walls, ceilings, and windows from the candles.

With my asthma becoming affected, we agreed to distinguish them, but left the altar intact, continuing with a nightly prayer and meditation.

As the days passed, Roberto became more despondent without his favorite kitty. I was just sick not being able to console his grief and felt worthless; I'd do whatever it took to see the sunshine in his face again.

Eighteen months to the day, washing dishes and scanning the property, as usual, I almost dropped the bowl I was holding when a black cat, more identical to Lucky than Fluke, came bounding up the walkway.

I turned to see Lucky sitting in the foyer and looked outside again. The cat paused, as if to assess he was at the correct location, and, without a care in the world, proceeded forward to our front door.

I muttered "Oh my God!"

That was all Roberto needed to hear. He ran to the kitchen to find out what the matter was and saw the cat.

He put his shoes on and dashed outside, but it was only a moment later when he returned.

The discouraged look on his face said it wasn't Fluke. I felt his sadness and disappointment and wanted to wrap him in my arms and tell him how sorry I was.

However, you must admit, it was beyond coincidence it was a tuxedo Norwegian Forest cat, the same breed as Fluke and Lucky.

I mean, how many big black felines, with long fluffy boa tails akin to Fluke's, are wandering around looking for a place to crash, and then happen upon a house where they'd just lost one identical to him?

Roberto scoffed at the idea it was a gift. He said we hadn't requested *a* carbon copy of Fluke, we'd asked *for* Fluke.

I tried to reason with him how it wasn't the kitty's fault for not being who we wanted him to be.

Ready to bail any second when approached, Roberto had a way of speaking to him he responded to. In a matter of days, he allowed him to pet him. Not long after that, I caught him cradling the kitty in his arms.

For me though, when I brought him water and nourishment, I had to walk on eggshells before he'd accept my offering. His growling tummy trumped his fearfulness, and he wolfed his food in a single bite. I was sure it would come back up, but it never did.

He made a temporary home for himself underneath the old, dilapidated gazebo, and adapted to our mealtime routine.

We didn't need to call him for meals, or the squirrels, as our front door groans loud when it's opened. Without missing a beat, his small, panther-like face would appear, prompt and expectant each time. If late, Lucky was sure to fetch him.

Overall, he took to him too. Although he'd growl at the sight of another cat and chase them off our property, he'd welcomed Fluke, as well as this stranger, and kept a close eye on the youngster as if reminding him about manners, respect, and the way things were around here.

Most important, birds, moles and rats were ok to hunt, but mom's squirrels, yes even the one that looks and squeaks like a brown rat, and the daily visits of a stellar jay were off limits.

The stray followed Lucky everywhere and sat as close as allowed, ten feet was pushing it, appearing to hang on every word of the ramblings of an old man.

The following week we called our vet. The morning of his appointment, Roberto gave him breakfast while I prepared a cat carrier with a clean towel, dousing it with Feliway spray.

He whispered for me to come as quiet as possible, and bring the box in a way that he could slide him in. Roberto scooped him in his arms and placed him inside.

The kitty complied without question, and Roberto closed the door behind him before he knew what had happened.

PART III

He didn't put up as much of a fight as we thought he might, but boy did he carry on as if he were being murdered.

Lucky wasn't anywhere to be seen.

We loaded the vagrant into the car and headed in to town. Just as we left, I spotted our eldest sitting in the neighbor's driveway waiting for us to leave.

We laughed. Lucky does not like to visit the doctor and might think it funny how the youngster got bamboozled into the carrier, unaware, this time, of where he was going.

On the way to the vet, Roberto said he hoped that the kitty had a microchip; he was a nice gift and, although he felt grateful, he only wanted Fluke, or no other cat, period, other than the ones we had at home.

Once in the examining room, I crossed my fingers as the vet scanned his muscular body from nose to tail for the incriminating chip.

Not finding one, she looked to Roberto for permission to proceed; he let out a defeated sigh, and agreed, nodding his approval for the exam and series of tests.

The vet assumed he was about a year old, and healthy as a horse through and through.

She asked if his remaining lab results turned out normal if we planned to keep him. You could have heard a pin drop; I held my breath for the verdict.

Roberto couldn't deny the coincidences surrounding the little orphan as he pondered the question, the seconds from the wall clock ticked loud and slow.

Just when I thought I'd pass out, the answer I was desperate to hear, echoed in mine and the kitty's hearts, "Yes."

Oh, happy day! The vet congratulated us as we laughed and loved on the little fur ball. She asked what birthday to give him. Roberto said he wanted him to have his father's, June 7.

And then she asked what name she should write on his medical record. I suggested Martin, after one of the patron saints of cats we had prayed to for Fluke.

He agreed for a second time; it was perfect. We consulted with the kitty. He purred as if giving his consent too but stopped when we returned him to an assistant for the *works*.

The following day, with the news of a normal blood test and an uncomplicated neuter, armed with special cat litter made of wood that wouldn't stick to his procedure site, we arrived again at the veterinary hospital to bring our bundle of joy home.

Although poked and prodded, not unlike that of an alien abduction, with the required shots and neutering, he was still so happy to see us and walked without argument into the safe confines of the carrier.

But just before he made it within its safe borders, they brought him out again for one final ritual, the insertion of the microchip, sealing his adoption, making him an official member of our family. Martin Martinez, how funny is that?

My office became his infirmary while he recovered. We had to protect everything with plastic sheets while the last of the male hormone left his body.

The vet warned us, since he was late to neuter, it might take a few weeks for the testosterone to cycle out, meaning he shouldn't go beyond the boundaries of the office until then.

He was quiet and slept most of the day while I worked and seemed most content when one of us was in the room with him. But it was a whole other ball game in the evenings when he was alone.

As our bedroom is on the other side of the paper-thin wall, his all-night yowling and pacing was maddening, not unlike having a newborn in the house.

Roberto got up throughout the evening to console him. We were relieved the day he was allowed back outside again.

After a month, he became one of the pack and only allowed Roberto to hold him in his arms, increasing the sessions with time.

He cradled him the same way he held Fluke, caressing and planting kisses on his little head, always reassuring him in soft and soothing whispers; nothing could be sweeter.

Roberto has called him Fluke several times, but Martin seems to understand, and doesn't mind in the least.

The peace in Roberto's heart is indescribable; I can see the light in his eyes again, and that's all that matters.

SEVENTEEN

Compared to our noisy neighbors, learning to cohabitate with the Zimmermans is nothing. Without insulation as a sound barrier, I hear every confounded tweet, quack, and daily deluge of my neighbor's nail pulling, cacophony of leaf blowers and lawn mowers along with anything else he can find that makes noise.

But the one that takes the cake, comes from the county park three properties away. Once school lets out in June until it resumes in September, from sun up to sun down, the YMCA day camp descends upon it. I swear I know all their agonizing cheers and war cries by heart.

Prayers for rainy days is all for naught, the dampness only brings the din down to a dull rumble. I've tried to work in a different room but can't escape it. Others have suggested I wear earplugs or headphones; it's obvious they don't write.

Because summer was out for any productive writing, I signed up as a vendor at a local farmers' market. Being a rookie, I reserved and paid for a space for all the weekends from May through September.

The first month was comical. We just had our camping tent, along with a table and some shelves to display our products, then waited with high hopes for customers.

A monsoon came instead, and about capsized our little production. Discouraged from leaving early, like the S.S. Minnow, Roberto and I hunkered down with our cribbage board, and braved the elements with the rest of the merchants until June.

As luck would have it, the weather didn't co-operate once during our first summer. It would be nice and sunny all week long, and then a hurricane would blow in on market day. It's a wonder we didn't get pneumonia.

Educated in the errors of our ways by veteran vendors, we bought a sturdier, climate-proof, marketplace canopy with weights; for fifty dollars more, they delivered it in our theme color.

It was the only orange tent among all the white ones and made me look tan.

We learned more tricks of the trade as we went along. The number one unwritten rule was not to sign up for a single market for the entire season.

Because Roberto worked an occasional weekend, he'd set me up before he left, and return at closing to pack up.

Scared of my own shadow, an introvert through and through, Roberto and my son used their excellent sales skills and wrote a short and sweet pitch to help me feel more confident.

Being on my own tested my social anxiety to the max. It was scary and fun all at once; it felt as if I were *on stage* whenever I had to speak with a customer. At the end of the day, I felt as if I'd run a 10K.

～

During our second summer, my vision became more and more blurry, and drug store readers no longer helped. With my daughter and Roberto's persistence, I saw Roberto's ophthalmologist.

In casual conversation, I mentioned the neck aches I had been having, unsure if our bed, my stationary steering wheel, or my worsening eyesight were the culprit.

He had me read a basic visual chart for the final test. I tilted my head back to focus on the symbols. He asked me not to, and to look straight ahead and recite them again. I couldn't. When I did, the letters doubled.

We'd found the cause for my neck ache. A weakened muscle in my left eye was causing the problem.

He showed me a little trick with a piece of glass with a prism in it, put it in the testing machine, and then had me read the chart again. It was amazing, I didn't see two of anything.

The special lens was thick, like Mommy's, but not as noticeable. Because it wasn't possible to combine it with the one for reading, like a bifocal, I had to buy two different pairs.

He recommended to wear them daily. Well, that was easier said than done. Whenever I walked with them on, it seemed as if I were walking in a funhouse.

Roberto helped me practice, but it didn't matter, I couldn't get used to them, and it took another month before I could even drive with them on. So, I just wear them for driving and watching TV.

～

The summers as vendors was uneventful, and the time passed by in a blink. By and by, I added a handful of large blow-up bugs, gathered a few cute props from eBay and second-hand stores, designed and printed a stack of pamphlets, postcards, and flyers, and created a company banner to display in the booth to make my space more interesting.

My creativity increased the time required to load and break down our production. I even had several mobile magnets made for further advertising.

When those arrived, once Roberto was home from work and distracted, I plastered our vehicle doors with them.

Because he drove all over the city for his job, I went a step further and bought a personalized license plate with our trademark for his car and affixed it while his back was turned.

The money made at the markets wasn't anything to write home about, but the comradery was. Our fellow vendors became extended family, and we looked forward to seeing them on the weekends.

⌒

One evening over burgers and onion rings at our favorite restaurant, taking advantage of the light mood of the busy summer, I brought up the subject of marriage for the umpteenth time.

I countered how I'd learned it would benefit his taxes, the opposite of what we'd always thought, and added how fun it would be to marry on our tenth anniversary the following year.

Hip deep into justifying my cause, he caught me by surprise when he interrupted in agreement.

"What?"

With a twinkle in his eye, he said, "Yes, it would be a great idea to marry on our tenth anniversary."

"Is that a proposal?"

"As close as your gonna get to one." He smiled a devilish grin.

I about leaped across the table. "Oh my God!"

Oblivious to the warmth leaving our food, we spent the next hour discussing the details and texting everyone we knew with the news.

Although I'd always dreamed of a flamboyant, heartfelt, on the knees and the whole works proposal, I was overjoyed he was ready.

I wanted the fairy tale, to be married in a church with friends and family, but it wasn't in the budget. After a friendly debate, we settled with his idea of a more practical destination wedding in Las Vegas, celebrating with friends when we returned.

I felt elated but terrified at the same time. I'd come close to walking down the aisle once before, but then, well, you know.

The gears in my brain were already churning. It would be the first ceremony for both of us, and I was going to make it as perfect as I could.

Besides summer markets, we also signed up for an annual winter festival held during the holiday season, beginning with a busy and grueling event the first weekend in October.

Our initial experience was so much fun we reserved a spot the following year. As opening day approached, Roberto learned he wouldn't get the time off. Thankfully, my son volunteered to manage the till in his place; whew.

The first day, when I stood to greet a customer, I about lost my balance, and had to grab for the corner of a table to maintain equilibrium. It seemed as if I were walking on a boat in rough seas.

To add insult to injury, my tongue felt twice its size when I spoke. In all sense, I appeared intoxicated.

The customer left without a purchase. I weaved back to my chair, embarrassed beyond all get out, and had a sip of water and a snack to see if they would help.

The next morning, I still hadn't improved, so Dale had to do most of the chatting for the duration of the event.

I rattled the symptoms around in my head, remembering how Mommy had a similar episode, and how she'd had an even bigger one a couple years later, and died two weeks after that.

Doctor phobic, seeing them only if I can't cure what's ailing me, like a bad asthma attack, the flu, or something, with my current state-of-affairs qualifying as that drastic, I made an appointment with a neurologist at a local hospital.

PART III

EIGHTEEN

I explained to the receptionist why I wanted to be seen, as if I said I had a minor cold, she told me her next opening wasn't for another month; go figure. The symptoms didn't improve while I waited, they only got worse.

When I spoke without thinking, my words came out an incomprehensible, jumbled mess.

Whenever I fight the thick sensation of my tongue, it only intensifies the slurring, and the more I freak out about it, the worse my speech becomes.

Most frustrating, since the beginning of our nine-year relationship, communication between me and Roberto had become an issue.

After a while, I quit trying so hard and was relieved when others finished my thoughts for me. To save face, I avoided situations where I was required to speak.

Thank goodness there's been only one other scary anomaly.

While waiting at a traffic light, for a mere split second, I couldn't comprehend what was written on a sandwich board on the side of the road.

My mind flickered like the lights do before the power goes out, and I squeezed my eyes shut to look again. That time I knew they *were* words but couldn't make sense of them.

I blinked again, admonishing myself for being so dumb, and forced my brain to think. My synapses reconnected as the light changed and I understood the words on the sign.

It was scary. Amen it hasn't happened again.

༄

Roberto accompanied me to the appointment. The doctor was friendly as he examined me. All was going well until he had me perform a kind of sobriety test, walking toe to toe across the room. I couldn't keep my balance no matter how hard I tried.

No family history of brain diseases. Yes, maternal aunt died of lupus at 53. Yes, father had a five-way cardiac bypass in his forties, but still living. Yes, high cholesterol on both sides of the family. Yes, mother died from a stroke at age 63.

He had me return to the table and look away while he tested my reaction to several sensations, some sharp, some soft. I didn't feel some of them on the left side of my body.

He asked me to explain the onset of symptoms. I was so nervous my speech ran together in unintelligible warbles, like coming off Novocain. I was sure he thought I was drunk.

My cheeks burned red hot and tears welled in my eyes; something was terribly wrong.

I was thankful Roberto was with me. He'd become an expert at finishing my thoughts as of late. Any other time it would have made me defensive, but now, I know it sounds funny, but now, it makes me feel loved beyond certainty.

The doctor scheduled an EEG and labs for a blood profile straight away, an MRI in another two weeks, a spinal tap, a cognitive neuro evaluation, and a referral for speech and physical therapy.

Roberto and I walked in silence across the hospital to the lab area where they plastered goopy paste in strategic mounds all over the top of my head, attached a handful of electrodes with wires, and hooked them to an EEG machine. I was so glad I couldn't see myself.

The tech reclined my chair and dimmed the lights. It wasn't long before I about started snoring, that is until I felt a needle in my vein to withdraw blood. I couldn't believe how much they took, it's a wonder I had any left at all.

Two weeks down the road, the MRI experience was uneventful, until they put dye in my IV. It felt as though my arm was being torn off and it burned something awful.

As hard as I tried, I could not fight back the tears, I was so embarrassed.

A few days later, Roberto and I returned to hear the verdict of the results in so far. The EEG and the labs proved negative. The MRI of my brain ruled out a Stroke, MS, Alzheimer's, and Parkinson's, but showed signs of deterioration in the cerebellum, the cause of my symptoms, and a pituitary adenoma.

His diagnosis, Cerebellar Ataxia of unknown origin.

He pointed to the image where the primary reduction was, stating further testing may show the reason for it, and to follow up with him in four weeks.

My head whirled with the news. Brain shrinkage? I veered straight for the computer as soon as I got home. What I read wasn't reassuring.

I started the therapies. The women were so nice and patient. The speech therapist showed me tricks with different textures of food to keep from choking on them, and some techniques to work around the slurring.

She said it was very important to slow my inner Ricochet Rabbit down, to give myself the same patience as I did with others, and to quit fighting with what I had no control over.

Easier said than done.

Gone forever was my superhuman ability to multi-task on a dime. My mind was that of a wild pony anymore, and if I didn't keep a conscious hold of it, it would wander off into the deep woods somewhere.

Like the many times I'd find myself in the middle of a chore, stop for no reason, stare at whatever I was doing for I don't know how long, and then ponder over what in the heck it was I was just doing a moment before, or wanted to do next. I was annoying the hell out of myself.

In the meanwhile, per doctor's orders, I had to cancel my Christmas travel plans to Mazatlán, where Roberto's cousins lived and where family members from all over Mexico were gathering to celebrate his younger sister's sixtieth birthday, and our engagement.

Roberto said he wouldn't go without me, but I insisted he did. With a reluctant and heavy heart, he agreed, and ventured on ahead.

It wasn't a total loss though. With his laptop and ingenious idea, I was able to attend the festivities through Skype.

I wore my party dress, and he set *me* on a table where I could see the family and dancing. One and all stopped by to say hi, and then he took me around to check out the surroundings.

It was just like being there, less the hugs and kisses, ok, not going there, or I'll cry.

Roberto Skyped me each morning and evening until he came home the following week.

⸻

Year two thousand and fifteen began with a spinal tap. It was worse than the MRI. I thought it would be comparable to the epidural I'd had with the birth of my kids, and positioned myself into the familiar fetal pose, and waited for the doctor to begin.

The technician patted my arm and corrected me, moving me to lie face down, showing me two handles underneath to brace myself with, and emphasized how important it was I lay motionless throughout the test. I thought she was making a bigger deal out of it than it was, until I was in the throes of it.

The kind doctor did his best to reassure me while my lower backbone felt like it was being snapped in half.

Tears stung my cheeks as I breathed through it; to say it was traumatizing would be an understatement. Labor pains must have distracted me back then because I don't recall it hurting as terrible as it did this time. When it was over, they gave me a coupon for a free latte.

Amid all the doctor appointments and the Quasimodo thing that had a grip on me, I continued with wedding planning.

PART III

NINETEEN

I found a rustic, old-fashioned chapel on the outskirts of Vegas. It wasn't a drive-by like some on the strip, and it had a la carte packages. The demo of the many ceremonies they'd performed along with the upbeat song, Pretty Thing, playing in the background, which I burned a copy of and put in our keepsake box, helped me make the final decision.

I couldn't believe how Vegas had the whole works for whatever type of wedding one wanted, all tailored to how grandiose or small a ceremony. It was the marriage capital of the world.

I chose a package that included a recording of the ceremony and an event planner; scores of ideas played out in my head kept me awake at night.

As Grandma Faye entered her ninth decade, she thought it best to live with her son's family, a hop, skip, and a jump from her beloved lake house.

While visiting her one day and discussing bridal details, her daughter-in-law, Sheryl, disappeared mid-conversation, and returned a short time later with the most fascinating, delicate and sheer, light periwinkle, peplum at the waist, matching lace on the décolletage, knee-length, long-sleeved vintage dress.

She said it was mine if I wanted. It was love at first sight. I had found my wedding gown.

The pearls Lexi gave me one Mother's Day and silver accessories matched the dress the best, and I emailed my color choices to the wedding planner.

She said she wouldn't have a problem finding like colors, and suggested ivory roses sprayed with a hint of light blue. Perfect.

Sheryl accompanied me to find a birdcage veil to match my time-classic theme. After some hunting, we found one at a bridal shop made of sheer netting with tiny silver flecks on it.

I asked the kids if they'd be our witnesses and they both agreed.

A good friend of mine moved two states over a while back and wanted to attend, as did Uncle Mike's son and his wife who resided in nearby Reno.

The guest of honor was the greatest surprise of all and my wedding gift to Roberto. One of his closest friends, Don, relocated out of state six years prior to help his aging parents, but met a girl while there, got married, and then decided to plant his roots in southern territory.

Roberto hadn't seen him since.

Of all the hats he wears, a counselor, and a firefighter to name a couple, he's also a chaplain and officiates at weddings. I contacted him through Facebook and asked if he would like to take part in ours.

My request floored him, he couldn't believe it, and was so honored I'd thought of him. Although they live a few states East of Nevada, he said they visit Vegas a couple of times a year and would plan their next trip around our wedding.

Since he and his wife are familiar with the area, we coordinated our honeymoon day to spend with them. With his know-how, we bought great discounts for the activities we'd planned —if I'm the coupon queen, he would be the king.

There was one activity I prearranged just for the two us to see at the end of the evening, a magician of the century, and couldn't believe my luck to find the tickets were sold through Ticketmaster.

We had held onto a gift card Roberto received from his employer two Christmases ago until something interesting came along. Now it was to become a wedding present!

Don said he had a clergy gown to co-ordinate with my colors and emailed me a picture of it and asked me what kind of service I wanted.

Other than having the kids involved and for it to be non-traditional, was all I had so far.

He suggested I might be interested in a Celtic theme with a Handfasting ceremony like the one he and his wife had. After some research, I fell in love with the idea and ran with it.

It would be the biggest secret I'd ever kept; put it in Guinness for sure. I couldn't wait to see the look on Roberto's face when he saw Don was to be the officiate.

With the event planner's assistance, I decided upon a quaint Italian restaurant for the celebration dinner. As with everything wedding in Vegas, they had meal packages too. Uncle Mike's son, a former Italian restaurateur, helped me create a mouthwatering menu for my guests.

Then I ordered a small cake with the Vegas theme from a local bakery who would deliver it to the restaurant just before we arrived.

Part of the chapel package not only included a limo ride from the hotel to the church but would also take us to the restaurant and the hotel afterward.

Since we might have a party of twelve, I reserved a snazzy stretch SUV for a tad more.

PART III

As Groupon had a great deal for The Golden Nugget, I called in a reservation for two nights for Roberto, Dale, and me to share. Lexi set aside another room for herself and her roommate.

I cut corners however possible to splurge on our honeymoon. As I was about to book a night at The Signature at MGM Grand, an email from my credit card company interrupted my transaction with a discount for that very same hotel; unbelievable.

Then, while I was researching the same credit card for our mileage point balance, I learned we had earned two free round-trip tickets to Vegas, wow. I half expected Gus-Gus to pop in from out of nowhere.

The event planner scheduled an appointment for a tux fitting for Dale and Roberto and a dress for Lexi, with a little boutique she recommended near the chapel.

It was all I could do to contain my excitement with how it all was coming together. Roberto had no idea what I was up to. Sure, it would take us a couple of years to catch up with the expense, but so what? A shop on Etsy made our Handfasting cord with my colors. Some other stores had the tokens I wanted to attach to the ends of it, a trinity symbol for each side, a pendant representing the Sacred Heart, and one more representing each of the Archangels.

Another store had some cute ivory and baby blue pearl with silver accents drop earrings along with a matching hair comb to hold my planned French twist in place. I love Etsy.

The wedding planner said newlyweds who wore t-shirts announcing their nuptials around Vegas sometimes received special treatment. With some research, I found a bridal website who made them and set about creating ours.

I chose a baseball jersey with black sleeves for both and added a black-tie bib on the front of Roberto's along with our names, and the wedding date in small script to the side.

On the back across the top, I wrote his last name and in the center; entered the year 2015 and a pair of wedding bands. I hoped he'd wear it.

For mine, the design was the same except it had the word Bride written in large script on the front, and the opposite side flaunted an outline of a large diamond ring.

‧⊘‧

The next month I followed up with the neurologist.

TWENTY

The doctor said all the tests had come back inconclusive, surmising the atrophy may be related to menopause, and suggested I have another MRI in a few years.

The first week of April concluded my eighth and final visit for the neuro evaluation. Overall, I performed well, my intelligence was in the normal range despite some processing issues.

That doctor disagreed with the neurologist's conclusion and encouraged me to seek a second opinion with a more advanced specialist in downtown Seattle.

∽

May was the soonest I could get an appointment. Roberto worked a half day and met me there. The doctor was to review my neurologist's findings prior, but they didn't know me from Adam when I arrived.

In addition, he said what I was seeking was above his head and referred me to someone else in the same office. That next available appointment was two weeks away.

When we returned, the endocrinologist, though unfamiliar with brain shrinkage, had examined the images of my pituitary adenoma and saw no reason for concern, stating most of the population had one, and pointed out a movement disorders specialist in the same building to address the atrophy.

That appointment was yet another week away.

I faced the third visit alone. It didn't make sense for Roberto to miss work if we ran into the same dead end as the previous two times.

Much to my surprise, that doctor *had* reviewed my history and was prepared to see me. The exam was more thorough than the one the first neurologist performed.

He worked methodically with a serious but friendly straight face and made notes between each test. After some mindful deliberation, he concluded my brain anomaly was caused by one of three things; genetics 10%, other 40%, or MSA-C 50%; then, scheduled me for a slew of tests to rule out one or the other.

I asked about the MSA. He said we'd discuss it further when the results came back, shook my hand, and left the room. My chin quivered; how I'd wished Roberto had come with me.

PART III

I held my tears back until I reached the threshold of the bathroom. I couldn't catch my breath. *It's never good when a doctor is evasive.* My nose was a red as Rudolph's and my legs felt like spaghetti.

Fully clothed, I sat on the toilet until I got a grip, took a hit off my inhaler, and made a beeline for my car.

When I arrived home, I spent the next few hours researching the ailment on the internet, which the doctor told me not to do, exactly what he shouldn't have said.

The more I read, the more upset I became. *MSA-C, a rare neurological disease that cannot be confirmed positively until death, upon autopsy. It is progressive; there is no treatment or cure.*

A positive time of death is not possible, but eventual, with a high variable survival, some cases up to 15 years.

I tried to figure out the math, but I couldn't make a figure without knowing the beginning date.

I was quiet during dinner and picked at my food, concentrating mostly on my supposed timeline. It didn't go unnoticed.

As usual afterwards we settled on the couch to watch TV. But rather than reaching for the remote, I buried my face into Roberto's chest and bawled.

He wrapped his arms around me and asked what the matter was.

Tripping over my tongue and in between tears I explained what the doctor said, and about what I'd read.

Then questioned if he still wanted to marry me.

He kissed my cherry red nose and planted kisses all over my face, between each he said, "What kind of question is that? I'd marry you today, or tomorrow, or next week if you wanted. In fact, I would trade a thousand tomorrows just to be married to you for even one day."

∽

Since the suspected disease was prevalent in older men, and I was neither, we set our hopes on the other percentages the doctor mentioned. The testing would begin the first week of June. The proceeding ones would consume the rest of the summer.

Inspired by Roberto's profound reserve, I wrote our vows and continued to plan the ceremony. I purposely left out, *Until Death Do Us Part.*

My son will walk me down the aisle, proclaim his blessings and that of the family, and give me to Roberto.

We'll be prayed over as we exchanged vows, with the binding of a cord around our clasped hands after each one.

Will you share each other's dreams and look for the brightness in life and the positive in each other?

Will you share each other's pain and burdens and seek to ease them so that your spirits may grow in this union?

Will you be a constant friend to one another and love each other wholly and completely without reservation?

Will you protect each other from harm, honoring and respecting one another as an equal, in all ways and at all times, and seek to never break that honor?

Then the cord will be tied, and we'll be blessed with these words:

Above you are stars and below you is earth. Like stars, your love should be a constant source of light, and like the earth, a firm foundation from which to grow.

May these hands be blessed this day and always to hold each other and have the strength to hang on during the storms of stress and the dark of disillusionment.

May they build a relationship founded in love and be free in giving affection and warmth to each other.

May these hands be healer, protector, shelter, and guide for each other.

May you be forever one, sharing in all things, in love and loyalty for all time to come and your love so endure that its flame remains a guiding light unto you both.

Then the cord will be removed, and we'll exchange rings, given by my children, with this blessing:

"Your hands beneath serve as a symbol of how Elise and Roberto and their marriage are supported upon this earth by the love of their friends and family as blessed from above.

"Holy Spirit and Guardians of all that is seen and unseen,

Bless these rings and this couple who shall wear them.

Keep them safe through adversity, forever supported

by your eternal blessing. Amen."

Perfect.

PART III

TWENTY-ONE

To keep my mind off the Black Box, I signed up to vendor at a variety of the summertime farmer's markets. As much as I tried to ignore the ensuing storm in my brain, the stress and heat made things worse.

On top of the embarrassing slurring, I had moments when I felt faint, when I'd forget how to make change, or when I'd forget what our products were about.

At times, it got so severe, I landed in the ER twice with heatstroke.

Unable to work the booth alone and because Roberto couldn't always be with me, I decided it best to cancel the remaining summer markets yet save our spot for the few easy winter bazaars.

It was devastating and demoralizing. When had I become such a fragile snowflake? It wasn't as if we made a boatload of money, but it was the association with the other vendors and the interesting people who came to my booth I'd miss the most.

∽

All the while, I worked on the creation of our rings. Since I knew what I wanted, I looked to a local designer to bring them to fruition. I admired his work and had decided the day we married, he would be the one to create them.

I called his shop to learn he'd moved to Oregon. My heart sank, but before I could panic, he said he still took custom orders; whew.

He mailed some sizers in the metals we were interested in. We settled for palladium, as it is more durable, with an extra width and thickness to incorporate the raised design for my ring, and a Celtic trinity knot pattern.

Because I have a slight webbing between my fingers and cannot wear a separate engagement ring with a band, I combined the two.

An Irish jeweler and close friend of the designer assisted him with the carving of the trinity chain motif in and around each of our bands, adding little trinity symbols spaced evenly apart on Roberto's and a pair of tiny ones into the shoulders of mine.

Nestled beneath the shoulders on either side of my creation are another miniature set of the holy signs, and in the center of the masterpiece are six little claws to keep my crown jewel in place.

Roberto asked the jeweler to create the setting for a carat sized diamond.

I couldn't believe it. My special pebble was to be a whopper!

The grand finale was to have our names engraved inside each of the other's ring.

I invited my friend's mom to help me pick out my stone, and we made a day of it. The broker's office was a renovated condo within a secure building on the outskirts of Seattle.

I gave him my ring and explained my budget. He laid a few diamonds out on a piece of cloth before us. One stood out from the others and shined like a disco ball.

But, it was a bit over my cost. *What the heck*, I thought, and put a down payment on it before my inner critic could have a say. I couldn't wait to show it off.

∽

With the end of summer, arose an onslaught of test results. The autonomic assessment came back abnormal; it showed sympathetic nervous system degeneration with slight orthostatic hypotension, explaining the dizzy spells, heat intolerance, and why I'd stopped sweating. I dropped it into the Black Box.

The genetics result was negative, eliminating it from the 10% possibility, and the sleep study was positive for sleep breathing disorder, one more for the Black Box.

Then I started having trouble focusing on objects around me while walking and zeroing in on a specific target, like looking out my peripheral for cars.

My eyes bobbed up and down inside of my skull in cadence with my steps. If I moved my head too suddenly, I'd become disoriented and lose my balance.

To keep from falling and to get a good look at what I wanted to see, I needed to stop and close one eye. It's so embarrassing when someone passes by and I can't meet their eyes when they greet me.

I followed up with the optometrist. He said the double vision had worsened and changed my prescription for a stronger prism, Black Box.

Undeterred, I delved further into finding other possibilities as a cause; it was beyond me why this wasn't being done already.

In my research, I discovered a direct correlation between paraneoplastic syndrome, cancer, and cerebellar atrophy. Because of my history of cervical and uterine cancer in 2000, which resulted in a partial hysterectomy, I hoped I had found the smoking gun, the other 40%.

I know it sounds morbid, but I'd rather have a tumor over the MSA any day. At least the progression would stop once it was removed. The downside was I might not live any longer than one over the other.

I presented my theory to the neurologist, but he didn't want to entertain the idea, even though just to rule it out. So, I fired him, and referred myself to the leading cancer care hospital in Seattle.

I wrote out my petition; but despite my preparedness, I couldn't get past the receptionist at the main clinic. Although no doctor, she was adamant they wouldn't be able to help me and refused to make me an appointment.

Going around her, I called a satellite treatment center, and they scheduled me in without question or duress.

Not wanting to cause anyone concern until there was a definite answer, I kept the illness from everyone but my family. In the same sense, I'd also hidden my fears and concerns from Roberto and the kids.

As much as I had tried to keep a lid on it, the clammy clutches of depression had me in its grips, and I couldn't shake it, any little thing made me cry and it was embarrassing.

I felt my optimism slipping and was busting at the seams with worry; it scared me to death to think something might be out of my control.

I felt like a hypochondriac, like Mommy. Yet, down deep I knew I had a legitimate reason to be concerned. My greatest fear was, if too much more time elapses before the mystery is solved, I'd succumb to whatever was ailing me.

One day, while standing at the kitchen sink preparing the applesauce Roberto can't get enough of, watching the quarterback squirrels have their breakfast, there were fifteen of them now, and the black-capped chickadees eating peanuts from the window sill, and worrying about the future, a stellar jay appeared and perched itself on the ladder propped in front of the window.

He remained frozen in the same spot for a good while, just sitting there and watching me work. Feeling self-conscious under his steely gaze, I said aloud, "Oh all right then, I'll knock it off, thanks for coming by." He stayed only a few moments more before flying away.

The following day I called to see a neuropsychologist.

༄

Like before, my initial visit with the oncologist didn't disappoint; the doctor was oblivious why I was there. I wanted to cry. In full-blown panic, I rattled off what I was facing, in hopes to sell her on my idea with the little time I suspected she had.

She cut me off mid-sentence and agreed every stone *should* be turned over and she would do the same. I couldn't believe my ears; tears welled in my eyes.

She said we'd start with a full body CT scan and some blood work and then do the rest after the wedding. She had no idea how close I came from giving her a hug that day.

A week before *show time*, I had to drink some icky crap prior to the scanning, just imagine they had three different *flavors,* all before eight a.m., what a way to start the day. Then, they put even more into an IV. It was the easiest test to date.

∽

My first neuropsychology appointment wasn't until later in the afternoon, so I drove home and took a nap. Not much got done that day.

Since the wedding was two weeks before my fiftieth birthday, we were going all out to celebrate both occasions. To help me through the grueling marathon I'd set myself up for in Vegas, I sought after a naturopath for acupuncture.

It hurt and wasn't helpful except to leave bruising.

There was another naturopath in the clinic, but at a different satellite office. I'd read that cranio-sacral therapy might relieve some of my symptoms and the doctor there specialized in it.

She was friendly, patient, and genuinely concerned, and I clicked with her right off the bat. She spoke in metaphysical terms I understood.

I liked how she picked up on that. I'm sure my black angora cape, leggings, and tall leather boots had nothing to do with it.

Just when I thought we'd be best friends forever, she burst my bubble when she explained how the massage wouldn't relieve my symptoms or help in the way I'd wanted.

Tears burned in my eyes. The wedding was only a week away and I needed to calm the heck down. But, she continued, there was something that would, and proceeded to ask me some strange questions, *did I like this, did I like that*, a mad inquiry for sure, and then popped out of the room.

She reappeared every so often for further questioning and then stepped out again. Upon her final return, she announced a medicine called Carsinosen would arrive in the mail, and how someone would call for payment of about $14.

She stated I'd be receiving a small glass vial of tiny white pills and I was to fill the bottle cap with them and put them under my tongue until they dissolved.

PART III

She said to do this only one time and to come back to see her in a month. It was if she had a cauldron somewhere in the bowels of the clinic.

Weird, okey dokey then. I don't like taking medication for anything, but something about her made me trust her.

And then she dropped a bombshell. She said I'd have to quit coffee for two weeks prior to beginning the medicine and then forever afterwards or it could affect the results.

WHAT? I've been a caffeine junky since I was fifteen. Ok, fine, I'll try. She said wine would be acceptable though. *Alrighty then, take me out back with a double barrel and pop the cork while you're at it. Geeze.*

She also recommended I apply for Social Security Disability.

The wedding was the following week; my illness was not invited.

TWENTY-TWO

*D*ale jinxed it. He said I shouldn't freak out if things didn't go as planned and that weddings never do. I didn't see why they wouldn't; I had it all under control, so I thought.

The Friday before the wedding, Roberto's boss told him he had to be in Los Angeles for a mandatory conference, regardless of his upcoming nuptials. He agreed to attend, adamant he was leaving on Monday, no matter what.

When I took our diabetic cat, Lucky, to board at our vet, he still wasn't home, and didn't arrive until one o'clock the next morning.

Because Dale's flight was at three and was carpooling with us, Roberto was home long enough to gather our luggage before returning to the airport.

We left Dale at his trip counter, checked our bags in with his, and processed through the maze of security.

Just as we made it to the other side, Dale texted me, "Mom, I won't be able to go."

I about died on the spot.

The airline didn't have record of his payment even though he had printed proof of it. I offered to pay, but he said not to worry, he would work something out.

I was a bundle of nerves when we boarded our plane. Once in my seat, I closed my eyes and bartered with God and all that was sacred, along with Mark and my mom, to get my son on an airplane.

When we reached San Francisco for our connecting flight, I received another text from Dale. He'd made it; he had passed security and was about to board.

Before I could breathe a collective sigh of relief, Lexi texted with problems. Her roommate's flight was booked to LA and not to Vegas. The airline was quicker to resolve that snafu, thank God and *everyone else over there*.

Since arriving later than planned meant we would be late for the fittings, I called the owner of the shop to explain our dilemma.

She said even if we came in the morning, it would still allow enough time to be ready for the ceremony and offered to pick us up at nine-thirty the next morning.

Somehow Roberto kept my marbles together, despite not having slept or eaten for almost eighteen hours, he had become quite proficient at keeping track of them as of late.

Since the kids wouldn't arrive for a while, we decided to seek out the courthouse to get the marriage license, but there wasn't a soul around to ask for directions.

We got out our trusty tourist map and followed it, and every finger-pointing way, all the while dodging salivating street corner hawkers, to the court.

When the clerk asked for Roberto's ID and he reached in his pocket for it, he came up empty-handed. He'd left it at the hotel.

The return trip was shorter as Roberto figured out a route to bypass the pushers, dragging me along like Christopher Robin to avoid them. Comical visual, isn't it?

We giggled as if we were kids as we filled out the papers and were just as excited when they gave us copies for the church; the trick now was not to lose them before the wedding.

Limited by choices of what to eat, we got a bite at one of the hotel bars, bought a bottle of wannabe Sangria, and headed to our room.

I drowned myself in a long hot bath, finished the wine, and slept until seven the next morning. Roberto and the kids saw to the fitting without me. I needed to chill somehow before the ceremony.

I turned down the lights, put my feet up, and tried to fall back asleep. But I just could not relax, my mind was breaking down the barn by now.

We had all made it and everything was going to be ok, but I still couldn't calm the heck down.

I was interrupted by a knock at the door. It was my longtime friend. My wedding day was extra special for us as the last event we'd shouldered was rather poignant and somber. I needed her now as much as I did then.

Unbeknownst of my illness, I rattled off what our trip had been like so far with no sense of direction. Familiar with my under-pressure craziness, she slapped the table and said, "That's it, come on, let's go get a drink."

Just then, Roberto and the kids walked in. More panic. I couldn't leave the room, the lady who was coming to do my hair and face in a couple of hours instructed me not to put makeup on prior, at my age I don't go anywhere without my war paint.

"Bullshit," was my friend's expression I believe; she dragged me downstairs and bought us all a congratulatory round.

It didn't take long for the tension to melt away. After two more glasses, we wandered across the lobby for the elevator to Lexi's room to prepare for show time.

Her suite was in the new section of the hotel. The little living area was quaint, yet classy, fancier than our digs across the way.

We were having fun until the lady who was to get me ready arrived. She was in a rush from the get-go and certainly wasn't dressed to impress, wearing faded jeans, flip-flops and a tank top; even worse, her hands smelled like cigarettes.

I was in no mood to be hurried. I would have dismissed her if I hadn't been on a time schedule. I explained how I wanted a bouffant hairdo like Brigitte Bardot's to match my vintage dress, just like the pictures I'd sent her, and to take ten years off when she did my makeup.

Lexi watched in fascination as my matchbox thin locks were renovated into a flammable four-story building and my face into a living Picasso.

My friend, Keeper of the Calm, kept giving me *courage*, assuring our glasses were never without the tiny pink bubbles as we scurried around to get pretty.

When she finished my transformation, the girls agreed in unison I was beautiful and fussed over the final creation; but I didn't *feel* like I was. I've never worn so much makeup in my life.

And when I smiled in the mirror, yikes, the crypt keeper grinned back at me. I might have looked lovely, but in a matronly way, or in a reincarnated Tammy Faye way, or, remember Madame the puppet? Yeah. My God!

I was trying for Bardot, but the lady was so young, it was doubtful she knew who that was. Instead I resembled a librarian, no offense, but it was not what I was going for, disappointed wasn't anywhere near how I felt. I hoped to be so pretty for Roberto. But there was no time to sulk, the limo had arrived.

It was a group effort to get me dressed. Lexi's expression said it all when I tossed her my itsy-bitsy body shaper.

"Mama, really. You don't need one of these."

The look on my face said it wasn't negotiable.

She knew she had her work cut out for her as she watched me determinedly wriggle into the micro piece of spandex with the skill of a contortionist, deftly squeezing my squishy parts into its small confinements.

With a vise grip on either side on the top of the straight jacket, the girls grimaced as they helped me pull it all the way up.

After some intense grunt work and sheer willpower, we got the straps over my shoulders; then, it was time for the stuffing.

"That goes in here, this can go up a little higher, oh no, now the bottom is too high, squish that part in…there, that ought to do the trick." I felt like a chorizo. *It hurts to be beautiful*, MB would say.

In contrast, the silk and chiffon of the slip and dress slipped right over the top without budging a single coifed hair on my head.

The front desk called again. I grabbed my silver glittery sandals and Lexi handed me the glass of wine.

"Have one more sip, mama," and out the door we flew.

In the elevator, I had a dreaded thought, the control garment didn't have a snap bottom, *how in the world would I manage the bathroom?*

Lexi assured me girdle duty was on the list as my MOH.

It was no less than a miracle we had only three tug-of-war pit stops to deal with the entire night, I made sure of that.

When we walked out to meet the limo, you'd think we were either movie stars or street walkers the way people gawked.

The stretch sedan was fun. The cool air-conditioning was a godsend.

Then we got stuck in traffic. The driver explained some politicians were in town for a convention. The car carrying the guys wasn't far behind us. I didn't want Roberto to see me until the ceremony.

I wrung my hands in anticipation. The Keeper of the Calm noticed and handed me the glass. When we arrived at last, the remainder of my excitement drained from my heart by what I saw.

TWENTY-THREE

*I*t was so different from the countryside picturesque photos portrayed on its web page. Instead of a sprawling landscape, there was only a patch of lawn, and the patio garden looked like a studio prop.

Rather than a serene little church tucked away from the hustle and bustle on the strip, this one sat on the side of a busy Vegas thoroughfare, wedged between the airport and a six-lane highway.

On the website, it appeared to be one oversized building, with a foyer reception and dressing rooms. But it was only a tiny chapel like the kind on Route 66.

The changing areas were to the right of it in a single story, cement block, refurbished hotel from the fifties.

As I entered the *bridal suite*, the event planner approached me and said we'd lost half of our allotted time and there were only fifteen minutes left for our ceremony and pictures. PANIC.

As she spoke, I felt my feet swell inside my silver, peep toe kitten heels, and my ankles weakened; I felt as if I were standing on stilts.

The sultry air made my girdle feel ten degrees hotter; threatening to swallow me whole any second. I was sure I'd faint.

Distress like a veil blanketed my face and it showed in the photos. They were ruined. I wasn't aware I had the *mask* expression I'd read about until I saw the pictures later.

All my careful planning to avoid being frazzled had gone out the window. What I had now was not any different from the drive by nuptials in town. Why was there a curse on a bride's wedding day, anyway? It wasn't fair.

The event planner was in full bore by now; no time to get my girdle in a wad.

Don and his wife, Amy, had been hiding in the bridal suite waiting for me. He said not to worry, he'd cut the ceremony back without missing a beat.

I wanted to cry. It wasn't supposed to be this way. It was akin to childbirth, baby's coming and off to delivery you go.

I gave our rings to my children, the wedding planner handed Lexi and me our bouquets, and the photographer continued to snap away.

PART III

I had her take a shot of the hands of the kids and me for a special Christmas gift I'd planned for them later, Dale's on the bottom, Lexi's on top of his, and mine over all.

Then, they shuffled us out towards the chapel.

Dale looked so handsome. It was the only time I had seen him in a tux.

They sent Lexi in to lead the parade, *go slow*, they said, *walk normal*, but she's a product of me what can I say, and she tore up the rug as she made a beeline down the aisle to stand alongside Roberto.

Then it was my turn.

I fought back tears as my baby boy took my right hand, tucked it into the crook of his left arm, and gave it a reassuring squeeze. It was so precious and meant more to me than he'll ever know.

White rose petals, just like my bouquet, carpeted our steps as we walked in pace to the wedding march down the Green Mile, I mean aisle.

Roberto stood at military ease on the goal line. He looked so handsome in his fancy black tux, silver vest, and shiny patent leather shoes. I bet he was as scared as I was.

I wanted to laugh at the look he gave me, he'd never seen me in such a get-up or with so much makeup on before.

In mere seconds, I was about to break his sixty-two-year bachelorhood record. He left Seattle a single man and would return to Seattle with a wife and a couple of kids.

Too funny. No wonder he appeared a bit ashen.

Don followed close behind Dale and me.

I found out later, while he and my son were waiting for me to arrive, they connived a change of plans of how the surprise for Roberto would go down.

My plan was once Dale and I reached the end of the aisle and separated, Don would walk nonchalantly between us and surprise him, but, that's not how *they* planned it.

Once we got to the altar and parted ways, I paused for Don to step through.

But he didn't.

Instead, while Roberto was trying to coax me to take his arm, poor thing confessed later he was sure I'd lost it by then, Don snuck around his other side to stand before him while the chapel clergy bowed out.

The expression on Roberto's face when he realized who the clergy was, was priceless.

Amy was the first to crack up, then the rest of our tiny group joined in and clapped. The church minister blocked the camera at that precise second, but the photos tell it all; I got the last laugh for sure.

I was a hot mess by the time it came to hitch Roberto's yoke. He gave me the wrong hand. Dale noticed and laughed. The subtle readjustment is only noticeable if you know to look for it.

Caught up in the magical moment, we were oblivious to the close airplane fly-by, the noise from the traffic, or the gunning of a motorcycle chopper, until we saw the clip later.

Talk about a ten-grand funniest video, we couldn't have planned it any better if we tried.

Even though we were rushed, and I didn't approve of most of the pictures I was in, it couldn't have been any more perfect. It was memorable, wonderful, and blessed all in one. A fairytale wedding just the way I wanted.

A limo drove our party to the restaurant. When we entered, my heart dropped. There wasn't room to breathe. The only available space was the one reserved for us. So much for being assured it would be quiet during the seven o'clock hour.

We stood out like sore thumbs among all the casual diners as we followed the hostess to our table. Several people snapped cell phone pics as if we were movie stars; headline, *Cheech Marin Marries Mary Kate Olson.*

We sat close to a little stage with a two-man band and a Sinatra impersonator, and danced our first dance in a small space next to our seats. It was straight out of a gangster classic for sure.

Cellphone flashes lit up the room once more. I'd had plenty of wine by then and was enjoying every Cinderella moment.

The waitress gave everyone a custom dinner menu with a brief thank you message I'd penned on the outside and poured champagne. We toasted our marriage, our ten years together, and my fiftieth birthday.

The meal began with fried calamari and bruschetta appetizers along with salad and bread. Followed by a choice of grilled NY Strip, grilled Salmon Florentine, Chicken Marsala with Penne Marinara, or Eggplant Di Amore.

Then we had mini Cannoli's and Crème Brûlées for dessert. It was a feast for sure. The meals were late, but so worth the wait.

Our wedding cake arrived just before the limo did.

Dale took several good shots of it as Roberto and I cut the first piece. Then the waitress brought it in the back and served it up. I think I got one bite when we had to go, there went $135!

They gave us the top, like what would we do with it in a hotel. Our room didn't come with a refrigerator; that was extra.

Ironically, where Don and Amy stayed was a much nicer place than ours; it not only included a fridge but had a microwave and other amenities too; and they paid less than we did.

Oh well, Dale brought it along to our room to snack on.

Like Cinderella's carriage, the driver of the stretch SUV dropped our guests off at their respective hotels, and then took us to the MGM Signature for our honeymoon.

Between the wine, the heels, the girdle, and the illness, I had a hell of a time getting out of the vehicle. The chauffeur laughed. He said, without naming names, a spoiled wannabe Hollywood elite was the most ungraceful person he'd ever seen, and I had nothing on her; still.

This cowboy boot wearing, home girl kicked off her Cinderella slippers as soon as she hit the elevator, *"OUCH!"*

It felt as if we were going to the moon as it climbed. The ascent was unnerving; I was so glad for the darkness and the inability to see below.

Our suite was exquisite, just like in the movies. I made a beeline for the bathroom and removed the death trap; good Lord, never again. I should have taken my daughter's advice.

Then I ran a nice hot Jacuzzi bath; it had a five-person capacity and then some.

The hotel sent up a bottle of champagne, so sweet. I brought out some candles, put them alongside the tub, and looked for some matches, but couldn't find any.

I called the front desk. They said our room was nonsmoking and lighting candles would set off the fire alarm and sprinklers.

What a redneck, goes to show how long it's been since I stayed in a hotel.

We laughed at the visual of the scene had I the foresight to bring a lighter. Oh well, they looked romantic alongside the tub all the same.

Our full-size bed at home was a joke compared to the king-sized one before us. It was two a.m. by the time we hit the sack, Don and Amy were due to pick us up at nine.

I guess I used up all the hot water the night before as there wasn't any left for bathing the next morning. I couldn't believe it.

The plaster in my hair from the wedding *needed* washing, so we bit the bullet and had a comical cold shower anyway; is that making memories or what?

We made it to the lobby with minutes to spare to wait for our friends. A little after nine they called to check on our whereabouts. They had been waiting at another section of the hotel.

We rolled our luggage through the back alleys and service entrances until we found them. I was already feeling my oats, and the day had just begun.

Don and I planned five activities; I made it through four and threw in the towel. Each attraction was at least the distance of a football field apart, it all had looked so close together on the map.

First, we ate breakfast at a yummy buffet, and then walked through Madame Tussaud's wax museum. Next, we strolled through the Venetian Hotel; its blue-sky painted ceiling and Italian scenery was fascinating.

Then we climbed aboard a gondola and glided across a lagoon on the outside of the hotel. We snuggled close as the gondolier sang, transporting us to Italy.

The grand finale was a ride on the world's tallest Ferris wheel, the High Roller.

Our day ended with Chinese food in the majestic lobby of the Luxor Hotel, then we parted ways with Don and Amy, and Roberto and I took the escalator down one floor to the magic show.

Just after midnight, we were returned to reality at the front door of our hotel where we had about five hours of sleep before it was time to head to the airport for home.

We waited at the designated post at the main entrance for shuttle, but after fifteen minutes and it still hadn't arrived, we panicked.

Should the delay cause us to miss our connecting flight, we worried about being charged for an additional day if we were late picking Lucky up from the vet.

Roberto rang the shuttle dispatcher and was reassured that it would arrive at any moment.

A half hour later he called again. Apparently, the driver had been waiting for us at a different entrance, and now we'd have to take the next one.

Although our transportation was prepaid, we flagged down a taxi; the man drove like a bat out of hell to get us to the airport on time.

Upon arrival, we jumped out and made a thirty-mile dash to the gate, Roberto dragging my sorry, worn-out carcass behind him the entire way. All in all, we arrived at the vet in the nick of time.

It took almost two weeks to recover from the trip. I lost five pounds in just those four days and Roberto gained that many.

It wouldn't break my heart if I never saw Vegas again.

✺

After the whirlwind celebration, Roberto accompanied me to the oncologist to hear the results.

PART III

TWENTY-FOUR

*A*nyone in their right mind would pray there wasn't anything, but we had hoped they had as it would mean a possible cure and stopping the brain deterioration.

Like game show contestants, our eyes lit up when we learned they'd found a significant sized nodule on my left thyroid, six in the lower lungs, and one on the left ovary.

Because I'd had cancer of the cervix and uterus removed fifteen years ago, it was probable it had returned. They scheduled me for an immediate ultrasound of my neck and abdomen followed by a CT of my chest in January.

The ovaries were first, early the next morning, internally, yuck.

The doctor said he'd found a few cysts on my right ovary but wasn't concerned about any of them, and recommended I repeat the test in eight weeks to see if there were any changes.

He said my blood tests were normal, with the exception that I was in the middle of menopause. Really? Well, I'll be. I hope the rest of the way is as smooth.

The imaging on the thyroid was later the same week. The following morning, the oncologist asked me to return for a fine needle biopsy.

It was the worst thing ever. Without question, I'd trade ten spinal taps for one of those puppies. As the doctor performed the procedure, I about squeezed the technician's hand off. He was heaven sent for sure and made the entire process bearable.

It wasn't painful per se, but it was the increasing dull ache it caused that made it horrible, and the anxiety of the whole *hold still or else* aspect was agonizing.

Afterwards, I got another coffee card.

The next day I waited on pins and needles for a call to come in for surgery, but it never came. Strike One.

I wasn't scheduled to see the oncologist again until after the second CT on the lungs in January, so, no news is good news, perhaps?

༄

I had been off caffeine for a few weeks, and it was time to take the magic pills. It has been *hell* waking up in the morning. I'm falling asleep watching the newscast right along with Roberto and sleeping through the night like a baby with clean diapers. Thank God for decaf, but it's not the same, I try to tell myself it is, but she doesn't believe me.

I waited until evening to take the little pills, just in case I saw pink elephants or something, and emptied a capful of the tiny white deco balls under my tongue and went to sleep.

The next morning, I bounded out of bed, no slurring, no thinking problems, no stumbling, nada; I forgot I was sick for three whole weeks. I had my Tigger back.

But then; *then*, Thanksgiving reared its ugly head, and a windstorm knocked the power out for three days, and I couldn't get warm for the life of me.

Roberto fed our all-consuming fireplace at a regular pace to keep a perpetual toasty fire for me and wrapped my feet in a heating pad.

In addition, I wore long johns under my jammies and buried myself under tons of blankets, but it was all for naught, I was miserable.

Even worse, as fall slipped into winter, my coveted daily walks became intolerable, regardless of how much I bundled up.

Ever vigilant of my body temp, when it's below fifty outside, my core temp registers at 93.6, making it crucial I hurry back inside.

So, because we live in Washington state, it's guaranteed I'll be stuck inside for the next six months. I watch the weather barometer hanging from the gazebo like Sally and Conrad in anticipation of warmer weather.

To make matters worse, I awoke one morning to find I'd relapsed back to my old sick self, stumbling, slurring and the whole nine yards.

It scared me, I thought I was cured. I was certain of it. But nope, something was still wrong.

I called the doctor. She was encouraged by the initial results of the remedy, and we discussed the supplements I was taking and my diet and adjusted both.

She instructed me to take another dose of the pills and to let her know if I wasn't feeling better. I asked when I could have leaded coffee again. She said not for the duration of the treatment.

It's not what I wanted to hear, but it made sense to give my body a rest from being on full tilt all the time; but still, dammit.

I took the pills that night. Nothing. I gave it a few days, and then called her. She assured me there was no cause for worry as it could take up to two weeks.

In the meanwhile, I kept my mind busy decorating our fake little tree, making a couple of batches of apple sauce, one with rhubarb and the other with pumpkin, and accomplished a few tasks with the business.

Overall, I made strides, but I still wanted to be the way I was before. By Christmas, I'd improved by only sixty percent.

Lexi tried to cheer me up, "It's better than nothing, right?"

No, it wasn't. I wanted it *all* to go away.

With the smidgeon of renewed health, I tackled the sales tax report. It took three times longer than usual. I couldn't make heads or tails of the numbers I typed the year before as a clue how to enter this year's report.

I found bookkeeping totals entered in wrong columns of my Excel sheets and documents in the file drawer before they were entered in to QuickBooks.

As I'm the only employee, I can't blame anyone else but myself. It's a real Alice in Wonderland experience I tell ya. I want to bash my head on my desk; it's as if I'm chasing a Woozle.

Like a thief in the night, my brain is slowly being pilfered away, it's so subtle, it isn't noticed until something becomes an issue.

For instance, from out of the blue, recipes and simple instructions have become time consuming riddles; then, another day multi-tasking turns problematic, like crocheting and watching TV at the same time.

Somehow, by the grace of God, I can still write. Not by hand so much anymore, but my creative ability to weave stories is still intact.

I'm trying not to dwell on this brain thing, but I can't help worrying if one day I'll awake to find my sense of reality has changed and won't know it.

Then again, who's to say, maybe it already has.

This type of thinking can drive a person nail-pulling nuts no doubt. And then they take away my coffee.

Amen for Roberto for sure; I know, no matter what my reality is or how scary things become, he is my wingman and I'm safe with him.

If only I could see what's broken in my thick skull maybe I could fix it.

It's unfortunate there isn't a reboot, program update, or internet solution to be had, no tech department to decipher the code, and no Hoo Doo Voodoo, magic potion, or prayer.

I'm frightened by the uncertainty of what *this* is, if where I am at is it or if it's progressive, and if it will get worse like they think. I hate the unknown.

I'm such a control freak; always have been and forever will be. I prefer having my ducks all in a row, and right now they are all over the frigging place.

I've tried to *Let Go and Let God*, but that's easier said than done; sometimes I pray for answers and healing until I'm blue in the face.

Funny how we take for granted the simplicity of even the littlest tasks, managing the clasp on a necklace, carrying a cup of coffee, working a needle into a stitch of yarn, until we are challenged by them.

Above all, I hate how Roberto sees me fighting with myself. He says he feels awful he can't do anything to help.

Oh, but there is, I tell him; *the best medicine ever is just to continue to be patient and love me.*

◦∽◦

I followed up with the ultrasound on the ovaries. The doctor was all smiles; he said he didn't see any cause for concern and return the following year for a follow-up.

It wasn't *good news* in my book. My lungs were the final chance for the 40% other.

◦∽◦

Before I knew it, New Year's Eve of two thousand and sixteen was upon me, we'd come full circle with all the inconclusive, painful, and expensive testing.

Adding to the pile was the follow-up CT on the lungs; just like the others that preceded it, there was no evidence of cancer. My last-ditch effort failed. One more ballot for the Black Box.

After all I'd read about the disease they wanted to label me with, I feared I'd waken one day and not be able to move or get out of bed the most.

Well, that premonition almost bit me in the butt when I awoke one morning with excruciating pain across my lower back. Nothing relieved it, and the more I freaked out about it, the more it intensified.

With sheer determination and Roberto's loving assistance, I rolled out of the sack, but I couldn't stand upright. After some time of working through the agony, I managed to straighten up, but became stuck again whenever I stood from a sitting or lying down position.

This charade lasted for almost a week until the doctor increased the dosage, four times that of the previous. With the stronger dose, I was only to take ten of the little white pills.

I was certain I'd see the pink elephants this time.

But nope, I bounded out of bed like before, free again from the slurring, dizziness, back pain, and leg cramps. Everything was coming along fine until I made another attempt at the stupid sales taxes and started to lose my mind again.

PART III

I was on the toboggan once more whether I wanted to be or not.

Roberto says it's not noticeable; but I hear it when I speak and see it in my lack of coordination, especially among strangers.

Then, I get self-conscious, and then, around and around we go, *they're coming to take me away*, no seriously. My God, how much more can I take?

So, I've decided to avoid any stress that might upset the apple cart, and that means not leaving the house anymore, except to visit friends, have an occasional lunch with Lexi, or my daily walks, weather permitting.

The effort of putting up a strong front and appearing upbeat, all the while carrying this annoying monkey on my back, isn't worth the grief. And since misery loves company, I choose to be alone.

As if things couldn't get worse, the groundhog saw his shadow, increasing my indoor solitary confinement by six weeks. I'd like to give him a piece of my mind for sure.

I once looked forward to the winter, but no more.

The naturopath changed my medicine all together and started me on phosphorus. It hasn't needed adjusting, yet, knock on wood, symptoms be damned.

Undeterred, like Wee Willie Winkie, I convinced myself to pursue the elusive 40% other, one last time. With tenacious and thorough research, I found what was touted to be the holy grail of neurologists in the Puget Sound and presented my situation to him.

It was my hope, with all his years of experience, my case would be familiar to him and he'd know of a cure.

But as with all the others, regardless of my tedious preparation, it turned out to be a waste of time and money. He had not read my history before my initial visit or before my next two visits, nor did he seem interested.

As a consolation prize, he performed a second autonomic test. When the results came back, he said although there was a slight increase of degeneration with the autonomic system; they hadn't changed much since the original one from the year before, except now my heart was affected.

On his way out of the exam room, as if rattling off the weather, he said how there may never be a reasonable explanation for what was happening inside my brain and suggested I might want to get my affairs in order, just in case, slipping his ballot into the Black Box as he closed the door behind him.

What?! He was so fired. What did he know? He hadn't even taken the time to research my history.

I wanted to climb on the coffee table in the center of the waiting room like Norma Rae did and scream, "What the hell folks, it's 2016, somebody must have seen these symptoms before, DO something!" But I'd probably fall off. I marched straight to my car and somehow made it home.

Ripped from the pages of *Your Worst Nightmare,* my eleventh hour slipping away and regardless of how many doors I pound on, no one in the medical field seems to care, all except my beloved naturopath.

As Roberto wasn't due home for a while, it left me time to take my frustrations out on my pillow, wash my face, and look put together before he arrived, but…He arrived home early to the sounds of mournful crying coming from our bedroom. He dropped his things, ran to my side, and gathered me to his chest in a fierce embrace.

"Roberto; oh, Roberto!" I sobbed.

He cradled my face in his gentle hands and kissed my tearful eyes.

"What is it, baby? What is it? What did the doctor say?"

The storm in my heart raged on, "Roberto…Oh, Roberto…"

He continued rocking me and said, "It's ok baby, it will be ok, whatever it is, we'll beat it, you'll see."

PART III

AFTERWORD

Some parts of this story haven't seen the light of day, until now. You may ask what compelled me to unlock the closet and let the skeletons loose.

Well, as I face my final curtain, I've spent a lot of time questioning the purpose of my life and why things happened the way they did. *Was I meant to serve as a sacrificial lamb for others to gain encouragement? To be a pillar of strength for others to look up to?*

I concluded, if I am right, then I must tell all, every bit of dirty laundry. If my convoluted journey helps at least one person, then it was worth the risk and I hope it reaches the souls for whom it was intended.

After I finished writing it, I searched my heart for why God had me go through so much. My answer was He'd donned me in a stone-clad armor the day of my conception to protect me throughout my life because I was to write a great story one day, a testimony of His love and grace, a story that would bring someone, or hopefully many, to salvation.

Although some parts are not suitable for Christian literature, one cannot deny the presence of Divine intervention in-between the lines throughout the story. Call it what you will, but I believe.

It took Mark's death to bring me to my knees; I was so far down in grief that when Christ reached His hand out to me, I was more than willing to cling to Him, for my children's sake if anything, and I'm so glad I did.

I intentionally lightened some of the sad parts with humor, to zap melancholy moments. It's what Lexi likes best about my writing.

In the end, I can say with certainty, I've found the love and acceptance I always longed for in the hearts of the many friends whom I consider family. Thank you, it's been real; it's been fun; it's been real fun.

For over a decade, Roberto and I have accomplished many incredible things. He has nurtured my independence and self-confidence and given me room to become the person who I've always wanted to be.

Roberto is the family I've yearned to be a part of, the DG I have always wished for, and the best friend I've always wanted.

I finally have discovered what true love is all about. My life began again when I met Roberto, he is my ultimate hero, and my happy ever after.

At publishing time, it saddens me to report Maggie is also battling a life-threatening illness. We have yet to reconcile to make the most of the uncertain time we have left.

In our last conversation, we discussed what heaven might be like, and, if it were a place of our choosing, somewhere we had been the happiest, where would that be? Without a second thought, we agreed MB's was the place for both of us.

Know this dear sister, if I am the first to go, I'll be waiting for you in MB's backyard on the swing set next to Daddy's roses.

Dearest reader, it would mean the world to me if you would post a review of this book.

Thank you!

ABOUT THE AUTHOR

E. R. Crawford, AKA Elise Crawford, was born on a cold and wet November day in the Motor City and moved with her mother and younger sister to Seattle in 1968.

Although not formally educated as a writer, Elise has been telling stories since she was eight years old. She holds several Associate of Arts degrees; one in Liberal Arts, two in Social Sciences, and one Technical.

When not writing, Elise loves to crochet. She recently taught herself the skill and has made hats, animals, a cloak for Lexi, and a few blankets. She also loves a good search-a-word puzzle and reading a nail-biting mystery.

A Promise Kept was Elise's first published book, her partial memoir, for which she won a gold medal for Readers Favorite in 2010.

Elise is currently working on several writing projects; a series of children's books, two ghostwriting projects, and a third book, With Only A Horse, a truth is stranger than fiction novel, based on true events, embellished with a fictitious flair.

Elise is a native of Washington; she and her husband Roberto reside in Woodinville Washington. Their CEDAR-AL business continues to flourish and prosper. Elise has two grown children; a son, Dale, and a daughter, Lexi.

www.ingramcontent.com/pod-product-compliance
Lightning Source LLC
Chambersburg PA
CBHW022123290426
44112CB00008B/794